AF444640

THE DEVIL IS AN ASS

by

Ben Jonson

Edited with Introduction, Notes, and Glossary

by

William Savage Johnson, Ph.D.

Instructor in English in Yale University

A Thesis presented to
the Faculty of the Graduate School of Yale University
in Candidacy for the Degree of
Doctor of Philosophy

TO MY MOTHER

NATAL PUBLISHING LLC
ARS LONGA, VITA BREVIS

Copyright© 2025 Natal Publishing

All rights reserved

PREFACE

In *The Devil is an Ass* Jonson may be studied, first, as a student; secondly, as an observer. Separated by only two years from the preceding play, *Bartholomew Fair*, and by nine from the following, *The Staple of News*, the present play marks the close of an epoch in the poet's life, the period of his vigorous maturity. Its relations with the plays of his earlier periods are therefore of especial interest.

The results of the present editor's study of these and other literary connections are presented, partly in the Notes, and partly in the Introduction to this book. After the discussion of the purely technical problems in Sections A and B, the larger features are taken up in Section C, I and II. These involve a study of the author's indebtedness to English, Italian, and classical sources, and especially to the early English drama; as well as of his own dramatic methods in previous plays. The more minute relations to contemporary dramatists and to his own former work, especially in regard to current words and phrases, are dealt with in the Notes.

As an observer, Jonson appears as a student of London, and a satirist of its manners and vices; and, in a broader way, as a critic of contemporary England. The life and aspect of London are treated, for the most part, in the Notes; the issues of state involved in Jonson's satire are presented in historical discussions in Section C, III. Personal satire is treated in the division following.

I desire to express my sincere thanks to Professor Albert S. Cook for advice in matters of form and for inspiration in the work; to Professor Henry A. Beers for painstaking discussion of difficult questions; to Dr. De Winter for help and criticism; to Dr. John M. Berdan for the privilege of consulting his copy of the Folio; to Mr. Andrew Keogh and to Mr. Henry A. Gruener, for aid in bibliographical matters; and to Professor George L. Burr for the loan of books from the Cornell Library.

A portion of the expense of printing this book has been borne by the Modern Language Club of Yale University from funds placed at its disposal by the generosity of Mr. George E. Dimock of Elizabeth, New Jersey, a graduate of Yale in the Class of 1874.

W. S. J.
Yale University,
August 30, 1905.

Contents

Introduction

A. Editions of the Text

B. Date and Presentation

C. The Devil is an Ass

    I. The Devil Plot
        1. The Devil in the pre-Shakespearian Drama
        2. Jonson's Treatment of the Devil
        3. The Influence of Robin Goodfellow and of Popular
           Legend
        4. Friar Rush and Dekker
        5. The Novella of *Belfagor* and the Comedy of *Grim*
        6. Summary
        7. The Figure of the Vice
        8. Jonson's Use of the Vice

    II. The Satirical Drama
        1. General Treatment of the Plot
        2. Chief Sources of the Plot
        3. Prototypes of the leading Characters
        4. Minor Sources

    III. Specific Objects of Satire
        1. The Duello
        2. The Monopoly System
        3. Witchcraft

    IV. Personal Satire
        Mrs. Fitzdottrel
        Fitzdottrel
        Wittipol
        Justice Eitherside
        Merecraft
        Plutarchus Guilthead

The Noble House

D. After-Influence of the Devil is an Ass

Appendix—Extracts from the Critics

Text

Notes

Glossary

Bibiliography

A. Editions of the Text

The Devil is an Ass was first printed in 1631, and was probably put into circulation at that time, either as a separate pamphlet or bound with *Bartholomew Fair* and *The Staple of News*. Copies of this original edition were, in 1640-1, bound into the second volume of the First Folio of Jonson's collected works.[1] In 1641 a variant reprint edition of *The Devil is an Ass*, apparently small, was issued in pamphlet form. The play reappears in all subsequent collected editions. These are: (1) the 'Third Folio', 1692; (2) a bookseller's edition, 1716 [1717]; (3) Whalley's edition, 1756; (4) John Stockdale's reprint of Whalley's edition (together with the works of Beaumont and Fletcher), 1811; (5) Gifford's edition, 1816; (6) Barry Cornwall's one-volume edition, 1838; (7) Lieut. Col. Francis Cunningham's three-volume reissue (with some minor variations) of Gifford's edition, 1871; (8) another reissue by Cunningham, in nine volumes (with additional notes), 1875. The *Catalogue* of the British Museum shows that Jonson's works were printed in two volumes at Dublin in 1729. Of these editions only the first two call for detailed description, and of the others only the first, second, third, fifth, and eighth will be discussed.

1631. Owing to irregularity in contents and arrangement in different copies, the second volume of the First Folio has been much discussed. Gifford speaks of it as the edition of 1631-41.[2] Miss Bates, copying from Lowndes, gives it as belonging to 1631, reprinted in 1640 and in 1641.[3] Ward says substantially the same thing.[4] In 1870, however, Brinsley Nicholson, by a careful collation,[5] arrived at the following results. (1) The so-called editions of the second volume assigned to 1631, 1640, and 1641 form only a single edition. (2) The belief in the existence of 'the so-called first edition of the second volume in 1631' is due to the dates prefixed to the opening plays. (3) The belief in the existence of the volume of 1641 arose from the dates of *Mortimer* and the *Discoveries*, 'all the copies of which are dated 1641', and of the variant edition of *The Devil is an Ass*, which will next be described. (4) The 1640 edition supplies for some copies a general title-page, 'R. Meighen, 1640', but

---

[1] The first volume of this folio appeared in 1616. A reprint of this volume in 1640 is sometimes called the Second Folio. It should not be confused with the 1631-41 Edition of the second volume.

[2] Note prefixed to *Bartholomew Fair*.

[3] *Eng. Drama*, p. 78.

[4] *Eng. Drama* 2. 296.

[5] *N. & Q.* 4th Ser. 5. 573.

the plays printed in 1631 are reprinted from the same forms. Hazlitt arrives at practically the same conclusions.[6]

The volume is a folio by measurement, but the signatures are in fours.

Collation: Five leaves, the second with the signature A_3 B-M in fours. Aa-Bb; Cc-Cc_2 (two leaves); C_3 (one leaf); one leaf; D-I in fours; two leaves. [N]-Y in fours; B-Q in fours; R (two leaves); S-X in fours; Y (two leaves); Z-Oo in fours. Pp (two leaves). Qq; A-K in fours. L (two leaves). [M]-R in fours. A-P in fours. Q (two leaves). [R]-V in fours.

The volume opens with *Bartholomew Fayre*, which occupies pages [1-10], 1-88 (pages 12, 13, and 31 misnumbered), or the first group of signatures given above.

2. *The Staple of Newes*, paged independently, [1]-[76] (pages 19, 22, and 63 misnumbered), and signatured independently as in the second group above.

3. *The Diuell is an Asse*, [N]-Y, paged [91]-170 (pages 99, 132, and 137 misnumbered). [N] recto contains the title page (verso blank). N_2 contains a vignette and the persons of the play on the recto, a vignette and the prologue on the verso. N_3 to the end contains the play proper; the epilogue being on the last leaf verso.

One leaf (pages 89-90) is thus unaccounted for; but it is evident from the signatures and pagination that *The Diuell is an Asse* was printed with a view to having it follow *Bartholomew Fayre*. These three plays were all printed by I. B. for Robert Allot in 1631. Hazlitt says that they are often found together in a separate volume, and that they were probably intended by Jonson to supplement the folio of 1616.[7]

Collation made from copy in the library of Yale University at New Haven.

It was the opinion of both Whalley and Gifford that the publication of *The Devil is an Ass* in 1631 was made without the personal supervision of the author. Gifford did not believe that Jonson 'concerned himself with the revision of the folio, ... or, indeed, ever saw it'. The letter to the Earl of Newcastle (*Harl. MS.* 4955), quoted in Gifford's memoir, sufficiently disproves this supposition, at least so far as *Bartholomew Fair* and *The Devil is an Ass* are concerned. In this letter, written according to Gifford about 1632, Jonson says: 'It is the lewd printer's fault that I can send your lordship no more of my book. I sent you one piece before, The Fair, ... and now I send you this other morsel, The fine gentleman that walks the town, The Fiend; but before he will perfect the rest I fear he will come himself to be a part under the title of The Absolute Knave, which he hath played with me'. In 1870 Brinsley Nicholson quoted this letter in *Notes and Queries* (4th S. 5. 574), and pointed out that the jocular allusions are evidently to *Bartholomew Fair* and *The Devil is an Ass*.

Although Gifford is to some extent justified in his contempt for the edition, it is on the whole fairly correct.

The misprints are not numerous. The play is overpunctuated. Thus the words 'now' and 'again' are usually marked off by commas. Occasionally the

---

[6] *Bibliog. Col.*, 2d Ser. p. 320.

[7] *Bibliog. Col.*, p. 320. For a more detailed description of this volume see Winter, pp. xii-xiii.

punctuation is misleading. The mark of interrogation is generally, but not invariably, used for that of exclamation. The apostrophe is often a metrical device, and indicates the blending of two words without actual elision of either. The most serious defect is perhaps the wrong assignment of speeches, though later emendations are to be accepted only with caution. The present text aims to be an exact reproduction of that of the 1631 edition.

1641. The pamphlet quarto of 1641 is merely a poor reprint of the 1631 edition. It abounds in printer's errors. Few if any intentional changes, even of spelling and punctuation, are introduced. Little intelligence is shown by the printer, as in the change 5. I. 34 SN. (references are to act, scene, and line) He flags] He stags. It is however of some slight importance, inasmuch as it seems to have been followed in some instances by succeeding editions (cf. the omission of the side notes 2. I. 20, 22, 33, followed by 1692, 1716, and W; also 2. I. 46 his] a 1641, f.).

The title-page of this edition is copied, as far as the quotation from Horace, from the title-page of the 1631 edition. For the wood-cut of that edition, however, is substituted the device of a swan, with the legend 'God is my helper'. Then follow the words: 'Imprinted at London, 1641.'

Folio by measurement; signatures in fours.

Collation: one leaf, containing the title-page on the recto, verso blank; second leaf with signature A_2 (?), containing a device (St. Francis preaching to the birds [?]), and the persons of the play on the recto, and a device (a saint pointing to heaven and hell) and the prologue on the verso. Then the play proper; B-I in fours; K (one leaf). The first two leaves are unnumbered; then 1-66 (35 wrongly numbered 39).

1692. The edition of 1692[8] is a reprint of 1631, but furnishes evidence of some editing. Most of the nouns are capitalized, and a change of speaker is indicated by breaking the lines; obvious misprints are corrected: e. g., 1. 1. 98, 101; the spelling is modernized: e. g., 1. 1. 140 Tiborne] Tyburn; and the punctuation is improved. Sometimes a word undergoes a considerable morphological change: e. g., 1. 1. 67 Belins-gate] Billings-gate; 1. 6. 172, 175 venter] venture. Etymology is sometimes indicated by an apostrophe, not always correctly: e. g., 2. 6. 75 salts] 'salts. Several changes are uniform throughout the edition, and have been followed by all later editors. The chief of these are: inough] enough; tother] t'other; coozen] cozen; ha's] has; then] than; 'hem] 'em (except G sometimes); injoy] enjoy. Several changes of wording occur: e.g., 2. 1. 53 an] my; etc.

1716. The edition of 1716 is a bookseller's reprint of 1692. It follows that edition in the capitalization of nouns, the breaking up of the lines, and usually in the punctuation. In 2. 1. 78-80 over two lines are omitted by both editions. Independent editing, however, is not altogether lacking. We find occasional new elisions: e. g., 1. 6. 121 I'have] I've; at least one change of wording: 2. 3. 25 where] were; and one in the order of words: 4. 2. 22 not love] love not. In 4. 4. 75-76 and 76-78 it corrects two wrong assignments of speeches. A regular

---

[8] For a collation of this edition, see Mallory, pp. xv-xvii.

change followed by all editors is wiues] wife's.

1756. The edition of Peter Whalley, 1756, purports to be 'collated with all the former editions, and corrected', but according to modern standards it cannot be called a critical text. Not only does it follow 1716 in modernization of spelling; alteration of contractions: e. g., 2. 8. 69 To'a] T'a; 3. 1. 20 In t'one] Int' one; and changes in wording: e. g., 1. 1. 24 strengths] strength: 3. 6. 26 Gentleman] Gentlewoman; but it is evident that Whalley considered the 1716 edition as the correct standard for a critical text, and made his correction by a process of occasional restoration of the original reading. Thus in restoring 'Crane', 1. 4. 50, he uses the expression,—'which is authorized by the folio of 1640.' Again in 2. 1. 124 he retains 'petty' from 1716, although he says: 'The edit. of 1640, as I think more justly,—*Some* pretty *principality*.' This reverence for the 1716 text is inexplicable. In the matter of capitalization Whalley forsakes his model, and he makes emendations of his own with considerable freedom. He still further modernizes the spelling; he spells out elided words: e. g., 1. 3. 15 H' has] he has; makes new elisions: e. g., 1. 6. 143 Yo' are] You're; 1. 6. 211 I am] I'm; grammatical changes, sometimes of doubtful correctness: e. g., 1. 3. 21 I'le] I'd; morphological changes: e. g., 1. 6. 121 To scape] T'escape; metrical changes by insertions: e. g., 1. 1. 48 'to'; 4. 7. 38 'but now'; changes of wording: e. g., 1. 6. 195 sad] said; in the order of words: e. g., 3. 4. 59 is hee] he is; and in the assignment of speeches: e. g., 3. 6. 61. Several printer's errors occur: e. g., 2. 6. 21 and 24.

1816. William Gifford's edition is more carefully printed than that of Whalley, whom he criticizes freely. In many indefensible changes, however, he follows his predecessor, even to the insertion of words in 1. 1. 48 and 4. 7. 38, 39 (see above). He makes further morphological changes, even when involving a change of metre: e.g., 1. 1. 11 Totnam] Tottenham; 1. 4. 88 phantsie] phantasie; makes new elisions: e. g., 1. 6. 226 I ha'] I've; changes in wording: e. g., 2. 1. 97 O'] O!; and in assignment of speeches: e. g., 4. 4. 17. He usually omits parentheses, and the following changes in contracted words occur, only exceptions being noted in the variants: fro'] from; gi'] give; h'] he; ha'] have; 'hem] them (but often 'em); i'] in; o'] on, of; t'] to; th'] the; upo'] upon; wi'] with, will; yo'] you. Gifford's greatest changes are in the stage directions and side notes of the 1631 edition. The latter he considered as of 'the most trite and trifling nature', and 'a worthless incumbrance'. He accordingly cut or omitted with the utmost freedom, introducing new and elaborate stage directions of his own. He reduced the number of scenes from thirty-six to seventeen. In this, as Hathaway points out, he followed the regular English usage, dividing the scenes according to actual changes of place. Jonson adhered to classical tradition, and looked upon a scene as a situation. Gifford made his alterations by combining whole scenes, except in the case of Act 2. 3, which begins at Folio Act 2. 7. 23 (middle of line); of Act 3. 2, which begins at Folio Act 3. 5. 65 and of Act 3. 3, which begins at Folio Act 3. 5. 78 (middle of line). He considered himself justified in his mutilation of the side notes on the ground that they were not from the hand of Jonson. Evidence has already been adduced to show that they were at any rate printed with his sanction. I am, however, inclined to believe with Gifford that they were written by another hand. Gifford's criticism of them is to a large extent just. The note on '*Niaise*', 1. 6. 18, is of especially doubtful value (see note).

1875. 'Cunningham's reissue, 1875, reprints Gifford's text without change. Cunningham, however, frequently expresses his disapproval of Gifford's licence in changing the text' (Winter).

B. Date and Presentation

We learn from the title-page that this comedy was acted in 1616 by the King's Majesty's Servants. This is further confirmed by a passage in 1. 1. 80-81:

Now? As Vice stands this present yeere? Remember,
What number it is. *Six hundred* and *sixteene.*

Another passage (1. 6. 31) tells us that the performance took place in the Blackfriars Theatre:

Today, I goe to the *Black-fryers Play-house.*

That Fitzdottrel is to see *The Devil is an Ass* we learn later (3. 5. 38). The performance was to take place after dinner (3. 5. 34).

At this time the King's Men were in possession of two theatres, the Globe and the Blackfriars. The former was used in the summer, so that *The Devil is an Ass* was evidently not performed during that season.[9] These are all the facts that we can determine with certainty.

Jonson's masque, *The Golden Age Restored*, was presented, according to Fleay, on January 1 and 6. His next masque was *Christmas, his Masque*, December 25, 1616. Between these dates he must have been busy on *The Devil is an Ass*. Fleay, who identifies Fitzdottrel with Coke, conjectures that the date of the play is probably late in 1616, after Coke's discharge in November. If Coke is satirized either in the person of Fitzdottrel or in that of Justice Eitherside (see Introduction, pp. lxx, lxxii), the conjecture may be allowed to have some weight.

In 1. 2. 1 Fitzdottrel speaks of Bretnor as occupying the position once held by the conspirators in the Overbury case. Franklin, who is mentioned, was not brought to trial until November 18, 1615. Jonson does not speak of the trial as of a contemporary or nearly contemporary event.

Act 4 is largely devoted to a satire of Spanish fashions. In 4. 2. 71 there is a possible allusion to the Infanta Maria, for whose marriage with Prince Charles secret negotiations were being carried on at this time. We learn that Commissioners were sent to Spain on November 9 (*Cal. State Papers, Dom. Ser.*), and from a letter of January 1, 1617, that 'the Spanish tongue, dress, etc. are all in fashion' (*ibid.*).

---

[9] Collier, *Annals* 3. 275, 302; Fleay, *Hist.* 190.

These indications are all of slight importance, but from their united evidence we may feel reasonably secure in assigning the date of presentation to late November or early December, 1616.

The play was not printed until 1631. It seems never to have been popular, but was revived after the Restoration, and is given by Downes[10] in the list of old plays acted in the New Theatre in Drury Lane after April 8, 1663. He continues: 'These being Old Plays, were Acted but now and then; yet being well Perform'd were very Satisfactory to the Town'. The other plays of Jonson revived by this company were *The Fox*, *The Alchemist*, *Epicoene*, *Catiline*, *Every Man out of his Humor*, *Every Man in his Humor*, and *Sejanus*. Genest gives us no information of any later revival.

C. The Devil is an Ass

Jonson's characteristic conception of comedy as a vehicle for the study of 'humors' passed in *Every Man out of his Humor* into caricature, and in *Cynthia's Revels* and *Poetaster* into allegory. The process was perfectly natural. In the humor study each character is represented as absorbed by a single vice or folly. In the allegorical treatment the abstraction is the starting-point, and the human element the means of interpretation. Either type of drama, by a shifting of emphasis, may readily pass over into the other. The failure of *Cynthia's Revels*, in spite of the poet's arrogant boast at its close, had an important effect upon his development, and the plays of Jonson's middle period, from *Sejanus* to *The Devil is an Ass*, show more restraint in the handling of character, as well as far greater care in construction. The figures are typical rather than allegorical, and the plot in general centres about certain definite objects of satire. Both plot and characterization are more closely unified.

The Devil is an Ass marks a return to the supernatural and allegorical. The main action, however, belongs strictly to the type of the later drama, especially as exemplified by *The Alchemist*. The fanciful motive of the infernal visitant to earth was found to be of too slight texture for Jonson's sternly moral and satirical purpose. In the development of the drama it breaks down completely, and is crowded out by the realistic plot. Thus what promised at first to be the chief, and remains in some respects the happiest, motive of the play comes in the final execution to be little better than an inartistic and inharmonious excrescence. Yet Jonson's words to Drummond seem to indicate that he still looked upon it as the real kernel of the play.[11]

The action is thus easily divisible into two main lines; the devil-plot, involving the fortunes of Satan, Pug and Iniquity, and the satirical or main plot. This division is the more satisfactory, since Satan and Iniquity are not once

---

[10] *Roscius Anglicanus*, p. 8.

[11] 'A play of his, upon which he was accused, The Divell is ane Ass; according to *Comedia Vetus*, in England the Divell was brought in either with one Vice or other: the play done the Divel caried away the Vice, he brings in the Divel so overcome with the wickedness of this age that thought himself ane Ass. Παρεργους [incidentally] is discoursed of the Duke of Drounland: the King desired him to conceal it.'— *Conversations with William Drummond*, Jonson's *Wks.* 9. 400-1.

brought into contact with the chief actors, while Pug's connection with them is wholly external, and affects only his own fortunes. He is, as Herford has already pointed out, merely 'the fly upon the engine-wheel, fortunate to escape with a bruising' (*Studies*, p. 320). He forms, however, the connecting link between the two plots, and his function in the drama must be regarded from two different points of view, according as it shares in the realistic or the supernatural element.

I. The Devil-Plot

Jonson's title, *The Devil is an Ass*, expresses with perfect adequacy the familiarity and contempt with which this once terrible personage had come to be regarded in the later Elizabethan period. The poet, of course, is deliberately archaizing, and the figures of devil and Vice are made largely conformable to the purposes of satire. Several years before, in the Dedication to *The Fox*,[12] Jonson had expressed his contempt for the introduction of 'fools and devils and those antique relics of barbarism', characterizing them as 'ridiculous and exploded follies'. He treats the same subject with biting satire in *The Staple of News*.[13] Yet with all his devotion to realism in matters of petty detail, of local color, and of contemporary allusion, he was, as we have seen, not without an inclination toward allegory. Thus in *Every Man out of his Humor* the figure of Macilente is very close to a purely allegorical expression of envy. In *Cynthia's Revels* the process was perfectly conscious, for in the Induction to that play the characters are spoken of as Virtues and Vices. In *Poetaster* again we have the purging of Demetrius and Crispinus. Jonson's return to this field in *The Devil is an Ass* is largely prophetic of the future course of his drama. The allegory of *The Staple of News* is more closely woven into the texture of the play than is that of *The Devil is an Ass*; and the conception of Pecunia and her retinue is worked out with much elaboration. In the Second Intermean the purpose of this play is explained as a refinement of method in the use of allegory. For the old Vice with his wooden dagger to snap at everybody he met, or Iniquity, appareled 'like Hokos Pokos, in a juggler's jerkin', he substitutes 'vices male and female', 'attired like men and women of the time'. This of course is only a more philosophical and abstract statement of the idea which he expresses in *The Devil is an Ass* (1. 1. 120 f.) of a world where the vices are not distinguishable by any outward sign from the virtues:

> They weare the same clothes, eate the same meate,
> Sleep i' the self-same beds, ride i' those coaches.
> Or very like, foure horses in a coach,
> As the best men and women.

The New Inn and *The Magnetic Lady* are also penetrated with allegory of a sporadic and trivial nature. Jonson's use of devil and Vice in the present play is threefold. It is in part earnestly allegorical, especially in Satan's long speech in

---

[12] *Wks.* 3. 158.
[13] *Wks.* 5. 105 f. Cf. also Shirley, Prologue to *The Doubtful Heir*.

the first scene; it is in part a satire upon the employment of what he regarded as barbarous devices; and it is, to no small extent, itself a resort for the sake of comic effect to the very devices which he ridiculed.

Jonson's conception of the devil was naturally very far from mediæval, and he relied for the effectiveness of his portrait upon current disbelief in this conception. Yet mediævalism had not wholly died out, and remnants of the morality-play are to be found in many plays of the Elizabethan and Jacobean drama. Rev. John Upton, in his *Critical Observations on Shakespeare*, 1746, was the first to point out the historical connection between Jonson's Vice and devils and those of the pre-Shakespearian drama. In modern times the history of the devil and the Vice as dramatic figures has been thoroughly investigated, the latest works being those of Dr. L.W. Cushman and Dr. E. Eckhardt, at whose hands the subject has received exhaustive treatment. The connection with Machiavelli's novella of *Belfagor* was pointed out by Count Baudissin,[14] *Ben Jonson und seine Schule*, Leipzig 1836, and has been worked out exhaustively by Dr. E. Hollstein in a Halle dissertation, 1901. Dr. C.H. Herford, however, had already suggested that the chief source of the devil-plot was to be found in the legend of Friar Rush.

1. The Devil in the pre-Shakespearian Drama

The sources for the conception of the devil in the mediæval drama are to be sought in a large body of non-dramatic literature. In this literature the devil was conceived of as a fallen angel, the enemy of God and his hierarchy, and the champion of evil. As such he makes his appearance in the mystery-plays. The mysteries derived their subjects from Bible history, showed comparatively little pliancy, and dealt always with serious themes. In them the devil is with few exceptions a serious figure. Occasionally, however, even at this early date, comedy and satire find place. The most prominent example is the figure of Titivillus in the Towneley cycle.

In the early moralities the devil is still of primary importance, and is always serious. But as the Vice became a more and more prominent figure, the devil became less and less so, and in the later drama his part is always subordinate. The play of *Nature* (c. 1500) is the first morality without a devil. Out of fifteen moralities of later date tabulated by Cushman, only four are provided with this character.

The degeneration of the devil as a dramatic figure was inevitable. His grotesque appearance, at first calculated to inspire terror, by its very exaggeration produced, when once familiar, a wholly comic effect. When the active comic parts were assumed by the Vice, he became a mere butt, and finally disappears.

One of the earliest comic figures in the religious drama is that of the clumsy or uncouth servant.[15] Closely allied to him is the under-devil, who appears as early as *The Harrowing of Hell*, and this figure is constantly employed as a

---

[14] Count Baudissin translated two of Jonson's comedies into German, *The Alchemist* and *The Devil is an Ass* (*Der Dumme Teufel*).

[15] Eckhardt, p. 42 f.

comic personage in the later drama.[16] The figure of the servant later developed into that of the clown, and in this type the character of the devil finally merged.[17]

2. Jonson's Treatment of the Devil

In the present play the devil-type is represented by the arch-fiend Satan and his stupid subordinate, Pug. Of these two Satan received more of the formal conventional elements of the older drama, while Pug for the most part represents the later or clownish figure. As in the morality-play Satan's chief function is the instruction of his emissary of evil. In no scene does he come into contact with human beings, and he is always jealously careful for the best interests of his state. In addition Jonson employs one purely conventional attribute belonging to the tradition of the church- and morality-plays. This is the cry of 'Ho, ho!', with which Satan makes his entrance upon the stage in the first scene.[18] Other expressions of emotion were also used, but 'Ho, ho!' came in later days to be recognized as the conventional cry of the fiend upon making his entrance.[19]

How the character of Satan was to be represented is of course impossible to determine. The devil in the pre-Shakespearian drama was always a grotesque figure, often provided with the head of a beast and a cow's tail.[20] In the presentation of Jonson's play the ancient tradition was probably followed. Satan's speeches, however, are not undignified, and too great grotesqueness of costume must have resulted in considerable incongruity.

In the figure of Pug few of the formal elements of the pre-Shakespearian devil are exhibited. He remains, of course, the ostensible champion of evil, but is far surpassed by his earthly associates, both in malice and in intellect. In personal appearance he is brought by the assumption of the body and dress of a human being into harmony with his environment. A single conventional episode, with a reversal of the customary proceeding, is retained from the morality-play. While Pug is languishing in prison, Iniquity appears, Pug mounts upon his back, and is carried off to hell. Iniquity comments upon it:

> The Diuell was wont to carry away the euill;

---

[16] *Ibid.*, p. 67 f.

[17] In general the devil is more closely related to the clown, and the Vice to the fool. In some cases, however, the devil is to be identified with the fool, and the Vice with the clown.

[18] In the Digby group of miracle-plays roaring by the devil is a prominent feature. Stage directions in *Paul* provide for 'cryeing and rorying' and Belial enters with the cry, 'Ho, ho, behold me.' Among the moralities *The Disobedient Child* may be mentioned.

[19] So in *Gammer Gurton's Needle*, c 1562, we read: 'But Diccon, Diccon, did not the devil cry ho, ho, ho?' Cf. also the translation of Goulart's Histories, 1607 (quoted by Sharp, p. 59): 'The fellow—coming to the stove—sawe the Diuills in horrible formes, some sitting, some standing, others walking, some ramping against the walles, but al of them, assoone as they beheld him, crying Hoh, hoh, what makest thou here?'

[20] Cf. the words of Robin Goodfellow in *Wily Beguiled* (*O. Pl.*, 4th ed., 9. 268): 'I'll put me on my great carnation-nose, and wrap me in a rowsing calf-skin suit and come like some hobgoblin, or some devil ascended from the grisly pit of hell.'

But, now, the Euill out-carries the Diuell.

That the practice above referred to was a regular or even a frequent feature of the morality-play has been disputed, but the evidence seems fairly conclusive that it was common in the later and more degenerate moralities. At any rate, like the cry of 'Ho, ho!' it had come to be looked upon as part of the regular stock in trade, and this was enough for Jonson's purpose.[21] This motive of the Vice riding the devil had changed from a passive to an active comic part. Instead of the devil's prey he had become in the eyes of the spectators the devil's tormentor. Jonson may be looked upon as reverting, perhaps unconsciously, to the original and truer conception.

In other respects Pug exhibits only the characteristics of the inheritor of the devil's comedy part, the butt or clown. As we have seen, one of the chief sources, as well as one of the constant modes of manifestation, of this figure was the servant or man of low social rank. Pug, too, on coming to earth immediately attaches himself to Fitzdottrel as a servant, and throughout his brief sojourn on earth he continues to exhibit the wonted stupidity and clumsy uncouthness of the clown. He appears, to be sure, in a fine suit of clothes, but he soon shows himself unfit for the position of gentleman-usher, and his stupidity appears at every turn. The important element in the clown's comedy part, of a contrast between intention and accomplishment, is of course exactly the sort of fun inspired by Pug's repeated discomfiture. With the clown it often takes the form of blunders in speech, and his desire to appear fine and say the correct thing frequently leads him into gross absurdities. This is brought out with broad humor in 4. 4. 219, where Pug, on being catechized as to what he should consider 'the height of his employment', stumbles upon the unfortunate

---

[21] Cushman points out that it occurs in only one drama, that of *Like will to Like*. He attributes the currency of the notion that this mode of exit was the regular one to the famous passage in Harsnet's *Declaration of Popish Impostures* (p. 114, 1603): 'It was a pretty part in the old church-playes, when the nimble Vice would skip up nimbly like a jackanapes into the devil's necke, and ride the devil a course, and belabour him with his wooden dagger, till he made him roare, whereat the people would laugh to see the devil so vice-haunted.' The moralities and tragedies give no indication of hostility between Vice and devil. Cushman believes therefore that Harsnet refers either to some lost morality or to 'Punch and Judy.' It is significant, however, that in 'Punch and Judy,' which gives indications of being a debased descendant of the morality, the devil enters with the evident intention of carrying the hero off to hell. The joke consists as in the present play in a reversal of the usual proceeding. Eckhardt (p. 85 n.) points out that the Vice's cudgeling of the devil was probably a mere mirth-provoking device, and indicated no enmity between the two. Moreover the motive of the devil as an animal for riding is not infrequent. In the *Castle of Perseverance* the devil carries away the hero, Humanum Genus. The motive appears also in Greene's *Friar Bacon and Friar Bungay* and Lodge and Greene's *Looking Glass for London and England*, and especially in *Histriomastix*, where the Vice rides a roaring devil (Eckhardt, pp. 86 f.). We have also another bit of evidence from Jonson himself. In *The Staple of News* Mirth relates her reminiscences of the old comedy. In speaking of the devil she says: 'He would carry away the Vice on his back quick to hell in every play.'

suggestion: 'To find out a good *Corne-cutter*'. His receiving blows at the hand of his master further distinguishes him as a clown. The investing of Pug with such attributes was, as we have seen, no startling innovation on Jonson's part. Moreover, it fell into line with his purpose in this play, and was the more acceptable since it allowed him to make use of the methods of realism instead of forcing him to draw a purely conventional figure. Pug, of course, even in his character of clown, is not the unrelated stock-figure, introduced merely for the sake of inconsequent comic dialogue and rough horse-play. His part is important and definite, though not sufficiently developed.

3. The Influence of Robin Goodfellow and of Popular Legend

A constant element of the popular demonology was the belief in the kobold or elfish sprite. This figure appears in the mysteries in the shape of Titivillus, but is not found in the moralities. Robin Goodfellow, however, makes his appearance in at least three comedies, *Midsummer Night's Dream*, 1593-4, *Grim, the Collier of Croyden*, c 1600, and *Wily Beguiled*, 1606. The last of these especially approaches Jonson's conception. Here Robin Goodfellow is a malicious intriguer, whose nature, whether human or diabolical, is left somewhat in doubt. His plans are completely frustrated, he is treated with contempt, and is beaten by Fortunatus. The character was a favorite with Jonson. In the masque of *The Satyr*, 1603,[22] that character is addressed as Pug, which here seems evidently equivalent to Puck or Robin Goodfellow. Similarly Thomas Heywood makes Kobald, Hobgoblin, Robin Goodfellow, and Pug practically identical.[23] Butler, in the *Hudibras*,[24] gives him the combination-title of good 'Pug-Robin'. Jonson's character of Pug was certainly influenced in some degree both by the popular and the literary conception of this 'lubber fiend'.

The theme of a stupid or outwitted devil occurred also both in ballad literature[25] and in popular legend. Roskoff[26] places the change in attitude toward the devil from a feeling of fear to one of superiority at about the end of the eleventh century. The idea of a baffled devil may have been partially due to the legends of the saints, where the devil is constantly defeated, though he is seldom made to appear stupid or ridiculous. The notion of a 'stupid devil' is not very common in English, but occasionally appears. In the Virgilius legend the fiend is cheated of his reward by stupidly putting himself into the physical power of the wizard. In the Friar Bacon legend the necromancer delivers an Oxford gentleman by a trick of sophistry.[27] In the story upon which the drama of *The Merry Devil of Edmonton* was founded, the devil is not only cleverly outwitted, but appears weak and docile in his indulgence of the wizard's plea for a temporary respite. It may be said in passing, in spite of Herford's assertion

---

[22] Cf. also *Love Restored*, 1610-11, and the character of Puck Hairy in *The Sad Shepherd*.
[23] *Hierarchie of the Blessed Angels* 9. 574.
[24] Part 3. Cant. 1, l. 1415.
[25] Cf. *Devil in Britain and America*, ch. 2.
[26] *Geschichte des Teufels* 1. 316, 395.
[27] Hazlitt, *Tales*, pp. 39, 83.

to the contrary, that the supernatural machinery in this play has considerably less connection with the plot than in *The Devil is an Ass*. Both show a survival of a past interest, of which the dramatist himself realizes the obsolete character.

4. *Friar Rush and Dekker*

It was the familiar legend of Friar Rush which furnished the groundwork of Jonson's play. The story seems to be of Danish origin, and first makes its appearance in England in the form of a prose history during the latter half of the sixteenth century. It is entered in the *Stationer's Register* 1567-8, and mentioned by Reginald Scot in 1584.[28] As early as 1566, however, the figure of Friar Rush on a 'painted cloth' was a familiar one, and is so mentioned in *Gammer Gurton's Needle*.[29] The first extant edition dates from 1620, and has been reprinted by W. J. Thoms.[30] The character had already become partially identified with that of Robin Goodfellow,[31] and this identification, as we have seen, Jonson was inclined to accept.

In spite of many variations of detail the kernel of the Rush story is precisely that of Jonson's play, the visit of a devil to earth with the purpose of corrupting men. Both Rush and Pug assume human bodies, the former being 'put in rayment like an earthly creature', while the latter is made subject 'to all impressions of the flesh'.

Rush, unlike his counterpart, is not otherwise bound to definite conditions, but he too becomes a servant. The adventure is not of his own seeking; he is chosen by agreement of the council, and no mention is made of the emissary's willingness or unwillingness to perform his part. Later, however, we read that he stood at the gate of the religious house 'all alone and with a heavie countenance'. In the beginning, therefore, he has little of Pug's thirst for adventure, but his object is at bottom the same, 'to goe and dwell among these religious men for to maintaine them the longer in their ungracious living'. Like Pug, whose request for a Vice is denied him, he goes unaccompanied, and presents himself at the priory in the guise of a young man seeking service: 'Sir, I am a poore young man, and am out of service, and faine would have a maister'.[32]

Most of the remaining incidents of the Rush story could not be used in Jonson's play. Two incidents may be mentioned. Rush furthers the amours of his master, as Pug attempts to do those of his mistress. In the later history of

---

[28] *Discovery*, p. 522.

[29] *O. Pl.*, 4th ed., 3. 213.

[30] *Early Eng. Prose Romances*, London 1858.

[31] See Herford's discussion, *Studies*, p. 305; also *Quarterly Rev.* 22. 358. The frequently quoted passage from Harsnet's *Declaration* (ch. 20, p. 134), is as follows: 'And if that the bowle of curds and cream were not duly set out for Robin Goodfellow, the Friar, and Sisse the dairy-maide, why then either the pottage was burnt the next day, or the cheese would not curdle,' etc. Cf. also Scot, *Discovery*, p. 67: 'Robin could both eate and drinke, as being a cousening idle frier, or some such roge, that wanted nothing either belonging to lecherie or knaverie, &c.'

[32] Cf. Pug's words, 1. 3. 1 f.

Rush the motive of demoniacal possession is worked into the plot. In a very important respect, however, the legend differs from the play. Up to the time of discovery Rush is popular and successful. He is nowhere made ridiculous, and his mission of corruption is in large measure fulfilled. The two stories come together in their conclusion. The discovery that a real devil has been among them is the means of the friars' conversion and future right living. A precisely similar effect takes place in the case of Fitzdottrel.

The legend of Friar Rush had already twice been used in the drama before it was adopted by Jonson. The play by Day and Haughton to which Henslowe refers[33] is not extant; Dekker's drama, *If this be not a good Play, the Diuell is in it*, appeared in 1612. Jonson in roundabout fashion acknowledged his indebtedness to this play by the closing line of his prologue.

If this Play doe not like, the Diuell is in't.

Dekker's play adds few new elements to the story. The first scene is in the infernal regions; not, however, the Christian hell, as in the prose history, but the classical Hades. This change seems to have been adopted from Machiavelli. Three devils are sent to earth with the object of corrupting men and replenishing hell. They return, on the whole, successful, though the corrupted king of Naples is finally redeemed.

In certain respects, however, the play stands closer to Jonson's drama than the history. In the first place, the doctrine that hell's vices are both old-fashioned and outdone by men, upon which Satan lays so much stress in his instructions to Pug in the first scene, receives a like emphasis in Dekker:

       ... 'tis thought
That men to find hell, now, new waies have sought,
As Spaniards did to the Indies.

and again:

... aboue vs dwell,Diuells brauer, and more subtill then in Hell.[34]

and finally:

They scorne thy hell, hauing better of their owne.

In the second place Lurchall, unlike Rush, but in the same way as Pug, finds himself inferior to his earthly associates. He acknowledges himself overreached by Bartervile, and confesses:

---

[33] See Herford, p. 308.

[34] A similar passage is found in Dekker, *Whore of Babylon, Wks.* 2. 355. The sentiment is not original with Dekker. Cf. Middleton, *Black Book*, 1604:
... And were it number'd well,There are more devils on earth than are in hell.

I came to teach, but now (me thinkes) must learne.

A single correspondence of lesser importance may be added. Both devils, when asked whence they come, obscurely intimate their hellish origin. Pug says that he comes from the Devil's Cavern in Derbyshire. Rufman asserts that his home is Helvetia.[35]

5. *The Novella of Belfagor and the Comedy of Grim*

The relation between Jonson's play and the novella attributed to Niccolò Machiavelli (1469-1522) has been treated in much detail by Dr. Ernst Hollstein. Dr. Hollstein compares the play with the first known English translation, that by the Marquis of Wharton in 1674.[36] It is probable, however, that Jonson knew the novella in its Italian shape, if he knew it at all.[37] The Italian text has therefore been taken as the basis of the present discussion, while Dr. Hollstein's results, so far as they have appeared adequate or important, have been freely used.

Both novella and play depart from the same idea, the visit of a devil to earth to lead a human life. Both devils are bound by certain definite conditions. Belfagor must choose a wife, and live with her ten years; Pug must return at midnight. Belfagor, like Pug, must be subject to 'ogni infortunio nel quale gli uomini scorrono'.

In certain important respects Machiavelli's story differs essentially from Jonson's. Both Dekker and Machiavelli place the opening scene in the classical Hades instead of in the Christian hell. But Dekker's treatment of the situation is far more like Jonson's than is the novella's. Herford makes the distinction clear: 'Macchiavelli's Hades is the council-chamber of an Italian Senate, Dekker's might pass for some tavern haunt of Thames watermen. Dekker's fiends are the drudges of Pluto, abused for their indolence, flogged at will, and peremptorily sent where he chooses. Machiavelli's are fiends whose advice he requests with the gravest courtesy and deference, and who give it with dignity and independence'. Further, the whole object of the visit, instead of being the corruption of men, is a mere sociological investigation. Pug is eager to undertake his mission; Belfagor is chosen by lot, and very loath to go. Pug becomes a servant, Belfagor a nobleman.

But in one very important matter the stories coincide, that of the general character and fate of the two devils. As Hollstein points out, each comes with a firm resolve to do his best, each finds at once that his opponents are too strong for him, each through his own docility and stupidity meets repulse after repulse, ending in ruin, and each is glad to return to hell. This, of course, involves the very essence of Jonson's drama, and on its resemblance to the novella must be based any theory that Jonson was familiar with the latter.

---

[35] Dekker makes a similar pun on Helicon in *News from Hell, Non-dram Wks.* 2. 95.

[36] A paraphrase of *Belfagor* occurs in the Conclusion of Barnaby Riche's *Riche his Farewell to Militarie Profession*, 1581, published for the Shakespeare Society by J. P. Collier, 1846. The name is changed to Balthasar, but the main incidents are the same.

[37] Jonson refers to Machiavelli's political writings in *Timber* (ed. Schelling, p. 38).

Of resemblance of specific details not much can be made. The two stories have in common the feature of demoniacal possession, but this, as we have seen, occurs also in the Rush legend. The fact that the princess speaks Latin, while Fitzdottrel surprises his auditors by his 'several languages', is of no more significance. This is one of the stock indications of witchcraft. It is mentioned by Darrel, and Jonson could not have overlooked a device so obvious. Certain other resemblances pointed out by Dr. Hollstein are of only the most superficial nature. On the whole we are not warranted in concluding with any certainty that Jonson knew the novella at all.

On the other hand, he must have been acquainted with the comedy of *Grim, the Collier of Croydon* (c 1600). Herford makes no allusion to this play, and, though it was mentioned as a possible source by A. W. Ward,[38] the subject has never been investigated. The author of *Grim* uses the Belfagor legend for the groundwork of his plot, but handles his material freely. In many respects the play is a close parallel to *The Devil is an Ass*. The same respect for the vices of earth is felt as in Dekker's and Jonson's plays. Belphegor sets out to

> ... make experiment
> If hell be not on earth as well as here.

The circumstances of the sending bear a strong resemblance to the instructions given to Pug:

> Thou shalt be subject unto human chance,
> So far as common wit cannot relieve thee.
> But whatsover happens in that time,
> Look not from us for succour or relief.
> This shalt thou do, and when the time's expired,
> Bring word to us what thou hast seen and done.

So in Jonson:

> ... but become subject
> To all impression of the flesh, you take,
> So farre as humane frailty: ...
> But as you make your soone at nights relation,
> And we shall find, it merits from the State, You shall haue both trust from vs, and imployment.

Belphegor is described as 'patient, mild, and pitiful'; and during his sojourn on earth he shows little aptitude for mischief, but becomes merely a butt and object of abuse. Belphegor's request for a companion, unlike that of Pug, is granted. He chooses his servant Akercock, who takes the form of Robin Goodfellow. Robin expresses many of the sentiments to be found in the mouth of Pug. With the latter's monologue (Text, 5. 2) compare Robin's exclamation:

---

[38] *Eng. Dram. Lit.* 2. 606.

> Zounds, I had rather be in hell than here.

Neither Pug (Text, 2. 5. 3-4) nor Robin dares to return without authority:

> What shall I do? to hell I dare not go,
> Until my master's twelve months be expir'd.

Like Pug (Text, 5. 6. 3-10) Belphegor worries over his reception in hell:

> How shall I give my verdict up to Pluto
> Of all these accidents?

Finally Belphegor's sensational disappearance through the yawning earth comes somewhat nearer to Jonson than does the Italian original. The English comedy seems, indeed, to account adequately for all traces of the Belfagor story to be found in Jonson's play.

6. Summary

It is certain that of the two leading ideas of Jonson's comedy, the sending of a devil to earth with the object of corrupting men is derived from the Rush legend. It is probable that the no less important motive of a baffled devil, happy to make his return to hell, is due either directly or indirectly to Machiavelli's influence. This motive, as we have seen, was strengthened by a body of legend and by the treatment of the devil in the morality play.

7. The Figure of the Vice

It is the figure of the Vice which makes Jonson's satire on the out-of-date moralities most unmistakable. This character has been the subject of much study and discussion, and there is to-day no universally accepted theory as to his origin and development. In the literature of Jonson's day the term Vice is almost equivalent to harlequin. But whether this element of buffoonery is the fundamental trait of the character, and that of intrigue is due to a confusion in the meaning of the word, or whether the element of intrigue is original, and that of buffoonery has taken its place by a process of degeneration in the Vice himself, is still a disputed question.

The theory of Cushman and of Eckhardt is substantially the same, and may be stated as follows. Whether or not the Vice be a direct descendant of the devil, it is certain that he falls heir to his predecessor's position in the drama, and that his development is strongly influenced by that character. Originally, like the devil, he represents the principle of evil and may be regarded as the summation of the seven deadly sins. From the beginning, however, he possessed more comic elements, much being ready made for him through the partial degeneration of the devil, while the material of the moralities was by no means so limited in scope as that of the mysteries. This comic element, comparatively slight at first, soon began to be cultivated intentionally, and gradually assumed the chief function, while the allegorical element was largely displaced. In course of time the transformation from the intriguer to the buffoon became complete.[39] Moreover, the rapidity of the transformation was hastened by the influence of the fool, a new dramatic figure of independent origin, but the partial successor upon the stage of the Vice's comedy part. As early as 1570 the union of fool and Vice is plainly visible.[40] In 1576 we find express stage directions given for the Vice to fill in the pauses with improvised jests.[41] Two years later a Vice plays the leading rôle for the last time.[42] By 1584 the Vice has completely lost his character of intriguer,[43] and in the later drama he appears only as an antiquated figure, where he is usually considered as identical with the fool or jester.[44] Cushman enumerates the three chief rôles of the Vice as the opponent of the Good; the corrupter of man; and the buffoon.

The Vice, however, is not confined to the moralities, but appears frequently in the comic interludes. According to the theory of Cushman, the name Vice stands in the beginning for a moral and abstract idea, that of the principle of evil in the world, and must have originated in the moralities; and since it is applied to a comic personage in the interludes, this borrowing must have taken place after the period of degeneration had already begun. To this theory Chambers[45] offers certain important objections. He points out that, although 'vices in the ordinary sense of the word are of course familiar personages in the morals', the term Vice is not applied specifically to a character in 'any pre-Elizabethan moral interlude except the Marian *Respublica*', 1553. Furthermore, 'as a matter of fact, he comes into the interlude through the avenue of the farce'. The term is first applied to the leading comic characters in the farces of John Heywood, *Love* and *The Weather*, 1520-30. These characters have traits more nearly resembling those of the fool and clown than those of the intriguer of the moralities. Chambers concludes therefore that 'the character of the vice is derived from that of the domestic fool or jester', and that the term was borrowed by the authors of the moralities from the comic interludes.

These two views are widely divergent, and seem at first wholly irreconcilable. The facts of the case, however, are, I believe, sufficiently clear to warrant the following conclusions: (1) The early moralities possessed many allegorical characters representing vices in the ordinary sense of the word. (2) From among these vices we may distinguish in nearly every play a single character as in a preëminent degree the embodiment of evil. (3) To this chief character the name of Vice was applied about 1553, and with increasing frequency after that date. (4) Whatever may have been the original meaning of

---

[39] Eckhardt, p. 195.

[40] In W. Wager's *The longer thou livest, the more fool thou art.*

[41] In Wapull's *The Tide tarrieth for No Man.*

[42] Subtle Shift in *The History of Sir Clyomon and Sir Clamydes.*

[43] In Wilson's *The Three Ladies of London.*

[44] He is so identified in Chapman's *Alphonsus, Emperor of Germany* c 1590 (*Wks.*, ed. 1873, 3. 216), and in Stubbes' *Anat.*, 1583. Nash speaks of the Vice as an antiquated figure as early as 1592 (*Wks.* 2. 203).

[45] *Med. Stage*, pp. 203-5.

the word, it must have been generally understood in the moralities in the sense now usually attributed to it; for (5) The term was applied in the moralities only to a character in some degree evil. Chambers instances *The Tide tarrieth for No Man* and the tragedy of *Horestes*, where the Vice bears the name of Courage, as exceptions. The cases, however, are misleading. In the former, Courage is equivalent to 'Purpose', 'Desire', and is a distinctly evil character.[46] In the latter he reveals himself in the second half of the play as Revenge, and although he incites Horestes to an act of justice, he is plainly opposed to 'Amyte', and he is finally rejected and discountenanced. Moreover he is here a serious figure, and only occasionally exhibits comic traits. He cannot therefore be considered as supporting the theory of the original identity of the fool and the Vice. (6) The Vice of the comic interludes and the leading character of the moralities are distinct figures. The former was from the beginning a comic figure or buffoon;[47] the latter was in the beginning serious, and continued to the end to preserve serious traits. With which of these two figures the term Vice originated, and by which it was borrowed from the other, is a matter of uncertainty and is of minor consequence. These facts, however, seem certain, and for the present discussion sufficient: that the vices of the earlier and of the later moralities represent the same stock figure; that this figure stood originally for the principle of evil, and only in later days became confused with the domestic fool or jester; that the process of degeneration was continuous and gradual, and took place substantially in the manner outlined by Cushman and Eckhardt; and that, while to the playwright of Jonson's day the term was suggestive primarily of the buffoon, it meant also an evil personage, who continued to preserve certain lingering traits from the character of intriguer in the earlier moralities.

8. Jonson's Use of the Vice

The position of the Vice has been discussed at some length because of its very important bearing on Jonson's comedy. It is evident, even upon a cursory reading, that Jonson has not confined himself to the conception of the Vice obtainable from a familiarity with the interludes alone, as shown in Heywood's farces or the comedy of *Jack Juggler*. The character of Iniquity, though fully identified with the buffoon of the later plays, is nevertheless closely connected in the author's mind with the intriguer of the old moralities. This is clear above all from the use of the name Iniquity, from his association with the devil, and from Pug's desire to use him as a means of corrupting his playfellows. Thus, consciously or unconsciously on Jonson's part, Iniquity presents in epitome the history of the Vice.

His very name, as we have said, links him with the morality-play. In fact, all the Vices suggested, Iniquity, Fraud, Covetousness, and Lady Vanity, are taken from the moralities. The choice of Iniquity was not without meaning, and was doubtless due to its more general and inclusive significance. In

---

[46] Eckhardt, p. 145.

[47] Sometimes he is even a virtuous character. See Eckhardt's remarks on *Archipropheta*, p. 170. Merry Report in Heywood's *Weather* constantly moralizes, and speaks of himself as the servant of God in contrast with the devil.

Shakespeare's time Vice and Iniquity seem to have been synonymous terms (see Schmidt), from which it has been inferred that Iniquity was the Vice in many lost moralities.[48]

Of the original Vice-traits Iniquity lays vigorous claim to that of the corrupter of man. Pug desires a Vice that he may 'practice there-with any playfellow', and Iniquity comes upon the stage with voluble promises to teach his pupil to 'cheat, lie, cog and swagger'. He offers also to lead him into all the disreputable precincts of the city. Iniquity appears in only two scenes, Act 1. Sc. 1 and Act 5. Sc. 6. In the latter he reverses the usual process and carries away the devil to hell. This point has already been discussed (p. xxiv).

Aside from these two particulars, Iniquity is far nearer to the fool than to the original Vice. As he comes skipping upon the stage in the first scene, reciting his galloping doggerel couplets, we see plainly that the element of buffoonery is uppermost in Jonson's mind. Further evidence may be derived from the particularity with which Iniquity describes the costume which he promises to Pug, and which we are doubtless to understand as descriptive of his own. Attention should be directed especially to the wooden dagger, the long cloak, and the slouch hat. Cushman says (p. 125): 'The vice enjoys the greatest freedom in the matter of dress; he is not confined to any stereotyped costume; ... the opinion that he is always or usually dressed in a fool's costume has absolutely no justification'. The wooden dagger, a relic of the Roman stage,[49] is the most frequently mentioned article of equipment. It is first found (1553-8) as part of the apparel of Jack Juggler in a print illustrating that play, reproduced by Dodsley. It is also mentioned in *Like Will to Like, Hickescorner, King Darius*, etc. The wooden dagger was borrowed, however, from the fool's costume, and is an indication of the growing identification of the Vice with the house-fool. That Jonson recognized it as such is evident from his *Expostulation with Inigo Jones*:

No velvet suit you wear will alter kind;
A wooden dagger is a dagger of wood.

The long cloak, twice mentioned (1. 1. 51 and 85), is another property borrowed from the fool. The natural fool usually wore a long gown-like dress,[50] and this was later adopted as a dress for the artificial fool. Muckle John, the court fool of Charles I., was provided with 'a long coat and suit of scarlet-colour serge'.[51]

Satan's reply to Pug's request for a Vice is, however, the most important passage on this subject. He begins by saying that the Vice, whom he identifies with the house fool, is fifty years out of date. Only trivial and absurd parts are left for Iniquity to play, the mountebank tricks of the city and the tavern fools.

---

[48] This designation for the Vice first appears in *Nice Wanton*, 1547-53, then in *King Darius*, 1565, and *Histriomastix*, 1599 (printed 1610).

[49] Wright, *Hist. of Caricature*, p. 106.

[50] Doran, p. 182.

[51] *Ibid.*, p. 210.

Douce (pp. 499 f.) mentions nine kinds of fools, among which the following appear: 1. The general domestic fool. 4. The city or corporation fool. 5. Tavern fools. Satan compares Iniquity with each of these in turn. The day has gone by, he says:

> When euery great man had his *Vice* stand by him,
> In his long coat, shaking his wooden dagger.

Then he intimates that Iniquity may be able to play the tavern fool:

> Where canst thou carry him? except to Tauernes?
> To mount vp ona joynt-stoole, with a *Iewes*-trumpe,
> To put downe *Cokeley*, and that must be to Citizens?

And finally he compares him with the city fool:

> Hee may perchance, in taile of a Sheriffes dinner,
> Skip with a rime o' the table, from *New-nothing*,
> And take his *Almaine*-leape into a custard.

Thus not only does Jonson identify the Vice with the fool, but with the fool in his senility. The characteristic functions of the jester in the Shakespearian drama, with his abundant store of improvised jests, witty retorts, and irresistible impudence, have no part in this character. He is merely the mountebank who climbs upon a tavern stool, skips over the table, and leaps into corporation custards.

Iniquity, then, plays no real part in the drama. His introduction is merely for the purpose of satire. In *The Staple of News* the subject is renewed, and treated with greater directness:

'*Tat*. I would fain see the fool, gossip; the fool is the finest man in the company, they say, and has all the wit: he is the very justice o' peace o' the play, and can commit whom he will and what he will, error, absurdity, as the toy takes him, and no man say black is his eye, but laugh at him'.

In *Epigram 115, On the Town's Honest Man*, Jonson again identifies the Vice with the mountebank, almost in the same way as he does in *The Devil is an Ass*:

> ... this is one
> Suffers no name but a description
> Being no vicious person but the Vice
> About the town;...
> At every meal, where it doth dine or sup,
> The cloth's no sooner gone, but it gets up,
> And shifting of its faces, doth play more
> Parts than the Italian could do with his door.
> Acts old Iniquity and in the fit

Of miming gets the opinion of a wit.

II. The Satirical Drama

It was from Aristophanes[52] that Jonson learned to combine with such boldness the palpable with the visionary, the material with the abstract. He surpassed even his master in the power of rendering the combination a convincing one, and his method was always the same. Fond as he was of occasional flights of fancy, his mind was fundamentally satirical, so that the process of welding the apparently discordant elements was always one of rationalizing the fanciful rather than of investing the actual with a far-away and poetic atmosphere. Thus even his purely supernatural scenes present little incongruity. Satan and Iniquity discuss strong waters and tobacco, Whitechapel and Billingsgate, with the utmost familiarity; even hell's 'most exquisite tortures' are adapted in part from the homely proverbs of the people. In the use of his sources three tendencies are especially noticeable: the motivation of borrowed incidents; the adjusting of action on a moral basis: the reworking of his own favorite themes and incidents.

1. General Treatment of the Plot

For the main plot we have no direct source. It represents, however, Jonson's typical method. It has been pointed out[53] that the characteristic Jonsonian comedy always consists of two groups, the intriguers and the victims. In *The Devil is an Ass* the most purely comic motive of the play is furnished by a reversal of the usual relation subsisting between these two groups. Here the devil, who was wont to be looked upon as arch-intriguer, is constantly 'fooled off and beaten', and thus takes his position as the comic butt. Pug, in a sense, represents a satirical trend. Through him Jonson satirizes the outgrown supernaturalism which still clung to the skirts of Jacobean realism, and at the same time paints in lively colors the vice of a society against which hell itself is powerless to contend. It is only, however, in a general way, where the devil stands for a principle, that Pug may be considered as in any degree satirical. In the particular incident he is always a purely comic figure, and furnishes the mirth which results from a sense of the incongruity between anticipation and accomplishment.

Fitzdottrel, on the other hand, is mainly satirical. Through him Jonson passes censure upon the city gallant, the attendant at the theatre, the victim of the prevalent superstitions, and even the pretended demoniac. His dupery, as in the case of his bargain with Wittipol, excites indignation rather than mirth, and his final discomfiture affords us almost a sense of poetic justice. This character stands in the position of chief victim.

In an intermediate position are Merecraft and Everill. They succeed in swindling Fitzdottrel and Lady Tailbush, but are in turn played upon by the chief intriguer, Wittipol, with his friend Manly. Jonson's moral purpose is here

---

[52] See Herford, p. 318.
[53] Woodbridge, *Studies*, p. 33.

plainly visible, especially in contrast to Plautus, with whom the youthful intriguer is also the stock figure. The motive of the young man's trickery in the Latin comedy is usually unworthy and selfish. That of Wittipol, on the other hand, is wholly disinterested, since he is represented as having already philosophically accepted the rejection of his advances at the hands of Mrs. Fitzdottrel.

In construction the play suffers from overabundance of material. Instead of a single main line of action, which is given clear precedence, there is rather a succession of elaborated episodes, carefully connected and motivated, but not properly subordinated. The plot is coherent and intricate rather than unified. This is further aggravated by the fact that the chief objects of satire are imperfectly understood by readers of the present day.

Jonson observes unity of time, Pug coming to earth in the morning and returning at midnight. With the exception of the first scene, which is indeterminate, and seems at one moment to be hell, and the next London, the action is confined to the City, but hovers between Lincoln's Inn, Newgate, and the house of Lady Tailbush. Unity of action is of course broken by the interference of the devil-plot and the episodic nature of the satirical plot. The main lines of action may be discussed separately.

In the first act chief prominence is given to the intrigue between Wittipol and Mrs. Fitzdottrel. This interest is continued through the second act, but practically dropped after this point. In Act 4 we find that both lovers have recovered from their infatuation, and the intrigue ends by mutual consent.

The second act opens with the episode of Merecraft's plot to gull Fitzdottrel. The project of the dukedom of Drownedland is given chief place, and attention is centred upon it both here and in the following scenes. Little use, however, is made of it in the motivation of action. This is left for another project, the office of the Master of Dependencies (quarrels) in the next act. This device is introduced in an incidental way, and we are not prepared for the important place which it takes in the development of the plot. Merecraft, goaded by Everill, hits upon it merely as a temporary makeshift to extort money from Fitzdottrel. The latter determines to make use of the office in prosecuting his quarrel with Wittipol. In preparation for the duel, and in accordance with the course of procedure laid down by Everill, he resolves to settle his estate. Merecraft and Everill endeavor to have the deed drawn in their own favor, but through the interference of Wittipol the whole estate is made over to Manly, who restores it to Mrs. Fitzdottrel. This project becomes then the real turning-point of the play.

The episode of Guilthead and Plutarchus in Act 3 is only slightly connected with the main plot. That of Wittipol's disguise as a Spanish lady, touched upon in the first two acts, becomes the chief interest of the fourth. It furnishes much comic material, and the characters of Lady Tailbush and Lady Eitherside offer the poet the opportunity for some of his cleverest touches in characterization and contrast.[54] The scene, however, is introduced for incidental purposes, the satirization of foreign fashions and the follies of London society, and is overelaborated. The catalogue of cosmetics is an instance of Jonson's intimate acquaintance with recondite knowledge standing in the way of his art.

Merecraft's 'after game' in the fifth act is of the nature of an appendix. The play might well have ended with the frustration of his plan to get possession of the estate. This act is introduced chiefly for the sake of a satire upon pretended demoniacs and witch-finders. It also contains the conclusion of the devil-plot.

The Devil is an Ass will always remain valuable as a historical document, and as a record of Jonson's own attitude towards the abuses of his times. In the treatment of Fitzdottrel and Merecraft among the chief persons, and of Plutarchus Guilthead among the lesser, this play belongs to Jonson's character-drama.[55] It does not, however, belong to the pure humor-comedy. Like *The Alchemist*, and in marked contrast to *Every Man out of his Humor*, interest is sought in plot development. In the scene between Lady Tailbush and Lady Eitherside, the play becomes a comedy of manners, and in its attack upon state abuses it is semi-political in nature. Both Gifford and Swinburne have observed the ethical treatment of the main motives.

With the exception of Prologue and Epilogue, the doggerel couplets spoken by Iniquity, Wittipol's song (2. 6. 94), and some of the lines quoted by Fitzdottrel in the last scene, the play is written in blank verse throughout. Occasional lines of eight (2. 2. 122), nine (2. 1. 1), twelve (1. 1. 33) or thirteen (1. 1. 113) syllables are introduced. Most of these could easily be normalized by a slight emendation or the slurring of a syllable in pronunciation. Many of the lines, however, are rough and difficult of scansion. Most of the dialogue is vigorous, though Wittipol's language is sometimes affected and unnatural (cf. Act 1. Sc. 1). His speech, 1. 6. 111-148, is classical in tone, but fragmentary and not perfectly assimilated. The song already referred to possesses delicacy and some beauty of imagery, but lacks Jonson's customary polish and smoothness.

As a work of art the play must rely chiefly upon the vigor of its satiric dialogue and the cleverness of its character sketches. It lacks the chief excellences of construction—unity of interest, subordination of detail, steady and uninterrupted development, and prompt conclusion.

2. Chief Sources of the Plot

The first source to be pointed out was that of Act 1. Sc. 4-6.[56] This was again noticed by Koeppel, who mentions one of the word-for-word borrowings, and points out the moralistic tendency in Jonson's treatment of the husband,

---

[54] Contrasted companion-characters are a favorite device with Jonson. Compare Corvino, Corbaccio, and Voltore in *The Fox*, Ananias and Tribulation Wholesome in *The Alchemist*, etc.

[55] It should be noticed that in the case of Merecraft the method employed is the caricature of a profession, as well as the exposition of personality.

[56] Langbaine, *Eng. Dram. Poets*, p. 289.

and his rejection of the Italian story's licentious conclusion.[57] The original is from Boccaccio's *Decameron*, the fifth novella of the third day. Boccaccio's title is as follows: 'Il Zima dona a messer Francesco Vergellesi un suo pallafreno, e per quello con licenzia di lui parla alla sua donna, ed ella tacendo, egli in persona di lei si risponde, e secondo la sua risposta poi l'effetto segue'. The substance of the story is this. Il Zima, with the bribe of a palfrey, makes a bargain with Francesco. For the gift he is granted an interview with the wife of Francesco and in the latter's presence. This interview, however, unlike that in *The Devil is an Ass*, is not in the husband's hearing. To guard against any mishap, Francesco secretly commands his wife to make no answer to the lover, warning her that he will be on the lookout for any communication on her part. The wife, like Mrs. Fitzdottrel, upbraids her husband, but is obliged to submit. Il Zima begins his courtship, but, though apparently deeply affected, she makes no answer. The young man then suspects the husband's trick (e poscia s'incominciò ad accorgere dell' arte usata dal cavaliere). He accordingly hits upon the device of supposing himself in her place and makes an answer for her, granting an assignation. As a signal he suggests the hanging out of the window of two handkerchiefs. He then answers again in his own person. Upon the husband's rejoining them he pretends to be deeply chagrined, complains that he has met a statue of marble (una statua di marmo) and adds: 'Voi avete comperato il pallafreno, e io non l'ho venduto'. Il Zima is successful in his ruse, and Francesco's wife yields completely to his seduction.

A close comparison of this important source is highly instructive. Verbal borrowings show either that Jonson had the book before him, or that he remembered many of the passages literally. Thus Boccaccio's 'una statua di marmo' finds its counterpart in a later scene[58] where Mrs. Fitzdottrel says: 'I would not haue him thinke hee met a statue'. Fitzdottrel's satisfaction at the result of the bargain is like that of Francesco: 'I ha' kept the contract, and the cloake is mine' (omai è ben mio il pallafreno, che fu tuo). Again Wittipol's parting words resemble Il Zima's: 'It may fall out, that you ha' bought it deare, though I ha' not sold it'.[59] In the mouths of the two heroes, however, these words mean exactly opposite things. With Il Zima it is a complaint, and means: 'You have won the cloak, but I have got nothing in return'. With Wittipol, on the other hand, it is an open sneer, and hints at further developments. The display of handkerchiefs at the window is another borrowing. Fitzdottrel says sarcastically:

> ... I'll take carefull order,
> That shee shall hang forth ensignes at the window.

Finally Wittipol, like Il Zima, suspects a trick when Mrs. Fitzdottrel refuses to answer:

---

[57] *Quellen Studien*, p. 15.
[58] 2. 2. 69.
[59] Mentioned by Koeppel, p. 15.

How! not any word? Nay, then, I taste a tricke in't.

But precisely here Jonson blunders badly. In Boccaccio's story the trick was a genuine one. Il Zima stands waiting for an answer. When no response is made he begins to suspect the husband's secret admonition, and to thwart it hits upon the device of answering himself. But in Jonson there is no trick at all. Fitzdottrel does indeed require his wife to remain silent, but by no means secretly. His command is placed in the midst of a rambling discourse addressed alternately to his wife and to the young men. There is not the slightest hint that any part of this speech is whispered in his wife's ear, and Wittipol enters upon his courtship with full knowledge of the situation. This fact deprives Wittipol's speech in the person of Mrs. Fitzdottrel of its character as a clever device, so that the whole point of Boccaccio's story is weakened, if not destroyed. I cannot refrain in conclusion from making a somewhat doubtful conjecture. It is noticeable that while Jonson follows so many of the details of this story with the greatest fidelity he substitutes the gift of a cloak for that of the original 'pallafreno' (palfrey).[60] The word is usually written 'palafreno' and so occurs in Florio. Is it possible that Jonson was unfamiliar with the word, and, not being able to find it in a dictionary, conjectured that it was identical with 'palla', a cloak?

In other respects Jonson's handling of the story displays his characteristic methods. Boccaccio spends very few words in description of either husband or suitor. Jonson, however, is careful to make plain the despicable character of Fitzdottrel, while Wittipol is represented as an attractive and high-minded young man. Further than this, both Mrs. Fitzdottrel and Wittipol soon recover completely from their infatuation.

Koeppel has suggested a second source from the *Decameron*, Day 3, Novella 3. The title is: 'Sotto spezie di confessione e di purissima coscienza una donna, innamorata d'un giovane, induce un solenne frate, senza avvedersene egli, a dar modo che'l piacer di lei avessi intero effetto'. The story is briefly this. A lady makes her confessor the means of establishing an acquaintance with a young man with whom she has fallen in love. Her directions are conveyed to him under the guise of indignant prohibitions. By a series of messages of similar character she finally succeeds in informing him of the absence of her husband and the possibility of gaining admittance to her chamber by climbing a tree in the garden. Thus the friar becomes the unwitting instrument of the very thing which he is trying to prevent. So in Act 2. Sc. 2 and 6, Mrs. Fitzdottrel suspects Pug of being her husband's spy. She dares not therefore send Wittipol a direct message, but requests him to cease his attentions to her

At the Gentlemans chamber-window in *Lincolnes-Inne* there,
That opens to my gallery.

---

[60] So spelled in 1573 ed. In earlier editions 'palafreno.'

Wittipol takes the hint, and promptly appears at the place indicated.

Von Rapp[61] has mentioned certain other scenes as probably of Italian origin, but, as he advances no proofs, his suggestions may be neglected. It seems to me possible that in the scene above referred to, where the lover occupies a house adjoining that of his mistress, and their secret amour is discovered by her servant and reported to his master, Jonson had in mind the same incident in Plautus' *Miles Gloriosus*, Act. 2. Sc. 1 f.

The trait of jealousy which distinguishes Fitzdottrel was suggested to some extent by the character of Euclio in the *Aulularia*, and a passage of considerable length[62] is freely paraphrased from that play. The play and the passage had already been used in *The Case is Altered*.

Miss Woodbridge has noticed that the scene in which Lady Tailbush and her friends entertain Wittipol disguised as a Spanish lady is similar to Act 3. Sc. 2 of *The Silent Woman*, where the collegiate ladies call upon Epicoene. The trick of disguising a servant as a woman occurs in Plautus' *Casina*, Acts 4 and 5.

For the final scene, where Fitzdottrel plays the part of a bewitched person, Jonson made free use of contemporary books and tracts. The motive of pretended possession had already appeared in *The Fox* (*Wks.* 3. 312), where symptoms identical with or similar to those in the present passage are mentioned—swelling of the belly, vomiting crooked pins, staring of the eyes, and foaming at the mouth. The immediate suggestion in this place may have come either through the Rush story or through Machiavelli's novella. That Jonson's materials can be traced exclusively to any one source is hardly to be expected. Not only were trials for witchcraft numerous, but they must have formed a common subject of speculation and discussion. The ordinary evidences of possession were doubtless familiar to the well-informed man without the need of reference to particular records. And it is of the ordinary evidences that the poet chiefly makes use. Nearly all these are found repeatedly in the literature of the period.

We know, on the other hand, that Jonson often preferred to get his information through the medium of books. It is not surprising, therefore, that Merecraft proposes to imitate 'little Darrel's tricks', and to find that the dramatist has resorted in large measure to this particular source.[63]

The Darrel controversy was carried on through a number of years between John Darrel, a clergyman (see note 5. 3. 6), on the one hand, and Bishop Samuel Harsnet, John Deacon and John Walker, on the other. Of the tracts produced in this controversy the two most important are Harsnet's *Discovery of the Fraudulent Practises of John Darrel*,[64] 1599, and Darrel's *True Narration of*

---

[61] *Studien*, p. 232.

[62] See note 2. 1. 168 f.

[63] Gifford points out the general resemblance. He uses Hutchinson's book for comparison.

[64] This book, so far as I know, is not to be found in any American library. My knowledge of its contents is derived wholly from Darrel's answer, *A Detection of that sinnful, shamful, lying and ridiculous Discours, of Samuel Harshnet, entituled: A Discoverie,*

the Strange and Grevous Vexation by the Devil of 7 Persons in Lancashire and William Somers of Nottingham, ... 1600. The story is retold in Francis Hutchinson's *Historical Essay concerning Witchcraft*, London, 1720.

Jonson follows the story as told in these two books with considerable fidelity. The accompaniments of demonic possession which Fitzdottrel exhibits in the last scene are enumerated in two previous speeches. Practically all of these are to be found in Darrel's account:

>   ... roule but wi' your eyes,
> And foam at th' mouth.   (Text, 5. 3. 2-3)
>   ... to make your belly swell,
> And your eyes turne, to foame, to stare, to gnash
> Your teeth together, and to beate your selfe,
> Laugh loud, and faine six voices.   (5. 5. 25 f.)

They may be compared with the description given by Darrel: 'He was often seene ... to beate his head and other parts of his body against the ground and bedstead. In most of his fitts, he did swell in his body; ... if he were standing when the fit came he wold be cast headlong upon the ground, or fall doune, drawing then his lips awry, gnashing with his teeth, wallowing and foaming.... Presently after he would laughe loud and shrill, his mouth being shut close'. (Darrel, p. 181.) 'He was also continually torne in very fearfull manner, and disfigured in his face ... now he gnashed with his teeth; now he fomed like to the horse or boare, ... not to say anything of his fearfull staring with his eyes, and incredible gaping'. (Darrel, p. 183.) The swelling, foaming, gnashing, staring, etc., are also mentioned by Harsnet (pp. 147-8), as well as the jargon of languages (p. 165).

The scene is prepared before Merecraft's appearance (Text, 5. 5. 40. Cf. *Detection*, p. 92), and Fitzdottrel is discovered lying in bed (Text, 5. 5. 39; 5. 8. 40). Similarly, Somers performed many of his tricks 'under a coverlet' (*Detection*, p. 104). Sir Paul Eitherside then enters and 'interprets all'. This is imitated directly from Harsnet, where we read: 'So. [Somers] acting those gestures M. Dar. did expound them very learnedlye, to signify this or that sinne that raigned in Nott. [Nottingham].' Paul's first words are: 'This is the *Diuell* speakes and laughes in him'. So Harsnet tells us that 'M. Dar. vpon his first comming vnto Som. affirmed that it was not So. that spake in his fitts, but the diuell by him'. Both Fitzdottrel (Text, 5. 8. 115) and Somers (*Narration*, p. 182) talk in Greek. The devil in Fitzdottrel proposes to 'break his necke in jest' (Text, 5. 8. 117), and a little later to borrow money (5. 8. 119). The same threat is twice made in the *True Narration* (pp. 178 and 180). In the second of these passages Somers is met by an old woman, who tries to frighten him into giving her money. Otherwise, she declares, 'I will throwe thee into this pit, and

---

etc.... Imprinted 1600, which apparently cites all of Harsnet's more important points for refutation. It has been lent me through the kindness of Professor George L. Burr from the Cornell Library. The quotations from Harsnet in the following pages are accordingly taken from the excerpts in the *Detection*.

breake thy neck'. The mouse 'that should ha' come forth' (Text, 5. 8. 144) is mentioned by both narrators (*Detection*, p. 140; *Narration*, p. 184), and the pricking of the body with pins and needles (Text, 5. 8. 49) is found in slightly altered form (*Detection*, p. 135; *Narration*, p. 174). Finally the clapping of the hands (Text. 5. 8. 76) is a common feature (*Narration*, p. 182). The last mentioned passage finds a still closer parallel in a couplet from the contemporary ballad, which Gifford quotes from Hutchinson (p. 249):

And by the clapping of his Hands
He shew'd the starching of our Bands.

Of the apparatus supplied by Merecraft for the imposture, the soap, nutshell, tow, and touchwood (Text, 5. 3. 3-5), the bladders and bellows (Text, 5. 5. 48), some are doubtless taken from Harsnet's *Discovery*, though Darrel does not quote these passages in the *Detection*. We find, however, that Darrel was accused of supplying Somers with black lead to foam with (*Detection*, p. 160), and Gifford says that the *soap* and *bellows* are also mentioned in the 'Bishop's book'.

Though Jonson drew so largely upon this source, many details are supplied by his own imagination. Ridiculous as much of it may seem to the modern reader, it is by no means overdrawn. In fact it may safely be affirmed that no such realistic depiction of witchcraft exists elsewhere in the whole range of dramatic literature.

3. Prototypes of the leading Characters

The position of the leading characters has already been indicated. Pug, as the comic butt and innocent gull, is allied to Master Stephen and Master Matthew of *Every Man in his Humor*, Dapper of *The Alchemist*, and Cokes of *Bartholomew Fair*. Fitzdottrel, another type of the gull, is more closely related to *Tribulation Wholesome* in *The Alchemist*, and even in some respects to Corvino and Voltore in *The Fox*. Wittipol and Manly, the chief intriguers, hold approximately the same position as Wellbred and Knowell in *Every Man in his Humor*, Winwife and Quarlous in *Bartholomew Fair*, and Dauphine, Clerimont, and Truewit in *The Silent Woman*. Merecraft is related in his character of swindler to Subtle in *The Alchemist*, and in his character of projector to Sir Politick Wouldbe in *The Fox*.

The contemptible 'lady of spirit and woman of fashion' is one of Jonson's favorite types. She first appears in the persons of Fallace and Saviolina in *Every Man out of his Humor*; then in *Cynthia's Revels*, where Moria and her friends play the part; then as Cytheris in *Poetaster*, Lady Politick in *The Alchemist*, the collegiate ladies in *The Silent Woman*, and Fulvia and Sempronia in *Catiline*. The same affectations and vices are satirized repeatedly. An evident prototype of Justice Eitherside is found in the person of Adam Overdo in *Bartholomew Fair*. Both are justices of the peace, both are officious, puritanical, and obstinate. Justice Eitherside's denunciation of the devotees of tobacco finds its counterpart in a speech in *Bartholomew Fair*, and his repeated 'I do detest it' reminds one of Overdo's frequent expressions of horror at the enormities which he constantly discovers.

4. Minor Sources

The Devil is an Ass is not deeply indebted to the classics. Jonson borrows twice from Horace, 1. 6. 131, and 2. 4. 27 f. The half dozen lines in which the former passage occurs (1. 6. 126-132) are written in evident imitation of the Horatian style. Two passages are also borrowed from Plautus, 2. 1. 168 f., already mentioned, and 3. 6. 38-9. A single passage (2. 6. 104 f.) shows the influence of Martial. These passages are all quoted in the notes.

The source of Wittipol's description of the 'Cioppino', and the mishap attendant upon its use, was probably taken from a contemporary book of travels. A passage in Coryat's *Crudities* furnishes the necessary information and a similar anecdote, and was doubtless used by Jonson (see note 4. 4. 69). Coryat was patronized by the poet. Similarly, another passage in the *Crudities* seems to have suggested the project of the forks (see note 5. 4. 17).

A curious resemblance is further to be noted between several passages in *The Devil is an Ass* and *Underwoods 62*. The first draft of this poem may have been written not long before the present play (see Fleay, *Chron.* 1. 329-30) and so have been still fresh in the poet's mind. The passage *DA.* 3. 2. 44-6 shows unmistakably that the play was the borrower, and not the poem. Gifford suggests that both passages were quoted from a contemporary posture-book, but the passage in the epigram gives no indication of being a quotation.

The chief parallels are as follows: *U. 62.* 10-14 and *DA.* 3. 3. 165-6; *U. 62.* 21-2 and *DA.* 3. 3. 169-72; *U. 62.* 25-6 and *DA.* 3. 2. 44-6; *U. 62.* 45-8 and *DA.* 2. 8. 19-22. These passages are all quoted in the notes. In addition, there are a few striking words and phrases that occur in both productions, but the important likenesses are all noted above. In no other poem except *Charis*, *The Gipsies*, and *Underwoods 36*,[65] where the borrowings are unmistakably intentional, is there any thing like the same reworking of material as in this instance.

III. Specific Objects of Satire

The Devil is an Ass has been called of all Jonson's plays since *Cynthia's Revels* the most obsolete in the subjects of its satire.[66] The criticism is true, and it is only with some knowledge of the abuses which Jonson assails that we can appreciate the keenness and precision of his thrusts. The play is a colossal exposé of social abuses. It attacks the aping of foreign fashions, the vices of society, and above all the cheats and impositions of the unscrupulous swindler. But we miss its point if we fail to see that Jonson's arraignment of the society which permitted itself to be gulled is no less severe than that of the swindler who practised upon its credulity. Three institutions especially demand an explanation both for their own sake and for their bearing upon the plot. These

---

[65] See Introduction, Section C. IV.
[66] Swinburne, p. 65.

are the duello, the monopoly, and the pretended demoniacal possession.

1. The Duello

The origin of private dueling is a matter of some obscurity. It was formerly supposed to be merely a development of the judicial duel or combat, but this is uncertain. Dueling flourished on the Continent, and was especially prevalent in France during the reign of Henry III. Jonson speaks of the frequency of the practice in France in *The Magnetic Lady*.

No private duel seems to have occurred in England before the sixteenth century, and the custom was comparatively rare until the reign of James I. Its introduction was largely due to the substitution of the rapier for the broadsword. Not long after this change in weapons fencing-schools began to be established and were soon very popular. Donald Lupton, in his *London and the Countrey carbonadoed*, 1632, says they were usually set up by 'some low-country soldier, who to keep himself honest from further inconveniences, as also to maintain himself, thought upon this course and practises it'.[67]

The etiquette of the duel was a matter of especial concern. The two chief authorities seem to have been Jerome Carranza, the author of a book entitled *Filosofia de las Armas*,[68] and Vincentio Saviolo, whose *Practise* was translated into English in 1595. It contained two parts, the first 'intreating of the vse of the rapier and dagger', the second 'of honor and honorable quarrels'. The rules laid down in these books were mercilessly ridiculed by the dramatists; and the duello was a frequent subject of satire.[69]

By 1616 dueling must have become very common. Frequent references to the subject are found about this time in the *Calendar of State Papers*. Under date of December 9, 1613, we read that all persons who go abroad to fight duels are to be censured in the Star Chamber. On February 17, 1614, 'a proclamation, with a book annexed', was issued against duels, and on February 13, 1617, the King made a Star Chamber speech against dueling, 'on which he before published a sharp edict'.

The passion for dueling was turned to advantage by a set of improvident bravos, who styled themselves 'sword-men' or 'masters of dependencies,' a *dependence* being the accepted name for an impending quarrel. These men undertook to examine into the causes of a duel, and to settle or 'take it up' according to the rules laid down by the authorities on this subject. Their prey were the young men of fashion in the city, and especially 'country gulls', who were newly come to town and were anxious to become sophisticated. The

---

[67] Cf. also Gosson, *School of Abuse*, 1579; Dekker, *A Knight's Conjuring*, 1607; Overbury, *Characters*, ed. Morley, p. 66.

[68] See *New Inn* 2. 2; *Every Man in* 1. 5; B. & Fl., *Love's Pilgrimage*, *Wks.* 11. 317, 320.

[69] Cf. *Albumazar*, *O. Pl.* 7. 185-6; *Rom. and Jul.* 2. 4. 26; *Twelfth Night* 3. 4. 335; *L. L. L.* 1. 2. 183; Massinger, *Guardian*, *Wks.*, p. 346. Mercutio evidently refers to Saviolo's book and the use of the rapier in *Rom. and Jul.* 3. 1. 93. Here the expression, 'fight by the book', first occurs, used again by B. & Fl., *Elder Brother*, *Wks.* 10. 284; Dekker, *Guls Horne-booke*, ch. 4; *As You Like it* 5. 4. Dekker speaks of Saviolo, *Non-dram. Wks.* 1. 120.

profession must have been profitable, for we hear of their methods being employed by the 'roaring boys'[70] and the masters of the fencing schools.[71] Fletcher in *The Elder Brother*, *Wks.* 10. 283, speaks of

> ... the masters of dependencies
> That by compounding differences 'tween others
> Supply their own necessities,

and Massinger makes similar comment in *The Guardian*, *Wks.*, p. 343:

> When two heirs quarrel,
> The swordsmen of the city shortly after
> Appear in plush, for their grave consultations
> In taking up the difference; some, I know,
> Make a set living on't.

Another function of the office is mentioned by Ford in *Fancies Chaste and Noble*, *Wks.* 2. 241. The master would upon occasion 'brave' a quarrel with the novice for the sake of 'gilding his reputation', and Massinger in *The Maid of Honor*, *Wks.*, p. 190, asserts that he would even consent 'for a cloak with thrice-died velvet, and a cast suit' to be 'kick'd down the stairs'. In *A King and No King*, B. & Fl., *Wks.* 2. 310 f., Bessus consults with two of these 'Gentlemen of the Sword' in a ridiculous scene, in which the sword-men profess the greatest scrupulousness in examining every word and phrase, affirming that they cannot be 'too subtle in this business'.

Jonson never loses an opportunity of satirizing these despicable bullies, who were not only ridiculous in their affectations, but who proved by their 'fomenting bloody quarrels' to be no small danger to the state. Bobadill, who is described as a Paul's Man, was in addition a pretender to this craft. Matthew complains that Downright has threatened him with the bastinado, whereupon Bobadill cries out immediately that it is 'a most proper and sufficient dependence' and adds: 'Come hither, you shall chartel him; I'll shew you a trick or two, you shall kill him with at pleasure'.[72] Cavalier Shift, in *Every Man out of his Humor*, among various other occupations has the reputation of being able to 'manage a quarrel the best that ever you saw, for terms and circumstances'. We have an excellent picture of the ambitious novice in the person of Kastrill in *The Alchemist*. Kastrill, who is described as an 'angry boy', comes to consult Subtle as to how to 'carry a business, manage a quarrel fairly'. Face assures him that Dr. Subtle is able to 'take the height' of any quarrel whatsoever, to tell 'in what degree of safety it lies', 'how it may be borne', etc.

From this description of the 'master of dependencies' the exquisite humor of the passage in *The Devil is an Ass* (3. 3. 60 f.) can be appreciated. Merecraft assures Fitzdottrel that this occupation, in reality the refuge only of the Shifts

---

[70] Overbury, ed. Morley, p. 72.

[71] *Ibid.*, p. 66.

[72] *Every Man in*, *Wks.* 1. 35.

and Bobadills of the city, is a new and important office about to be formally established by the state. In spite of all their speaking against dueling, he says, they have come to see the evident necessity of a public tribunal to which all quarrels may be referred. It is by means of this pretended office that Merecraft attempts to swindle Fitzdottrel out of his entire estate, from which disaster he is saved only by the clever interposition of Wittipol.

2. The Monopoly System

Jonson's severest satire in *The Devil is an Ass* is directed against the projector. Through him the whole system of Monopolies is indirectly criticised. To understand the importance and timeliness of this attack, as well as the poet's own attitude on the subject, it is necessary to give a brief historical discussion of the system as it had developed and then existed.

Royal grants with the avowed intention of instructing the English in a new industry had been made as early as the fourteenth century,[73] and the system had become gradually modified during the Tudor dynasty. In the sixteenth century a capitalist middle class rose to wealth and political influence. During the reign of Elizabeth a large part of Cecil's energies was directed toward the economic development of the country. This was most effectually accomplished by granting patents to men who had enterprise enough to introduce a new art or manufacture, whether an importation from a foreign country or their own invention. The capitalist was encouraged to make this attempt by the grant of special privileges of manufacture for a limited period.[74] The condition of monopoly did not belong to the mediaeval system, but was first introduced under Elizabeth. So far the system had its economic justification, but unfortunately it did not stop here. Abuses began to creep in. Not only the manufacture, but the exclusive trade in certain articles, was given over to grantees, and commodities of the most common utility were 'ingrossed into the hands of these blood-suckers of the commonwealth.[75] A remonstrance of Parliament was made to Elizabeth in 1597, and again in 1601, and in consequence the Queen thought best to promise the annulling of all monopolies then existing, a promise which she in large measure fulfilled. But the immense growth of commerce under Elizabeth made it necessary for her successor, James I., to establish a system of delegation, and he accordingly adapted the system of granting patents to the existing needs.[76] Many new monopolies were granted during the early years of his reign, but in 1607 Parliament again protested, and he followed Elizabeth's example by revoking them all. After the suspension of Parliamentary government in 1614 the system grew up again, and the old abuses became more obnoxious than ever. In 1621 Parliament addressed a second remonstrance to James. The king professed ignorance, but promised redress, and in 1624 all the existing monopolies were abolished by the Statute 21 James I. c. 3. In Parliament's address to James 'the tender point of

---

[73] Letters to John Kempe, 1331, Rymer's *Foedera*; Hulme, *Law Quarterly Rev.*, vol. 12.
[74] Cunningham, *Eng. Industry*, Part I, p. 75.
[75] D'Ewes, *Complete Journal of the Houses of Lords and Commons*, p. 646.
[76] Cunningham, p. 21.

prerogative' was not disturbed, and it was contrived that all the blame and punishment should fall on the patentees.[77]

Of all the patents granted during this time, that which seems to have most attracted the attention of the dramatists was one for draining the Fens of Lincolnshire. Similar projects had frequently been attempted during the sixteenth century. In the list of patents before 1597, catalogued by Hulme, seven deal with water drainage in some form or other. The low lands on the east coast of England are exposed to inundation.[78] During the Roman occupation large embankments had been built, and during the Middle Ages these had been kept up partly through a commission appointed by the Crown, and partly through the efforts of the monasteries at Ramsey and Crowland. After the dissolution of these monasteries it became necessary to take up anew the work of reclaiming the fen-land. An abortive attempt by the Earl of Lincoln had already been made when the Statute 43 Eliz. c. 10. 11. was passed in the year 1601. This made legal the action of projectors in the recovery of marsh land. Many difficulties, however, such as lack of funds and opposition on the part of the inhabitants and neighbors of the fens, still stood in their way. In 1605 Sir John Popham and Sir Thomas Fleming headed a company which undertook to drain the Great Level of the Cambridgeshire fens, consisting of more than 300,000 acres, at their own cost, on the understanding that 130,000 acres of the reclaimed land should fall to their share. The project was a complete failure. Another statute granting a patent for draining the fens is found in the seventh year of Jac. I. c. 20, and the attempt was renewed from time to time throughout the reigns of James and Charles I. It was not, however, until the Restoration that these efforts were finally crowned with success.

When the remonstrance was made to James in 1621, the object of the petitioners was gained, as we have seen, by throwing all the blame upon the patentees and projectors. Similarly, the dramatists often prefer to make their attack, not by assailing the institution of monopolies, but by ridicule of the offending subjects.[79] Two agents are regularly distinguished. There is the patentee, sometimes also called the projector, whose part it is to supply the funds for the establishment of the monopoly, and, if possible, the necessary influence at Court; and the actual projector or inventor, who undertakes to furnish his patron with various projects of his own device.

Jonson's is probably the earliest dramatic representation of the projector. Merecraft is a swindler, pure and simple, whose schemes are directed not so much against the people whom he aims to plunder by the establishment of a monopoly as against the adventurer who furnishes the funds for putting the project into operation:

> ... Wee poore Gentlemen, that want acres,
> Must for our needs, turne fooles vp and plough *Ladies*.

---

[77] Craik 2. 24. Rushworth, *Collection* 1. 24.

[78] For a more detailed account of the drainage of the Lincolnshire fens see Cunningham, pp. 112-119.

[79] Cf. Dekker, *Non-dram. Wks.* 3. 367.

Both Fitzdottrel and Lady Tailbush are drawn into these schemes so far as to part with their money. Merecraft himself pretends that he possesses sufficient influence at Court. He flatters Fitzdottrel, who is persuaded by the mere display of projects in a buckram bag, by demanding of him 'his count'nance, t'appeare in't to great men' (2. 1. 39). Lady Tailbush is not so easily fooled, and Merecraft has some difficulty in persuading her of the power of his friends at Court (Act 4. Sc. 1).

Merecraft's chief project, the recovery of the drowned lands, is also satirized by Randolph:

> I have a rare device to set Dutch windmills
> Upon Newmarket Heath, and Salisbury Plain,
> To drain the fens.[80]

and in *Holland's Leaguer*, Act 1. Sc. 5 (cited by Gifford):

> Our projector
> Will undertake the making of bay salt,
> For a penny a bushel, to serve all the state;
> Another dreams of building waterworkes,
> Drying of fenns and marshes, like the Dutchmen.

In the later drama the figure of the projector appears several times, but it lacks the timeliness of Jonson's satire, and the conception must have been largely derived from literary sources. Jonson's influence is often apparent. In Brome's *Court Beggar* the patentee is Mendicant, a country gentleman who has left his rustic life and sold his property, in order to raise his state by court-suits. The projects which he presents at court are the invention of three projectors. Like Merecraft, they promise to make Mendicant a lord, and succeed only in reducing him to poverty. The character of the Court Beggar is given in these words: 'He is a Knight that hanckers about the court ambitious to make himselfe a Lord by begging. His braine is all Projects, and his soule nothing but Court-suits. He has begun more Knavish suits at Court, then ever the Kings Taylor honestly finish'd, but never thriv'd by any: so that now hee's almost fallen from a Palace Begger to a Spittle one'.

In the *Antipodes* Brome introduces 'a States-man studious for the Commonwealth, solicited by Projectors of the Country'. Brome's list of projects (quoted in Gifford's edition) is a broad caricature. Wilson, in the Restoration drama, produced a play called *The Projectors*, in which Jonson's influence is apparent (see Introduction).

Among the *characters*, of which the seventeenth century writers were so fond, the projector is a favorite figure. John Taylor,[81] the water-poet, furnishes

---

[80] *Muse's Looking Glass, O. Pl.* 9. 180 (cited by Gifford).
[81] *Works*, 1641, reprinted by the Spenser Society.

us with a cartoon entitled 'The complaint of M. Tenterhooke the *Projector* and Sir *Thomas* Dodger the Patentee'. In the rimes beneath the picture the distinction between the projector, who 'had the Art to cheat the Commonweale', and the patentee, who was possessed of 'tricks and slights to pass the seale', is brought out with especial distinctness. Samuel Butler's character[82] of the projector is of less importance, since it was not published until 1759. The real importance of Jonson's satire lies in the fact that it appeared in the midst of the most active discussion on the subject of monopolies. Drummond says that he was 'accused upon' the play, and that the King 'desired him to conceal it'. Whether the subject which gave offense was the one which we have been considering or that of witchcraft, it is, however, impossible to determine.

3. Witchcraft

Witchcraft in Jonson's time was not an outworn belief, but a living issue. It is remarkable that the persecutions which followed upon this terrible delusion were comparatively infrequent during the Middle Ages, and reached their maximum only in the seventeenth century.

The first English Act against witchcraft after the Norman Conquest was passed in 1541 (33 Hen. VIII. c. 8). This Act, which was of a general nature, and directed against various kinds of sorceries, was followed by another in 1562 (5 Eliz. c. 16). At the accession of James I. in 1603 was passed 1 Jac. I. c. 12, which continued law for more than a century.

During this entire period charges of witchcraft were frequent. In Scotland they were especially numerous, upwards of fifty being recorded during the years 1596-7.[83] The trial of Anne Turner in 1615, in which charges of witchcraft were joined with those of poisoning, especially attracted the attention of Jonson. In 1593 occurred the trial of the 'three Witches of Warboys', in 1606 that of Mary Smith, in 1612 that of the earlier Lancashire Witches, and of the later in 1633. These are only a few of the more famous cases. Of no less importance in this connection is the attitude of the King himself. In the famous *Demonology*[84] he allied himself unhesitatingly with the cause of superstition. Witchcraft was of course not without its opponents, but these were for the most part obscure men and of little personal influence. While Bacon and Raleigh were inclining to a belief in witchcraft, and Sir Thomas Browne was offering his support to persecution, the cause of reason was intrusted to such champions as Reginald Scot, the author of the famous *Discovery of Witchcraft*, 1584, a work which fearlessly exposes the prevailing follies and crimes. It is on this side that Jonson places himself. That he should make a categorical statement as to his belief or disbelief in witchcraft is not to be expected. It is enough that he presents a picture of the pretended demoniac, that he makes it as sordid and hateful as possible, that he draws for us in the person of Justice Eitherside the portrait of the bigoted, unreasonable, and unjust judge, and that

---

[82] *Character Writings*, ed. Morley, p. 350.
[83] See *Trials for Witchcraft 1596-7*, vol. 1, *Miscellany of the Spalding Club*, Aberdeen, 1841.
[84] First appeared in 1597. *Workes*, fol. ed., appeared 1616, the year of this play.

he openly ridicules the series of cases which he used as the source of his witch scenes (cf. Act. 5. Sc. 3).

To form an adequate conception of the poet's satirical purpose in this play one should compare the methods used here with the treatment followed in Jonson's other dramas where the witch motive occurs. In *The Masque of Queens*, 1609, and in *The Sad Shepherd*, Jonson employed the lore of witchcraft more freely, but in a quite different way. Here, instead of hard realism with all its hideous details, the more picturesque beliefs and traditions are used for purely imaginative and poetical purposes.

The Masque of Queens was presented at Whitehall, and dedicated to Prince Henry. Naturally Jonson's attitude toward witchcraft would here be respectful. It is to be observed, however, that in the copious notes which are appended to the masque no contemporary trials are referred to. The poet relies upon the learned compilations of Bodin, Remigius, Cornelius Agrippa, and Paracelsus, together with many of the classical authors. He is clearly dealing with the mythology of witchcraft. Nightshade and henbane, sulphur, vapors, the eggshell boat, and the cobweb sail are the properties which he uses in this poetic drama. The treatment does not differ essentially from that of Middleton and Shakespeare.

In *The Sad Shepherd* the purpose is still different. We have none of the wild unearthliness of the masque. Maudlin is a witch of a decidedly vulgar type, but there is no satirical intent. Jonson, for the purpose of his play, accepts for the moment the prevailing attitude toward witchcraft, and the satisfaction in Maudlin's discomfiture doubtless assumed an acquiescence in the popular belief. At the same time the poetical aspect is not wholly forgotten, and appears with especial prominence in the beautiful passage which describes the witch's forest haunt, beginning: 'Within a gloomy dimble she doth dwell'. *The Sad Shepherd* and the masque are far more akin to each other in their treatment of witchcraft than is either to *The Devil is an Ass*.

IV. Personal Satire

The detection of personal satire in Jonson's drama is difficult, and at best unsatisfactory. Jonson himself always resented it as an impertinence.[85] In the present case Fleay suggests that the motto, *Ficta, voluptatis causa, sint proxima veris*, is an indication that we are to look upon the characters as real persons. But Jonson twice took the pains to explain that this is precisely the opposite of his own interpretation of Horace's meaning.[86] The subject of personal satire was a favorite one with him, and in *The Magnetic Lady* he makes the sufficiently explicit statement: 'A play, though it apparel and present vices in general, flies from all particularities in persons'.

On the other hand we know that Jonson did occasionally indulge in

---

[85] See Dedication to *The Fox*, Second Prologue to *The Silent Woman*, Induction to *Bartholomew Fair*, *Staple of News* (Second Intermean), *Magnetic Lady* (Second Intermean).

[86] See the note prefixed to *Staple of News*, Act 3, and the second Prologue for *The Silent Woman*.

personal satire. Carlo Buffone,[87] Antonio Balladino,[88] and the clerk Nathaniel[89] are instances sufficiently authenticated. Of these Jonson advances a plea of justification: 'Where have I been particular? where personal? except to a mimic, cheater, bawd or buffoon, creatures, for their insolencies, worthy to be taxed? yet to which of these so pointingly, as he might not either ingenuously have confest, or wisely dissembled his disease?'[90]

In only one play do we know that the principal characters represent real people. But between *Poetaster* and *The Devil is an Ass* there is a vast difference of treatment. In *Poetaster* (1) the attitude is undisguisedly satirical. The allusions in the prologues and notices to the reader are direct and unmistakable. (2) The character-drawing is partly caricature, partly allegorical. This method is easily distinguishable from the typical, which aims to satirize a class. (3) Jonson does not draw upon historical events, but personal idiosyncrasies. (4) The chief motive is in the spirit of Aristophanes, the great master of personal satire. These methods are what we should naturally expect in a composition of this sort. Of such internal evidence we find little or nothing in *The Devil is an Ass*. Several plausible identifications, however, have been proposed, and these we must consider separately.

The chief characters are identified by Fleay as follows: Wittipol is Jonson. He has returned from travel, and had seen Mrs. Fitzdottrel before he went. Mrs. Fitzdottrel is the Lady Elizabeth Hatton. Fitzdottrel is her husband, Sir Edward Coke.

Mrs. Fitzdottrel. The identification is based upon a series of correspondences between a passage in *The Devil is an Ass* (2. 6. 57-113) and a number of passages scattered through Jonson's works. The most important of these are quoted in the note to the above passage. To them has been added an important passage from *A Challenge at Tilt*, 1613. Fleay's deductions are these: (1) *Underwoods 36* and *Charis* must be addressed to the same lady (cf. especially *Ch.*, part 5). (2) Charis and Mrs. Fitzdottrel are identical. The song (2. 6. 94 f.) is found complete in the *Celebration of Charis*. In Wittipol's preceding speech we find the phrases 'milk and roses' and 'bank of kisses', which occur in *Charis* and in *U. 36*, and a reference to the husband who is the 'just excuse' for the wife's infidelity, which occurs in *U. 36*. (3) Charis is Lady Hatton. Fleay believes that *Charis*, part 1, in which the poet speaks of himself as writing 'fifty years', was written c 1622-3; but that parts 2-10 were written c 1608. In reference to these parts he says: 'Written in reference to a mask in which Charis represented Venus riding in a chariot drawn by swans and doves (*Charis*, part 4), at a marriage, and leading the Graces in a dance at Whitehall, worthy to be envied of the Queen (6), in which Cupid had a part (2, 3, 5), at which Charis kissed him (6, 7), and afterwards kept up a close intimacy with him (8, 9, 10). The mask of 1608, Feb. 9, exactly fulfils these conditions, and the Venus of that mask was probably L. Elizabeth Hatton, the most beautiful of

---

[87] *Ev. Man in.*
[88] *Case is Altered.*
[89] *Staple of News.*
[90] Dedication to *The Fox.*

the then court ladies. She had appeared in the mask of Beauty, 1608, Jan. 10, but in no other year traceable by me. From the Elegy, G. 36, manifestly written to the same lady (compare it with the lines in 5 as to "the bank of kisses" and "the bath of milk and roses"), we learn that Charis had "a husband that is the just excuse of all that can be done him". This was her second husband, Sir Edward Coke, to whom she was married in 1593'.

Fleay's theory rests chiefly upon (1) his interpretation of *The Celebration of Claris*; (2) the identity of Charis and Mrs. Fitzdottrel. A study of the poem has led me to conclusions of a very different nature from those of Fleay. They may be stated as follows:

Charis 1. This was evidently written in 1622-3. Jonson plainly says: 'Though I now write fifty years'. Charis is here seemingly identified with Lady Purbeck, daughter of Lady Hatton. Compare the last two lines with the passage from *The Gipsies*. Fleay believes the compliments were transferred in the masque at Lady Hatton's request.

Charis 4 and 7 have every mark of being insertions. (1) They are in different metres from each other and from the other sections, which in this respect are uniform. (2) They are not in harmony with the rest of the poem. They entirely lack the easy, familiar, half jocular style which characterizes the eight other parts. (3) Each is a somewhat ambitious effort, complete in itself, and distinctly lyrical. (4) In neither is there any mention of or reference to Charis. (5) It is evident, therefore, that they were not written for the *Charis* poem, but merely interpolated. They are, then, of all the parts the least valuable for the purpose of identification, nor are we justified in looking upon them as continuing a definite narrative with the rest of the poem. (6) The evident reason for introducing them is their own intrinsic lyrical merit.

Charis 4 was apparently written in praise of some pageant, probably a court masque. The representation of Venus drawn in a chariot by swans and doves, the birds sacred to her, may have been common enough. That this is an accurate description of the masque of February 9, 1608 is, however, a striking fact, and it is possible that the lady referred to is the same who represented Venus in that masque. But (1) we do not even know that Jonson refers to a masque of his own, or a masque at all. (2) We have no trustworthy evidence that Lady Hatton was the Venus of that masque. Fleay's identification is little better than a guess. (3) Evidence is derived from the first stanza alone. This does not appear in *The Devil is an Ass*, and probably was not written at the time. Otherwise there is no reason for its omission in that place. It seems to have been added for the purpose of connecting the lyric interpolation with the rest of the poem.

Charis 5 seems to be a late production. (1) Jonson combines in this single section a large number of figures used in other places. (2) That it was not the origin of these figures seems to be intimated by the words of the poem. Cupid is talking. He had lately found Jonson describing his lady, and Jonson's words, he says, are descriptive of Cupid's own mother, Venus. So Homer had spoken of her hair, so Anacreon of her face. He continues:

> By her looks I do her know
> *Which you call* my shafts.

The italicized words may refer to *U. 36.* 3-4. They correspond, however, much more closely to *Challenge, 2 Cup.* The 'bath your verse discloses' (l. 21) may refer to *DA.* 2. 6. 82-3. *U. 36.* 7-8 or *Gipsies* 15-6.

> ... the bank of kisses,
> Where *you say* men gather blisses

is mentioned in *U. 36.* 9-10. 'The passages in *DA.* and *Gipsies*[91] are less close. The 'valley *called* my nest' may be a reference to *DA.* 2. 6. 74 f. Jonson had already spoken of the 'girdle 'bout her waist' in *Challenge, 2 Cup. Charis* 5 seems then to have been written later than *U. 36, Challenge,* 1613, and probably *Devil is an Ass,* 1616. The evidence is strong, though not conclusive.

Charis 6 evidently refers to a marriage at Whitehall. That Cupid, who is referred to in 2, 3, 5, had any part in the marriage of *Charis* 6 is nowhere even intimated. That Charis led the Graces in a dance is a conjecture equally unfounded. Jonson of course takes the obvious opportunity (ll. 20, 26) of playing on the name Charis. That this occasion was the same as that celebrated in 4 we have no reason to believe. It applies equally well, for instance, to *A Challenge at Tilt,* but we are by no means justified in so limiting it. It may have been imaginary.

Charis 7 was written before 1618, since Jonson quoted a part of it to Drummond during his visit in Scotland (cf. *Conversations* 5). It was a favorite of the poet's and this furnishes sufficient reason for its insertion here. It is worthy of note that the two sections of *Charis,* which we know by external proof to have been in existence before 1623, are those which give internal evidence of being interpolations.

Summary. The poem was probably a late production and of composite nature. There is no reason for supposing that the greater part was not written in 1622-3. The fourth and seventh parts are interpolations. The first stanza of the fourth part, upon which the identification largely rests, seems not to have been written until the poem was put together in 1622-3. If it was written at the same time as the other two stanzas, we cannot expect to find it forming part of a connected narrative. The events described in the fourth and sixth parts are not necessarily the same. There is practically no evidence that Lady Hatton was the Venus of 1608, or that *Charis* is addressed to any particular lady.

The other link in Fleay's chain of evidence is of still weaker substance. The mere repetition of compliments does not necessarily prove the recipient to be

---

[91] The passage from the *Gipsies* especially finds a close parallel in the fragment of a song in Marston's *Dutch Courtezan,* 1605, *Wks.* 2. 46:

> Purest lips, soft banks of blisses
> Self alone deserving kisses.

Are not these lines from Jonson's hand? This was the year of his collaboration with Marston in *Eastward Ho.*

the same person. In fact we find in these very pieces the same phrases applied indiscriminately to Lady Purbeck, Lady Frances Howard, Mrs. Fitzdottrel, perhaps to Lady Hatton, and even to the Earl of Somerset. Of what value, then, can such evidence be?

Fleay's whole theory rests on this poem, and biographical evidence is unnecessary. It is sufficient to notice that Lady Hatton was a proud woman, that marriage with so eminent a man as Sir Edward Coke was considered a great condescension (*Chamberlain's Letters*, Camden Soc., p. 29), and that an amour with Jonson is extremely improbable.

Fitzdottrel. Fleay's identification of Fitzdottrel with Coke rests chiefly on the fact that Coke was Lady Hatton's husband. The following considerations are added. Fitzdottrel is a 'squire of Norfolk'. Sir E. Coke was a native of Norfolk, and had held office in Norwich. Fitzdottrel's rôle as sham demoniac is a covert allusion to Coke's adoption of the popular witch doctrines in the Overbury trial. His jealousy of his wife was shown in the same trial, where he refused to read the document of 'what ladies loved what lords', because, as was popularly supposed, his own wife's name headed the list. Jonson is taking advantage of Coke's disgrace in November, 1616. He had flattered him in 1613 (*U. 64*).

Our reasons for rejecting this theory are as follows: (1) The natural inference is that Jonson would not deliberately attack the man whom he had highly praised three years before. I do not understand Fleay's assertion that Jonson was always ready to attack the fallen. (2) The compliment paid to Coke in 1613 (*U. 64*) was not the flattery of an hour of triumph. The appointment to the king's bench was displeasing to Coke, and made at the suggestion of Bacon with the object of removing him to a place where he would come less often into contact with the king. (3) Fitzdottrel is a light-headed man of fashion, who spends his time in frequenting theatres and public places, and in conjuring evil spirits. Coke was sixty-four years old, the greatest lawyer of his time, and a man of the highest gifts and attainments. (4) The attempted parallel between Fitzdottrel, the pretended demoniac, and Coke, as judge in the Overbury trial, is patently absurd. (5) If Lady Hatton had not been selected for identification with Mrs. Fitzdottrel, Coke would never have been dreamed of as a possible Fitzdottrel.

Wittipol. He is a young man just returned from travel, which apparently has been of considerable duration. He saw Mrs. Fitzdottrel once before he went, and upon returning immediately seeks her out. How does this correspond to Jonson's life? *The Hue and Cry* was played February 9, 1608. According to Fleay's interpretation, this was followed by an intimacy with Lady Hatton. Five years later, in 1613, Drummond tells us that Jonson went to France with the son of Sir Walter Raleigh. He returned the same year in time to compose *A Challenge at Tilt*, December 27. Three years later he wrote *The Devil is an Ass* at the age of forty-three.

Wittipol intimates that he is Mrs. Fitzdottrel's equal in years, in fashion (1. 6. 124-5), and in blood (1. 6. 168). For Jonson to say this to Lady Hatton would have been preposterous.

Justice Eitherside.   Only the desire to prove a theory at all costs could have prevented Fleay from seeing that Coke's counterpart is not Fitzdottrel, but Justice Eitherside. In obstinacy, bigotry, and vanity this character represents the class of judges with which Coke identified himself in the Overbury trial. Nor are these merely class-traits. They are distinctly the faults which marred Coke's career from the beginning. It is certain that Coke is partially responsible for this portraiture. Overbury was a personal friend of the poet, and the trial, begun in the previous year, had extended into 1616. Jonson must have followed it eagerly. On the other hand, it is improbable that the picture was aimed exclusively at Coke. He merely furnished traits for a typical and not uncommon character. As we have seen, it is in line with Jonson's usual practise to confine personal satire to the lesser characters.

Merecraft.   Fleay's identification with Sir Giles Mompesson has very little to commend it. Mompesson was connected by marriage with James I.'s powerful favorite, George Villiers, later Duke of Buckingham. In 1616 he suggested to Villiers the creation of a special commission for the purpose of granting licenses to keepers of inns and ale-houses. The suggestion was adopted by Villiers; Mompesson was appointed to the Commission in October, 1616, and knighted on November 18 of that year. The patent was not sealed until March, 1617. His high-handed conduct soon became unpopular, but he continued in favor with Villiers and James, and his disgrace did not come until 1621.

It will readily be seen that Mompesson's position and career conform in no particular to those of Merecraft in the present play. Mompesson was a knight, a friend of the king's favorite, and in favor with the king. Merecraft is a mere needy adventurer without influence at court, and the associate of ruffians, who frequent the 'Straits' and the 'Bermudas'. Mompesson was himself the recipient of a patent (see section III. 2). Merecraft is merely the projector who devises clever projects for more powerful patrons. Mompesson's project bears no resemblance to those suggested by Merecraft, and he could hardly have attracted any popular dislike at the time when *The Devil is an Ass* was presented, since, as we have seen, his patent was not even sealed until the following year. Finally, Jonson would hardly have attacked a man who stood so high at court as did Mompesson in 1616.

It is evident that Jonson had particularly in mind those projectors whose object it was to drain the fens of Lincolnshire. The attempts, as we have seen, were numerous, and it is highly improbable that Jonson wished to satirize any one of them more severely than another. In a single passage, however, it seems possible that Sir John Popham (see page lx) is referred to. In Act 4. Sc. 1 Merecraft speaks of a Sir John Monie-man as a projector who was able to 'jump a business quickly' because 'he had great friends'. That Popham is referred to seems not unlikely from the fact that he was the most important personage who had embarked upon an enterprise of this sort, that his scheme was one of the earliest, that he was not a strict contemporary (d. 1607), and that his scheme had been very unpopular. This is proved by an anonymous letter to the king, in which complaint is made that 'the "covetous bloody Popham" will ruin many poor men by his offer to drain the fens' (*Cal. State Papers*, Mar. 14?, 1606).

Plutarchus Guilthead. Fleay's identification with Edmund Howes I am prepared to accept, although biographical data are very meagre. Fleay says: 'Plutarchus Gilthead, who is writing the lives of the great men in the city; the captain who writes of the Artillery Garden "to train the youth", etc. [3. 2. 45], is, I think, Edmond Howes, whose continuation of Stow's Chronicle was published in 1615.'

Howes' undertaking was a matter of considerable ridicule to his acquaintances. In his 1631 edition he speaks of the heavy blows and great discouragements he received from his friends. He was in the habit of signing himself 'Gentleman' and this seems to be satirized in 3. 1, where Guilthead says repeatedly: 'This is to make you a Gentleman' (see *N. & Q.* 1st Ser. 6. 199.).

The Noble House. Two proposed identifications of the 'noble house', which pretends to a duke's title, mentioned at 2. 4. 15-6. have been made. The expenditure of much energy in the attempt to fix so veiled an allusion is hardly worth while. Jonson of course depended upon contemporary rumor, for which we have no data.

Cunningham's suggestion that Buckingham is referred to is not convincing. Buckingham's father was Sir George Villiers of Brooksby in Leicestershire. He was not himself raised to the nobility until August 27, 1616, when he was created Viscount Villiers and Baron Waddon. It was not until January 5, 1617 (not 1616, as Cunningham says), that he became Earl of Buckingham, and it is unlikely that before this time any allusion to Villiers' aspiration to a dukedom would have been intelligible to Jonson's audience.

Fleay's theory that the 'noble house' was that of Stuart may be accepted provisionally. Lodowick was made Earl of Richmond in 1613, and Duke in 1623. He was acceptable to king and people, and in this very year was made steward of the household.

D. After-Influence of the Devil is an Ass

A few instances of the subsequent rehandling of certain motives in this play are too striking to be completely overlooked. John Wilson, 1627-c 1696, a faithful student and close imitator of Jonson, produced in 1690 a drama called *Belphegor*, or *The Marriage of the Devil, a Tragi-comedy*. While it is founded on the English translation of Machiavelli's novella, which appeared in 1674, and closely adheres to the lines of the original, it shows clear evidence of Jonson's influence. The subject has been fully investigated by Hollstein (cf. *Verhältnis*, pp. 22-24, 28-30, 35, 43, 50).

The Cheats, 1662, apparently refers to *The Devil is an Ass* in the *Prologue*. The characters of Bilboe and Titere Tu belong to the same class of low bullies as Merecraft and Everill, but the evident prototypes of these characters are Subtle and Face in *The Alchemist*.

A third play of Wilson's, *The Projectors*, 1664, shows unmistakable influence of *The Devil is an Ass*. The chief object of satire is of course the same, and the character of Sir Gudgeon Credulous is modeled after that of Fitzdottrel. The scenes in which the projects are explained, 2. 1 and 3. 1, are similar to the corresponding passages in Jonson. The *Aulularia* of Plautus is a partial source, so that the play in some features resembles *The Case is Altered*. In 2. 1 Wilson imitates the passage in the *Aulularia*, which closes Act 2. Sc. 1 of *The Devil is an Ass* (see note 2. 1. 168).

Brome, Jonson's old servant and friend, also handled the subject of monopolies. Jonson's influence is especially marked in *The Court Beggar*. The project of perukes (*Wks.* 1. 192) should be compared with Merecraft's project of toothpicks.

Mrs. Susanna Centlivre's *Busie Body* uses the motives borrowed from Boccaccio. The scenes in which these appear must have been suggested by Jonson's play (Genest 2. 419), though the author seems to have been acquainted with the *Decameron* also. In Act. 1. Sc. 1 Sir George Airy makes a bargain with Sir Francis Gripe similar to Wittipol's bargain with Fitzdottrel. In exchange for the sum of a hundred guineas he is admitted into the house for the purpose of moving his suit to Miranda. 'for the space of ten minutes, without lett or molestation', provided Sir Francis remain in the same room, though out of ear shot (2d ed., p. 8). In Act 2. Sc. 1 the bargain is carried out in much the same way as in Boccaccio and in Jonson. Miranda remaining dumb and Sir George answering for her.

In Act 3. Sc. 4 (2d ed., p. 38) Miranda in the presence of her guardian sends a message by Marplot not to saunter at the garden gate about eight o'clock as he has been accustomed to do, thus making an assignation with him (compare *DA.* 2. 2. 52).

Other motives which seem to show some influence of *The Devil is an Ass* are Miranda's trick to have the estate settled upon her, Charles' disguise as a Spaniard, and Traffick's jealous care of Isabinda. The character of Marplot as comic butt resembles that of Pug.

The song in *The Devil is an Ass* 2. 6. 94 was imitated by Sir John Suckling.

APPENDIX
EXTRACTS FROM THE CRITICS

Gifford: There is much good writing in this comedy. All the speeches of Satan are replete with the most biting satire, delivered with an appropriate degree of spirit. Fitzdottrel is one of those characters which Jonson delighted to draw, and in which he stood unrivalled, a *gull*, i. e., a confident coxcomb, selfish, cunning, and conceited. Mrs. Fitzdottrel possesses somewhat more interest than the generality of our author's females, and is indeed a well sustained character. In action the principal amusement of the scene (exclusive of the admirable burlesque of witchery in the conclusion) was probably derived from the mortification of poor Pug, whose stupid stare of amazement at finding himself made an *ass* of on every possible occasion must, if portrayed as some then on the stage were well able to portray it, have been exquisitely comic.

This play is strictly moral in its conception and conduct. Knavery and folly are shamed and corrected, virtue is strengthened and rewarded, and the ends of dramatic justice are sufficiently answered by the simple exposure of those whose errors are merely subservient to the minor interests of the piece.

Herford (*Studies in the Literary Relations of England and Germany*, pp. 318-20): Jonson had in fact so far the Aristophanic quality of genius, that he was at once a most elaborate and minute student of the actual world, and a poet of the airiest and boldest fancy, and that he loved to bring the two rôles into the closest possible combination. No one so capable of holding up the mirror to contemporary society without distorting the slenderest thread of its complex tissue of usages; no one, on the other hand, who so keenly delighted in startling away the illusion or carefully undermining it by some palpably fantastic invention. His most elaborate reproductions of the everyday world are hardly ever without an infusion of equally elaborate caprice,—a leaven of recondite and fantastic legend and grotesque myth, redolent of old libraries and antique scholarship, furtively planted, as it were, in the heart of that everyday world of London life, and so subtly blending with it that the whole motley throng of merchants and apprentices, gulls and gallants, discover nothing unusual in it, and engage with the most perfectly matter of fact air in the business of working it out. The purging of Crispinus in the *Poetaster*, the Aristophanic motive of the *Magnetic Lady*, even the farcical horror of noise which is the mainspring of the *Epicœne*, are only less elaborate and sustained examples of this fantastic realism than the adventure of a Stupid Devil in the play before us. Nothing more anomalous in the London of Jonson's day could be conceived; yet it is so managed that it loses all its strangeness. So perfectly is the supernatural element welded with the human, that it almost ceases to appear supernatural. Pug, the hero of the adventure, is a pretty, petulant boy, more human by many degrees than the half fairy Puck of Shakespeare, which doubtless helped to suggest him, and the arch-fiend Satan is a bluff old politician, anxious to ward off the perils of London from his young simpleton of a son, who is equally eager to plunge into them. The old savage horror fades away before Jonson's humanising touch, the infernal world loses all its privilege of peculiar terror and strength, and sinks to the footing of a mere rival state, whose merchandise can be kept out of the market and its citizens put in the Counter or carted to Tyburn.

A. W. Ward (*Eng. Dram. Lit.*, pp. 372-3): The oddly-named comedy of *The Devil is an Ass*, acted in 1616, seems already to exhibit a certain degree of decay in the dramatic powers which had so signally called forth its predecessor. Yet this comedy possesses a considerable literary interest, as adapting both to Jonson's dramatic method, and to the general moral atmosphere of his age, a theme connecting itself with some of the most notable creations of the earlier Elizabethan drama.... The idea of the play is as healthy as its plot is ingenious; but apart from the circumstance that the latter is rather slow in preparation, and by no means, I think, gains in perspicuousness as it proceeds, the design itself suffers from one radical mistake. Pug's intelligence is so much below par that he suffers as largely on account of his clumsiness as on account of his viciousness, while remaining absolutely without influence upon the course of the action. The comedy is at the same time full of humor, particularly in the entire character of Fitzdottrel.

Swinburne (*Study of Ben Jonson*, pp. 65-7): If *The Devil is an Ass* cannot be ranked among the crowning masterpieces of its author, it is not because the play shows any sign of decadence in literary power or in humorous invention. The writing is admirable, the wealth of comic matter is only too copious, the characters are as firm in outline or as rich in color as any but the most triumphant examples of his satirical or sympathetic skill in finished delineation and demarcation of humors. On the other hand, it is of all Ben Jonson's comedies since the date of *Cynthia's Revels* the most obsolete in subject of satire, the most temporary in its allusions and applications: the want of fusion or even connection (except of the most mechanical or casual kind) between the various parts of its structure and the alternate topics of its ridicule makes the action more difficult to follow than that of many more complicated plots: and, finally, the admixture of serious sentiment and noble emotion is not so skilfully managed as to evade the imputation of incongruity. [The dialogue between Lady Tailbush and Lady Eitherside in Act 4. Sc. 1 has some touches 'worthy of Molière himself.' In Act 4. Sc. 3 Mrs. Fitzdottrel's speech possesses a 'a noble and natural eloquence,' but the character of her husband is 'almost too loathsome to be ridiculous,' and unfit 'for the leading part in a comedy of ethics as well as of morals.'] The prodigality of elaboration lavished on such a multitude of subordinate characters, at the expense of all continuous interest and to the sacrifice of all dramatic harmony, may tempt the reader to apostrophize the poet in his own words:

You are so covetous still to embrace
More than you can, that you lose all.

Yet a word of parting praise must be given to Satan: a small part as far as extent goes, but a splendid example of high comic imagination after the order of Aristophanes, admirably relieved by the low comedy of the asinine Pug and the voluble doggrel by the antiquated Vice.

TEXT

Editor's Note

The text here adopted is that of the original edition of 1631. No changes of reading have been made; spelling, punctuation, capitalization, and italics are reproduced. The original pagination is inserted in brackets; the book-holder's marginal notes are inserted where 1716 and Whalley placed them. In a few instances modern type has been substituted for archaic characters. The spacing of the contracted words has been normalized.

1641 =	Pamphlet folio of 1641.
1692 =	The Third Folio, 1692.
1716 =	Edition of 1716 (17).
W =	Whalley's edition, 1756.
G =	Gifford's edition, 1816.
SD. =	Stage directions at the beginning of a scene.
SN. =	Side note, or book-holder's note.
om. =	omitted.
ret. =	retained.
f. =	and all later editions.
G§ =	a regular change. After a single citation only exceptions are noted. See Introduction.

Mere changes of spelling have not been noted in the variants. All changes of form and all suggestive changes of punctuation have been recorded.

THE DIUELL
IS
AN ASSE:

A COMEDIE
ACTED IN THE
YEARE, 1616.
BY HIS MAIESTIES
Servants.

The Author BEN: IONSON

HOR. *de* ART. POET.
Ficta voluptatis Cauſâ, ſint proxima veris.

The Persons of the Play[92]

Satan.	*The great diuell.*[93]
Pvg.	*The leſſe diuell.*[94]
Iniqvity.	*The Vice.*
Fitz-dottrell.[95]	*A Squire of Norfolk.*
Miſtreſſe Frances.[96]	*His wife.*
Meere-craft.	*The Proiector.*
Everill.	*His champion.*
Wittipol.	*A young Gallant.*
Manly.[97]	*His friend.*
Ingine.[98]	*A Broaker.*
Traines.	*The Proiectors man.*
Gvilt-head.[99]	*A Gold-ſmith.*
Plvtarchvs.[100]	*His ſonne.*
Sir Povle Either-side.	*A Lawyer, and Iuſtice.*
Lady Either-side.	*His wife.*
Lady Taile-bvsh.	*The Lady Proiectreſſe.*
Pit-fall.	*Her woman.*
Ambler.[101]	*Her Gentlemanvſher.*
Sledge.	*A Smith, the conſtable.*
Shackles.	*Keeper of Newgate.*

Serieants.[102]

The Scene, London.[103]

---

[92] Dramatis Personæ 1716, f. G places the women's names after those of the men.
[93] Devil 1692, f.
[94] Devil 1692, f.
[95] Fabian Fitzdottrel G
[96] Mrs. Frances Fitzdottrel G || His wife] om. G
[97] Eustace Manly G
[98] Engine 1716, f.
[99] Thomas Gilthead G
[100] His wife] om. G
[101] Gentleman-usher to lady Tailbush G
[102] Serjeants, officers, servants, underkeepers, &c. G
[103] The] om. 1716, W

THE PROLOGUE[104]

The Divell *is an* Aſſe. *That is, to day,*
The name of what you are met for, a new Play.
Yet, Grandee's, would you were not come to grace
Our matter, with allowing vs no place.
Though you preſume Satan *a ſubtill[105] thing,*   5

And may haue heard hee's worne in a thumbe-ring;
Doe not on theſe preſumptions, force vs act,
In compaſſe of a cheeſe-trencher. This tract
Will ne'er admit our vice, *becauſe of yours.*
Anone, who, worſe then[106] you, the fault endures   10

That your ſelues make? when you will thruſt and ſpurne,
And knocke vs o'[107] the elbowes, and bid, turne;
As if, when wee had ſpoke, wee muſt be gone,
Or, till[108] wee ſpeake, muſt all runne in, to one,
Like the young adders, at the old ones mouth?   15

Would wee could ſtand due North; *or had no* South,
If that offend: or were Muſcouy *glaſſe,*
That you might looke our Scenes *through as they paſſe.*
We know not how to affect you. If you'll come
To ſee new Playes, pray you affoord vs roome,   20

And ſhew this, but the ſame face you haue done
Your deare delight, the Diuell *of* Edmunton.
Or, if, for want of roome it muſt miſ-carry,
'Twill be but Iuſtice, that your cenſure tarry,
Till you giue ſome. And when ſixe times you ha'[109] ſeen't,   25

If this Play *doe not like, the Diuell is in't.*

---

[104] The Prologue.] follows the title-page 1716, W
[105] *subtle* 1692 f.
[106] than 1692, f. passim in this sense. Anon 1692, f.
[107] o'] on G§
[108] till] 'till 1716
[109] ha'] have G§

ACT. I. SCENE. I.
Divell. Pvg. Iniqvity.[110]

Hoh, hoh, hoh, hoh, hoh, hoh, hoh, hoh, &c.[111]
To earth? and, why to earth, thou fooolifh Spirit?
What wold'ft thou do on earth? Pvg. For that, great Chiefe!
As time fhal work. I do but ask my mon'th.
Which euery petty *pui'nee Diuell* has;   5

Within that terme, the Court of *Hell* will heare
Some thing, may gaine a longer grant, perhaps.
Sat. For what? the laming a poore Cow, or two?
Entring[112] a Sow, to make her caft her farrow?
Or croffing of a Mercat-womans Mare,[113]   10

Twixt this, and *Totnam[114]*? thefe were wont to be
Your maine atchieuements, *Pug*, You haue fome plot, now,
Vpon a tonning of Ale, to ftale the yeft,
Or keepe the churne fo, that the buttter come not;
Spight o' the houfewiues[115] cord, or her hot fpit?   15

Or fome good Ribibe, about *Kentifh* Towne,
Or *Hogfden*, you would hang now, for a witch,
Becaufe fhee will not let you play round *Robbin*:
And you'll goe fowre the Citizens Creame 'gainft Sunday?
That fhe may be accus'd for't, and condemn'd,   20

By a *Middlefex* Iury, to the fatisfaction
Of their offended friends, the *Londiners* wiues
Whofe teeth were fet on edge with it[116]? Foolifh feind,
Stay i'[117] your place, know your owne ftrengths, and put not
Beyond the fpheare of your actiuity.   25

You are too dull a Diuell to be trufted
Forth in thofe parts, *Pug*, vpon any affayre
That may concerne our name, on earth. It is not

---

[110] Divell] *Devil*, 1692 || *Satan* 1716, W || Divell ...] *Enter* Satan *and* Pug. G
[111] &c. om. G
[112] entering G
[113] Market 1641, 1692, 1716 || market W, G
[114] Tottenham G
[115] Housewive's 1716 || housewife's W, f.
[116] with't W, G
[117] i'] in G§ || strength 1692, f.

Euery ones worke. The ſtate of *Hell* muſt care
Whom it imployes[118], in point of reputation,   30

Heere about *London*. You would make, I thinke
An Agent, to be ſent, for *Lancaſhire*,
Proper inough[119]; or ſome parts of *Northumberland*,
So yo' had[120] good inſtructions, *Pug.Pvg. O Chiefe!*
You doe not know, deare *Chiefe*, what there is in mee.   35

Proue me but for a fortnight, for a weeke,
And lend mee but a *Vice*, to carry with mee,
To practice there-with[121] any play-fellow,
And, you will ſee, there will come more vpon't,
Then you'll imagine, pretious *Chiefe. Sat.* What *Vice*?   40

What kind wouldſt th' haue it of?
Pvg. Why, any *Fraud[122]*; Or *Couetouſneſſe*;
or Lady *Vanity*; Or old *Iniquity*: I'll[123] call him hither.
Ini. What is he, calls vpon me, and would ſeeme to lack a *Vice*?
Ere his words be halfe ſpoken, I am with him in a trice;   45

Here, there, and euery where, as the Cat is with the mice:
True *vetus Iniquitas*. Lack'ſt thou Cards, friend, or Dice?
I will teach thee cheate,[124] Child, to cog, lye, and ſwagger,
And euer and anon, to be drawing forth thy dagger:
To ſweare by Gogs-nownes, like a lusty *Iuuentus*,   50

In a cloake to thy heele, and a hat like a pent-houſe.
Thy breeches of three fingers, and thy doublet all belly,
With a Wench that shall feede thee, with cock-ſtones and gelly.
Pvg. Is it not excellent, *Chiefe*? how nimble he is!
Ini. Child of hell, this is nothing! I will fetch thee a leape.   55

From the top of *Pauls*-ſteeple, to the Standard in *Cheepe*:
And lead thee a daunce,[125] through the ſtreets without faile,
Like a needle of *Spaine*, with a thred at my tayle.
We will ſuruay the *Suburbs*, and make forth our ſallyes,
Downe *Petticoate-lane*, and vp the *Smock-allies*,   60

---

[118] employs W, G
[119] enough 1692, f.
[120] you 'ad 1716 you had W, G
[121] there with 1692, f.
[122] th'] thou G Why any, Fraud, 1716 Why any: Fraud, W, G
[123] I'll ...] *Sat.* I'll ... W, G] *Enter* Iniquity. G
[124] cheate] to cheat W [to] cheat G
[125] Dance 1716 ‖ dance 1641. W, G

To *Shoreditch, Whitechappell,* and so to Saint *Kathernes.*
To drinke with the *Dutch* there, and take forth their patternes:
From thence, wee will put in at *Cuſtome-houſe* key there,
And ſee, how the Factors, and Prentizes play there,
Falſe with their Maſters; and gueld many a full packe,   65

To ſpend it in pies, at the *Dagger,* and the *Wool-ſacke.*
Pvg. Braue, braue, *Iniquity*! will not this doe, *Chiefe*?
Ini. Nay, boy, I wil bring thee to the Bawds, and the Royſters,
At *Belins-gate,*[126] feaſting with claret-wine, and oyſters,
From thence ſhoot the *Bridge,* childe, to the Cranes i' the *Vintry,*   70

And ſee, there the gimblets, how they make their entry!
Or, if thou hadſt rather, to the *Strand* downe to fall,
'Gainſt the Lawyers come dabled from *Weſtminſter-hall*
And marke how they cling, with their clyents together,
Like Iuie to Oake; so Veluet to Leather: 75

Ha, boy, I would ſhew thee.[127] Pvg. Rare, rare! Div. Peace, dotard,
And thou more ignorant thing, that ſo admir'ſt.
Art thou the ſpirit thou ſeem'ſt? ſo poore? to chooſe
This, for a *Vice,* t'[128]aduance the cauſe of *Hell,*
Now? as Vice ſtands this preſent yeere? Remember,   80

What number it is. *Six hundred* and *ſixteene.*
Had it but beene *fiue hundred,* though ſome *ſixty*
Aboue; that's *fifty* yeeres agone, and *ſix,*
(When euery great man had his *Vice* ſtand by him,[129]
In his long coat, ſhaking his wooden dagger)   85

I could conſent, that, then this your graue choice
Might haue done that with his Lord *Chiefe,* the which
Moſt of his chamber can doe now. But *Pug,*
As the times are, who is it, will receiue you?
What company will you goe to? or whom mix with?   90

Where canſt thou carry him? except to Tauernes?
To mount vp ona joynt-ſtoole, with a *Iewes*-trumpe,
To put downe *Cokeley,* and that muſt be to Citizens?
He ne're will be admitted, there, where *Vennor* comes.
Hee may perchance, in taile of a Sheriffes dinner,   95

---

[126] *Billings-gate* 1692 *Billingsgate* 1716 Billingsgate W Billingsgate G
[127] thee.] thee—G || Div.] Dev. 1692 || *Sat.* 1716, f.
[128] t'] to G
[129] 5 () om. G§

Skip with a rime o' the Table, from *New-nothing*,
And take his *Almaine*-leape into a cuſtard,
Shall make my Lad[130] *Maioreſſe*, and her ſiſters,
Laugh all their hoods ouer their shoulders. But,
This is not that will doe, they are other things   100

That are receiu'd now vpon earth, for Vices[131];
Stranger, and newer: and chang'd euery houre.
They ride 'hem[132] like their horſes off their legges,
And here they come to *Hell*, whole legions of 'hem,
Euery weeke tyr'd. Wee, ſtill ſtriue to breed,   105

And reare 'hem vp new ones; but they doe not ſtand,[133]
When they come there[134]: they turne 'hem on our hands.
And it is fear'd they haue a ſtud o' their owne
Will put downe ours. Both our breed, and trade
VVill ſuddenly decay, if we preuent not.   110

Vnleſſe it be a *Vice* of quality,
Or faſhion, now, they take none from vs. Car-men
Are got into the yellow ſtarch, and Chimney-ſweepers
To their tabacco, and ſtrong-waters, *Hum*,
Meath, and *Obarni*. VVe muſt therefore ayme   115

At extraordinary ſubtill[135] ones, now,
When we doe ſend to keepe vs vp in credit.
Not old *Iniquities*. Get you e'ne backe, Sir,
To making of your rope of ſand againe.
You are not for the manners[136], nor the times: 120

They haue their *Vices*, there, moſt like to *Vertues*;
You cannnot know 'hem, apart, by any difference:
They weare the ſame clothes, eate the ſame meate,
Sleepe i' the ſelfe-ſame beds, rid i' thoſe coaches.
Or very like, foure horſes in a coach,   125

As the beſt men and women. Tiſſue gownes,
Garters and roſes, foureſcore pound a paire,

---

[130] Lady 1692, 1716 lady W, G
[131] Vices 1641, 1692, 1716, G vices W
[132] 'hem] 'em 1692, 1716, W passim them G§
[133] 'hem om. G stand,] stand; G
[134] there:] there W there, G
[135] subtle 1692, f.
[136] manner G

Embroydred[137] ſtockings, cut-worke ſmocks, and ſhirts,
More certaine marks of lechery, now, and pride,
Then ere they were of true nobility![138]   130

But *Pug*, ſince you doe burne with ſuch deſire
To doe the Common-wealth of Hell ſome ſeruice;
I am content, aſſuming of a body,
You goe to earth, and viſit men, a day.
But you muſt take a body ready made, *Pug*,   135

I can create you none: nor ſhall you forme
Your ſelfe an aery[139] one, but become ſubiect
To all impreſſion of the fleſh, you take,
So farre as humane[140] frailty. So, this morning,
There is a handſome Cutpurſe hang'd at *Tiborne*,[141]   140

Whoſe ſpirit departed, you may enter his body:
For clothes imploy[142] your credit, with the Hangman,
Or let our tribe of Brokers furniſh you.
And, looke, how farre your ſubtilty can worke
Thorow thoſe organs, with that body, ſpye   145

Amongſt mankind, (you cannot there want vices,[143]
And therefore the leſſe need to carry 'hem wi'[144] you)
But as you make your ſoone at nights relation,
And we ſhall find, it merits from the State,
Your ſhall haue both truſt from vs, and imployment.[145]   150

Pvg. Most gracious *Chiefe*![146]
Div. Onely, thus more I bind you,
To ſerue the firſt man that you meete; and him
I'le ſhew you, now[147]: Obſerue him. Yon' is hee,
He ſhewes Fitz-dottrel *to him, comming forth.*[148]
You ſhall ſee, firſt, after your clothing. Follow him:

---

[137] Embrothered 1641 Embroider'd 1716, f. stockins 1641
[138] [*Exit Iniq.* G
[139] airy 1692, f. passim
[140] human W, G
[141] *Tyburn* 1692, f. passim
[142] employ W, G
[143] 7 () ret. G
[144] wi'] with G§
[145] employment W, G
[146] Div.] *Dev.* 1692 *Sat.* 1716, f.
[147] now] new 1716
[148] SN.] *Shews him Fitzdottrel coming out of his house at a distance.* G

But once engag'd, there you muſt ſtay and fixe;
Not ſhift, vntill the midnights cocke doe crow.

Pvg. Any conditions to be gone.

Div. Away, then.[149]   157

---

149 *Exeunt severally.* G

ACT. I.   SCENE. II.
Fitz-Dottrell.[150]

I, they doe, now, name *Bretnor*, as before,
They talk'd of *Gresham*, and of Doctor *Fore-man*,
Francklin, and *Fiske*, and *Sauory* (he was in too)
But there's not one of thefe, that euer could
Yet fhew a man the *Diuell*, in true fort.   5

They haue their chriftalls, I doe know, and rings,
And virgin parchment, and their dead-mens fculls
Their rauens wings, their lights, and *pentacles*,
With *characters*; I ha' feene all thefe. But—
Would I might fee the *Diuell*. I would giue   10

A hundred o' thefe pictures, to fee him
Once out of picture[151]. May I proue a cuckold,
(And that's the one maine mortall thing I feare)
If I beginne not, now, to thinke, the Painters
Haue onely made him. 'Slight, he would be feene,   15

One time or other elfe. He would not let
An ancient gentleman, of a good[152] houfe,
As moft are now in *England*, the *Fitz-Dottrel's*
Runne wilde, and call vpon him thus in vaine,
As I ha' done this twelue mone'th. If he be not,   20

At all, why, are there Coniurers? If they be not,[153]
Why, are there lawes againft 'hem? The beft artifts
Of *Cambridge*, *Oxford*, *Middlesex*, and *London*,
Essex, and *Kent*, I haue had in pay to raife him,
Thefe fifty weekes, and yet h'[154]appeares not. 'Sdeath,   25

I fhall fufpect, they, can make circles[155] onely
Shortly, and know but his hard names. They doe fay,
H'will meet a man (of himfelfe) that has a mind to him.
If hee would fo, I haue a minde and a halfe for him:

---

[150] SD. Act. I. om. 1716, f. (as regularly, after Sc. I. of each act.) Act ...] Scene II. *The street before Fitzdottrel's House. Enter* Fitzdottrel. G
[151] picture, 1641
[152] a] as W [as] G ‖ good] good a G
[153] comma om. after 'why' and 'Why' 1692 f.
[154] h'] he G
[155] circle 1641

He fhould not be long abfent. Pray thee[156], come   30

I long for thee. An'[157] I were with child by him, And my wife too;
I could not more. Come, yet, *He expreffes[158] a longing to fee the Diuell*
Good *Beelezebub*. Were hee a kinde diuell,
And had humanity in him, hee would come, but
To faue ones longing. I fhould vfe him well,   35

I fweare, and with refpect (would he would try mee)
Not, as the Conjurers doe, when they ha' rais'd him.
Get him in bonds, and fend him poft, on errands.
A thoufand miles, it is prepofterous, that;
And I beleeue, is the true caufe he comes not.   40

And hee has reafon. Who would be engag'd,
That might liue freely, as he may doe? I fweare,
They are wrong all. The burn't child dreads the fire.
They doe not know to entertaine the *Diuell*.
I would fo welcome him, obferue his diet,   45

Get him his chamber hung with *arras*, two of 'hem,[159]
I' my own houfe; lend him my wiues[160] wrought pillowes:
And as I am an honeft man, I thinke,
If he had a minde to her, too; I should grant him,
To make our friend-fhip perfect. So I would not   50

To euery man. If hee but heare me, now?
And fhould come to mee in a braue young fhape,
And take me at my word[161]? ha! Who is this?

---

[156] Prithee G
[157] An'] an G
[158] SN. *expresseth* 1692, 1716, W || SN. om. G
[159] 'hem] 'em G
[160] Wife's 1716 wife's W, G passim
[161] word?—*Enter* Pug *handsomely shaped and apparelled.* G

ACT. I. SCENE. III.
Pvg.   Fitz-dottrell.

Sir, your good pardon, that I thus prefume
Vpon[162] your priuacy. I am borne a Gentleman,
A younger brother; but, in fome difgrace,
Now, with my friends: and want fome little meanes,
To keepe me vpright, while things be reconcil'd.   5

Pleafe you, to let my feruice be of vfe to you, Sir.
Fit. Seruice? 'fore hell, my heart was at my mouth,
Till I had view'd his fhooes well: for, thofe rofes
Were bigge inough to hide a clouen foote.
Hee lookes and furuay's[163] his feet: ouer and ouer.
No, friend, my number's full. I haue one feruant,   10

Who is my all, indeed; and, from the broome
Vnto the brufh: for, iuft so farre, I truft him.
He is my Ward-robe man, my Cater,[164] Cooke,
Butler, and Steward; lookes vnto my horfe:
And helpes to watch my wife. H'has[165] all the places,   15

That I can thinke on, from the garret downward,
E'en[166] to the manger, and the curry-combe.
Pvg. Sir, I fhall put your worfhip to no charge,
More then my meate, and that but very little,
I'le ferue you for your loue. Fit. Ha? without wages?   20

I'le[167] harken o' that eare, were I at leafure.
But now, I'm[168] bufie. 'Pr'y the, friend forbeare mee,
And'[169] thou hadft beene a *Diuell*, I fhould fay
Somewhat more to thee. Thou doft hinder, now,
My meditations. Pvg. Sir, I am a *Diuell*.   25

Fit. How! Pvg. A true *Diuell*, S^r.[170]

---

162 on. G
163 SN. on. G || *Aside.* G
164 m'acater W
165 He has W, G
166 Even G
167 I'd W, G
168 I am G 'Prythe 1692 'Prithee 1716, W Prithee G
169 An' 1716, W An G || hadft] hast 1692, 1716
170 Sir 1641. f. passim

Fit. Nay, now, you ly:
Vnder your fauour, friend, for, I'll not quarrell.
I look'd o' your feet, afore, you cannot coozen[171] mee,
Your ſhoo's[172] not clouen, Sir, you are whole hoof'd.
He viewes his feete againe.
Pvg. Sir, that's a popular error, deceiues many: 30

But I am that, I[173] tell you. Fit. What's your name?
Pvg. My name is *Diuell*, S[r]. Fit. Sai'ſt thou true.
Pvg. in-deed, S[r]. Fit. 'Slid! there's ſome *omen* i' this! what countryman?
Pvg. Of *Derby-ſhire*, S[r]. about the *Peake*.
Fit. That HoleBelong'd to your Anceſtors? Pvg. Yes, *Diuells* arſe, S[r].   35

Fit. I'll entertaine him for the name ſake. Ha?
And turne away my tother[174] man? and ſaue
Foure pound a yeere by that? there's lucke, and thrift too!
The very *Diuell* may come, heereafter, as well.[175]
Friend, I receiue you: but (withall) I acquaint you,   40

Aforehand, if yo'[176] offend mee, I muſt beat you.
It is a kinde of exerciſe, I vſe. And cannot be without.
Pvg. Yes, if I doe not Offend, you can, ſure.
Fit. Faith, *Diuell*, very hardly:
I'll call you by your ſurname, 'cauſe I loue it.   45

---

171 cozen 1692, f. passim
172 SN. om. G
173 that, I] that I 1692, f.
174 t'other 1692, f.
175 [*Aside.* G
176 you W, G

ACT. I.   SCENE. IIII.
Ingine.   Wittipol.   Manly.
Fitzdottrell.   Pvg.[177]

Yonder hee walkes, Sir, I'll goe lift him for you.
Wit. To him, good *Ingine*, raiſe him vp by degrees,
Gently, and hold him there too, you can doe it.
Shew your ſelfe now, a *Mathematicall* broker.
Ing. I'll warrant you for halfe a piece.
Wit. 'Tis done, Sʳ.[178]   5

Man. Is't poſſible there ſhould be ſuch a man?
Wit. You ſhall be your owne witneſſe, I'll not labour
To tempt you paſt your faith.
Man. And is his wifeSo very handſome, ſay you?
Wit. I ha' not ſeene her,
Since I came home from trauell: and they ſay,   10

Shee is not alter'd. Then, before I went,
I ſaw her once; but ſo, as ſhee hath ſtuck
Still i' my view, no obiect hath remou'd her.
Man. 'Tis a faire gueſt, Friend, beauty: and once lodg'd
Deepe in the eyes, ſhee hardly leaues the Inne.   15

How do's he keepe her?
Wit. Very braue. Howeuer,
Himselfe be fordide, hee is ſenſuall that way.
In euery dreſſing, hee do's ſtudy her.
Man. And furniſh forth himselfe ſo from the *Brokers*?[179]
Wit. Yes, that's a hyr'd ſuite, hee now has one,[180]   20

To ſee the *Diuell* is an *Aſſe*, to day, in:
(This *Ingine* gets three or foure pound a weeke by him)
He dares not miſſe a new *Play*, or a *Feaſt*,
What rate ſoeuer clothes be at; and thinks
Himſelfe ſtill new, in other mens old. Man. But ſtay,   25

Do's he loue meat ſo?
Wit. Faith he do's not hate it.
But that's not it. His belly and his palate

---

[177] Act. ...] *Enter, behind,* Engine, *with a cloke on his arm,* Wittipol, *and* Manly. G
[178] [*Engine goes to Fitzdottrel and takes him aside.* G
[179] *Broker* 1692, 1716 broker W
[180] on 1641, f.

Would be compounded with for reafon. Mary,[181]
A wit he has, of that ftrange credit with him,
'Gainft all mankinde; as it doth make him doe   30

Iuft what it lift: it rauifhes him forth,
Whither[182] it pleafe, to any affembly'or place,
And would conclude him ruin'd, fhould hee fcape
One publike meeting, out of the beliefe
He has of his owne great, and Catholike ftrengths,   35

In arguing, and difcourfe. It takes, I fee:[183]
H'has got the cloak vpon him.
Ingine *hath won* Fitzdottrel, *to 'fay on the cloake.*[184]
Fit. A faire garment, By my faith, *Ingine!*
Ing. It was neuer made, Sir,
For three fcore pound, I affure you: 'Twill yeeld thirty.
The plufh, Sir, coft three pound, ten fhillings a yard!   40

And then the lace, and veluet.
Fit. I fhall, *Ingine,* Be look'd at, pretitly,[185] in it! Art thou fure
The *Play* is play'd to day?
Ing. O here's the bill, S^r.*Hee giues him the* Play-*bill.*
I', had forgot to gi't you.[186]
Fit. Ha? the *Diuell!* I will not lofe you, Sirah! But, *Ingine,* thinke you,   45

The Gallant is fo furious in his folly?
So mad vpon the matter, that hee'll part
With's cloake vpo'[187] thefe termes?
Ing. Truft not your *Ingine,*
Breake me to pieces elfe, as you would doe
A rotten *Crane,*[188] or an old rufty *Iacke,*   50

That has not one true wheele in him. Doe but talke with him.[189]
Fit. I fhall doe that, to fatisfie you, *Ingine,*
And my felfe too.[190] With your leaue, Gentlemen.
Hee turnes to Wittipol.

---

[181] Marry 1692, f.
[182] whether 1716
[183] SN. 'say] say 1641, f. SN. om. G
[184] *Fitz. [after saying on the cloke.]* G
[185] prettily 1641. f.
[186] I', had] I'd 1716 I had W, G gi't] give it G
[187] upon 1716, f.
[188] *Cain* 1692 *Cane* 1716
[189] with him] with W
[190] too. *[comes forward.]* G SN. om. G

Which of you is it, is fo meere Idolater
To my wiues beauty, and fo very prodigall   55

Vnto my patience, that, for the fhort parlee?
Of one fwift houres quarter, with my wife,
He will depart with (let mee fee) this cloake here
The price of folly? Sir, are you the man?
Wit. I am that vent'rer,[191] Sir.
Fit. Good time! your name   60

Is *Witty-pol*?
Wit. The fame, S^r.
Fit. And 'tis told me, Yo'[192] haue trauell'd lately?
Wit. That I haue, S^r.
Fit. Truly, Your trauells may haue alter'd your complexion;
But fure, your wit ftood ftill.
Wit. It may well be, Sir. All heads ha' not like growth.
Fit. The good mans grauity,   65

That left you land, your father, neuer taught you Thefe pleafant matches?
Wit. No, nor can his mirth, With whom I make 'hem, put me off.
Fit. You are Refolu'd then?
Wit. Yes, S^r.
Fit. Beauty is the *Saint*, You'll facrifice your felfe,[193] into the fhirt too?   70

Wit. So I may ftill cloth, and keepe warme your wifdome?
Fit. You lade me S^r!
Wit. I know what you wil beare, S^r.
Fit. Well, to the point. 'Tis only, Sir, you fay,
To fpeake vnto my wife?
Wit. Only, to fpeake to her.
Fit. And in my prefence?
Wit. In your very prefence.   75

Fit. And in my hearing?
Wit. In your hearing: fo,
You interrupt vs not.
Fit. For the fhort fpace
You doe demand, the fourth part of an houre,
I thinke I fhall, with fome conuenient ftudy,
And this good helpe to boot, bring my felfe to't.[194]   80

---

191 venturer G
192 You G§
193 comma om. after 'selfe' 1692, f. to W, G
194 SN. *Hee* om. G

Hee fhrugs himfelfe vp in the cloake.
Wit. I aske no more.
Fit. Pleafe you, walk to'ard my houfe,
Speake what you lift; that time is[195] yours: My right
I haue departed with. But, not beyond,
A minute, or a fecond, looke for. Length,
And drawing out, ma'aduance[196] much, to thefe matches.   85

And I except all kiffing. Kiffes are
Silent petitions ftill with willing *Louers.*
Wit. *Louers?* How falls that o' your phantfie?[197]
Fit. Sir.I doe know fomewhat. I forbid all lip-worke.
Wit. I am not eager at forbidden dainties.   90

Who couets vnfit things, denies him felfe.
Fit. You fay well, Sir, 'Twas prettily faid, that fame,
He do's, indeed. I'll haue no touches, therefore,
Nor takings by the armes, nor tender circles
Caft 'bout the waft, but all be done at diftance.   95

Loue is brought vp with thofe foft *migniard* handlings;
His pulfe lies in his palme: and I defend
All melting ioynts, and fingers, (that's my bargaine)
I doe defend 'hem, any thing like action.[198]
But talke, Sir, what you will. Vfe all the *Tropes*   100

And *Schemes*, that Prince *Quintilian* can afford you:
And much good do your *Rhetoriques* heart. You are welcome, Sir.[199]
Ingine, God b'w'you.[200]
Wit. Sir, I muft condition To haue this Gentleman by, a witneffe.
Fit. Well, I am content, fo he be filent.
Man. Yes, S r.   105

Fit. Come *Diuell*, I'll make you roome, ftreight. But I'll fhew you
Firft, to your Miftreffe, who's no common one,
You muft conceiue, that brings this[201] game to fee her.
I hope thou'ft brought me good lucke.
Pvg. I fhall do't. Sir.[202]

---

[195] is om. 1641
[196] may W, G
[197] phant'sie W phantasy G o'ret. G
[198] comma om. W, G
[199] [*Opens the door of his house.* G
[200] b'w'] be wi' G
[201] this om. 1641
[202] [*They all enter the house.* G

ACT. I. SCENE. V.
VVittipol.   Manly.[203]

Ingine, you hope o' your halfe piece? 'Tis there, Sir.
Be gone.[204] Friend *Manly*, who's within here? fixed?
Wittipol *knocks his friend o' the breſt.*
Man. I am directly in a fit of wonder
What'll[205] be the iſſue of this conference!
Wit. For that, ne'r vex your ſelfe, till the euent.   5

How like yo' him?
Man. I would faine ſee more of him.
Wit. What thinke you of this?
Man. I am paſt degrees of thinking.
Old *Africk*, and the new *America*,
With all their fruite of Monſters cannot ſhew
So iuſt a prodigie.
Wit. Could you haue beleeu'd,   10

Without your ſight, a minde ſo ſordide inward,
Should be ſo ſpecious, and layd forth abroad,
To all the ſhew, that euer ſhop, or ware was?
Man. I beleeue any thing now, though I confeſſe
His *Vices* are the moſt extremities   15

I euer knew in nature. But, why loues hee
The *Diuell* ſo?
Wit. O Sʳ! for hidden treaſure,
Hee hopes to finde: and has propos'd himſelfe
So infinite a Maſſe, as to recouer,
He cares not what he parts with, of the preſent,   20

To his men of Art, who are the race, may coyne him.
Promiſe gold-mountaines, and the couetous
Are ſtill moſt prodigall.
Man. But ha' you faith,
That he will hold his bargaine?
Wit. O deare, Sir!
He will not off on't. Feare him not. I know him.   25

---

[203] Act. ...] om. Scene III. *A Room in* Fitzdottrel's *House. Enter* Wittipol, Manly, *and*
Engine. G
[204] SN.] gone. [*Exit Engine.*] ‖ fixed! [*knocks him on the breast.* G
[205] 'll] will G

One bafeneffe ftill accompanies another.
See! he is heere already, and his wife too.
Man. A wondrous handfome creature, as I liue!

ACT. I.   SCENE. VI.
Fitz-dottrell. Miftreffe Fitz-dottrell.[206]

Wittipol. Manly.
Come wife, this is the Gentleman. Nay, blufh not.
M[rs]. Fi. Why, what do you meane Sir? ha' you your reafon?
Fit. Wife,I do not know, that I haue lent it forth
To any one; at leaft, without a pawne, wife:
Or that I'haue eat or drunke the thing, of late,   5

That fhould corrupt it. Wherefore gentle wife,
Obey, it is thy vertue: hold no acts
Of difputation.
M[rs]. Fi. Are you not enough
The talke, of feafts, and meetingy,[207] but you'll ftill
Make argument for frefh?
Fit. Why, carefull wedlocke,   10

If I haue haue[208] a longing to haue one tale more
Goe of mee, what is that to thee, deare heart?
Why fhouldft thou enuy my delight? or croffe it?
By being folicitous, when it not concernes thee?
M[rs]. Fi. Yes, I haue fhare in this. The fcorne will fall   15

As bittterly on me, where both are laught at.
Fit. Laught at, fweet bird? is that the fcruple? Come, come,
Thou art a *Niaife.*
A Niaife *is a young Hawke, tane crying out of the neft.*[209]
Which of your great houfes, (I will not meane at home, here, but abroad)[210]
Your families in *France*, wife, fend not forth   20

Something, within the feuen yeere, may be laught at?
I doe not fay feuen moneths, nor feuen weekes,
Nor feuen daies, nor houres: but feuen yeere wife.
I giue 'hem time. Once, within feuen yeere,
I thinke they may doe fomething may be laught at.   25

In *France*, I keepe me there, ftill. Wherefore, wife,
Let them that lift, laugh ftill, rather then weepe

---

[206] om. *Enter* Fitzdottrell, *with Mrs.* Frances *his wife.* G
[207] Meetings 1692, 1716 meetings 1641, W, G
[208] I haue] I've W haue a] a 1641. f.
[209] SN. om. G
[210] () ret. G

For me; Heere is a cloake coſt fifty pound, wife,
Which I can ſell for thirty, when I ha' ſeene
All *London* in't, and *London* has ſeene mee.   30

To day, I goe to the *Black-fryers Play-houſe*,
Sit ithe[211] view, ſalute all my acquaintance,
Riſe vp betweene the *Acts*, let fall my cloake,
Publiſh a handſome man, and a rich ſuite
(As that's a ſpeciall end, why we goe thither,   35

All that pretend, to ſtand for't o' the *Stage*)
The Ladies aske who's that? (For, they doe come
To ſee vs, *Loue*, as wee doe to ſee them)
Now, I ſhall loſe all this, for the falſe feare
Of being laught at? Yes, wuſſe. Let 'hem laugh, wife,   40

Let me haue ſuch another cloake to morrow.
And let 'hem laugh againe, wife, and againe,
And then grow fat with laughing, and then fatter,
All my young Gallants, let 'hem[212] bring their friends too:
Shall I forbid 'hem? No, let heauen forbid 'hem: 45

Or wit, if't haue any charge on 'hem.[213] Come, thy eare, wife,
Is all, I'll borrow of thee. Set your watch, Sir,
Thou, onely art to heare, not ſpeake a word, *Doue*,
To ought he ſayes. That I doe gi'[214] you in precept,
No leſſe then councell, on your wiue-hood, wife,   50

Not though[215] he flatter you, or make court, or *Loue*
(As you muſt looke for theſe)[216] or ſay, he raile;
What ere his arts be, wife, I will haue thee
Delude 'hem with a trick, thy obſtinate ſilence;
I know aduantages; and I loue to hit   55

Theſe pragmaticke young men, at their owne weapons.
Is your watch ready? Here my ſaile beares, for you:
Tack toward him, ſweet *Pinnace*, where's your watch?
He diſpoſes his wife to his place,[217] and ſets his watch.
Wit. I'le ſet it. Sir, with yours.

---

[211] i' the 1641, 1692, 1716, W in the G
[212] 'hem] 'em G
[213] 't] it G || 'hem] 'em G
[214] gi'] give G
[215] though 1641, f.
[216] () om. G
[217] SN.] *He disposes his wife to her place.* G

M^{rs}. Fi. I muſt obey.[218]
Man. Her modeſty ſeemes to ſuffer with her beauty,   60

And ſo, as if his folly were away, It were worth pitty.
Fit. Now, th'are[219] right, beginne, Sir.
But firſt, let me repeat the contract, briefely.
Hee repeats his contract againe.
I am, Sir, to inioy[220] this cloake, I ſtand in,
Freely, and as your gift; vpon condition   65

You may as freely, ſpeake here to my ſpouſe,
Your quarter of an houre alwaies keeping
The meaſur'd diſtance of your yard, or more,
From my ſaid Spouſe: and in my ſight and hearing.
This is your couenant?
Wit. Yes, but you'll allow   70

For this time ſpent, now?
Fit. Set 'hem ſo much backe.
Wit. I thinke, I ſhall not need it.
Fit. Well, begin, Sir,There is your bound, Sir. Not beyond that ruſh.
Wit. If you interrupt me, Sir, I ſhall diſcloake you.
Wittipol *beginnes.*[221]
The time I haue purchaſt, Lady, is but ſhort;   75

And, therefore, if I imploy[222] it thriftily,
I hope I ſtand the neerer to my pardon.
I am not here, to tell you, you are faire,
Or louely, or how well you dreſſe you, Lady,
I'll ſaue my ſelfe that eloquence of your glaſſe,   80

Which can ſpeake these things better to you then I.
And 'tis a knowledge, wherein fooles may be
As wiſe as a *Count Parliament*. Nor come[223] I,
With any preiudice, or doubt, that you
Should, to the notice of your owne worth, neede   85

Leaſt reuelation. Shee's a ſimple woman,
Know's not her good: (who euer knowes her ill)

---

[218] [*Aside.* G
[219] th'art 1641, 1692, 1716 they are W, G SN. om. G
[220] enjoy 1692, f.
[221] SN. om. G
[222] employ W, G
[223] came W

And at all caracts.[224] That you are the wife,
To fo much blafted flefh, as fcarce hath foule,
In ftead of falt, to keepe it fweete; I thinke,   90

Will aske no witneffes, to proue. The cold
Sheetes that you lie in, with the watching candle,
That fees, how dull to any thaw of beauty,
Pieces, and quarters, halfe, and whole nights, fometimes,
The Diuell-giuen *Elfine* Squire, your husband,   95

Doth leaue you, quitting heere his proper circle,
For a much-worfe i' the walks of *Lincolnes Inne,*
Vnder the Elmes, t'expect the feind in vaine, there
Will confeffe for you.
Fit. I did looke for this geere.[225]
Wit. And what a daughter of darkneffe, he do's make you,   100

Lock'd vp from all fociety, or object;
Your eye not let to looke vpon a face,
Vnder a Conjurers (or fome mould for one,
Hollow, and leane like his) but, by great meanes,
As I now make; your owne too fenfible fufferings,   105

Without the extraordinary aydes,
Of fpells, or fpirits, may affure you, Lady.
For my part, I proteft 'gainft all fuch practice,
I worke by no falfe arts, medicines, or charmes
To be said forward and backward.
Fit. No, I except: 110

Wit. Sir I fhall ease you.
He offers to difcloake him.
Fit. Mum.
Wit. Nor haue I ends, Lady,
Vpon you, more then this: to tell you how *Loue*
Beauties good Angell, he that waits vpon her
At all occafions, and no leffe then *Fortune,*
Helps th' aduenturous,[226] in mee makes that proffer,   115

Which neuer faire one was fo fond, to lofe;
Who could but reach a hand forth[227] to her freedome:
On the firft fight, I lou'd you: fince which time,

---

[224] charats 1692 Characts 1716
[225] jeer W, G
[226] adventrous 1692, 1716 advent'rous W || th'] the G
[227] forth] out 1641

Though I haue trauell'd, I haue beene in trauell
More for this second blessing of your eyes   120

Which now I'haue[228] purchas'd, then for all aymes elſe.
Thinke of it, Lady, be your minde as actiue,
As is your beauty: view your object well.
Examine both my faſhion, and my yeeres;
Things, that are like, are ſoone familiar: 125

And Nature ioyes, ſtill in equality.
Let not the ſigne o'[229] the husband fright you, Lady.
But ere your ſpring be gone, inioy it. Flowers,
Though faire, are oft but of one morning. Thinke,
All beauty doth not laſt vntill the *autumne*.   130

You grow old, while I tell you this.
And ſuch, As cannot vſe the preſent, are not wiſe.
If Loue and Fortune will take care of vs,
Why ſhould our will be wanting? This is all.
What doe you anſwer, Lady?
Shee stands mute.[230]
Fit. Now, the sport comes.[231]   135

Let him ſtill waite, waite, waite: while the watch goes,
And the time runs. Wife!
Wit. How! not any word?
Nay, then, I taſte a tricke in't. Worthy Lady,
I cannot be ſo falſe to mine[232] owne thoughts
Of your preſumed goodneſſe, to conceiue   140

This, as your rudeneſſe, which I ſee's impos'd.
Yet, ſince your cautelous *Iaylor*, here ſtands by you,
And yo' are[233] deni'd the liberty o' the houſe,
Let me take warrant, Lady, from your ſilence,
(Which euer is interpreted conſent)   145

To make your anſwer for you: which ſhall be
To as good purpoſe, as I can imagine,
And what I thinke you'ld ſpeake.
Fit. No, no, no, no.

---

[228] I' haue] I have 1692 I've 1716, f.
[229] o'] of G
[230] misplaced t adjusted 1692. f.
[231] SN. om. G
[232] my G
[233] you're 1716, W you are G

Wit. I ſhall reſume, Sʳ.
Man. Sir, what doe you meane?
He ſets Mʳ. Manly, *his friend, in her place.*[234]
Wit. One interruption more, Sir, and you goe   150

Into your hoſe and doublet, nothing ſaues you.
And therefore harken. This is for your wife.
Man. You muſt play faire, Sʳ.
Wit. Stand for mee, good friend.
And ſpeaks for her.
Troth, Sir, tis more then true, that you haue vttred[235]
Of my vnequall, and ſo ſordide match heere,   155

With all the circumſtances of my bondage.
I haue a husband, and a two-legg'd one,
But ſuch a moon-ling, as no wit of man
Or roſes can redeeme from being an Aſſe.
H'is[236] growne too much, the ſtory of mens mouthes,   160

To ſcape[237] his lading: ſhould I make't my ſtudy,
And lay all wayes, yea, call mankind to helpe,
To take his burden off, why, this one act
Of his, to let his wife out to be courted,
And, at a price, proclaimes his aſinine nature   165

So lowd, as I am weary of my title to him.
But Sir, you ſeeme a Gentleman of vertue,
No leſſe then blood; and one that euery way
Lookes as he were of too good quality,
To intrap a credulous woman, or betray her: 170

Since you haue payd thus deare, Sir, for a viſit,
And made ſuch venter,[238] on your wit, and charge
Meerely to ſee mee, or at moſt to ſpeake to mee,
I were too ſtupid; or (what's worſe) ingrate
Not to returne your venter. Thinke, but how,   175

I may with ſafety doe it; I ſhall truſt
My loue and honour to you, and preſume;
You'll euer huſband both, againſt this huſband;
Who, if we chance to change his liberall eares,

---

[234] SN. [*Sets Manly in his place, and speaks for the lady.* (after 'friend.' 153) G
[235] utt'red 1692 utter'd 1716, f.
[236] He's 1716, f.
[237] T' escape W To 'scape 1716
[238] venture 1692, f.

To other enſignes, and with labour make   180

A new beaſt of him, as hee ſhall deſerue,
Cannot complaine, hee is vnkindly dealth[239] with.
This day hee is to goe to a new play, Sir.
From whence no feare, no, nor authority,
Scarcely the *Kings* command, Sir, will reſtraine him,   185

Now you haue fitted him with a *Stage*-garment,
For the meere names ſake, were there nothing elſe:[240]
And many more ſuch iourneyes, hee will make.
Which, if they now, or, any time heereafter,
Offer vs opportunity, you heare, Sir,   190

Who'll be as glad, and forward to imbrace,[241]
Meete, and enioy it chearefully as you.I humbly thanke you, Lady.
Hee ſhifts to his owne place againe[242]
Fit. Keepe your ground Sir.
Wit. Will you be lightned?[243]
Fit. Mum.
Wit. And but I am,
By the ſad[244] contract, thus to take my leaue of you   195

At this ſo enuious distance, I had taught
Our lips ere this, to ſeale the happy mixture
Made of our ſoules. But we muſt both, now, yield
To the neceſſity. Doe not thinke yet, Lady,
But I can kiſſe, and touch, and laugh, and whiſper,   200

And doe those crowning court-ſhips too, for which,
Day, and the publike haue allow'd no name
But, now, my bargaine binds me. 'Twere rude iniury,
T'importune more, or vrge a noble nature,
To what of it's owne bounty it is prone to: 205

Elſe, I ſhould ſpeake—But, Lady, I loue ſo well,
As I will hope, you'll doe ſo to. I haue done, Sir.
Fit. Well, then, I ha' won?
Wit. Sir, And I may win, too.
Fit. O yes! no doubt on't. I'll take carefull order,

---

[239] dealt 1692, f.
[240] nothing] no things 1692, 1716
[241] embrace 1692, f.
[242] SN. om. 1641, 1692, 1716 ǁ *Hee* om. G
[243] lighten'd 1716, f.
[244] sad] said W, G

That fhee fhall hang forth enfignes at the window,   210

To tell you when I am[245] abfent. Or I'll keepe
Three or foure foote-men, ready ftill of purpofe,
To runne and fetch you, at her longings, Sir.
I'll goe befpeake me ftraight a guilt caroch,
For her and you to take the ayre in. Yes,   215

Into *Hide-parke*, and thence into *Black-Fryers*,
Vifit the painters, where you may fee pictures,
And note the propereft limbs, and how to make 'hem.
Or what doe you fay vnto a middling Goffip
To bring you aye together, at her lodging?   220

Vnder pretext of teaching o' my wife
Some rare receit of drawing *almond* milke? ha?
It shall be a part of my care. Good Sir, God b'w'you.[246]
I ha' kept the contract, and the cloake is mine.[247]
Wit. Why, much good do't you S^r; it may fall out,   225

That you ha' bought it deare, though I ha'[248] not fold it.
Fit. A pretty riddle! Fare you well, good Sir.
Wife, your face this way, looke on me: and thinke
Yo' haue[249] had a wicked dreame, wife, and forget it.
Hee turnes his wife about.
Man. This is the ftrangeft motion I ere faw.[250]   230

Fit. Now, wife, fits this faire cloake the worfe vpon me,
For my great fufferings, or your little patience? ha?
They laugh, you thinke?
M^rs. Fi. Why S^r. and you might fee't.
What thought, they haue of you, may be foone collected
By the young Genlemans fpeache.
Fit. Youug Gentleman?[251]   235

Death! you are in loue with him, are you? could he not
Be nam'd the Gentleman, without the young?
Vp to your Cabbin againe.
M^rs. Fi. My cage, yo' were beftTo call it?

---

[245] I am] I'm W
[246] be wi' G
[247] is mine] is mine owne 1641 is mine own 1692 's mine own 1716, W, G
[248] I ha'] I've G [*Exit.* G
[249] Ya' have 1692 You've 1716 You W, G SN. om. G
[250] [*Exit.* G
[251] Youug] Young 1641, f. ‖ Gentlmans 1641 Gentleman's 1692, 1716 gentleman's W, G

Fit. Yes, fing there. You'ld faine be making
Blanck Manger with him[252] at your mothers! I know you.   240

Goe get you vp.[253] How now! what fay you, *Diuell*?

---

[252] him] it 1641
[253] up.—[*Exit Mrs. Fitz. Enter* Pug. G

ACT. I.   SCENE. VII.
Pvg.   Fitzdottrel.   Ingine.[254]

Heere is one *Ingine*, Sir, defires to fpeake with you.
Fit. I thought he brought fome newes, of a broker! Well,
Let him come in, good *Diuell*: fetch him elfe.[255]
O, my fine *Ingine*! what's th'affaire?[256] more cheats?
Ing. No Sir, the Wit, the Braine, the great *Proiector*,   5

I told you of, is newly come to towne.
Fit. Where, *Ingine*?
Ing. I ha' brought him (H'is[257] without)
Ere hee pull'd off his boots, Sir, but fo follow'd,
For bufineffes:[258]
Fit. But what is a *Proiector*?
I would conceiue.
Ing. Why, one Sir, that proiects   10

Wayes to enrich men, or to make 'hem great,
By fuites, by marriages, by vndertakings:[259]
According as he fees they humour it.
Fit. Can hee not coniure at all?
Ing. I thinke he can, Sir.
(To tell you true) but, you doe know, of late,   15

The State hath tane fuch note of 'hem,[260] and compell'd 'hem,
To enter fuch great bonds, they dare not practice.
Fit. 'Tis true, and I lie fallow for't, the while!
Ing. O, Sir! you'll grow the richer for the reft.
Fit. I hope I fhall: but *Ingine*, you doe talke   20

Somewhat too much, o'[261] my courfes. My Cloake-cuftomer
Could tell mee ftrange particulars.
Ing. By my meanes?
Fit. How fhould he haue 'hem elfe?
Ing. You do not know, S^r,

---

[254] om. G
[255] *Exit Pug. Re-enter* Engine. G
[256] th'] the G§
[257] H'is] he's 1716, f. () ret. G
[258] businesse 1641
[259] undertaking 1641
[260] 'hem] 'em G
[261] o' ret. G

What he has: and by what arts! A monei'd man, Sir,
And is as great with your *Almanack-Men,* as you are!   25

Fit. That Gallant?
Ing. You make the other wait too long, here:
And hee is extreme punctuall.
Fit. Is he a[262] gallant?
Ing. Sir, you ſhall ſee: He'is[263] in his riding ſuit,
As hee comes ńow from Court. But heere him ſpeake:
Miniſter matter to him, and then tell mee.[264]   30

---

[262] a om. 1692, 1716, W
[263] He'is] He's 1716 he's W, G
[264] [*Exeunt.* G

Act. II. Scene. I.
Meer-craft. Fitz-dottrel. Ingine.
Traines. Pvg.[265]

Sir, money's[266] a whore, a bawd, a drudge;
Fit to runne out on errands: Let her goe.
Via pecunia! when fhe's runne and gone,
And fled and dead; then will I fetch her, againe,
With *Aqua-vitæ*, out of an old Hogs-head!   5

While there are lees of wine, or dregs of beere,
I'le neuer want her! Coyne her out of cobwebs,
Duft, but I'll haue her! Raife wooll vpon egge-fhells,
Sir, and make grafe grow out o' marro-bones.
To make her come. (Commend mee to[267] your Miftreffe,   10

To a waiter.
Say, let the thoufand pound but be had ready,
And it is done)[268] I would but fee the creature
(Of flefh, and blood) the man, the *prince*, indeed,
That could imploy[269] fo many millions
As I would help him to.
Fit. How, talks he?[270] millions?   15

Mer. (I'll giue you an account of this to morrow.)
Yes, I will talke no leffe, and doe it too;
To another.[271]
If they were *Myriades*:[272] and without the *Diuell*,
By direct meanes, it fhall be good in law.
Ing. Sir.
Mer. Tell M^r. *Wood-cock*, I'll not faile to meet him[273]   20

To a third.
Vpon th' *Exchange* at night. Pray him to haue

---

[265] Meer. ...] *A Room in* Fitzdottrel's *House. Enter* Fitzdottrel, Engine, *and* Meercraft, *followed by* Trains *with a bag, and three or four Attendants.* G
[266] 's] is G
[267] SN. *To* ...] [*To 1 Attendant.*] G
[268] done. [*Exit 1 Attend.*] G
[269] employ W, G
[270] How, talks] How talks 1716, f.
[271] SN.] [*To 2 Attendant.*] [*Exit 2 Atten.* G || talke] take 1641, 1716, f.
[272] *Myriads* 1716 Myriads W myriads G
[273] SN. om. 1641, 1692. 1716, W [*to 3 Atten.*] G || M^r.] master G passim

The writings there, and wee'll difpatch it.[274] Sir,
He turnes to Fitz-dottrel.
You are a Gentleman of a good prefence,
A handfome man (I haue confidered you)[275]
As a fit ftocke to graft honours vpon: 25

I haue a proiect to make you a *Duke*, now.
That you muft be one, within fo many moneths,
As I fet downe, out of true reafon[276] of ftate,
You fha'[277] not auoyd it. But you muft harken, then.
Ing. Harken? why S[r], do you doubt his eares? Alas!   30

You doe not know Mafter *Fitz-dottrel*.
Fit. He do's not know me indeed. I thank you, *Ingine*,
For rectifying him.
Mer. Good! Why, *Ingine*, then
He turnes to Ingine.[278]
I'le tell it[279] you. (I see you ha' credit, here,
And, that you can keepe counfell, I'll not queftion.)[280]   35

Hee fhall but be an vndertaker with mee,
In a moft feafible bus'neffe. It shall cost him
Nothing.
Ing. Good, S[r].
Mer. Except he pleafe, but's count'nance;
(That I will haue) t'appeare in't, to great men,
For which I'll make him one. Hee fhall not draw   40

A ftring of's purfe. I'll driue his pattent for him.
We'll take in Cittizens, *Commoners*, and *Aldermen*,
To beare the charge, and blow 'hem off againe,
Like fo many dead flyes, when 'tis[281] carryed.
The thing is for recouery of drown'd land,   45

Whereof the *Crowne's* to haue his[282] moiety,
If it be owner; Elfe, the *Crowne* and Owners
To fhare that moyety: and the recouerers

---

[274] it. [*Exit 3 Atten.*] G || SN. om. 1641, f.
[275] () om. W
[276] reasons G
[277] sha'] shall G
[278] SN. om. 1641. f.
[279] it om. 1641
[280] () ret. G (same for line 39)
[281] 'tis] it is G
[282] his] a 1641, f.

T'enioy the tother moyety, for their charge.
Ing. Thorowout[283] *England*?
Mer. Yes, which will arife   50

To eyghteene *millions*, feuen the firft yeere:
I haue computed all, and made my furuay
Vnto an[284] acre. I'll beginne at the Pan,
Not, at the skirts: as fome ha' done, and loft,
All that they wrought, their timber-worke, their trench,   55

Their bankes all borne away, or elfe fill'd vp
By the next winter. Tut, they neuer went
The way: I'll haue it all.
Ing. A gallant tract
Of land it is!
Mer. 'Twill yeeld a pound an acre.
Wee muft let cheape, euer, at firft. But Sir,   60

This lookes too large for you, I fee. Come hither,
We'll haue a leffe. Here's a plain fellow,[285] you fee him,
Has his black bag of papers, there, in Buckram,
Wi'[286] not be fold for th'Earledome of *Pancridge*: Draw,
Gi' me out one, by chance.[287] Proiect. 4. *Dog-skinnes?*   65

Twelue thoufand pound! the very worft, at firft.
Fit. Pray, you let's fee't[288] Sir.
Mer. 'Tis a toy, a trifle!
Fit. Trifle! 12. thoufand pound for dogs-skins?
Mer. Yes,[289] But, by my[290] way of dreffing, you muft know, Sir,
And med'cining the leather, to a height   70

Of improu'd ware, like your *Borachio*
Of *Spaine*, Sir. I can fetch nine thoufand for't—
Ing. Of the Kings glouer?
Mer. Yes, how heard you that?
Ing. Sir, I doe know you can.

---

[283] Throughout 1641, 1692, 1716, W Thoroughout G
[284] an] my 1692, f.
[285] fellow, [*points to Trains*] G
[286] Wi'] Will W, G
[287] chance. [*Trains gives him a paper out of the bag.*] G || Project; foure 1641 Project: four 1692, 1716 Project four; W Project four: G || Dog-skinnes] dogs-skins 1641 Dogs Skins 1692, 1716 dogs skins W Dogs' skins G
[288] see't] see it G
[289] Mer. Yes,] included in line 69 1692, 1716, W
[290] my om. 1641

Mer. Within this houre:
And referue halfe my fecret. Pluck another;　　　　　　　　75

See if thou haft a happier hand: I thought fo.
Hee[291] pluckes out the 2. Bottle-ale.
The very next worfe to it! Bottle-ale.
Yet, this is two and twenty thoufand! Pr'y thee[292]
Pull out another, two or three.
Fit. Good, ftay, friend,
By bottle-ale, two and twenty thoufand pound?[293]　　　　80

Mer. Yes, Sir, it's caft to penny-hal'[294]penny-farthing,
O' the back-fide, there you may fee it, read,
I will not bate a *Harrington* o' the fumme.
I'll winne it i' my water, and my malt,
My furnaces, and hanging o' my coppers,　　　　　　　85

The tonning, and the fubtilty o' my yeft;
And, then the earth of my bottles, which I dig,
Turne vp, and fteepe, and worke, and neale, my felfe,
To a degree of *Porc'lane.*[295] You will wonder,
At my proportions, what I will put vp　　　　　　　90

In feuen yeeres! for fo long time, I aske
For my inuention. I will faue in cork,
In my mere ftop'ling, 'boue[296] three thoufand pound,
Within that terme: by googing of 'hem out
Iuft to the fize of my bottles, and not flicing,　　　　95

There's infinite loffe i' that. What haft thou there?
O'[297] making wine of raifins: this is in hand, now,
Hee drawes out another. Raifines.
Ing. Is not that ftrange, S[r], to make wine of raifins?
Mer. Yes, and as true a[298] wine, as the wines of *France*,
Or *Spaine*, or *Italy*, Looke of what grape　　　　　　100

My raifin is, that wine I'll render perfect,
As of the *mufcatell* grape, I'll render *mufcatell*;

---

[291] SN. *Hee ...*] [*Trains draws out another.*] (after 'hand:' 76) G
[292] Pr'y thee] Pry'thee W Prithee G
[293] Pr'y thee—pound? om. 1692, 1716
[294] hal'] half G
[295] Proc'lane 1641 porcelane G
[296] above G
[297] O'] O! G ǁ SN.] [*Trains draws out another.*] G
[298] a om. 1641

Of the[299] *Canary*, his; the *Claret*, his;
So of all kinds: and bate you of the prices,
Of wine, throughout the kingdome, halfe in halfe.   105

Ing. But, how, S[r], if you raife the other commodity, Rayfins?
Mer. Why, then I'll make it out of blackberries:
And it fhall doe the fame. 'Tis but more art,
And the charge leffe. Take out another.
Fit. No, good Sir.Saue you the trouble, I'le not looke, nor heare   110

Of any, but your firft, there; the *Drown'd-land*:
If't will doe, as you fay.
Mer. Sir, there's not place,
To gi' you demonftration of thefe things.
They are a little to fubtle.[300] But, I could fhew you
Such a neceffity in't,[301] as you muft be   115

But what you pleafe: againft the receiu'd herefie,
That *England* beares no Dukes. Keepe you the land, S[r],
The greatneffe of th' eftate fhall throw't vpon you.
If you like better turning it to money,
What may not you, S[r], purchafe with that wealth?   120

Say, you fhould part with two o' your millions,
To be the thing you would, who would not do't?
As I proteft, I will, out of my diuident,[302]
Lay, for fome pretty[303] principality,
In *Italy*, from the Church: Now, you perhaps,   125

Fancy the fmoake of *England*, rather? But—
Ha' you no priuate roome, Sir, to draw to,
T'enlarge our felues more vpon.
Fit. O yes, *Diuell*!
Mer. Thefe, Sir, are bus'neffes, aske to be carried
With caution, and in cloud.
Fit. I apprehend,   130

They doe fo,[304] S[r]. *Diuell*, which way is your Miftreffe?
Pvg. Aboue, S[r]. in her chamber.
Fit. O that's well.Then, this way, good, Sir.

---

[299] Of the] Of 1641
[300] subtile 1692, 1716, W
[301] in't] in it G
[302] Dividend 1716 dividend W, G
[303] petty 1692, 1716, W
[304] so om. G sir.—*Enter* Pug. G

Mer. I fhall follow you; *Traines*,
Gi' mee the bag, and goe you prefently,
Commend my feruice to my Lady *Tail-bufh*.   135

Tell her I am come from Court this morning; fay,
I'haue got our bus'neffe mou'd, and well: Intreat[305] her,
That fhee giue you the four-fcore Angels, and fee 'hem
Difpos'd of to my Councel, Sir *Poul Eytherfide*.
Sometime, to day, I'll waite vpon her Ladifhip,   140

With the relation.[306]
Ing. Sir, of what difpatch,
He is! Do you marke?[307]
Mer. *Ingine*, when did you fee
My coufin *Euer-ill*? keepes he ftill your quarter?
I' the *Bermudas*?
Ing. Yes, Sir, he was writing
This morning, very hard.
Mer. Be not you knowne to him,
That I am come to Towne: I haue effected   146

A bufineffe for him, but I would haue it take him,
Before he thinks for't.
Ing. Is it paft?
Mer. Not yet.'Tis well o' the way.
Ing. O Sir! your worfhip takesInfinit paines.
Mer. I loue[308] Friends, to be actiue: 150

A fluggish nature puts off man, and kinde.
Ing. And fuch a bleffing followes it.
Mer. I thankeMy fate. Pray you let's be priuate, Sir?
Fit. In, here.
Mer. Where none may interrupt vs.[309]
Fit. You heare, *Diuel*,Lock the ftreete-doores faft, and let no one in   155

(Except they be this Gentlemans followers)
To trouble mee. Doe you marke? Yo' haue[310] heard and feene
Something, to day; and, by it, you may gather
Your Miftreffe is a fruite, that's worth the ftealing
And therefore worth the watching. Be you fure, now

---

[305] entreat W, G
[306] relation. [*Exit Trains.* G
[307] mark? [*Aside to Fitz.* G
[308] love] love, 1716, W
[309] us. [*Exeunt Meer. and Engine.* G
[310] Yo'haue] You've 1716, W (also on line 161)

Yo' haue all your eyes about you; and let in   161

No lace-woman; nor bawd, that brings French-maſques,
And cut-works. See you? Nor old croanes, with wafers,
To conuey letters. Nor no youths, diſguis'd
Like country-wiues, with creame, and marrow-puddings.   165

Much knauery may be vented in a pudding,
Much bawdy intelligence: They'are ſhrewd ciphers.
Nor turne the key to any neyghbours neede;
Be't[311] but to kindle fire, or begg a little,
Put it out, rather: all out, to an aſhe,   170

That they may ſee no ſmoake. Or water, ſpill it:
Knock o' the empty tubs, that by the ſound,
They may be forbid entry. Say, wee are robb'd,
If any come to borrow a ſpoone, or ſo.
I wi' not haue good fortune, or gods bleſſing[312]   175

Let in, while I am buſie.
Pvg. I'le take care, Sir:They ſha' not trouble you, if they would.
Fit. Well, doe ſo.[313]

---

[311] 't] it G
[312] will G§ good fortune, gods blessing] G capitalizes throughout.
[313] *Exit.* G SD. om. G

ACT. II.   SCENE. II.
Pvg.   Miſtreſſe Fitzdottrell.

I haue no ſingular ſeruice of this, now?
Nor no ſuperlatiue Maſter? I ſhall wiſh
To be in hell againe, at leaſure? Bring,
A *Vice* from thence? That had bin ſuch a ſubtilty,
As to bring broad-clothes[314] hither: or tranſport   5

Freſh oranges into *Spaine*. I finde it, now:
My *Chiefe* was i' the right. Can any feind
Boaſt of a better *Vice*, then heere by nature,
And art, th'are owners of? Hell ne'r owne mee,[315]
But I am taken! the fine tract of it   10

Pulls mee along! To heare men ſuch profeſſors
Growne in our ſubtleſt *Sciences*! My firſt *Act*, now,
Shall be, to make this Maſter of mine cuckold:
The primitiue worke of darkneſſe, I will practiſe!
I will deſerue ſo well of my faire Miſtreſſe,   15

By my diſcoueries, firſt; my counſells after;
And keeping counſell, after that: as who,
So euer, is one, I'le[316] be another, ſure,
I'll ha' my ſhare. Most delicate damn'd fleſh!
Shee will be! O! that I could ſtay time, now,   20

Midnight will come too faſt vpon mee, I feare,
To cut my pleaſure[317]—
Mʳˢ. Fi. Looke at the back-doore,
Shee ſends Diuell *out*.[318] One knocks, ſee who it is.
Pvg. Dainty *ſhe-Diuell*!
Mʳˢ. Fi. I cannot get this venter[319] of the cloake,
Out of my fancie; nor the Gentlemans way,   25

He tooke, which though 'twere ſtrange, yet 'twas[320] handſome,
And had a grace withall, beyond the newneſſe.

---

[314] cloths G
[315] they're 1716, f. ‖ never G
[316] I will G
[317] pleasure—*Enter Mrs.* Fitzdottrel. SN. om. G
[318] [*Aside and exit.* G
[319] venture 1692, f.
[320] it was G

Sure he will thinke mee that dull ſtupid creature,
Hee ſaid, and may conclude it; if I finde not
Some thought to thanke th' attemp.[321] He did preſume,   30

By all the carriage of it, on my braine,
For anſwer; and will ſweare 'tis very barren,
If it can yeeld him no returne. Who is it?
Diuell *returnes*.[322]
Pvg. Miſtreſſe, it is,[323] but firſt, let me aſſure
The excellence, of Miſtreſſes, I am,   35

Although my Maſters man, my Miſstreſſe ſlaue,
The ſeruant of her ſecrets, and ſweete turnes,
And know, what fitly will conduce to either.
M[rs]. Fi. What's this? I pray you come to your ſelfe and thinke
What your part is: to make an anſwer. Tell,   40

Who is it at the doore?
Pvg. The Gentleman, M[rs],[324]
Who was at the cloake-charge to ſpeake with you,
This morning, who expects onely to take
Some ſmall command'ments from you, what you pleaſe,
Worthy your forme, hee ſaies, and gentleſt manners.   45

M[rs]. Fi. O! you'll anon proue his hyr'd man, I feare,
What has he giu'n you, for this meſſage? Sir,
Bid him put[325] off his hopes of ſtraw, and leaue
To ſpread his nets, in view, thus. Though they take
Maſter *Fitz-dottrell*, I am no ſuch foule,   50

Nor faire one, tell him, will be had with ſtalking.
And wiſh him to for-beare his acting to mee,
At the Gentlemans chamber-window in *Lincolnes-Inne* there,
That opens to my gallery: elſe, I ſweare
T'acquaint my huſband with his folly, and leaue him   55

To the iuſt rage of his offended iealouſie.
Or if your Maſters ſenſe be not ſo quicke
To right mee, tell him, I ſhall finde a friend
That will repaire mee. Say, I will be quiet.[326]

---

[321] attempt 1641, f.
[322] SN.] *Re-enter* Pug. G
[323] it is,] it is—W
[324] it om. 1692, f. ‖ M[rs]] Mistresse 1641 Mistris 1692 Mistress 1716 mistress W, G
[325] put 1641, f.
[326] Period om. after 'quiet' 1716, f.

In mine owne houfe? Pray you, in thofe words giue it him.   60

Pvg. This is fome foole turn'd!
He goes out.[327]
M^rs. Fi. If he be the Mafter,
Now, of that ftate and wit, which I allow him;
Sure, hee will vnderftand mee: I durft not
Be more direct. For this officious fellow,
My husbands new groome, is a fpie vpon me,   65

I finde already. Yet, if he but tell him
This in my words, hee cannot but conceiue
Himfelfe both apprehended, and requited.
I would not haue him thinke hee met a *ftatue*:
Or fpoke to one, not there, though I were filent.[328]   70

How now? ha' you told him?
Pvg. Yes.
M^rs. Fi. And what faies he?
Pvg. Sayes he? That which my felf would fay to you, if I durft.
That you are proude, fweet Miftreffe? and with-all,
A little ignorant, to entertaine
The good that's proffer'd; and (by your beauties leaue)   75

Not all fo wife, as fome true politique wife
Would be: who hauing match'd with fuch a *Nupfon*
(I fpeake it with my Mafters peace)[329] whofe face
Hath left t'accufe him, now, for't[330] doth confeffe him,
What you can make him; will yet (out of fcruple,   80

And a fpic'd confcience) defraud the poore Gentleman,
At leaft delay him in the thing he longs for,
And makes it hs whole ftudy, how to compaffe,
Onely a title. Could but he write *Cuckold*,
He had his[331] ends. For, looke you—
M^rs. Fi. This can be   85

None but my husbands wit.[332]
Pvg. My pretious M^rs.
M. Fi. It creaks his *Ingine*: The groome neuer durft

---

[327] SN.] [*Exit.* G
[328] *Re-enter* Pug. G
[329] () ret. G (Same for lines 80 and 81)
[330] 't] it G
[331] hs] his 1641, f.
[332] M^rs. as in 2. 2. 41 || wit. [*Aside.* G

Be, elfe, so faucy[333]—
Pvg. If it were not clearely,
His worſhipfull ambition; and the top of it;
The very forked top too: why ſhould hee   90

Keepe you, thus mur'd vp in a back-roome,[334] Miſtreſſe,
Allow you ne'r a caſement to the ſtreete,
Feare of engendering[335] by the eyes, with gallants,
Forbid you paper, pen and inke, like Rats-bane.
Search your halfe pint of *muſcatell*, leſt a letter   95

Be ſuncke i' the pot: and hold your new-laid egge
Againſt the fire, leſt any charme be writ there?
Will you make benefit of truth, deare Miſtreſſe,
If I doe tell it you: I do't not often?
I am ſet ouer you, imploy'd,[336] indeed,   100

To watch your ſteps, your lookes, your very breathings,
And to report them to him. Now, if you
Will be a true, right, delicate ſweete Miſtreſſe,
Why, wee will make a *Cokes* of this *Wiſe Maſter*,
We will, my Miſtreſſe, an abſolute fine *Cokes*,   105

And mock, to ayre, all the deepe diligences
Of ſuch a ſolemne, and effectuall Aſſe,
An Aſſe to ſo good purpoſe, as wee'll vſe him.
I will contriue it ſo, that you ſhall goe
To *Playes*, to *Maſques*, to *Meetings*, and to *Feaſts*.   110

For, why is all this Rigging, and fine Tackle, Miſtris,
If you neat handſome veſſells, of good ſayle,
Put not forth euer, and anon, with your[337] nets
Abroad into the world. It is your fiſhing.
There, you ſhal chooſe your friends, your ſeruants, Lady,
Your ſquires of honour; I'le conuey your letters,   116

Fetch anſwers, doe you all the offices,
That can belong to your bloud, and beauty. And,
For the variety, at my times, although
I am not in due *ſymmetrie*, the man   120

---

[333] saucy. [*Aside.* G
[334] black Room 1716
[335] engendring 1641
[336] employ'd 1716, f.
[337] your G

Of that proportion; or in rule
Of *phyficke*, of the iuft complexion:
Or of that truth of *Picardill*,[338] in clothes,
To boaft a foueraignty o're Ladies: yet
I know, to do my turnes, fweet Miftreffe. Come, kiffe—
M^{rs}. Fi. How now!
Pvg. Deare delicate Mift.[339] I am your flaue,   126

Your little *worme*, that loues you: your fine *Monkey*;
Your *Dogge*, your *Iacke*, your *Pug*, that longs to be
Stil'd, o' your pleafures.
M^{rs}. Fit. Heare you all this? Sir, Pray you,
Come from your ftanding, doe, a little, fpare[340]   130

Shee thinkes her hufband watches.[341]
Your felfe, Sir, from your watch, t'applaud your *Squire*,
That fo well followes your inftructions!

---

[338] *Piccardell* 1641
[339] Mist.] as in 2. 2. 41
[340] *Mrs. Fitz. [aloud]*
[341] SN. om. G

Act. II.   Scene. III.
Fitz-dottrell.   Miſtreſſe Fitz-dottrel.   Pvg.[342]

How now, ſweet heart? what's[343] the matter?
M[rs]. Fi. Good!
You are a ſtranger to the plot! you ſet[344] not
Your fancy *Diuell*, here, to tempt your wife,
With all the inſolent vnciuill language,
Or action, he could vent?
Fit. Did you so, *Diuell*?   5

M[rs]. Fit. Not you? you were not planted i' your hole to heare him,
Vpo'[345] the ſtayres? or here, behinde the hangings?
I doe not know your qualities? he durſt doe it,
And you not giue directions?
Fit. You shall ſee, wife, Whether he durſt, or no: and what it was,   10

I did direct.[346]
Her huſband goes out, and enters presently with a cudgell vpon him.[347]
Pvg. Sweet Miſtreſſe, are you mad?
Fit. You moſt mere Rogue! you open manifeſt Villaine!
You Feind apparant you! you declar'd Hel-hound!
Pvg. Good S[r].
Fit. Good Knaue, good Raſcal, and good Traitor.
Now, I doe finde you parcel-*Diuell*, indeed.   15

Vpo' the point of truſt? I' your firſt charge?
The very day o' your probation?
To tempt your Miſtreſſe?[348] You doe ſee, good wedlocke,
How I directed him.
M[rs]. Fit. Why, where S[r]? were you?
Fit. Nay, there is one blow more,[349] for exerciſe: 20

After a pause. He ſtrikes him againe
I told you, I ſhould doe it.
Pvg. Would you had done, Sir.

---

[342] SD. om. *Enter* Fitzdottrel. G
[343] 's] is G
[344] set] see W
[345] upon G§
[346] Whether ... direct.] All in line 10. 1692, 1716
[347] SN.] [*Exit. Re-enter* Fitzdottrel *with a cudgel.* G
[348] mistress! [*Beats Pug.* G
[349] SN.] [*Strikes him again.* G

43

Fit. O wife, the rareſt man! yet[350] there's another
To put you in mind o'[351] the laſt, ſuch a braue man, wife!
Within, he has his proiects, and do's vent 'hem, *and againe.*[352]
The gallanteſt! where[353] you *tentiginous*? ha?   25

Would you be acting of the *Incubus*?
Did her ſilks ruſtling moue you?
Pvg. Gentle Sir.
Fit. Out of my ſight. If thy name were not *Diuell*,
Thou ſhouldſt not ſtay a minute with me. In,
Goe, yet ſtay: yet goe too. I am reſolu'd.   30

What I will doe: and you ſhall know't afore-hand.
Soone as the Gentleman is gone, doe you heare?
I'll helpe your liſping. Wife, ſuch a man, wife!
Diuell *goes out.*[354]
He has ſuch plots! He will make mee a *Duke*!
No leſſe, by heauen! ſix Mares, to your coach, wife!   35

That's your proportion! And your coach-man bald!
Becauſe he ſhall be bare, inough. Doe not you laugh,
We are looking for a place, and all, i' the map
What to be of. Haue faith, be not an Infidell.
You know, I am not eaſie to be gull'd.   40

I ſweare, when I haue my *millions*, elſe. I'll make
Another *Dutcheſſe*: if you ha' not faith.
Mʳˢ. Fi. You'll ha' too much, I feare, in theſe falſe ſpirits.
Fit. Spirits? O, no such thing! wife! wit, mere wit!
This man defies the *Diuell*, and all his works!   45

He dos't by *Ingine*,[355] and deuiſes, hee!
He has his winged ploughes, that goe with ſailes,
Will plough you forty acres, at once! and mills.
Will ſpout you water, ten miles off! All *Crowland*
Is ours, wife; and the fens, from vs, in *Norfolke*,   50

To the vtmoſt bound[356] of *Lincoln-ſhire*! we haue view'd it,
And meaſur'd it within all; by the ſcale!

---

[350] yet ... laſt] euclosed by () W, G
[351] o' ret. G
[352] SN.] [*Beats him again.*] G
[353] where] were 1716, W Were G
[354] SN.] [*Exit Pug.*] G
[355] *Engine* 1716 Engine W engine G
[356] bounds 1692, f. || of] in G

The richeſt tract of land, Loue, i' the kingdome!
There will be made feuenteene, or eighteene *millions*;
Or more, as't may be handled! wherefore, thinke,   55

Sweet heart, if th'[357] haſt a fancy to one place,
More then another, to be *Dutcheſſe* of;
Now, name it: I will ha't[358] what ere it coſt,
(If't will be had for money) either here,   59

Or'n[359] *France*, or *Italy*.
M[rs]. Fi. You ha' ſtrange phantaſies!

---

[357] th'] thou G
[358] have 't G
[359] Or'n] Or'in 1692 Or in 1716, f.

ACT. II.   SCENE. IV.

Mere-craft.   Fitz-dottrell.[360]

Ingine. Where are you, Sir?
Fit. I ſee thou haſt no *talent*
This way, wife. Vp to thy gallery; doe, *Chuck*,
Leaue vs to talke of it, who vnderſtand it.[361]
Mer. I thinke we ha' found a place to fit you, now, Sir.
Gloc'ſter.
Fit. O, no, I'll none!
Mer. Why, Sʳ?
Fit. Tis fatall.   5

Mer. That you ſay right in. *Spenſer*, I thinke,[362] the younger,
Had his laſt honour thence. But, he was but *Earle*.
Fit. I know not that, Sir. But *Thomas* of *Woodſtocke*,
I'm ſure, was *Duke*, and he was made away,
At *Calice*; as *Duke Humphrey* was at *Bury*:   10

And *Richard* the third, you know what end he came too.
Mer. By m'faith[363] you are cunning i' the *Chronicle*, Sir.
Fit. No, I confeſſe I ha't[364] from the *Play-bookes*,
And thinke they'are more *authentique*.
Ing. That's[365] ſure, Sir.
Mer. What ſay you (to this then)
He whiſpers him[366] *of a place*.
Fit. No, a noble houſe.[367]   15

Pretends to that. I will doe no man wrong.
Mer. Then take one propoſition more, and heare it
As paſt exception.
Fit. What's that?
Mer. To be
Duke of thoſe lands, you ſhall recouer; take
Your title, thence, Sir, *Duke* of the *Drown'd lands*,   20

---

[360] SD. Act. ...] om. *Enter* Meercraft *and* Engine. G
[361] [*Exit Mrs. Fitz.* G
[362] comma after 'thinke' om. 1692, f.
[363] m'] my W, G
[364] have it G
[365] 's] is W, G
[366] SN.] [*whispers him.*] G
[367] period after 'house' om. 1716, f.

Or *Drown'd-land.*
Fit. Ha? that laſt has a good ſound!
I like it well. The *Duke* of *Drown'd-land*?
Ing. Yes;
It goes like *Groen-land*, Sir, if you marke it.
Mer. I,
And drawing thus your honour from the worke,
You make the reputation of that, greater;   25

And ſtay't the longer i'[368] your name.
Fit. 'Tis true.*Drown'd-lands* will liue in *Drown'd-land*!
Mer. Yes, when you
Ha' no foote left; as that muſt be, Sir, one day.
And, though it tarry in your heyres, some *forty*,
Fifty deſcents, the longer liuer, at laſt, yet,   30

Muſt thruſt 'hem out on't: if no quirk in law,
Or odde *Vice* o' their owne not do'it[369] firſt.
Wee ſee thoſe changes, daily: the faire lands,
That were the *Clyents*, are the *Lawyers*, now:
And thoſe rich Mannors, there, of good man *Taylors*,   35

Had once more wood vpon 'hem, then the yard,
By which th'[370] were meaſur'd out for the laſt purchaſe.
Nature hath theſe viciſſitudes. Shee makes
No man a ſtate of perpetuety, Sir.
Fit. Yo' are[371] i' the right. Let's in then, and conclude. 40

Hee ſpies Diuell.I my ſight, againe? I'll talke with you, anon.[372]

---

[368] 't] it G
[369] do't 1641
[370] th'] they G
[371] You're 1716, W ‖ SN.] *Re-enter* Pug. G
[372] [*Exeunt Fitz. Meer. and Engine.* G ‖ I] I' 1716, W In G

ACT. II.   SCENE. V.
Pvg.[373]

Svre hee will geld mee, if I stay: or worſe,
Pluck out my tongue, one o' the two. This Foole,
There is no truſting of him: and to quit him,
Were a contempt againſt my *Chiefe*, paſt pardon.
It was a ſhrewd diſheartning[374] this, at firſt!   5

Who would ha' thought a woman ſo well harneſs'd,
Or rather well-capariſon'd, indeed,
That weares ſuch petticoates, and lace to her ſmocks,
Broad ſeaming laces (as I ſee 'hem hang there)[375]
And garters which are loſt, if ſhee can ſhew 'hem,   10

Could ha' done this? *Hell!* why is ſhee ſo braue?
It cannot be to pleaſe *Duke Dottrel*, ſure,
Nor the dull pictures, in her gallery,
Nor her owne deare reflection, in her glaſſe;
Yet that may be: I haue knowne many of 'hem,   15

Beginne their pleaſure, but none end it, there:
(That I conſider, as I goe a long with it)[376]
They may, for want of better company,
Or that they thinke the better, ſpend an houre;
Two, three, or foure, diſcourſing with their ſhaddow: 20

But ſure they haue a farther ſpeculation.
No woman dreſt with ſo much care, and ſtudy,
Doth dreſſe her ſelfe in vaine. I'll vexe this *probleme*,
A little more, before I leaue it, ſure.[377]

---

[373] om. G
[374] disheartening G
[375] () ret. G
[376] () ret. G
[377] [*Exit.* G

ACT. II.   SCENE. VI.
Wittipol.   Manly.   Miſtreſſe Fitz-dottrel.
Pvg.[378]

This was a fortune, happy aboue thought,
That this ſhould proue thy chamber: which I fear'd
Would be my greateſt trouble! this muſt be
The very window, and that the roome.
Man. It is.I now remember, I haue often ſeene there   5

A woman, but I neuer mark'd her much.
Wit. Where was your ſoule, friend?
Man. Faith, but now, and then,
Awake vnto thoſe obiects.
Wit. You pretend ſo.
Let mee not liue, if I am not in loue
More with her wit, for this direction, now,   10

Then with her forme, though I ha' prais'd that prettily,
Since I ſaw her, and you, to day. Read thoſe.
Hee giues him a paper, wherein is the copy of a Song.[379]
They'll goe vnto the ayre you loue ſo well.
Try 'hem vnto the note, may be the muſique
Will call her ſooner; light, ſhee's here. Sing quickly.[380]   15

M[rs]. Fit. Either he vnderſtood him not: or elſe,
The fellow was not faithfull in deliuery,
Of what I bad. And, I am iuſtly pay'd,
That might haue made my profit of his ſeruice,
But, by miſ-taking, haue drawne on his enuy,   20

And done the worſe defeate vpon my ſelfe.
Manly *ſings,* Pug *enters perceiues it.[381]*
How! Muſique? then he may be there: and is ſure.
Pvg. O! Is it ſo? Is there the enter-view?[382]

---

[378] Act. ...] om. Scene II. Manly's *Chambers in Lincoln's Inn, opposite* Fitzdottrel's *House. Enter* Wittipol *and* Manly. G

[379] SN.] [*Gives him the copy of a song.* G

[380] *Mrs.* Fitzdottrel *appears at a window of her house fronting that of Manly's Chambers.* G

[381]   worst W || SN. *enters*] *enters and* 1716, W || Manly ...] *Manly sings. Enter* Pug *behind.* G

[382] interview W, G

49

Haue I drawne to you, at laſt,[383] my cunning *Lady*?
The *Diuell* is an *Aſſe*! fool'd off! and beaten!   25

Nay, made an inſtrument! and could not ſent it!
Well, ſince yo' haue[384] ſhowne the malice of a woman,
No leſſe then her true wit, and learning, Miſtreſſe,
I'll try, if little *Pug* haue the malignity
To recompence it, and ſo ſaue his danger.   30

'Tis not the paine, but the diſcredite of it,
The *Diuell* ſhould not keepe a body intire.[385]
Wit. Away, fall backe, ſhe comes.
Man. I'll[386] leaue you, Sir,
The Maſter of my chamber. I haue buſineſſe.[387]
Wit. M^rs!
M^rs. Fi. You make me paint, S^r.
Wit. The'are faire colours,[388]   35

Lady, and naturall! I did receiue[389]
Some commands from you, lately, gentle *Lady*,[390]
This Scene is acted at two windo's as out of two contiguous buildings.
But ſo perplex'd, and wrap'd in the deliuery,
As I may feare t'haue[391] miſ-interpreted:
But muſt make ſuit ſtill, to be neere your grace.   40

M^rs. Fi. Who is there with you, S^r?
Wit. None, but my ſelfe.
It falls out. *Lady*, to be a deare friends lodging.
Wherein there's ſome conſpiracy of fortune
With your poore ſeruants bleſ affections.
M^rs. Fi. Who was it ſung?
Wit. He, *Lady*, but hee's gone,   45

Vpon my entreaty of him, ſeeing you
Approach the window. Neither need you doubt him,
If he were here. He is too much a gentleman.

---

383 least W
384 you've 1716, W
385 entire W, G || [*Aside and exit.* G
386 I'll] I W, G
387 [*Exit.* G
388 M^rs!] Mis! 1641 the rest as in 2. 2. 41 || They're 1716, W they are G || *Mrs. Fitz.* [*advances to the window.*] G
389 The'are ... receiue] one line 1692, 1716, W
390 SN. om. G
391 t'] to 1692, f.

Mrs. Fi. Sir, if you iudge me by this fimple action,
And by the outward habite, and complexion   50

Of eafineffe, it hath, to your defigne;
You may with Iuftice, fay, I am a woman:
And a ftrange woman. But when you fhall pleafe,
To bring but that concurrence of my fortune,
To memory, which to day your felfe did vrge: 55

It may beget fome fauour like excufe,
Though none like reafon.
Wit. No, my tune-full Miftreffe?
Then, furely, *Loue* hath none: nor *Beauty* any;
Nor *Nature* violenced, in both thefe:
With all whofe gentle tongues you fpeake, at once.   60

I thought I had inough remou'd, already,
That fcruple from your breft, and left yo' all[392] reafon;
When, through my mornings perfpectiue I fhewd you
A man fo aboue excufe, as he is[393] the caufe,
Why any thing is to be done vpon him: 65

And nothing call'd an iniury, mif-plac'd.
I'rather, now had hope, to fhew you how *Loue*
By his acceffes, growes more naturall:
And, what was done, this morning, with fuch force
Was but deuis'd to ferue the prefent, then.   70

That fince *Loue* hath the honour to approach[394]
He grows more familiar in his Court-fhip.
Thefe fifter-fwelling brefts; and touch this foft,
And rofie hand; hee hath the skill to draw
Their *Nectar* forth, with kiffing; and could make
More wanton falts,[395] from this braue promontory,   75

Downe to this valley, then the nimble *Roe*;
playes with her paps, kiffeth her hands, &c.
Could play the hopping *Sparrow*, 'bout thefe nets;
And fporting *Squirell* in thefe crifped groues;
Bury himfelfe in euery *Silke-wormes* kell,
Is here vnrauell'd; runne into the fnare,   80

---

[392] y'all 1716, W
[393] he's W, G
[394] SN. om. G
[395] 'salts 1692 'saults 1716

Which euery hayre is, caſt[396] into a curle,
To catch a *Cupid* flying: Bath himself
In milke, and roſes, here, and dry him, there;
Warme his cold hands, to play with this ſmooth, round,
And well torn'd chin, as with the *Billyard* ball;   85

Rowle on theſe lips, the banks of loue, and there
At once both plant, and gather kiſſes. *Lady*,
Shall I, with what I haue[397] made to day here, call
All ſenſe to wonder, and all faith to ſigne
The myſteries reuealed in your forme?   90

And will *Loue* pardon mee the blasphemy
I vtter'd, when I ſaid, a glaſſe could ſpeake
This beauty, or that fooles had power to iudge it?
Doe but looke, on her eyes! They doe light—
All that Loue's *world comprizeth!*   95

Doe but looke on her hayre! it is bright,
As Loue's *ſtarre, when it riſeth!*
Doe but marke, her fore-head's[398] ſmoother,
Then words that ſooth her!
And from her arched browes, ſuch a[399] grace   100

Sheds it ſelfe through the face;
As alone, there triumphs to the life,
All the gaine, all the good, of the elements ſtrife!
Haue you ſeene but a bright Lilly grow,
Before rude hands haue touch'd it?   105

Haue you mark'd but the fall of the[400] Snow,
Before the ſoyle hath ſmuch'd it?
Haue you felt the wooll o'[401] the Beuer?[402]
Or Swans downe, euer?
Or, haue ſmelt[403] o' the bud o' the Bryer?   110

Or the Nard i' the fire?
Or, haue taſted the bag o' the Bee?

---

[396] is, cast] is cast 1716, W
[397] I've W
[398] head's] head 1641
[399] a om. 1641
[400] of the] the 1641
[401] o'] of W (Same on line 112)
[402] Beuer] beaver W, G
[403] smelt o'ret. G

O, ſo white! O, ſo ſoft! O, ſo ſweet is ſhee!

53

O, ſo white! O, ſo ſoft! O, ſo ſweet is ſhee!

ACT. II.   SCENE. VII.
Fitz-dottrell.   Wittipol.   Pvg.[404]

Her huſband appeares at her back.
Is shee ſo, Sir? and, I will keepe her ſo.
If I know how, or can: that wit of man
Will doe't, I'll goe no farther. At this windo'
She ſhall no more be *buz'd* at. Take your leaue on't.
If you be ſweet meates, wedlock, or ſweet fleſh,   5

All's one: I doe not loue this *hum* about you.
A flye-blowne wife is not ſo proper, In:
For you, [405]S^r, looke to heare from mee.
Hee ſpeakes out of his wiues window.
Wit. So, I doe, Sir.
Fit. No, but in other termes. There's no man offers
This to my wife, but paies for't.
Wit. That haue I, Sir.
Fit. Nay, then, I tell you, you are.[406]
Wit. What am I, Sir?   11

Fit. Why, that I'll thinke on, when I ha' cut your throat.
Wit. Goe, you are an *Aſſe*.
Fit. I am reſolu'd on't, Sir.[407]
Wit. I thinke you are.
Fit. To call you to a reckoning.
Wit. Away, you brokers blocke, you property.   15

Fit. S'light, if you ſtrike me, I'll[408] ſtrike your Miſtreſſe.
Hee ſtrikes his wife.[409]
Wit. O! I could ſhoote mine[410] eyes at him, for that, now;
Or leaue my teeth in'him, were they cuckolds bane,
Inough to kill him. What prodigious,
Blinde, and moſt wicked change of fortune's this?   20

I ha' no ayre of patience: an my vaines

---

[404] om. SN.] Fitz-dottrell *appears at his Wife's back.* G
[405] SN. om. G || you,] you, you, W, G
[406] are.] are—W, G
[407] Sir.] Sir—Ed.
[408] I will W, G
[409] SN.] [*Strikes Mrs. Fitz. and leads her out.* G
[410] my 1641

Swell, and my finewes ftart at iniquity[411] of it.
I fhall breake, breake.
The Diuell *fpeakes below.*[412]
Pvg. This for the malice of it,
And my reuenge may paffe! But, now, my confcience
Tells mee, I haue profited the caufe of Hell   25

But little, in the breaking-off their loues.
Which, if some other act of mine repaire not,
I fhall heare ill of in my accompt.
Fitz-dottrel *enters with his wife[413] as come downe.*
Fit. O, Bird! Could you do this? 'gainft me? and at this time, now?
When I was fo imploy'd,[414] wholly for you,   30

Drown'd i' my care (more, then the land, I fweare,
I'haue hope to win)[415] to make you peere-leffe? ftudying,
For footemen for you, fine pac'd huifhers, pages,
To ferue you o' the knee; with what Knights wife,
To beare your traine, and fit with your foure women   35

In councell, and receiue intelligences,
From forraigne parts, to dreffe you at all pieces!
Y'haue[416] (a'moft) turn'd my good affection, to you;
Sowr'd my fweet thoughts; all my pure purpofes:
I could now finde (i' my very heart) to make   40

Another, *Lady Dutcheffe*; and depofe you.
Well, goe your waies in. *Diuell*, you haue redeem'd all.[417]
I doe forgiue you. And I'll doe you good.[418]

---

[411] th'iniquity G
[412] SN. om [*Exit.* Scene III. *Another Room in* Fitzdottrel's *House. Enter* Pug. G
[413] in om. 1641 || SN.] *Enter* Fitzdottrel *and his wife.* G
[414] employ'd 1716, f.
[415] () ret. G
[416] You've 1716, f. || almost W, G
[417] [*Exit Mrs. Fitz.*] G
[418] [*Exit Pug.* G

ACT. II.   SCENE. VIII.
Mere-craft.   Fitz-dottrel.   Ingine.   Traines.[419]

Why ha you thefe excurfions? where ha' you beene, Sir?
Fit. Where I ha' beene vex'd a little, with a toy!
Mer. O Sir! no toyes muft trouble your graue head,
Now it is growing to be great. You muft
Be aboue all thofe things.
Fit. Nay, nay, fo I will.   5

Mer. Now you are to'ard the Lord, you muft put off
The man, Sir.[420]
Ing. He faies true.
Mer. You muft do nothing
As you ha' done it heretofore; not know,
Or falute any man.
Ing. That was your bed-fellow,
The other moneth.
Mer. The other moneth? the weeke.   10

Thou doft not know the priueledges, *Ingine*,
Follow that Title; nor how fwift: To day,
When he has put on his Lords face once, then—
Fit. Sir, for thefe things I fhall doe well enough,
There is no feare of me. But then, my wife is   15

Such an vntoward thing! fhee'll neuer learne
How to comport with it. I am out of all
Conceipt, on her behalfe.
Mer. Beft haue her taught, Sir.
Fit. Where? Are there any Schooles for *Ladies*? Is there
An *Academy* for women? I doe know,   20

For men, there was: I learn'd in it, my felfe,
To make my legges, and doe my poftures.
Ing. Sir. Doe you remember the conceipt you had—
O' the Spanifh gowne, at home?
Ingine *whifpers* Merecraft,[421] Merecraft *turnes to* Fitz-dottrel.
Mer. Ha! I doe thanke thee,
With all my heart, deare *Ingine*. Sir, there is   25

---

[419] Act. ...] om. *Enter* Meercraft *and* Engine. G ‖ II] III 1641
[420] Now ... Sir.] "Now ... sir." W
[421] SN.] [*whispers Meercraft.*] G

A certaine *Lady*, here about the Towne,
An *Englifh* widdow, who hath lately trauell'd,
But fhee's[422] call'd the *Spaniard*; caufe fhe came
Lateft from thence: and[423] keepes the *Spanifh* habit.
Such a rare woman! all our women heere,   30

That are of fpirit, and fafhion flocke,[424] vnto her,
As to their Prefident; their *Law*; their *Canon*;
More then they euer did, to *Oracle-Foreman*.
Such rare receipts fhee has, Sir, for the face;
Such *oyles*; such *tinctures*; such *pomatumn's*;   35

Such *perfumes*; *med'cines*; *quinteffences*, &c.[425]
And fuch a Miftreffe of behauiour;
She knowes, from the *Dukes* daughter, to the Doxey,
What is their due iuft: and no more!
Fit. O Sir! You pleafe me i' this, more then mine owne greatneffe,   40

Where is fhee? Let vs haue her.
Mer. By your patience,
We muft vfe meanes; caft how to be acquainted—
Fit. Good, S^r, about it.
Mer. We muft think how, firft.
Fit. O! I doe not loue to tarry for a thing,
When I haue a mind to't.[426] You doe not know me.   45

If you doe offer it.
Mer. Your wife muft fend
Some pretty token to her, with a complement,
And pray to be receiu'd in her good graces,
All the great *Ladies* do't.[427]
Fit. She fhall, fhe fhall, What were it beft to be?
Mer. Some little toy,   50

I would not haue it any great matter, Sir:
A *Diamant*[428] ring, of *forty* or *fifty* pound,
Would doe it handfomely: and be a gift
Fit for your wife to fend, and her to take.

---

[422] she is W, G
[423] and om. 1641
[424] fashion flocke,] fashion, flock 1692, f.
[425] &c.] *et caetera*; G
[426] to it G
[427] do it G
[428] *Diamond* 1692, 1716 diamond W, G passim

Fit. I'll goe, and tell my wife on't, ſtreight.[429]   55

Fitz-dottrel *goes out.*
Mer. Why this
Is well! The clothes we'haue now: But, where's this *Lady*?
If we could get a witty boy, now, *Ingine*;
That were an excellent cracke: I could inſtruct him,
To the true height. For any thing takes this *dottrel.*
Ing. Why, Sir your beſt will be one o' the players!   60

Mer. No, there's no truſting them. They'll talke on't,[430]
And tell their *Poets.*
Ing. What if they doe? The ieſt
will brooke the Stage. But, there be ſome of 'hem
Are very honeſt Lads. There's *Dicke[431] Robinſon*
A very pretty fellow, and comes often   65

To a Gentlemans chamber, a friends[432] of mine. We had
The merrieſt ſupper of it there, one night,
The Gentlemans Land-lady invited him
To'a[433] Goſſips feaſt. Now, he Sir brought *Dick Robinſon,*
Dreſt like a Lawyers wife, amongſt 'hem all;   70

(I lent him cloathes) but, to ſee him behaue it;
And lay the law; and carue; and drinke vnto 'hem;
And then talke baudy: and ſend frolicks! o!
It would haue burſt your buttons, or not left you
A ſeame.
Mer. They ſay hee's an ingenious youth!   75

Ing. O Sir! and dreſſes himſelfe, the beſt! beyond
Forty o' your very *Ladies*! did you ne'r ſee him?
Mer. No, I do ſeldome ſee thoſe toyes. But thinke you,
That we may haue him?
Ing. Sir, the young Gentleman
I tell you of, can command him. Shall I attempt it?   80

Mer. Yes, doe it.
Enters againe.
Fit.[434] S'light, I cannot get my wife

---

[429] SN.] [*Exit.* G
[430] of it G
[431] *Dick* 1692, 1716 Dick W Dickey G
[432] friend W, G
[433] T'a 1716, W
[434] SN....] Fit.... 1716 Fitz-dottrel ... W *Re-enter* Fitzdottrel. G

To part with a ring, on any termes: and yet,
The ſollen *Monkey* has two.[435]
Mer. It were 'gainst reaſon
That you ſhould vrge it; Sir, ſend to a Gold-ſmith,
Let not her loſe by't.
Fit. How do's ſhe loſe by't[436]?   85

Is't not for her?
Mer. Make it your owne bounty,
It will ha' the better ſucceſſe; what is a matter
Of *fifty* pound to you, S[r].
Fit. I'haue but a hundred
Pieces, to ſhew here; that I would not breake—
Mer. You ſhall ha' credit, Sir. I'll ſend a ticket   90

Vnto my Gold-ſmith. Heer, my man comes too,
To carry it fitly. How now, *Traines*? What birds?
Traines *enters.*[437]
Tra. Your Couſin *Euer-ill* met me, and has beat mee,
Becauſe I would not tell him where you were:
I thinke he has dogd me to the houſe too.
Fit.[438] Well—   95

You ſhall goe out at the back-doore, then, *Traines*.
You muſt get *Guilt-head* hither, by ſome meanes:
Tra. 'Tis[439] impoſſible!
Fit. Tell him, we haue *veniſon*,
I'll g'[440] him a piece, and ſend his wife a *Pheſant*.
Tra. A Forreſt moues not, till that *forty* pound,   100

Yo' had of him, laſt, be pai'd. He keepes more ſtirre,
For that ſame petty ſumme, then for your bond
Of *ſixe*; and *Statute* of *eight* hundred!
Fit. Tell him
Wee'll hedge in that. Cry vp *Fitz-dottrell* to him,
Double his price: Make him a man of mettall.   105

Tra. That will not need, his bond is current inough.[441]

---

[435] sullen 1692, f.
[436] 't] it G
[437] SN.] *Enter* Trains. G
[438] Fit.] *Meer.* W, G (Same for line 103)
[439] 'T] It G
[440] gi' 1716, W give G [*Exit.* G
[441] 106 [*Exeunt.* G

Act. III.   Scene. I.
Gvilt-head.   Plvtarchvs.[442]

All this is to make you a Gentleman:
I'll haue you learne, Sonne. Wherefore haue I plac'd you
With S^r. *Poul*[443] *Either-fide*, but to haue fo much Law
To keepe your owne? Befides, he is a *Iuftice*,
Here i' the Towne; and dwelling, Sonne, with him,   5

You fhal learne that in a yeere, fhall be worth twenty
Of hauing ftay'd you at *Oxford*, or at *Cambridge*,
Or fending you to the *Innes* of *Court*, or *France*.
I am[444] call'd for now in hafte, by Mafter *Meere-craft*
To truft Mafter *Fitz-dottrel*, a good man: 10

I'haue inquir'd him, eighteene hundred a yeere,
(His name is currant)[445] for a diamant ring
Of forty, fhall not be worth thirty (thats gain'd)
And this is to make you a Gentleman!
Plv. O, but good father, you truft too much!
Gvi. Boy, boy,[446]   15

We liue, by finding fooles out, to be trufted.
Our fhop-bookes are our paftures, our corn-grounds,
We lay 'hem op'n for them to come into:
And when wee haue 'hem there, wee driue 'hem vp
In t'one[447] of our two Pounds, the *Compters*, ftreight,   20

And this is to make you a Gentleman!
Wee Citizens neuer truft, but wee doe coozen:
For, if our debtors pay, wee coozen them;
And if they doe not, then we coozen our felues.
But that's a hazard euery one muft runne,   25

That hopes to make his Sonne a Gentleman!
Plv. I doe not wifh to be one, truely, Father.
In a defcent, or two, wee come to be

---

[442] SD. Act. ... I. ...] Act. ... I. *A Room in* Fitzdottrel's *House. Enter* Thomas Gilthead *and* Plutarchus. G
[443] to om. 1692 t' 1716 || *Poul*] Pould 1641
[444] I'm W, G
[445] () ret. G
[446] Boy, boy] Boy, by 1692
[447] two om. 1692, 1716 || Int'one 1716, W into one G

Iuſt 'itheir[448] ſtate, fit to be coozend, like 'hem.
And I had rather ha' tarryed i' your trade: 30

For, ſince the *Gentry* ſcorne the Citty ſo much,
Me thinkes we ſhould in time, holding together,
And matching in our owne tribes, as they ſay,
Haue got an *Act* of *Common Councell*, for it,
That we might coozen them out of *rerum natura*.   35

Gvi. I, if we had an *Act* firſt to forbid
The marrying of our wealthy heyres vnto 'hem:
And daughters, with ſuch lauiſh portions.
That confounds all.
Plv. And makes a *Mungril* breed, Father.
And when they haue your money, then they laugh at you: 40

Or kick you downe the ſtayres. I cannot abide 'hem.
I would faine haue 'hem coozen'd, but not truſted.

---

[448] i' their 1716, W in their G

ACT. III.   SCENE. II.
Mere-craft.   Gvilt-head.
Fitz-dottrell.   Plvtarchvs.[449]

O, is he come! I knew he would not faile me.
Welcome, good *Guilt-head*, I muſt ha' you doe
A noble Gentleman, a courteſie, here:
In a mere toy (ſome pretty Ring, or Iewell)
Of fifty, or threeſcore pound (Make it a hundred,   5

And hedge in the laſt forty, that I owe you,
And your owne price for the Ring)[450] He's a good man, S^r,
And you may hap' ſee him a great one! Hee,
Is likely to beſtow hundreds, and thouſands,
Wi' you; if you can humour him. A great prince   10

He will be ſhortly. What doe you ſay?
Gvi. In truth, Sir
I cannot. 'T has beene a long vacation with vs?
Fit. Of what, I pray thee? of wit? or honesty?
Thoſe are your Citizens long vacations.
Plv. Good Father do not truſt 'hem.
Mer. Nay, *Thom.*[451] *Guilt-head.*   15

Hee will not buy a courteſie and begge it:
Hee'll rather pay, then pray. If you doe for him,
You muſt doe cheerefully. His credit, Sir,
Is not yet proſtitute! Who's this? thy ſonne?
A pretty youth, what's[452] his name?
Plv. *Plutarchus*, Sir,   20

Mer. *Plutarchus!* How came that about?
Gvi. That yeere S^r, That I begot him, I bought *Plutarch's* liues,
And fell ſ in[453] loue with the booke, as I call'd my ſonne
By'his name; In hope he ſhould be like him:
And write the liues of our great men!
Mer. I' the City?   25

And you do breed him, there?

---

[449] SD. Act. ...] *Enter* Meercraft. G
[450] ring. [*Aside to Gilthead.*
[451] Tom G
[452] 's] is G
[453] so in W, G

Gvi. His minde, Sir, lies Much to that way.
Mer. Why, then, he is[454] i' the right way.
Gvi. But, now, I had rather get him a good wife,
And plant him i' the countrey; there to vſe
The bleſſing I ſhall leaue him:
Mer. Out vpon't!   30

And loſe the laudable meanes, thou haſt at home, heere,
T'aduance, and make him a young *Alderman*?
Buy him a Captaines place, for ſhame; and let him
Into the world, early, and with his plume,
And Scarfes, march through *Cheapſide*, or along *Cornehill*,
And by the vertue'of thoſe, draw downe a wife   36

There from a windo', worth ten thouſand pound!
Get him the poſture booke, and's leaden men,
To ſet vpon a table, 'gainst his Miſtreſſe
Chance to come by, that hee may draw her in,   40

And ſhew her *Finsbury* battells.
Gvi. I haue plac'd him
With Iustice *Eytherſide*, to get so much law—
Mer. As thou haſt conſcience. Come, come, thou doſt wrong
Pretty *Plutarchus*, who had not his name,
For nothing: but was borne to traine the youth   45

Of *London*, in the military truth[455]—
That way his *Genius* lies.[456] My Couſin *Euerill*!

---

[454] he's W, G
[455] to ... truth] in italics G
[456] lies.—*Enter* Everill.

ACT. III. SCENE. III.

Ever-ill. Plvtarchvs. Gvilt-head.

Mere-craft. Fitzdottrell.[457]

O, are you heere, Sir?[458] 'pray you let vs whifper.
Plv. Father, deare Father, truſt him if you loue mee.
Gvi. Why, I doe meane it, boy; but, what I doe,
Muſt not come eaſily from mee: Wee muſt deale
With *Courtiers*, boy, as *Courtiers* deale with vs.   5

If I haue a *Buſineſſe* there, with any of them,
Why, I muſt wait, I'am[459] ſure on't, Son: and though
My *Lord* diſpatch me, yet his worſhipfull man—
Will keepe me for his ſport, a moneth, or two,
To ſhew mee with my fellow Cittizens.   10

I muſt make his traine long, and full, one quarter;
And helpe the ſpectacle of his greatneſſe. There,
Nothing is done at once, but iniuries, boy:
And they come head-long! an their good turnes moue not,
Or very ſlowly.
Plv. Yet ſweet father, truſt him.   15

Gvi. VVell, I will thinke.[460]
Ev. Come, you muſt do't, Sir.
I am[461] vndone elſe, and your *Lady Tayle-buſh*
Has ſent for mee to dinner, and my cloaths
Are all at pawne. I had ſent out this morning,
Before I heard you were come to towne, ſome twenty   20

Of my epiſtles, and no one returne—
Mere-craft *tells him of his faults*.[462]
Mer. VVhy, I ha' told you o' this. This comes of wearing
Scarlet, gold lace, and cut-works! your fine gartring![463]
VVith your blowne roſes, Couſin! and your eating
Pheſant, and *Godwit*, here in *London*! Haunting   25

---

[457] SD. om. G
[458] [*takes Meer. aside.* G
[459] I'm 1716, W I am G
[460] think. [*They walk aside.* G
[461] I'm 1716 I am W
[462] SN. om. G
[463] gartering W, G

The *Globes*, and *Mermaides*! wedging in with *Lords*,
Still at the table! and affecting lechery,
In veluet! where could you ha' contented your felfe
With cheefe, falt-butter, and a pickled hering,
I' the Low-countries; there worne cloth, and fuftian!   30

Beene fatisfied with a leape o' your Hoft's daughter,
In garrifon, a wench of a ftoter![464] or,
Your *Sutlers*[465] wife, i' the leaguer, of two blanks!
You neuer, then, had runne vpon this flat,
To write your letters miffiue, and fend out   35

Your priuy feales, that thus haue frighted off
All your acquaintance; that they fhun you at diftance,
VVorse, then you do the Bailies![466]
Ev. Pox vpon you.
I come not to you for counfell, I lacke money.
Hee repines.[467]
Mer. You doe not thinke, what you owe me already?
Ev. I?   40

They owe you, that meane to pay you. I'll befworne,
I neuer meant it. Come, you will proiect,
I fhall vndoe your practice, for this moneth elfe:
You know mee.
and threatens him.
Mer. I, yo' are[468] a right fweet nature!
Ev. Well, that's all one!
Mer. You'll leaue this Empire, one day?   45

You will not euer haue this tribute payd,
Your fcepter o' the fword?
Ev. Tye vp your wit,
Doe, and prouoke me not—
Mer. Will you, Sir, helpe,
To what I fhall prouoke another for you?
Ev. I cannot tell; try me: I thinke I am not   50

So vtterly, of an ore vn-to-be-melted,
But I can doe my felfe good, on occafions.

---

[464] Storer 1716 storer W, G
[465] Sulters 1641
[466] Bayliffs 1716 bailiffs W, G
[467] SN. om. G (Same on line 43)
[468] you're 1716, W

They ioyne.[469]
Mer. Strike in then, for your part. Mᵣ. *Fitz-dottrel*[470]
If I tranſgreſſe in point of manners, afford mee
Your beſt conſtruction; I muſt beg my freedom   55

From your affayres, this day.
Fit. How, Sᵣ.
Mer. It isIn ſuccour of this Gentlemans occaſions,
My kinſ-man—Mere-craft *pretends* buſineſſe.[471]
Fit. You'll not do me that affront, Sᵣ.
Mer. I am ſory you ſhould ſo interpret it,
But, Sir, it ſtands vpon his being inueſted   60

In a new *office*, hee has ſtood for, long:
Mere-craft *describes the* office *of* Dependancy.
Maſter of the *Dependances*! A place
Of my proiection too, Sir, and hath met
Much oppoſition; but the State, now, ſee's
That great neceſſity of it, as after all   65

Their writing, and their ſpeaking, againſt *Duells*,
They haue erected it. His booke is drawne—
For, ſince,[472] there will be differences, daily,
'Twixt Gentlemen; and that the roaring manner
Is growne offenſiue; that thoſe few, we call   70

The ciuill men o' the ſword, abhorre the vapours;
They ſhall refer now, hither, for their *proceſſe*;
And ſuch as treſſpaſe 'gainſt the rule of *Court*,
Are to be fin'd—
Fit. In troth, a pretty place!
Mer. A kinde of arbitrary *Court* 'twill be, Sir.   75

Fit. I ſhall haue matter for it, I beleeue,
Ere it be long: I had a diſtaſt.
Mer. But now, Sir,
My learned councell, they muſt haue a feeling,
They'll part, Sir, with no bookes, without the hand-gout
Be oyld, and I muſt furniſh. If't be money,   80

To me ſtreight. I am Mine, *Mint* and *Exchequer*.
To ſupply all. What is't? a hundred pound?

---

[469] *Enter* Fitzdottrel. || SN. om. G
[470] part. [*They go up to Fitz.*] G
[471] SN. om. G (Same on line 61)
[472] since 1641, f.

Eve. No, th' *Harpey*, now, ſtands on a hundred pieces.
Mer. Why, he muſt haue 'hem, if he will. To morrow, Sir,
Will equally ſerue your occaſion's,——   85

And therefore, let me obtaine, that you will yield
To timing a poore Gentlemans diſtreſſes,
In termes of hazard.—
Fit. By no meanes!
Mer. I muſt
Get him this money, and will.—
Fit. Sir, I proteſt,
I'd[473] rather ſtand engag'd for it my ſelfe: 90

Then you ſhould leaue mee.
Mer. O good Sʳ. do you thinke
So courſely of our manners, that we would,
For any need of ours, be preſt to take it:
Though you be pleas'd to offer it.
Fit. Why, by heauen,I meane it!
Mer. I can neuer beleeue leſſe.   95

But wee, Sir, muſt preferue our dignity,
As you doe publiſh yours. By your faire leaue, Sir.
Hee[474] offers to be gone.
Fit. As I am a Gentleman, if you doe offer
To leaue mee now, or if you doe refuſe mee,   99

I will not thinke you loue mee.
Mer. Sir, I honour you.
And with iuſt reaſon, for theſe noble notes,
Of the nobility, you pretend too! But, Sir—
I would know, why? a motiue (he a ſtranger)[475]
You ſhould doe this?
(Eve. You'll mar all with your fineneſſe)[476]
Fit. Why, that's all one, if 'twere, Sir, but my fancy.   105

But I haue a *Buſineſſe*, that perhaps I'd[477] haue
Brought to his *office*.
Mer. O, Sir! I haue done, then;
If hee can be made profitable, to you.
Fit. Yes, and it ſhall be one of my ambitions

---

[473] I had G
[474] SN. *Hee* om. G
[475] () ret. G
[476] *Ever.* [*Aside to Meer.*]
[477] 'd] would G

To haue it the firſt *Buſineſſe*? May I not?   110

Eve. So you doe meane to make't, a perfect *Buſineſſe*.
Fit. Nay, I'll doe that, aſſure you: ſhew me once.
Mer. S[r], it concernes, the firſt be a perfect *Buſineſſe*,
For his owne honour!
Eve. I, and th'[478] reputation
Too, of my place.
Fit. Why, why doe I take this courſe, elſe?   115

I am not altogether, an *Aſſe*, good Gentlemen,
Wherefore ſhould I conſult you? doe you thinke?
To make a ſong on't? How's your manner? tell vs.
Mer. Doe, ſatisfie him: giue him the whole courſe.
Eve. Firſt, by requeſt, or otherwiſe, you offer   120

Your *Buſineſſe* to the *Court*: wherein you craue:
The iudgement of the *Maſter* and the *Aſſiſtants*.
Fit. Well, that's[479] done, now, what doe you vpon it?
Eve. We ſtreight S[r], haue recourſe to the ſpring-head;
Viſit the ground; and, ſo diſcloſe the nature: 125

If it will carry, or no. If wee doe finde,
By our[480] proportions it is like to proue
A ſullen, and blacke *Bus'neſſe* That it be
Incorrigible; and out of, treaty; then.
We file it, a *Dependance*!
Fit. So 'tis fil'd.   130

What followes? I doe loue the order of theſe things.
Eve. We then aduiſe the party, if he be
A man of meanes, and hauings, that forth-with,
He ſettle his eſtate: if not, at leaſt
That he pretend it. For, by that, the world   135

Takes notice, that it now is a *Dependance*.
And this we call, Sir, *Publication*.
Fit. Very ſufficient! After *Publication*, now?
Eve. Then we grant out our *Proceſſe*, which is diuers;
Eyther by *Chartell*, Sir, or *ore-tenus*,   140

Wherein the Challenger, and Challengee
Or (with your *Spaniard*) your *Prouocador*,

---

[478] the W
[479] 's] is G
[480] our] your 1641

And *Prouocado*, haue their feuerall courfes—
Fit. I haue enough on't! for an hundred pieces?
Yes, for two hundred, vnder-write me, doe.   145

Your man will take my bond?
Mer. That he will, fure.
But, thefe fame Citizens, they are fuch fharks!
There's an old debt of forty, I ga'[481] my word
For one is runne away, to[482] the *Bermudas*,
And he will hooke in that, or he wi' not doe.   150

He whifpers Fitz-dottrell *afide.*[483]
Fit. Why, let him. That and the ring, and a hundred pieces,
Will all but make two hundred?
Mer. No, no more, Sir.
What ready *Arithmetique* you haue? doe you heare?
And then Guilt-head.[484]
A pretty mornings worke for you, this? Do it,
You fhall ha' twenty pound on't.
Gvi. Twenty pieces?   155

(Plv. Good Father, do't)
Mer. You will hooke ftill? well,
Shew vs your ring. You could not ha' done this, now
With gentleneffe, at firft, wee might ha' thank'd you?
But groane, and ha' your[485] courtefies come from you
Like a hard ftoole, and ftinke? A man may draw   160

Your teeth out eafier, then your money? Come,
Were little *Guilt-head* heere, no better a nature,
I fhould ne'r loue him, that could pull his lips off, now!
He pulls Plutarchus *by the lips.*[486]
Was not thy mother a Gentlewoman?
Plv. Yes, Sir.
Mer. And went to the Court at *Chriftmas*, and S^t. *Georges-tide?*[487]   165

And lent the Lords-men,[488] chaines?
Plv. Of gold, and pearle, S^r.

---

481 gave G
482 to] into 1641
483 SN.] [*Aside to Fitz.* G he wi'] he'll G
484 SN.] [*Aside to Gilthead.* G
485 you] your 1641, f.
486 SN.] [*Pulls him by the lips.* G
487 George-G
488 Lords-] lords W lords' G

Mer. I knew, thou muſt take, after ſome body!
Thou could'ſt not be elfe. This was no ſhop-looke!
I'll ha' thee Captaine *Guilt-head*, and march vp,
And take in *Pimlico*, and kill the buſh,   170

At euery tauerne! Thou shalt haue a wife,
If ſmocks will mount, boy. How now? you ha' there now
Some *Briſto-ſtone,*[489] or *Corniſh* counterfeit
You'ld put vpon vs.*He turns to old*[490] Guilt-head.
Gvi. No, Sir I aſſure you:
Looke on his luſter! hee will ſpeake himſelfe!   175

I'le gi' you leaue to put him i' the Mill,
H'is[491] no great, large ſtone, but a true *Paragon*,
H'has[492] all his corners, view him well.
Mer. H'is[493] yellow.
Gvi. Vpo' my faith, S^r, o' the right black-water,
And very deepe! H'is ſet without a foyle, too.   180

Here's one o' the yellow-water, I'll ſell cheape.
Mer. And what do you valew this, at? thirty pound?
Gvi. No, Sir, he cost me forty, ere he was ſet.
Mer. Turnings, you meane? I know your *Equinocks*:[494]
You'are[495] growne the better Fathers of 'hem o' late.   185

Well, where't[496] muſt goe, 'twill be iudg'd, and, therefore,
Looke you't be right. You ſhall haue fifty pound for't.
Now to Fitz-dottrel.[497]
Not a deneer[498] more! And, becauſe you would
Haue things diſpatch'd, Sir, I'll goe preſently,
Inquire out this *Lady*. If you thinke good, Sir.   190

Hauing an hundred pieces ready, you may
Part with thoſe, now, to ſerue my kinſmans turnes,
That he may wait vpon you, anon, the freer;
And take 'hem when you ha' ſeal'd, a game, of *Guilt-head*.

---

[489] Bristol stone W, G
[490] SN. *He, old* om. G
[491] He is W, G
[492] He has W, G
[493] He's W, G
[494] equivokes W, G
[495] You're 1716, W You are G || 'hem] 'em G || o' ret. G
[496] where it G
[497] SN.] [*To Fitz.*] G
[498] dencer 1641 Denier 1716 denier W, G

Fit. I care not if I do!
Mer. And difpatch all,   195

Together.
Fit. There, th'are iuft:[499] a hundred pieces!
I' ha' told 'hem ouer, twice a day, thefe two moneths.
Hee turnes 'hem out together.[500] And Euerill *and hee fall to fhare.*
Mer. Well, go, and feale, then, S[r], make your returne
As fpeedy as you can.
Eve. Come gi' mee.[501]
Mer. Soft, Sir.
Eve. Mary, and faire too, then. I'll no delaying, Sir.   200

Mer. But, you will heare?
Eve. Yes, when I haue my diuident.[502]
Mer. Theres forty pieces for you.
Eve. What is this for?
Mer. Your halfe. You know, that *Guilt-head* muft ha' twenty.
Eve. And what's your ring there? fhall I ha' none o'[503] that?
Mer. O, thats[504] to be giuen to a *Lady*!   205

Eve. Is't[505] fo?
Mer. By that good light, it is.
Ev. Come, gi' meTen pieces more, then.
Mer. Why?
Ev. For *Guilt-head*? Sir,
Do'you thinke, I'll 'low[506] him any fuch fhare:
Mer. You muft.
Eve. Muft I? Doe you[507] your mufts, Sir, I'll doe mine,
You wi' not part with the whole, Sir? Will you? Goe too.   210

Gi' me ten pieces!
Mer. By what law, doe you this?
Eve. E'n[508] Lyon-law, Sir, I muft roare elfe.
Mer. Good!

---

[499] they're just a 1716, W they are just a G
[500] SN.] [*Turns them out on table.* G
[501] can. [*Exeunt Fitzdottrel, Gilthead, and Plutarchus.*] me. [*They fall to sharing.* G
[502] Dividend 1716 dividend W, G
[503] o' ret. G
[504] that is G
[505] Is it W, G
[506] allow 1692, f.
[507] you om. 1692, 1716, W
[508] E'n] Even G

Eve. Yo' haue[509] heard, how th' *Aſſe* made his diuiſions, wiſely?
Mer. And, I am he: I thanke you.
Ev. Much good do you, S[r].
Mer. I ſhall be rid o' this tyranny, one day?
Eve. Not,
While you doe eate; and lie, about the towne, here;   216

And coozen i' your bullions; and I ſtand
Your name of credit, and compound your[510] buſineſſe;
Adiourne your beatings euery terme; and make
New parties for your proiects. I haue, now,   220

A pretty taſque, of it, to hold you in
Wi' your *Lady Tayle-buſh*: but the toy will be,
How we ſhall both come off?
Mer. Leaue you[511] your doubting.
And doe your portion, what's aſſign'd you: I
Neuer fail'd yet.
Eve. With reference to your aydes?   225

You'll ſtill be vnthankfull. Where ſhall I meete you, anon?
You ha' ſome feate to doe[512] alone, now, I ſee;
You wiſh me gone, well, I will finde you out,
And bring you after to the audit.[513]
Mer. S'light!
There's *Ingines* ſhare too, I had forgot! This raigne   230

Is too-too-vnſuportable! I muſt
Quit my ſelfe of this vaſſalage![514] *Ingine!* welcome.

---

[509] You've 1716, W
[510] your om. 1641
[511] you om. 1641
[512] to doe] to be done 1641
[513] audit. [*Exit.* G
[514] vassalage!—*Enter* Engine, *followed by* Wittipoll. G

ACT. III.   SCENE. IV.
Mere-craft.   Ingine.   VVittipol.[515]

How goes the cry?
Ing. Excellent well!
Mer. Wil't[516] do?
VVhere's *Robinſon*?
Ing. Here is the Gentleman, Sir.
VVill vndertake t'[517]himſelfe. I haue acquainted him.
Mer. VVhy did you ſo?
Ing. VVhy, *Robinſon* would ha' told him,
You know. And hee's a pleaſant wit! will hurt   5

Nothing you purpoſe. Then, he'is[518] of opinion,
That *Robinſon* might want[519] audacity,
She being ſuch a gallant. Now, hee has beene,
In *Spaine*, and knowes the faſhions there; and can
Diſcourſe; and being but mirth (hee ſaies) leaue much,   10

To his care:
Mer. But he is too tall!
He excepts at his ſtature.[520]
Ing. For that,
He has the braueſt deuice! (you'll loue him for't)[521]
To ſay, he weares *Cioppinos*: and they doe ſo
In *Spaine*. And *Robinſon's* as tall, as hee.
Mer. Is he ſo?
Ing. Euery iot.
Mer. Nay, I had rather   15

To truſt a Gentleman with it, o' the two.
Ing. Pray you goe to[522] him, then, Sir, and ſalute him.
Mer. Sir, my friend *Ingine* has acquainted you
With a ſtrange *buſineſſe*, here.
Wit. A merry one, Sir.
The *Duke* of *Drown'd-land*, and his *Dutcheſſe*?

---

[515] SD. om. G
[516] 't] it G
[517] t'] 't 1716, W it G
[518] he's 1692, f.
[519] want] have 1641
[520] SN. om. G
[521] () ret. G
[522] you to go 1716, W

Mer. Yes, Sir.   20

Now, that the *Coniurers* ha' laid him by,
I ha' made bold, to borrow him a while;
Wit. With purpofe, yet, to put him out I hope
To his beft vfe?
Mer. Yes, Sir.
Wit. For that fmall part,
That I am trufted with, put off your care: 25

I would not lofe to doe it, for the mirth,
Will follow of it; and well, I haue a fancy.
Mer. Sir, that will make it well.
Wit. You will report it fo.
Where muft I haue my dreffing?
Ing. At my houfe, Sir.
Mer. You fhall haue caution, Sir, for what he yeelds,   30

To fix pence.
Wit. You fhall pardon me. I will fhare, Sir,
I' your fports, onely: nothing i' your purchafe.
But you muft furnifh mee with complements,
To th' manner of *Spaine*; my coach, my *guarda duenn'as*;
Mer. *Ingine's* your *Pro'uedor*.[523] But, Sir, I muft   35

(Now I'haue entred truft wi' you, thus farre)
Secure ftill i' your quality, acquaint you
With fomewhat, beyond this. The place, defign'd
To be the *Scene*, for this our mery matter,
Becaufe it muft haue countenance of women,   40

To draw difcourse, and offer it, is here by,
At the *Lady Taile-bufhes*.
Wit. I know her, Sir. And her Gentleman *huifher*.[524]
Mer. Mr *Ambler*?
Wit. Yes, Sir.
Mer. Sir, It fhall be no fhame to mee, to confeffe
To you, that wee poore Gentlemen, that want acres,   45

Muft for our needs, turne fooles vp, and plough *Ladies*
Sometimes,[525] to try what glebe they are: and this
Is no vnfruitefull piece. She, and I now,
Are on a proiect, for the fact, and venting

---

[523] *Provedore* 1716 provedore W provedoré G
[524] Usher 1716 usher W, G
[525] Sometime 1692, 1716, W

Of a new kinde of *fucus* (paint, for *Ladies*)   50

To ſerue the kingdome: wherein ſhee her ſelfe
Hath trauell'd, ſpecially, by way of ſeruice
Vnto her ſexe, and hopes to get the *Monopoly*,
As the reward of her inuention.
Wit. What is her end, in this?
Ev. Merely[526] ambition,   55

Sir, to grow great, and court it with the ſecret:
Though ſhee pretend ſome other. For, ſhe's dealing,
Already, vpon caution for the ſhares,
And M^r. *Ambler*, is hee[527] nam'd *Examiner*
For the ingredients; and the *Register*   60

Of what is vented; and ſhall keepe the *Office*.
Now, if ſhee breake with you, of this (as I
Muſt make the leading thred to your acquaintance,
That, how experience gotten i' your being
Abroad, will helpe our buſineſſe)[528] thinke of ſome   65

Pretty additions, but to keep her floting:
It may be, ſhee will offer you a part,
Any ſtrange names of—
Wit. S^r, I haue my inſtructions.
Is it not high time to be making ready?
Mer. Yes, Sir.
Ing. The foole's in ſight, *Dottrel*.
Mer. Away, then.[529]   70

---

⁵²⁶ Ev.] *Meer.* 1716, f.
⁵²⁷ is hee] he is W, G
⁵²⁸ () ret. G
⁵²⁹ [*Exeunt Engine and Wittipol.* G

ACT. III.   SCENE. V.
Mere-craft.   Fitz-dottrel.   Pvg.[530]

Return'd fo foone?
Fit. Yes, here's the ring: I ha' feal'd.
But there's not fo much gold in all the row, he faies—
Till't[531] come fro' the Mint. 'Tis tane vp for the gamefters.
Mer. There's a fhop-fhift! plague on 'hem.
Fit. He do's fweare it.
Mer. He'll fweare, and forfweare too, it is his trade,   5

You fhould not haue left him.
Fit. S'lid, I can goe backe,
And beat him, yet.
Mer. No, now let him alone.
Fit. I was fo earneft,[532] after the maine *Bufineffe*,
To haue this ring, gone.
Mer. True, and 'tis[533] time.
I'haue learned, Sir, fin'[534] you went, her *Ladi-fhip* eats   10

With the *Lady Tail-bufh*, here, hard by.
Fit. I' the lane here?
Mer. Yes, if you'had a feruant, now of prefence,
Well cloth'd, and of an aëry voluble tongue,
Neither too bigge, or[535] little for his mouth,
That could deliuer your wiues complement;   15

To fend along withall.
Fit. I haue one Sir,
A very handfome, gentleman-like-fellow,
That I doe meane to make my *Dutcheffe Vfher*—
I entertain'd him, but this morning, too:
I'll call him to you. The worft of him, is his name!   20

Mer. She'll take no note of that, but of his meffage.
Hee fhewes him his Pug.[536]

---

[530] Act. ...] *Re-enter* Fitzdottrel. G
[531] Till it G ‖ from G§
[532] comma after 'earnest' om. 1716, f.
[533] it is W, G
[534] since G
[535] or] nor W, G
[536] SN. om. G (Same on lines 27 and 35.)

Fit. *Diuell!*[537] How like you him, Sir. Pace, go a little.
Let's fee you moue.
Mer. He'll ferue, S[r], giue it him:
And let him goe along with mee, I'll helpe
To prefent him, and it.
Fit. Looke, you doe firah,   25

Difcharge this well, as you expect your place.
Do'you[538] heare, goe on, come off with all your honours.
Giues him inftructions.
I would faine fee him, do it.
Mer. Truft him, with it;
Fit. Remember kiffing of your hand, and anfwering
With the *French*-time, in[539] flexure of your body.   30

I could now[540] fo inftruct him—and for his words—
Mer. I'll put them in his mouth.
Fit. O, but I haue 'hem
O' the very *Academies*.
Mer. Sir, you'll haue vfe for 'hem,
Anon, your felfe, I warrant you: after dinner,
When you are call'd.
Fit. S'light, that'll be iuft *play*-time.   35

He longs to fee the play.
It cannot be, I muft not lofe the *play*!
Mer. Sir, but you muft, if fhe appoint to fit.
And, fhee's[541] prefident.
Fit. S'lid, it is the *Diuell*.[542]
Becaufe it is the Diuell.
Mer. And,[543] 'twere his Damme too, you muft now apply
Your felfe, Sir, to this, wholly; or lofe all.   40

Fit. If I could but fee a piece—
Mer. S[r]. Neuer think on't.
Fit. Come but to one act, and I did not care—
But to be feene to rife, and goe away,
To vex the Players, and to punifh their *Poet*—
Keepe him in awe!

---

[537] Devil!—*Enter* Pug. G
[538] Do'you] D'you 1692, 1716, W
[539] in] and W, G
[540] now] not 1641
[541] she is W, G
[542] SN. om. G (Same on line 51)
[543] And,] An G

Mer. But ſay, that he be one,   45

Wi' not be aw'd! but laugh at you. How then?
Fit. Then[544] he ſhall pay for his' dinner himſelfe.
Mer. Perhaps,
He would doe that twice, rather then thanke you.
Come, get the *Diuell* out of your head, my *Lord*,
(I'll call you ſo in priuate ſtill)[545] and take   50

Your *Lord-ſhip* i' your minde. You were, ſweete *Lord*,
He puts him in mind of his quarrell.
In talke to bring a *Buſineſſe* to the *Office*.
Fit. Yes.
Mer. Why ſhould not you, Sʳ, carry it o'[546] your ſelfe,
Before the *Office* be vp? and ſhew the world,
You had no need of any mans direction;   55

In point, Sir, of ſufficiency. I ſpeake
Againſt a kinſman, but as one that tenders
Your graces good.
Fit. I thanke you; to proceed—
Mer. To *Publications*:[547] ha' your *Deed* drawne preſently.
And leaue[548] a blancke to put in your *Feoffees*   60

One, two, or more, as you ſee cauſe—
Fit. I thank you
Heartily, I doe thanke you. Not a word more,
I pray you, as you loue mee. Let mee alone.
That I could not thinke o' this, as well, as hee?
O, I could beat my infinite blocke-head—![549]   65

He is angry with himſelfe.
Mer. Come, we muſt this way.
Pvg. How far is't.
Mer. Hard by here Ouer the way.[550] Now, to atchieue this ring,
From this ſame fellow, that is to aſſure it;
He thinkes how to coozen the bearer, of the ring.[551]

---

[544] Then] That 1692, 1716 || for's 1692, f.
[545] () ret. G
[546] o'] on G
[547] publication G
[548] leave me a 1692, 1716, W
[549] SN.] [*Exeunt.* Scene II. *The Lane near the Lady* Tailbush's *House. Enter* Meercraft *followed by* Pug. G
[550] way. [*They cross over.*] G
[551] SN. om. G || is] is, W, G

Before hee giue it. Though my *Spanish Lady*,
Be a young Gentleman of meanes, and scorne 70

To share, as hee doth say, I doe not know
How such a toy may tempt his *Lady-ship*:
And therefore, I thinke best, it be assur'd.[552]
Pvg. Sir, be the *Ladies* braue, wee goe vnto?
Mer. O, yes.
Pvg. And shall I see 'hem, and speake to 'hem? 75

Mer. What else?[553] ha' you your false-beard about you? *Traines.*
Questions his man.
Tra. Yes.
Mer. And is this one of your double Cloakes?
Tra. The best of 'hem.
Mer. Be ready then.[554] Sweet *Pitfall*!

---

[552] [*Aside.* G

[553] else? *Enter* Trains. || SN. om. G

[554] then. [*Exeunt.* Scene III. *A Hall in Lady* Tailbush's *House. Enter* Meercraft *and* Pug, *met by* Pitfall. G

ACT. III.   SCENE. VI.

Mere-craft.   Pitfall.   Pvg.

Traines.[555]

Come, I muſt buſſe—
Offers to kiſſe.[556]
Pit. Away. Mer. I'll ſet thee vp again.
Neuer feare that: canſt thou get ne'r a bird?
No *Thruſhes* hungry? Stay, till cold weather come,
I'll help thee to an *Ouſell*, or, a *Field-fare.*
Who's within, with Madame?
Pit. I'll tell you ſtraight.[557]   5

She runs in, in haſte: he followes.
Mer. Pleaſe you ſtay here, a while Sir, I'le goe in.
Pvg. I doe ſo long to haue a little venery,
While I am in this body! I would taſt
Of euery ſinne, a little, if it might be
After the māner of man! *Sweet-heart!*[558]
Pit. What would you, Sʳ?   10

Pug *leaps at* Pitfall's *comming in.*
Pvg. Nothing but fall in, to you, be your Black-bird,
My pretty pit (as the Gentleman ſaid) your *Throſtle*:
Lye tame, and taken with you; here'is gold!
To buy you ſo much new ſtuffes, from the ſhop,
As I may take the old vp—
Tra. You muſt ſend, Sir.   15

The Gentleman the ring.
Traine's *in his falſe cloak, brings a falſe meſſage, and gets the ring.*
Pvg. There 'tis.[559] Nay looke,Will you be fooliſh, *Pit.*
Pit. This is ſtrange rudeneſſe.
Pvg. Deare *Pit.*
Pit. I'll call, I ſweare.
Mere-craft *followes preſently, and askes for it.*
Mer. Where are you, Sʳ?[560]

---

555 SD. om.
556 SN.] [*Offers to kiss her.* G
557 SN. [*Exit hastily.* (after 5) [*Exit.* (after 6) G
558 SN.] Sweetheart! *Re-enter* Pitfall. || sir? [*Pug runs to her.* G
559 SN.] *Enter* Trains *in his false beard and cloke.* (after 'vp—'15) [*Exit Trains.*] (after
'tis' 16) G
560 SN. *Enter* Meercraft. G

Is your ring ready? Goe with me.
Pvg. I fent it you.
Mer. Me? When? by whom?
Pvg. A fellow here, e'en now,   20

Came for it[561] i' your name.
Mer. I fent none, fure.
My meaning euer was, you fhould deliuer it,
Your felfe: So was your Mafters charge, you know.
Ent. Train's *as himfelfe againe.*[562]
What fellow was it, doe you know him?
Pvg. Here,
But now, he had it.
Mer. Saw you any? *Traines*?   25

Tra. Not I.
Pvg. The Gentleman[563] faw him.
Mer. Enquire.
Pvg. I was fo earneft vpon her, I mark'd not!
The Diuell *confeffeth himfelfe coozen'd.*[564]
My diuellifh *Chiefe* has put mee here in flesh,
To fhame mee! This dull body I am in,
I perceiue nothing with! I offer at nothing,   30

That will fucceed![565]
Tra. Sir, fhe faw none, fhe faies.
Pvg. *Satan* himfelfe, has tane a fhape t'abufe me.
It could not be elfe.[566]
Mer. This is aboue ftrange!
Mere-craft *accufeth him of negligence.*
That you fhould be fo retchleffe. What'll[567] you do, Sir?
How will you anfwer this, when you are queftion'd?   35

Pvg. Run from my flefh, if I could: put off mankind!
This's[568] fuch a fcorne! and will be a new exercife,
For my *Arch-Duke*! Woe to the feuerall cudgells,
Muft suffer, on this backe![569] Can you no fuccours? Sir?   39

---

[561] for't W
[562] SN.] *Re-enter* Trains *dressed as at first.* G
[563] Gentlewoman 1716 gentlewoman W, G
[564] SN. om. G (Same on lines 33 and 39.)
[565] succeed! [*Aside.* G
[566] else! [*Aside.* G
[567] 'll] will G
[568] 's] is G
[569] back! [*Aside.*] G

He asketh ayde.
Mer. Alas! the vſe of it is ſo preſent.
Pvg. I aske,
Sir, credit for another, but till to morrow?
Mer. There is not ſo much time, Sir. But how euer,
The lady is a noble Lady, and will
(To ſaue a Gentleman from check) be intreated[570]
Mere-craft *promiſeth faintly, yet comforts him.*[571]
To ſay, ſhe ha's[572] receiu'd it.
Pvg. Do you thinke ſo?   45

Will ſhee be won?
Mer. No doubt, to ſuch an office,
It will be a Lady's brauery, and her pride.
Pvg. And not be knowne on't after, vnto him?
Mer. That were a treachery! Vpon my word,
Be confident. Returne vnto your maſter,   50

My *Lady Preſident* ſits this after-noone,
Ha's tane the ring, commends her ſeruices
Vnto your *Lady-Dutcheſſe.* You may ſay
She's a ciuill *Lady,* and do's giue her
All her reſpects, already: Bad you, tell her   55

She liues, but to receiue her wiſh'd commandements,
And haue the honor here to kiſſe her hands:
For which ſhee'll ſtay this houre yet. Haſten you
Your *Prince,* away.
Pvg. And Sir, you will take care
Th' excuſe be perfect?
Mer. You confeſſe your feares.[573]   60

The Diuel *is doubtfull.* Too much.
Pvg. The ſhame is more, I'll[574] quit you of either.[575]

---

[570] entreated W, G
[571] SN. om. G (Same on line 60)
[572] has 1692, f. passim
[573] period om. 1716, f.
[574] I'll ...] *Meer.* I'll ... W, G
[575] *[Exeunt* G

Act. IIII.   Scene. I.
Taile-bvsh.   Mere-craft.   Manly.[576]

A Pox vpo' referring to *Commiſsioners*,
I'had rather heare that it were paſt the ſeales:
Your *Courtiers* moue ſo Snaile-like i' your *Buſineſſe*.
Wuld I had begun wi' you.
Mer. We muſt moue,*Madame*, in order, by degrees: not iump.   5

Tay. Why, there was S^r. *Iohn Monie-man* could iump
A *Buſineſſe* quickely.
Mer. True, hee had great friends,
But, becauſe ſome, ſweete *Madame*, can leape ditches,
Wee muſt not all ſhunne to goe ouer bridges.
The harder parts, I make account are done:[577]   10

He flatters her.
Now, 'tis referr'd. You are infinitly bound
Vnto'the *Ladies*, they ha' so cri'd it vp!
Tay. Doe they like it then?
Mer. They ha' ſent the *Spaniſh-Lady*,
To gratulate with you—
Tay. I must ſend 'hem thankes
And ſome remembrances.
Mer. That you muſt, and viſit 'hem.   15

Where's *Ambler*?
Tay. Loſt, to day, we cannot heare of him.
Mer. Not *Madam*?
Tay. No in good faith. They ſay he lay not
At home, to night. And here has fall'n a *Buſineſſe*
Betweene your Couſin, and Maſter *Manly*, has
Vnquieted vs all.
Mer. So I heare, *Madame*.   20

Pray you how was it?
Tay. Troth, it but appears
Ill o' your Kinſmans part. You may haue heard,
That *Manly* is a ſutor to me, I doubt not:
Mer. I gueſs'd it, *Madame*.

---

[576] SD. IIIJ] VI. 1641 Taile. ...] *A room in Lady* Tailbush's *House. Enter Lady* Tailbush
and Meercraft. G
[577] SN. om. G

Tay. And it ſeemes, he truſted
Your Couſin to let fall some faire reports   25

Of him vnto mee.
Mer. Which he did!
Tay. So farre
From it, as hee came in, and tooke him rayling
Againſt him.
Mer. How! And what said *Manly* to him?
Tay. Inough, I doe aſſure you: and with that ſcorne
Of him, and the iniury, as I doe wonder   30

How *Euerill* bore it! But that guilt vndoe's
Many mens valors.[578]
Mer. Here comes *Manly*.
Man. *Madame*,
I'll take my leaue—
Manly *offers to be gone.*[579]
Tay. You ſha' not goe, i' faith.
I'll ha' you ſtay, and ſee this *Spaniſh* miracle,
Of our *Engliſh Ladie.*
Man. Let me pray your *Ladiſhip*,   35

Lay your commands on me, some other time.
Tay. Now, I proteſt: and I will haue all piec'd
And friends againe.
Man. It will be but ill ſolder'd!
Tay. You are too much affected with it.
Man. I cannot
Madame, but thinke on't for th' iniuſtice.
Tay. Sir,   40

His kinſman here is ſorry.
Mer. Not I, *Madam*,
I am no kin to him, wee but call Couſins,
Mere-craft *denies him.*[580]
And if wee[581] were, Sir, I haue no relation
Vnto his crimes.
Man. You are not vrged with 'hem.
I can accuſe, Sir, none but mine owne iudgement,   45

For though it were his crime, ſo to betray mee:

---

[578] valours. *Enter* Manly. G
[579] SN. om. G
[580] SN. om. G
[581] wee] he G

I am[582] fure, 'twas more mine owne, at all to truft him.
But he, therein, did vfe but his old manners,
And fauour ftrongly what hee was before.
Tay. Come, he will change!
Man. Faith, I muft neuer think it.   50

Nor were it reafon in mee to expect
That for my fake, hee fhould put off a nature
Hee fuck'd in with his milke. It may be *Madam*,
Deceiuing truft, is all he has to truft to:
If fo, I fhall be loath, that any hope   55

Of mine, fhould bate him of his meanes.
Tay. Yo'[583] are fharp, Sir.
This act may make him honeft!
Man. If he were
To be made honeft, by an act of *Parliament*,
I fhould not alter, i' my faith of him.[584]
Tay. *Eyther-fide!*
Welcome, deare *Either-fide*! how haft thou done, good wench?
She spies the Lady Eyther-fide.[585]
Thou haft beene a ftranger! I ha' not feene thee, this weeke.   61

---

[582] I'm 1716, W
[583] Y'are 1716, W
[584] him. *Enter Lady* Eitherside.
[585] SN. om. G

ACT. IIII.   SCENE. II.[586]

Eitherside. {*To them*
Ever your feruant, *Madame*.
Tay. Where hast 'hou [587]beene?
I did fo long to fee thee.
Eit. Vifiting, and fo tyr'd!
I proteft, *Madame*, 'tis a monftrous trouble!
Tay. And fo it is. I fweare I muft to morrow,
Beginne my vifits (would they were ouer) at *Court*.   5

It tortures me, to thinke on 'hem.
Eit. I doe heare
You ha' caufe, Madam, your fute goes on.
Tay. Who told thee?
Eyt. One, that can tell: M&#r. *Eyther-fide*.
Tay. O, thy hufband!
Yes, faith, there's life in't, now: It is referr'd.
If wee once fee it vnder the feales, wench, then,   10

Haue with 'hem for the great *Carroch*, fixe horfes,
And the two *Coach-men*, with my *Ambler*, bare,
And my three women: wee will liue, i' faith,
The examples o' the towne, and gouerne it.
I'le lead the fafhion ftill.
Eit. You doe that, now,   15

Sweet *Madame*.
Tay. O, but then, I'll euery day
Bring vp fome new deuice. Thou and I, *Either-fide*,
Will firft be in it. I will giue it thee;
And they fhall follow vs. Thou fhalt, I fweare,
Weare euery moneth a new gowne, out of it.   20

Eith. Thanke you good *Madame*.
Tay. Pray thee call mee *Taile-bufh*
As I thee, *Either-fide*: I not loue[588] this, *Madame*.
Ety. Then I proteft to you, *Taile-bufh*, I am glad
Your *Bufineffe* fo fucceeds.
Tay. Thanke thee, good *Eyther-fide*.

---

586 SD. om. G
587 thou 1692, f.
588 not loue] love not 1716, f.

Ety. But Maſter *Either-ſide* tells me, that he likes   25

Your other *Buſineſſe* better.
Tay. Which?
Eit. O'[589] the Tooth-picks.
Tay. I neuer heard on't.[590]
Eit. Aske M[r]. *Mere-craft*.
Mer. *Madame?*[591] H'is one, in a word, I'll truſt his malice,
With any mans credit, I would haue abus'd!
Mere-craft *hath whiſper'd with the while.*[592]
Man. Sir, if you thinke you doe pleaſe mee, in this,   30

You are deceiu'd!
Mer. No, but becauſe my *Lady*,
Nam'd him my kinſman; I would ſatisfie you,
What I thinke of him: and pray you, vpon it
To iudge mee!
Man. So I doe: that ill mens friendſhip,
Is as vnfaithfull, as themſelues.
Tay. Doe you heare?   35

Ha' you a *Buſineſſe* about Tooth-picks?
Mer. Yes, *Madame*.
Did I ne'r tell't[593] you? I meant to haue offer'd it
Your *Lady-ſhip*, on the perfecting the pattent.
Tay. How is't![594]
Mer. For ſeruing the whole ſtate with Tooth-picks;
The Proiect *for* Tooth-picks.
(Somewhat an[595] intricate *Buſineſſe* to diſcourſe) but—   40

I ſhew, how much the Subiect is abus'd,
Firſt, in that one commodity? then what diſeaſes,[596]
And putrefactions in the gummes are bred,
By thoſe are made of adultrate,[597] and falſe wood?
My plot, for reformation of theſe, followes.   45

To haue all Tooth-picks, brought vnto an *office*,

---

[589] O'] O, 1641
[590] on't] of it G
[591] Madam! [*Aside to Manly.*] G || He is G
[592] SN. *with him the* 1692, 1716, W SN. om. G
[593] tell it G
[594] is it G || SN. om. G
[595] an] in 1641
[596] disease W
[597] adulterate G

There ſeal'd; and ſuch as counterfait 'hem, mulcted.
And laſt, for venting 'hem to haue a booke
Printed, to teach their vſe, which euery childe
Shall haue throughout the kingdome, that can read,   50

And learne to picke his teeth by. Which beginning
Earely to practice, with ſome other rules,
Of neuer ſleeping with the mouth open, chawing[598]
Some graines of *maſticke*, will preſerue the breath
Pure, and ſo free from taynt[599]—ha' what is't? ſaiſt thou?
Traines *his man whiſpers him*.
Tay. Good faith, it ſounds a very pretty *Buſ'neſſe*!   56

Eit. So Mr. *Either-ſide* ſaies, *Madame*.
Mer. The *Lady* is come.
Tay. Is ſhe? Good, waite vpon her in.[600] My *Ambler*
Was neuer ſo ill abſent. *Either-ſide*,
How doe I looke to day? Am I not dreſt,   60

Spruntly?
She[601] lookes in her glaſſe.
Eit. Yes, verily, *Madame*.
Tay. Pox o' *Madame*, Will you not leaue that?
Eit. Yes, good *Taile-buſh*.
Tay. So? Sounds not that better? What vile *Fucus* is this,
Thou haſt got on?
Eit. 'Tis *Pearle*.
Tay. *Pearle? Oyſter-ſhells*:
As I breath, *Either-side*, I know't. Here comes   65

(They say) a wonder, ſirrah, has beene in *Spaine*!
Will teach vs all; ſhee's ſent to mee, from *Court*.
To gratulate with mee! Pr'y thee,[602] let's obſerue her,
What faults ſhe has, that wee may laugh at 'hem,
When ſhe is gone.
Eit. That we will heartily, *Tail-buſh*.[603]   70

Wittipol *enters*.
Tay. O, mee! the very *Infanta* of the *Giants*!

---

[598] chewing 1716, f.
[599] SN.] taint—*Enter* Trains, *and whispers him*. G
[600] in. [*Exit Meercraft*.] G
[601] SN.] *She* om. G ǁ o' ret. G
[602] Prythee 1692 Prithee 1716 prithee W, G
[603] SN.] *Re-enter* Meercraft, *introducing* Wittipol *dressed as a Spanish Lady*. G

ACT. IIII.   SCENE. III.

Mere-craft.   Wittipol. } to them.[604]

Wittipol is[605] *dreſt like a* Spaniſh Lady.
Mer. Here is a noble *Lady*, *Madame*, come,
From your great friends, at *Court*, to ſee your *Ladi-ſhip*:
And haue the honour of your acquaintance.
Tay. Sir.
She do's vs honour.
Wit. Pray you, ſay to her *Ladiſhip*,
It is the manner of *Spaine*, to imbrace[606] onely,   5

Neuer to kiſſe. She will excuſe the cuſtome!
Excuſes him ſelfe for not kiſſing.[607]
Tay. Your vſe of it is law. Pleaſe you, ſweete, *Madame*,
To take a ſeate.
Wit. Yes, *Madame*. I'haue had
The fauour, through a world of faire report
To know your vertues, *Madame*; and in that   10

Name, haue deſir'd the happineſſe of preſenting
My ſeruice to your *Ladiſhip*!
Tay. Your loue, *Madame*,
I muſt not owne it elſe.
Wit. Both are due, *Madame*,
To your great vndertakings.
Tay. Great? In troth, *Madame*,
They are my friends, that thinke 'hem any thing: 15

If I can doe my ſexe (by 'hem[608]) any ſeruice,
I'haue my ends, *Madame*.
Wit. And they are noble ones,
That make a multitude beholden, *Madame*:
The common-wealth of *Ladies*, muſt acknowledge from you.
Eit. Except ſome enuious, *Madame*.
Wit. Yo'[609] are right in that, *Madame*,   20

Of which race, I encountred ſome but lately.

---

[604] SD. om. G
[605] SN. is om. 1692, 1716, W ‖ For G see 70 above.
[606] embrace 1716, f.
[607] SN. om. G
[608] 'em G
[609] Yo'] Y' 1716, W

89

Who ('t[610] ſeemes) haue ſtudyed reaſons to diſcredit
Your *buſineſſe*.
Tay. How, ſweet *Madame*.
Wit. Nay, the parties
Wi' not be worth your pauſe—Moſt ruinous things, *Madame*,
That haue put off all hope of being recouer'd   25

To a degree of handſomeneſſe.
Tay. But their reaſons, *Madame*?
I would faine heare.
Wit. Some *Madame*, I remember.
They ſay, that painting quite deſtroyes the face—
Eit. O, that's an old one, *Madame*.
Wit. There are new ones, too.
Corrupts the breath; hath left ſo little ſweetneſſe   30

In kiſſing, as 'tis now vſ'd, but for faſhion:
And ſhortly will be taken for a puniſhment.
Decayes the fore-teeth, that ſhould guard the tongue;
And ſuffers that runne riot euer-laſting!
And (which is worſe) ſome *Ladies* when they meete   35

Cannot be merry, and laugh, but they doe ſpit
In one anothers faces!
Man. I ſhould know
This voyce, and face too:
Manly *begins to know him*.
VVit. Then they ſay, 'tis dangerous[611]
To all the falne, yet well diſpos'd *Mad-dames*,[612]
That are induſtrious, and deſire to earne   40

Their liuing with their ſweate! For any diſtemper
Of heat, and motion, may diſplace the colours;
And if the paint once runne about their faces,
Twenty to one, they will appeare ſo ill-fauour'd,
Their ſeruants run away, too,[613] and leaue the pleaſure   45

Imperfect, and the reckoning all vnpay'd.
Eit. Pox, theſe are *Poets* reaſons.
Tay. Some old *Lady*
That keepes a *Poet*, has deuis'd theſe ſcandales.
Eit. Faith we muſt haue the *Poets* baniſh'd, *Madame*,

---

[610] 't] it G
[611] SN.] [*Aside.* G
[612] *Mad-dams* 1692, 1716 mad-dams W mad-ams G
[613] also G

As Maſter *Either-ſide* ſaies.
Mer. Maſter *Fitz-dottrel*?   50

And his wife:[614] where? *Madame*, the *Duke* of *Drown'd-land*,
That will be ſhortly.
VVit. Is this my *Lord*?
Mer. The ſame.

---

[614] wife! *Wit.* Where? *Enter Mr. and Mrs.*Fitzdottrel, *followed by* Pug. *Meer.* [*To Wit.*] Madam, G

Act. IIII.   Scene. IV.
Fitz-dottrel.   Miſtreſſe Fitz-dottrell.   Pvg. } *to them.*[615]

Your ſeruant, *Madame*!
VVit. How now? Friend? offended,
That I haue found your haunt here?
Wittipol *whiſpers with* Manly.[616]
Man. No, but wondering[617]
At your ſtrange faſhion'd venture, hither.
VVit. It isTo ſhew you what they are, you ſo purſue.
Man. I thinke 'twill proue a med'cine againſt marriage;
To know their manners.
VVit. Stay, and profit then.   6

Mer. The *Lady*, *Madame*, whose *Prince* has brought her, here,
To be inſtructed.
Hee[618] *preſents Miſtreſſe* Fitz-dottrel.
VVit. Pleaſe you ſit with vs, *Lady*.
Mer. That's *Lady-Preſident*.
Fit. A goodly woman!
I cannot ſee the ring, though.
Mer. Sir, ſhe has it.   10

Tay. But, *Madame*, theſe are very feeble reaſons!
Wit. So I vrg'd *Madame*, that the new complexion,
Now to come forth, in name o'[619] your *Ladiſhip's fucus*,
Had[620] no *ingredient*—
Tay. But I durſt eate, I aſſure you.
Wit. So do they, in *Spaine*.
Tay. Sweet *Madam* be ſo liberall,   15

To giue vs ſome o' your *Spaniſh Fucuſes*!
VVit. They are infinit, *Madame*.
Tay. So I heare,[621] they hau
VVater of *Gourdes*, of *Radiſh*, the white *Beanes*,
Flowers of *Glaſſe*, of *Thiſtles*, *Roſe-marine*.
Raw *Honey*, *Muſtard-ſeed*, and Bread dough-bak'd,   20

---

[615] om. G
[616] *Wit. [Takes Manly aside.]*
[617] SN. om. G wondering G
[618] SN. *Hee* om. G
[619] o'] of W
[620] had] has W, G
[621] hear. *Wit.* They G

The crums o' bread, *Goats-milke*, and whites of *Egges*,
Campheere,[622] and *Lilly-roots*, the fat of *Swannes*,
Marrow of *Veale*, white *Pidgeons*, and pine-*kernells*,
The ſeedes of *Nettles*, *perse'line*, and *hares gall*.
Limons, thin-skind—
Eit. How, her *Ladiſhip* has ſtudied   25

Al excellent things!
VVit. But ordinary, *Madame*.
No, the true rarities, are th' *Aluagada*,
And *Argentata* of Queene *Isabella*!
Tay. I, what are their *ingredients*, gentle *Madame*?
Wit. Your *Allum Scagliola*, or *Pol-dipedra*;   30

And *Zuccarino*; *Turpentine* of *Abezzo*,
Wash'd in nine waters: *Soda di leuante*,[623]
Or your *Ferne* aſhes; *Beniamin di gotta*;
Graſſo[624] *di ſerpe*; *Porcelletto marino*;
Oyles of *Lentiſco*; *Zucche*[625] *Mugia*; make   35

The admirable *Verniſh*[626] for the face,
Giues the right luſter; but two drops rub'd on
VVith a piece of ſcarlet, makes a *Lady* of ſixty
Looke at[627] ſixteen. But, aboue all, the water
Of the white *Hen*, of the *Lady Eſtifanias*!   40

Tay. O, I, that ſame, good *Madame*, I haue heard of:
How is it done?
VVit. *Madame*, you take your *Hen*,
Plume it, and skin it, cleanſe it o'[628] the inwards:
Then chop it, bones and all: adde to foure ounces
Of *Carrauicins*, *Pipitas*, *Sope* of *Cyprus*,   45

Make the decoction, ſtreine it. Then diſtill it,
And keep it in your galley-pot well glidder'd:
Three drops preſerues from wrinkles, warts, ſpots, moles,
Blemiſh, or Sun-burnings, and keepes the skin
In decimo ſexto, euer bright, and ſmooth,   50

---

[622] Camphire 1716, f.
[623] *leuante ... di* om. 1641
[624] *Grosia* 1641
[625] *Zucchi* 1641
[626] varnish G
[627] at] as 1716, f.
[628] o' ret. G

As any looking-glaſſe; and indeed, is call'd
The Virgins milke for the face, *Oglio reale*;
A Ceruſe, neyther cold or[629] heat, will hurt;
And mixt with oyle of *myrrhe*, and the red *Gilli-flower*
Call'd *Cataputia*; and flowers of *Rouiſtico*;   55

Makes the beſt *muta*, or dye of the whole world.
Tay. Deare *Madame*, will you let vs be familiar?
Wit. Your *Ladiſhips* ſeruant.
Mer. How do you like her.
Fit. Admirable!
But, yet, I cannot ſee the ring.
Hee is iealous about his ring, *and* Mere-craft *deliuers it.*[630]
Pvg. Sir.
Mer. I muſt Deliuer it, or marre all. This foole's ſo iealous.[631]   60

Madame[632]—Sir, weare this ring, and pray you take knowledge,
'Twas ſent you by his wife. And giue her thanks,
Doe not you dwindle, Sir, beare vp.[633]
Pvg. I thanke you, Sir.
Tay. But for the manner of *Spaine*! Sweet, *Madame*, let vs
Be bold, now we are in: Are all the *Ladies*,   65

There, i' the faſhion?
VVit. None but *Grandee's, Madame*,
O' the claſp'd traine, which may be worne at length, too,
Or thus, vpon my arme.
Tay. And doe they weare *Cioppino's* all?
VVit. If they be dreſt in *punto, Madame*.
Eit. Guilt as thoſe are? *madame?*
Wit. Of Goldſmiths work, *madame;*[634]   70

And ſet with diamants:[635] and their *Spaniſh* pumps
Of perfum'd leather.
Tai. I ſhould thinke it hard
To go in 'hem, *madame*.
Wit. At the firſt, it is, *madame*.
Tai. Do you neuer fall in 'hem?

---

629 or] nor W, G
630 SN. om. G
631 [*Aside.* G
632 Madam—[*whispers Wit.*] G
633 up. [*Aside to Pug.* G
634 Eit.] *Lady T.* G
635 Diamonds 1692, 1716 diamonds W, G

Wit. Neuer.
Ei. I fweare, I fhould
Six times an houre.
Wit.[636] But you haue men at hand, fstill,
To helpe you, if you fall?
Eit.[637] Onely one, madame,   76

The *Guardo-duennas*,[638] fuch a little old man,
As this.
Eit. Alas! hee can doe nothing! this![639]
Wit. I'll tell you, madame, I faw i' the[640] *Court* of *Spaine* once,
A *Lady* fall i' the Kings fight, along,   80

And there fhee lay, flat fpred, as an *Vmbrella*,
Her hoope here crack'd; no man durft reach a hand
To helpe her, till the *Guarda-duenn'as* came,
VVho is the perfon onel'[641] allow'd to touch
A *Lady* there: and he but by this finger.   85

Eit. Ha' they no feruants, *madame*, there? nor friends?
Wit. An *Efcudero*, or fo *madame*, that wayts
Vpon 'hem in another Coach, at diftance,
And when they walke, or daunce, holds by a hand-kercher,[642]
Neuer prefumes to touch 'hem.
Eit. This's[643] fciruy!   90

And a forc'd grauity! I doe not like it.
I like our owne much better.
Tay. 'Tis more *French*,
And *Courtly* ours.
Eit. And tafts more liberty.
VVe may haue our doozen[644] of vifiters, at once,
Make loue t'vs.
Tay. And before our husbands?
Eit. Hufband?   95

As I am honeft, *Tayle-bufh* I doe thinke

---

[636] Wit. ...] speech given to Tai. 1716, f.
[637] Eit. ...] speech given to Wit. 1716, f.
[638] guarda W, G
[639] this. [*Points to Trains.* G
[640] in the 1716, f.
[641] onl' 1692, 1716 only W, G
[642] dance 1692, f. || Handkerchief 1716 handkerchief W, G
[643] This is W, G
[644] dozen 1692, f.

If no body ſhould loue mee, but my poore husband,
I ſhould e'n hang my ſelfe.
Tay. Fortune forbid, wench:
So faire a necke ſhould haue ſo foule a neck-lace.
Eit. 'Tis true, as I am handſome!
Wit. I receiu'd, *Lady,*   100

A token from you, which I would not bee
Rude to refuſe, being your firſt remembrance.
(Fit. O, I am ſatisfied now![645]
Mer. Do you ſee it, Sir.)
Wit. But ſince you come, to know me, neerer, *Lady,*
I'll begge the honour, you will weare for mee,   105

It muſt be ſo.
Wittipol *giues it Miſtreſſe* Fitz-dottrel.
M[rs]. Fit. Sure I haue heard this tongue.[646]
Mer. What do you meane, S[r]?
Mere-craft *murmures,*[647]
Wit. Would you ha' me mercenary?
We'll recompence it anon, in ſomewhat elſe.
He is ſatisfied, now he ſees it.[648]
Fit. I doe not loue to be gull'd, though in a toy.
VVife, doe you heare? yo' are come into the Schole,[649] wife,
VVhere you may learne, I doe perceiue it, any thing!   111

How to be fine, or faire, or great, or proud,
Or what you will, indeed, wife; heere 'tis taught.
And I am glad on't, that you may not ſay,
Another day, when honours come vpon you,   115

You wanted meanes. I ha' done my parts: beene,
Today at fifty pound charge, firſt, for a ring,
He vpbraids her, with his Bill of coſts.[650]
To get you entred.[651] Then left my new *Play,*
To wait vpon you, here, to ſee't confirm'd.
That I may ſay, both to mine owne[652] eyes, and eares,   120

---

[645] now! [*Aside to Meer.* G
[646] SN.] [*Gives the ring to Mrs. Fitzdottrel.* G Surely 1641 tongue. [*Aside.* G
[647] SN.] [*Aside to Wit.* G
[648] SN. om. [*Exeunt Meer, and Trains* G
[649] heare? [*Takes Mrs. Fitz. aside.*] G You're 1716, W into] in 1641 schoole 1641 School
1692, 1716 school W, G
[650] SN. om. G
[651] left] let 1641 entered W enter'd G
[652] owne om. G

Senſes, you are my witneſſe, ſha' hath inioy'd[653]
All helps that could be had, for loue, or money—
M[rs]. Fit. To make a foole of her.
Fit. Wife, that's your malice,
The wickedneſſe o' you[654] nature to interpret
Your husbands kindeſſe[655] thus. But I'll not leaue;   125

Still to doe good, for your deprau'd affections:
Intend it. Bend this ſtubborne will; be great.
Tay. Good *Madame*, whom do they vſe in meſſages?
Wit. They comonly vſe their ſlaues, *Madame*.
Tai. And do's your *Ladiſhip*.Thinke that ſo good, *Madame*?
Wit. no, indeed, *Madame*; I,   130

Therein preferre the faſhion of *England* farre,
Of your young delicate Page, or diſcreet Vſher.
Fit. And I goe with your *Ladiſhip*, in opinion,
Directly for your Gentleman-vſher.
There's not a finer *Officer* goes on ground.   135

Wit. If hee be made and broken to his place, once.
Fit. Nay, ſo I preſuppoſe him.
Wit. And they are fitter
Managers too, Sir, but I would haue 'hem call'd
Our *Eſcudero's*.
Fit. Good.
Wit. Say, I ſhould ſend
To your *Ladiſhip*, who (I preſume) has gather'd   140

All the deare ſecrets, to know how to make
Paſtillos of the *Dutcheſſe* of *Braganza*,
Coquettas, Almoiauana's, Mantecada's,
Alcoreas, Muſtaccioli; or ſay it were
The *Peladore* of *Isabella*, or *balls*   145

Againſt the itch, or *aqua nanfa*, or *oyle*
Of *Ieſſamine* for gloues, of the *Marqueſſe*[656] *Muja*:
Or for the head, and hayre: why, theſe are *offices*.
Fit. Fit for a gentleman, not a ſlaue. They[657] onely
Might aske for your *pineti, Spaniſh*-cole,   150

---

[653] sha'] she' 1692 she 1716, f. enjoy'd 1692, f.
[654] your 1641, f.
[655] kindnesse 1641 Kindness 1692, 1716 kindness W, G
[656] Marquess 1692, 1716 marquess W
[657] Fit.] *Eith.* 1716, W *Wit.* They G

To burne, and sweeten a roome; but the *Arcana*
Of *Ladies* Cabinets—
Fit. Should be else-where trusted.
Yo' are[658] much about the truth. Sweet honoured *Ladies*,
He enters himselfe with the Ladies.
Let mee fall in wi' you. I'ha' my female wit,
As well as my male. And I doe know what sutes   155

A *Lady* of spirit, or a woman of fashion!
Wit. And you would haue your wife such.
Fit. Yes, *Madame*, aërie,
Light; not to plaine dishonesty, I meane:
But, somewhat o' this side.
Wit. I take you, Sir.
H'has[659] reason *Ladies*. I'll not giue this rush   160

For any *Lady*, that cannot be honestWithin a thred.
Tay. Yes, *Madame*, and yet venter[660]
As far for th'other, in her Fame—
Wit. As can be;
Coach it to *Pimlico*; daunce[661] the *Saraband*;
Heare, and talke bawdy; laugh as loud, as a larum;   165

Squeake, spring, do any thing.
Eit. In young company, *Madame*.
Tay. Or afore gallants. If they be braue, or *Lords*,
A woman is ingag'd.[662]
Fit. I say so, *Ladies*,It is ciuility to deny vs nothing.
Pvg. You talke of a *Vniuersity*! why, *Hell* is   170

A Grammar-schoole to this![663]
The Diuell *admires him*.
Eit. But then,
Shee must not lose a looke on stuffes, or cloth, *Madame*.
Tay. Nor no course fellow.
Wit. She must be guided, *Madame*
By the clothes he weares, and company he is in;
Whom to salute, how farre—
Fit. I ha' told her this.   175

---

658 SN. om. G ‖ You're 1716, W
659 He 'as 1716, W
660 venture 1692, f.
661 dance 1641, f.
662 engag'd W engaged G
663 SN.] [*Aside.* G

And how that bawdry[664] too, vpo' the point,
Is (in it felfe) as ciuill a difcourfe—
Wit. As any other affayre of flefh, what euer.
Fit. But fhee will ne'r be capable, fhee is not
So much as comming, *Madame*; I know not how   180

She lofes all her opportunities
With hoping to be forc'd. I'haue entertain'd[665]
He fhews his Pug. A gentleman, a younger brother, here,
Whom I would faine breed vp, her *Efcudero*,
Againft fome expectation's that I haue,   185

And fhe'll not countenance him.
Wit. What's his name?
Fit. *Diuel, o' Darbi-fhire.*
Eit. Bleffe us from him!
Tay. *Diuell?*
Call him *De-uile*, fweet *Madame*.
M^rs. Fi. What you pleafe, *Ladies*.
Tay. *De-uile's* a prettier name!
Eit. And founds, me thinks,
As it came in with the *Conquerour*—
Man. Ouer fmocks!   190

What things they are? That nature fhould be at leafure
Euer to make 'hem! my woing is at an end.
Manly *goes out with indignation.*[666]
Wit. What can he do?
Eit. Let's heare him.
Tay. Can he manage?
Fit. Pleafe you to try him, *Ladies*. Stand forth, *Diuell*.
Pvg. Was all this but the preface to my torment?[667]   195

Fit. Come, let their *Ladifhips*[668] fee your honours.
Eit. O,Hee makes a wicked leg.
Tay. As euer I faw!
Wit. Fit for a *Diuell*.
Tay. Good *Madame*, call him *De-uile*.
Wit. *De-uile*, what property is there moft required

---

[664] baudery 1641
[665] SN. om. G
[666] SN.] [*Aside, and exit with indignation.* G || Wooing 1692, 1716 wooing W, G
[667] [*Aside.* G
[668] Ladiship 1641

I' your conceit, now, in the *Escudero*?[669]   200

They begin their Catechisme.
Fit. Why doe you not speake?
Pvg. A setled discreet pase,[670] *Madame*.
Wit. I thinke, a barren head, Sir, Mountaine-like,
To be expos'd to the cruelty of weathers—
Fit. I, for his Valley is beneath the waste, *Madame*,
And to be fruitfull there, it is sufficient.   205

Dulnesse vpon you! Could not you hit this?
Pvg. Good Sir—
He strikes him.[671]
Wit. He then had had no barren head.
You daw[672] him too much, in troth, Sir.
Fit. I must walke
With the *French* sticke, like an old vierger[673] for you.
Pvg. O, *Chiefe*, call mee to *Hell* againe, and free mee.[674]   210

The Diuell *prayes*.
Fit. Do you murmur now?
Pvg. Not I, S^r.
Wit. What do you take
M^r. *Deuile*,[675] the height of your employment,
In the true perfect *Escudero*?
Fit. When? What doe you answer?
Pvg. To be able, *Madame*, First to enquire, then report the working,   215

Of any *Ladies* physicke, in sweete phrase.
Wit. Yes, that's an act of elegance, and importance.
But what aboue?
Fit. O, that I had a goad for him.
Pvg. To find out a good *Corne-cutter*.
Tay. Out on him!
Eit. Most barbarous!
Fit. Why did you doe this, now?   220

Of purpose to discredit me? you damn'd *Diuell*.
Pvg. Sure, if I be not yet, I shall be. All

---

[669] SN. om. G (same on line 210)
[670] pase] pause 1641
[671] SN.] [*Fit strikes Pug.* W ‖ *He* om. G
[672] draw 1716
[673] Virger W verger G
[674] [*Aside.* G
[675] Divele 1641

My daies in *Hell*, were holy-daies to this!
Tay. 'Tis labour loſt, *Madame*?[676]
Eit. H'is[677] a dull fellow Of no capacity!
Tai. Of no diſcourſe!   225

O, if my *Ambler* had beene here!
Eit. I, *Madame*; You talke of a man, where is there ſuch another?
Wit. Mr. *Deuile*, put caſe, one of my *Ladies*, heere,
Had a fine brach: and would imploy[678] you forth
To treate 'bout a conuenient match for her.   230

What would you obſerue?
Pvg. The color, and the ſize, *Madame*.
Wit. And nothing elſe?
Fit. The Moon, you calfe, the Moone!
Wit. I, and the Signe.
Tai. Yes, and receits for proneneſſe.
Wit. Then when the *Puppies* came, what would you doe?
Pvg. Get their natiuities caſt!
Wit. This's[679] wel. What more?   235

Pvg. Conſult the *Almanack-man* which would be leaſt?
Which cleanelieſt?
Wit. And which ſilenteſt?[680] This's wel, *madame*!
Wit. And while ſhe were with[681] puppy?
Pvg. Walke her out, And ayre her euery morning!
Wit. Very good! And be induſtrious to kill her fleas?   240

Pvg. Yes!
Wit. He will make a pretty proficient.
Pvg. Who, Comming from *Hell*, could looke for ſuch[682] Catechiſing?
The *Diuell* is an *Aſſe*. I doe acknowledge it.[683]
Fit. The top of woman! All her ſexe in abſtract!
Fitz-dottrel *admires* Wittipol.[684]
I loue her, to each ſyllable, falls from her.   245

Tai. Good *madame* giue me leaue to goe aſide with him!

---

[676] [*Aside.* G
[677] He's 1716, W He is G
[678] employ 1692, f.
[679] This's] This is 1716, f. (also on line 237)
[680] cleanliest 1692, f. silent'st 1692. f.
[681] Wit. om. 1692, f.
[682] such] such a W, G
[683] [*Aside.* G
[684] SN.] [*Aside, and looking at Wittipol.* G

And try him a little!
Wit. Do, and I'll with-draw, *Madame,*
VVith this faire *Lady*: read to her, the while.
Tai. Come, S^r.
Pvg. Deare *Chiefe*, relieue me, or I perifh.[685]
The Diuel *praies again.*
Wit. *Lady*, we'll follow. You are not iealous Sir? 250

Fit. O, *madame*! you fhall fee. Stay wife, behold,
I giue her vp heere, abfolutely, to you,
She is your owne.[686] Do with her what you will!
He giues his wife to him, taking him to be a Lady.
Melt, caft, and forme her as you fhall thinke good!
Set any ftamp on! I'll receiue her from you 255

As a new thing, by your owne ftandard!
VVit. Well, Sir![687]

---

[685] SN.] [*Aside.* G
[686] SN. om. G
[687] [*Exit Wit.* Well, sir! [*Exeunt Wittipol with Mrs. Fitz. and Tailbush and Eitherside with Pug.* G

ACT. IIII.   SCENE. V.

Mere-craft.   Fitz-dottrel.   Pit-Fal.

Ever-ill.   Plvtarchus.[688]

But what ha' you done i' your *Dependance*, ſince?
Fit. O, it goes on, I met your Couſin, the *Maſter*—
Mer. You did not acquaint him, S^r?
Fit. Faith, but I did, S^r.
And vpon better thought, not without reaſon!
He being chiefe *Officer*, might ha' tane[689] it ill, elſe,   5

As a *Contempt* againſt his Place, and that
In time Sir, ha' drawne on another *Dependance*.
No, I did finde him in good termes, and ready
To doe me any ſeruice.[690]
Mer. So he said, to you?
But S^r, you do not know him.
Fit. VVhy, I presum'd   10

Becauſe this *bus'neſſe* of my wiues, requir'd mee,
I could not ha' done better: And hee told
Me, that he would goe preſently to your *Councell*,
A Knight, here, i' the Lane—
Mer. Yes, *Iuſtice Either-ſide*.
Fit. And get the *Feoffment* drawne, with a letter of *Atturney*,   15

For *liuerie* and *ſeiſen*!
Mer. That I knowe's the courſe.
But Sir, you meane not to make him *Feoffee*?
Fit. Nay, that I'll pauſe on!
Mer. How now little *Pit-fall*.[691]
Pit. Your Couſin Maſter *Euer-ill*, would come in—
But he would know if Maſter[692] *Manly* were heere.   20

Mer. No, tell him, if he were, I ha' made his peace!
Mere-craft whiſpers againſt him.[693]
Hee's one, Sir, has no State, and a man knowes not,

---

[688] V] III. 1641 Act. ...] Scene II. *Another Room in the same. Enter* Meercraft *and* Fitzdottrel. G
[689] taken G
[690] service 1641, W, G Service 1692, 1716
[691] on. *Enter* Pitfall. G
[692] Mr. 1692, 1716 mr. W
[693] [*Exit Pitfall.* SN. om. G

103

How such a trust may tempt him.
Fit. I conceiue you.[694]
Eve. S^r. this fame deed is done here.
Mer. Pretty *Plutarchus*?
Art thou come with it? and has Sir *Paul*[695] view'd it?   25

Plv. His hand is to the draught.
Mer. VVill you step in, S^r.And read it?
Fit. Yes.
Eve. I pray you a word wi' you.
Eueril *whifpers against* Mere-craft.[696]
Sir *Paul Eitherside* will'd mee gi'[697] you caution,
Whom you did make *Feoffee*: for 'tis the truft
O' your whole State: and though my Cousin here   30

Be a worthy Gentleman, yet his valour has
At the tall board bin queftion'd: and we hold
Any man fo impeach'd, of doubtfull honesty!
I will not iuftifie this; but giue it you
To make your profit of it: if you vtter it,   35

I can forfweare it!
Fit. I beleeue you, and thanke you, Sir.[698]

---

[694] *Enter* Everill *and* Plutarchus. G
[695] *Poul* 1692, 1716 Poul W
[696] SN.] [*Aside to Fitz.* G
[697] give 1641, G *Paul*] as in 4.5.25
[698] [*Exeunt.* G

ACT. IIII.   SCENE. VI.
VVittipol.   Mistresse Fitz-dottrel.
Manly.   Mere-craft.[699]

Be not afraid, fweet *Lady*: yo'[700] are trufted
To loue, not violence here; I am no rauifher,
But one, whom you, by your faire truft againe,
May of a feruant make a moft true friend.[701]
M[rs]. Fi. And fuch a one I need, but not this way: 5

Sir, I confeffe me to you, the meere manner
Of your attempting mee, this morning tooke mee,
And I did hold m'inuention,[702] and my manners,
Were both engag'd, to giue it a requitall;
But not vnto your ends: my hope was then,   10

(Though interrupted, ere it could be vtter'd)
That whom I found the Mafter of fuch language,
That braine and fpirit, for fuch an enterprife,
Could not, but if thofe fuccours were demanded
To a right vfe, employ them vertuoufly!   15

And make that profit of his noble parts,
Which they would yeeld. S[r], you haue now the ground,
To exercife them in: I am a woman:
That cannot fpeake more wretchedneffe of my felfe,
Then you can read; match'd to a maffe of folly;   20

That euery day makes hafte to his owne ruine;
The wealthy portion, that I brought him, fpent;
And (through my friends neglect) no ioynture made me.
My fortunes ftanding in this precipice,
'Tis *Counfell* that I want, and honeft aides: 25

And in this name, I need you, for a friend!
Neuer in any other; for his ill,
Muft not make me, S[r], worfe.
Manly, *conceal'd this while, fhews himfelf.*[703]
Man. O friend! forfake not

---

[699] Scene III *Another Room in the same. Enter* Wittipol, *and Mrs.* Fitzdottrel. G
[700] Yo'] you W
[701] Manly *enters behind.* G
[702] m'] W, G
[703] SN.] [*comes forward.*] G

The braue occaſion, vertue offers you,
To keepe you innocent: I haue fear'd for both;   30

And watch'd you, to preuent the ill I fear'd.
But, ſince the weaker ſide hath ſo aſſur'd mee,
Let not the ſtronger fall by his owne vice,
Or be the leſſe a friend, cauſe vertue needs him.
Wit. Vertue ſhall neuer aske my ſuccours twice;   35

Moſt friend, moſt man: your *Counſells* are commands:
Lady, I can loue *goodnes* in you, more
Then I did *Beauty*; and doe here intitle
Your vertue, to the power, vpon a life
You ſhall engage in any fruitfull[704] ſeruice,   40

Euen to forfeit.[705]
Mer. *Madame*: Do you heare, Sir,
Mere-craft *takes* Wittipol *aſide, & moues a proiect for himſelfe.*
We haue another leg-ſtrain'd,[706] for this *Dottrel.*
He'ha's[707] a quarrell to carry, and ha's cauſ'd
A deed of *Feoffment*, of his whole eſtate
To be drawne yonder; h'ha'ſt[708] within: And you,   45

Onely, he meanes to make *Feoffee.* H'is[709] falne
So deſperatly enamour'd on you, and talks
Moſt like a mad-man: you did neuer heare
A *Phrentick*,[710] ſo in loue with his owne fauour!
Now, you doe know, 'tis of no validity   50

In your name, as you ſtand; Therefore aduiſe him
To put in me.[711] (h'is come here:) You ſhall ſhare Sir.

---

[704] faithfull 1641
[705] SN.] *Enter* Meercraft. (after 'forfeit.') *Aside to Wittipol.* (after 'Sir,') G
[706] leg-strain'd] hyphen om. 1692, f.
[707] He'] H' 1692, 1716
[708] h' om. 1641 he W, G
[709] H'is He's 1716, W He is G
[710] phrenetic G
[711] me!—*Enter* Fitzdottrel, Everill, *and* Plutarchus. G ‖ h'is] He's 1716, f.

ACT. IV.   SCENE. VIJ.
Wittipol.   Miſtreſſe Fitz-dottrel.   Manly.
Mere-craft.   Fitz-dottrell.   Everill.
Plvtarchvs.[712]

Fit. *Madame*, I haue a ſuit to you; and afore-hand,
I doe beſpeake you; you muſt not deny me,
I will be graunted.[713]
Wit. Sir, I muſt know it, though.
Fit. No *Lady*; you muſt not know it: yet, you muſt too.
For the truſt of it, and the fame indeed,   5

Which elſe were loſt me. I would vſe your name,
But in a *Feoffment*: make my whole eſtate
Ouer vnto you: a trifle, a thing of nothing,
Some eighteene hundred.
Wit. Alas! I vnderſtand not
Thoſe things Sir. I am a woman, and moſt loath,   10

To embarque my ſelfe—
Fit. You will not ſlight me, *Madame*?
Wit. Nor you'll not quarrell me?
Fit. No, ſweet *Madame*, I haue
Already a *dependance*; for which cauſe
I doe this: let me put you in, deare *Madame*,
I may be fairely kill'd.
Wit. You haue your friends, Sir,   15

About you here, for choice.
Eve. She tells you right, Sir.
Hee hopes to be the man.[714]
Fit. Death, if ſhe doe, what do I care for that?
Say, I would haue her tell me wrong.
Wit. Why, Sir,
If for the truſt, you'll let me haue the honor
To name you one.
Fit. Nay, you do me the honor, *Madame*:   20

Who is't?
Wit. This Gentleman:

---

[712] SD. om. G
[713] granted 1692, f.
[714] SN. om. G

Shee defignes Manly.[715]
Fit. O, no, sweet *Madame*,
H'is[716] friend to him, with whom I ha' the *dependance*.
Wit. Who might he bee?
Fit. One *Wittipol*: do you know him?
Wit. Alas Sir, he, a toy: This Gentleman
A friend to him? no more then I am Sir!   25

Fit. But will your *Ladyfhip* vndertake that, *Madame*?
Wit. Yes, and what elfe, for him, you will engage me.
Fit. What is his name?
VVit. His name is *Euftace Manly*.
Fit. VVhence do's he write himfelfe?
VVit. of *Middle-fex, Efquire*.
Fit. Say nothing, *Madame. Clerke*, come hether[717]   30

VVrite *Euftace Manly*, Squire o' *Middle-fex*.
Mer. What ha' you done, Sir?[718]
VVit. Nam'd a gentleman,
That I'll be anfwerable for, to you, Sir.
Had I nam'd you, it might ha' beene fufpected:
This way, 'tis fafe.
Fit. Come Gentlemen, your hands,   35

For witnes.
Man. VVhat is this?
Eve. You ha' made *Election*
Eueril *applaudes it*.[719]
Of a moft worthy *Gentleman*!
Man. VVould one of worth
Had fpoke it: whence[720] it comes, it is
Rather a fhame to[721] me, then a praife.
Eve. Sir, I will giue you any Satisfaction.   40

Man. Be filent then: "falfhood commends not truth".
Plv. You do deliuer this, Sir, as your deed.
To th' vfe of M[r]. *Manly*?[722]
Fit. Yes: and Sir—VVhen did you fee yong *Wittipol*? I am ready,

---

[715] SN. *She* om. W *She* ...] [*Pointing to Manly.* G
[716] He's 1716, f.
[717] [*To Plutarchus.* G || hither 1692, f.
[718] sir? [*Aside to Wit.* G
[719] SN. om. G
[720] it! but now whence W, G
[721] to] unto W, G
[722] [*To Manly.* G

For proceſſe now; Sir, this is *Publication.*   45

He ſhall heare from me, he would needes be courting
My wife, Sir.
Man. Yes: So witneſſeth his Cloake there.
Fit. Nay good Sir,—*Madame*, you did vndertake—
Fitz-dottrel *is ſuſpicious of* Manly *ſtill.*[723]
VVit. VVhat?[724]
Fit. That he was not *Wittipols* friend.
VVit. I heare S[r]. no confeſſion of it.
Fit. O ſhe know's not;   50

Now I remember, *Madame!* This young *Wittipol,*
VVould ha' debauch'd my wife, and made me *Cuckold,*
Through[725] a caſement; he did fly her home
To mine owne window: but I think I fou't[726] him,
And rauiſh'd her away, out of his pownces.   55

I ha' ſworne to ha' him by the eares: I feare
The toy, wi' not do me right.
VVit. No? that were pitty!
VVhat right doe you aske, Sir? Here he is will do't you?
Wittipol[727] *diſcouers himſelfe.*
Fit. Ha? *Wittipol?*
VVit. I Sir, no more *Lady* now,Nor *Spaniard!*
Man. No indeed, 'tis *Wittipol.*   60

Fit. Am I the thing I fear'd?
VVit. A *Cuckold?* No Sir,
But you were late in poſſibility,
I'll tell you ſo much.
Man. But your wife's too vertuous!
VVit. VVee'll ſee her Sir, at home, and leaue you here,
To be made *Duke o' Shore-ditch* with a proiect.   65

Fit. Theeues, rauiſhers.
VVit. Crie but another note, Sir,
I'll marre the tune, o' your pipe!
Fit. Gi' me my deed, then.
He would haue his deed *again.*[728]

---

[723] SN. om. G
[724] VVit. *What.* 1641
[725] Thorow 1692 Thorough 1716, f.
[726] sou't] fou't 1692 fought 1716, W sous'd G
[727] SN. Wittipol om. G
[728] SN. om. G

VVit. Neither: that fhall be kept for your wiues good,
VVho will know, better how to vfe it.
Fit. Ha'[729]To feaft you with my land?
VVit. Sir, be you quiet,   70

Or I fhall gag you, ere I goe, confult
Your Mafter of dependances; how to make this
A fecond bufineffe, you haue time Sir.
VVitipol *bafflees him, and goes out.*[730]
Fit. Oh!
VVhat will the ghoft of my wife Grandfather,
My learned *Father*, with my worfhipfull *Mother*,   75

Thinke of me now, that left me in this world
In ftate to be their *Heire*? that am become
A *Cuckold*, and an *Affe*, and my wiues Ward;
Likely to loofe my land; ha' my throat cut:
All, by her practice!
Mer. Sir, we are all abus'd!   80

Fit. And be fo ftill! VVho hinders you, I pray you,
Let me alone, I would enioy[731] my felfe,
And be the *Duke o' Drown'd-Land*, you ha' made me.
Mer. Sir, we muft play an *after-game* o' this.
Fit. But I am not in cafe to be a *Gam-fter*:   85

I tell you once againe—
Mer. You muft be rul'd
And take some counfell.
Fit. Sir, I do hate counfell,
As I do hate my wife, my wicked wife!
Mer. But we may thinke how to recouer all:If you will act.
Fit. I will not think; nor act;   90

Nor yet recouer; do not talke to me?
I'll runne out o' my witts, rather then heare;
I will be what I am, *Fabian Fitz-Dottrel*,
Though all the world fay nay to't.[732]
Mer. Let's follow him.

---

[729] Ha! 1692, f.
[730] SN.] [*Baffles him, and exit with Manly.* G
[731] injoy 1641
[732] to't. [*Exit.* G || Let's   Let us W, G || him. [*Exeunt.* G

ACT. V.   SCENE. I.
Ambler.   Pitfall.   Mere-craft.[733]

Bvt ha's my Lady mift me?
Pit. Beyond telling!
Here ha's been that infinity of ftrangers!
And then fhe would ha' had you, to ha' fampled you
VVith one within, that they are now a teaching;
And do's pretend to your ranck.
Amb. Good fellow *Pit-fall*,   5

Tel M^r. *Mere-craft*, I intreat[734] a word with him.
Pitfall *goes out*.
This most vnlucky accident will goe neare
To be the loffe o' my place; I am in doubt![735]
Mer. VVith me? what fay you Mr *Ambler*?
Amb. Sir,
I would befeech your worfhip ftand between   10

Me, and my *Ladies* difpleafure, for my abfence.
Mer. O, is that[736] all? I warrant you.
Amb. I would tell you Sir
But how it happened.
Mer. Brief, good Mafter *Ambler*,
Put your felfe to your rack: for I haue tafque[737]
Of more importance.
Mere-craft *feemes full of bufineffe*.[738]
Amb. Sir you'll laugh at me?   15

But (fo is *Truth*)[739] a very friend of mine,
Finding by conference with me, that I liu'd
Too chaft for my complexion (and indeed
Too honeft for my place, Sir) did aduife me
If I did loue my felfe (as that I do,   20

I muft confeffe)
Mer. Spare your *Parenthefis*.

---

[733] SD. Ambler ...] *A Room in* Tailbush's *House. Enter* Ambler *and* Pitfall. G
[734] entreat W, G ‖ SN.] [*Exit Pitfall.* G
[735] *Enter* Meercraft. G
[736] that] this 1641
[737] a tasque 1641
[738] SN. om. G
[739] () ret. G.

Amb. To gi' my body a little euacuation—
Mer. Well, and you went to a whore?
Amb.[740] No, S[r]. I durſt not
(For feare it might arriue at ſome body's eare,
It ſhould not) truſt my ſelfe to a common houſe;   25

Ambler *tels this with extraordinary ſpeed.*
But got the Gentlewoman to goe with me,
And carry her bedding to a *Conduit-head*,
Hard by the place toward *Tyborne*, which they call
My L. Majors[741] *Banqueting-houſe.* Now Sir, This morning
Was *Execution*; and I ner'e[742] dream't on't   30

Till I heard the noiſe o' the people, and the horſes;
And neither I, nor the poore Gentlewoman
Durſt ſtirre, till all was done and paſt: ſo that
I' the *Interim*, we fell a ſleepe againe.
He flags.[743]
Mer. Nay, if you fall, from your gallop, I am gone S[r].   35

Amb. But, when I wak'd, to put on my cloathes, a ſute,
I made new for the action, it was gone,
And all my money, with my purſe, my ſeales,
My hard-wax, and my table-bookes, my ſtudies,
And a fine new deuiſe, I had to carry   40

My pen, and inke, my ciuet, and my tooth-picks,
All vnder one. But, that which greiu'd me, was
The Gentlewoman's ſhoes (with a paire of roſes,
And garters, I had giuen her for the buſineſſe)[744]
So as that made vs ſtay, till it was darke.   45

For I was faine to lend her mine, and walke
In a rug, by her, barefoote, to Saint *Giles'es*.
Mer. A kind of Iriſh penance! Is this all, Sir?
Amb. To ſatisfie my *Lady*.
Mer. I will promiſe you, S[r].
Amb. I ha' told the true *Diſaſter*.
Mer. I cannot ſtay wi' you   50

---

[740] SN. Ambler om. G
[741] Mayor's 1716, f.
[742] never W, G
[743] SN. *slags* 1641
[744] (with ... garters,) W ‖ () ret. G

Sir, to condole; but gratulate your returne.[745]
Amb. An honeſt gentleman, but he's neuer at leiſure
To be himſelfe: He ha's ſuch tides of buſineſſe.

---

[745] [*Exit.* G (Also on line 53)

Act. V.   Scene. II.
Pvg.   Ambler.[746]

O, Call me home againe, deare *Chiefe*, and put me
To yoaking foxes, milking of Hee-goates,
Pounding of water in a morter, lauing
The fea dry with a nut-fhell, gathering all
The leaues are falne this *Autumne*, drawing farts   5

Out of dead bodies, making ropes of fand,
Catching the windes together in a net,
Muftring[747] of ants, and numbring atomes; all
That hell, and you thought exquifite torments, rather
Then ftay me here, a thought more: I would fooner   10

Keepe fleas within a circle, and be accomptant
A thoufand yeere, which of 'hem and how far
Out leap'd the other, then endure a minute
Such as I haue within. There is no hell
To a *Lady* of fafhion. All your torture there   15

Are paftimes to it. 'T would be a refrefhing
For me, to be i' the fire againe, from hence.
Ambler *comes in, & furuayes him*.[748]
Amb. This is my fuite, and thofe the fhoes and rofes![749]
Pvg. Th'[750] haue such impertinent vexations,
A generall Councell o' *diuels* could not hit[751]—   20

Pug *perceiues it, and ftarts*.
Ha! This is hee, I tooke a fleepe with his *Wench*,
And borrow'd his cloathes. What might I doe to balke him?
Amb. Do you heare, S^r?
Pvg. Answ. him[752] but not to th'purpofe[753]
Amb. What is your name, I pray you Sir.
Pvg. Is't fo late Sir?

---

[746] SD.] Scene II. *Another Room in the Same. Enter* Pug. G
[747] mustering G numbering G
[748] SN.] *Enter* Ambler, *and surveys him.* G
[749] [*Aside.* G
[750] They've W They have G
[751] SN. om. 1641 [*sees Ambler.*] G
[752] him om. 1641
[753] [*Aside.* G

He anſwers quite from the purpoſe.[754]
Amb. I aske not o' the time, but of your name, Sir.   25

Pvg. I thanke you, Sir. Yes it dos hold Sir, certaine.
Amb. Hold, Sir? what holds? I muſt both hold, and talke to you
About theſe clothes.
Pvg. A very pretty lace! But the
Taylor coſſend me.
Amb. No, I am coſſend
By you! robb'd.
Pvg. Why, when you pleaſe Sir, I am   30

For three peny *Gleeke*, your man.
Amb. Pox o'[755] your *gleeke*,
And three pence. Giue me an anſwere.
Pvg. Sir,My maſter is the beſt at it.
Amb. Your maſter! Who is your Maſter.
Pvg. Let it be friday night.
Amb. What ſhould be then?
Pvg. Your beſt ſongs *Thom. o'Bet'lem*[756]   35

Amb. I thinke, you are he. Do's he mocke me trow, from purpoſe?
Or do not I ſpeake to him, what I meane?
Good Sir your name.
Pvg. Only a couple a'[757] *Cocks* Sir,
If we can get a *Widgin*, 'tis in ſeaſon.
Amb. He hopes to make on[758] o' theſe *Scipticks* o' me   40

For Scepticks.(I thinke I name 'hem right)[759] and do's not fly me.
I wonder at that! 'tis a ſtrange confidence!
I'll prooue another way, to draw his anſwer.[760]

---

[754] SN. om. G (Same on line 40)
[755] o' ret. G
[756] *Tom* 1641, G ‖ o' ret. G ‖ *Bethlem* 1716, G Bethlem W
[757] a'] o' 1692, 1716, W of G
[758] on] one 1641, f.
[759] () ret. G
[760] [*Exeunt severally.* G

Act. V.   Scene. III.
Mere-craft.   Fitz-dottrel.
Everill.   Pvg.[761]

It is the eafieſt thing Sir, to be done.
As plaine, as fizzling: roule[762] but wi’ your eyes,
And foame at th’ mouth. A little caſtle-ſoape
Will do’t, to rub your lips: And then a nutſhell,
With toe, and touch-wood in it to ſpit fire,   5

Did you ner’e read, Sir, little *Darrels* tricks,
With the boy o’ *Burton*, and the 7. in *Lancaſhire,*
Sommers at *Nottingham*? All theſe do teach it.
And wee’ll giue out, Sir, that your wife ha’s bewitch’d you:
They repaire their old plot.[763]
Eve. And practiſed with thoſe two, as *Sorcerers*.   10

Mer. And ga’[764] you potions, by which meanes you were
Not *Compos mentis*, when you made your *feoffment*.
There’s no recouery o’ your ſtate,[765] but this:
This, Sir, will ſting.
Eve. And moue in a Court of equity.
Mer. For, it is more then manifeſt, that this was   15

A plot o’ your wiues, to get your land.
Fit. I thinke it.
Eve. Sir it appeares.
Mer. Nay, and my coſſen has knowne
Theſe gallants in theſe ſhapes.[766]
Eve. T’haue don ſtrange things, Sir.
One as the *Lady*, the other as the *Squire*.
Mer. How, a mans honeſty may be fool’d! I thought him   20

A very *Lady*.
Fit. So did I: renounce me elſe.
Mer. But this way, Sir, you’ll be reueng’d at height.
Eve. Vpon ’hem all.

---

[761] SD.] Scene III. *A Room in* Fitzdottrel’s *House. Enter* Meercraft, Fitzdottrel, *and* Everill. G
[762] Roll 1692, 1716 roll W, G
[763] SN. om. G
[764] gave G
[765] estate 1641
[766] shapes—G

Mer. Yes faith, and ſince your Wife
Has runne the way of woman thus, e'en giue her—
Fit. Loſt by this hand, to me, dead to all ioyes   25

Of her deare *Dottrell*, I ſhall neuer pitty her:
That could, pitty[767] her ſelfe.
Mer. Princely reſolu'd Sir,
And like your ſelfe ſtill, in *Potentiâ*.

---

[767] could not pity W could [not] pity G

Act. V. Scene. IV.

Mere-craft, &c. *to them.* Gvilt-head.[768]

Sledge. Plvtarchvs. Serieants.[769]

Gvilt-head What newes?
Fit. O Sir, my hundred peices:
Let me ha' them yet.
Fitz-dottrel *aſkes for his money.*[770]
Gvi. Yes Sir,[771] officersArreſt him.
Fit. Me?
Ser. I arreſt you.
Sle. Keepe the peace,
I charge you gentlemen.
Fit. Arreſt me? Why?
Gvi. For better ſecurity, Sir. My ſonne *Plutarchus*　　　　　5

Aſſures me, y'are[772] not worth a groat.
Plv. Pardon me, *Father*,
I said his worſhip had no foote of Land left:
And that I'll iuſtifie, for I writ the deed.
Fit. Ha' you theſe tricks i' the citty?
Gvi. Yes, and more.
Arreſt this gallant too, here, at my ſuite.[773]　　　　　10

Meaning Mere-craft.
Sle. I, and at mine. He owes me for his lodging
Two yeere and a quarter.
Mer. Why M. *Guilt-head*, Land-Lord,
Thou art not mad, though th'art[774] *Constable*
Puft vp with th' pride of the place? Do you heare, Sirs.
Haue I deſeru'd this from you two? for all　　　　　15

My paines at *Court*, to get you each a patent.
Gvi. For what?
Mer. Vpo' my proiect o' the *forkes*,
Sle. *Forkes?* what be they?

---

[768] Act. ...] *Enter* Gilthead, Plutarchus, Sledge, *and* Serjeants. G
[769] SD. Mere. ... *them*] *To them.* Mere-craft &c. 1692 Mere-craft, &c. om. 1716. W
[770] SN. om. G
[771] Ser.] I *Serj.* G
[772] y'] you W, G
[773] SN.] [*Points to Meercraft.* G
[774] th'] thou W, G

The Project *of forks.*[775]
Mer. The laudable vfe of forkes,
Brought into cuftome here, as they are in *Italy*,
To th' fparing o' *Napkins*. That, that fhould haue made   20

Your bellowes goe at the forge, as his at the fornace.
I ha' procur'd it, ha' the Signet for it,
Dealt with the *Linnen-drapers*, on my priuate,[776]
By cause, I fear'd, they were the likelyeft euer
To ftirre againft, to croffe it; for 'twill be   25

A mighty fauer of *Linnen* through the kingdome
(As that is one o' my grounds, and to[777] fpare wafhing)
Now, on you two, had I layd all the profits.
Guilt-head to haue the making of all thofe
Of gold and filuer, for the better perfonages;   30

And you, of thofe of *Steele* for the common fort.
And both by *Pattent*, I had brought you your feales in.
But now you haue preuented me, and I thanke you.
Sledge *is brought about.*[778]
Sle. Sir, I will bayle you, at mine owne ap-perill.
Mer. Nay choofe.
Plv. Do you fo too, good Father.   35

And Guilt-head *comes.*
Gvi. I like the fafhion o' the proiect, well,
The forkes! It may be a lucky one! and is not
Intricate,[779] as one would fay, but fit for
Plaine heads, as ours, to deale in. Do you heare
Officers, we difcharge you.[780]
Mer. Why this fhewes   40

A little good nature in you, I confeffe,
But do not tempt your friends thus. Little *Guilt-head*,
Aduife your fire, great *Guilt-head* from thefe courfes:
And, here, to trouble a great man in reuerfion,
For a matter o' fifty on[781] a falfe *Alarme*,   45

---

[775] SN. om. G
[776] private Bie, 'cause 1692, 1716 private, Because W, G
[777] to] so 1641
[778] SN. om. G
[779] Not intricate (l. 38) G
[780] you. [*Exeunt Serjeants.* G
[781] on] in W, G

Away, it ſhewes not well. Let him get the pieces
And bring 'hem. Yo'll[782] heare more elſe.
Plv. *Father.*

G

---

[782] You'll 1692, 1716 You'll W ‖ *Exeunt Gilt. and Plut. Enter* Ambler, *dragging in* Pug.

Act. V.   Scene. V.
Ambler.   { *To them.*[783]

O Mafter *Sledge*, are you here? I ha' been to feeke you.
You are the *Conftable*, they fay. Here's one
That I do charge with *Felony*, for the fuite
He weares, Sir.
Mer. Who? M. *Fitz-Dottrels* man?
Ware what you do, M. *Ambler*.[784]
Amb. Sir, thefe clothes   5

I'll fweare, are mine: and the fhooes the gentlewomans
I told you of: and ha' him afore a *Iuftice*,
I will.
Pvg. My mafter, Sir, will paffe his word for me.
Amb. O, can you fpeake to purpofe now?
Fit. Not I,
If you be fuch a one Sir, I will leaue you   10

To your *God fathers* in Law. Let twelue men worke.
Fitz-dottrel *difclaimes him*.[785]
Png. Do you heare Sir, pray, in priuate.[786]
Fit. well, what fay you?
Briefe, for I haue no time to loofe.
Pvg. Truth is, Sir,
I am the very *Diuell*, and had leaue
To take this body, I am in, to ferue you;   15

Which was a *Cutpurfes*, and hang'd this Morning.
And it is likewife true, I ftole this fuite
To cloth me with. But Sir let me not goe
To prifon for it. I haue hitherto
Loft time, done nothing; fhowne, indeed, no part   20

O' my *Diuels* nature. Now, I will fo helpe
Your malice, 'gainft thefe parties; fo aduance
The bufineffe, that you haue in hand of *witchcraft*,
And your *poffeffion*, as my felfe were in you.
Teach you fuch tricks, to make your belly fwell,   25

---

[783] SD. om. G
[784] *Ambler. Enter* Fitzdottrel. G
[785] SN. om. G
[786] private. [*Takes him aside.* G

And your eyes turne, to foame, to ftare, to gnafh
Your teeth together, and to beate your felfe,
Laugh loud,[787] and faine fix voices—
Fit. Out you Rogue!
You moft infernall counterfeit wretch! Auant!
Do you thinke to gull me with your *Æfops Fables*?   30

Here take him to you, I ha' no part in him.
Pvg. Sir.
Fit. Away, I do difclaime, I will not heare you.
And fends him away.[788]
Mer. What faid he to you, Sir?
Fit. Like a lying raskall
Told me he was the *Diuel*.
Mer. How! a good ieft!
Fit. And that he would teach me, fuch fine *diuels* tricks   35

For our new refolution.
Eve. O'[789] pox on him,'Twas excellent wifely done, Sir, not to truft him.
Mere-craft *giues the instructions to him and the reft*.[790]
Mer. Why, if he were the Diuel, we fha' not need him,
If you'll be rul'd. Goe throw your felfe on a bed, Sir,
And faine you ill. Wee'll not be feene wi' you,   40

Till after, that you haue a fit: and all
Confirm'd within. Keepe you with the two *Ladies*[791]
And perfwade them. I'll[792] to *Iuftice Either-fide*,
And poffeffe him with all. *Traines* fhall feeke out *Ingine*,
And they two[793] fill the towne with't, euery cable   45

Is to be veer'd. We muft employ[794] out all
Our *emiffaries* now; Sir, I will fend you
Bladders and *Bellowes*. Sir, be confident,
'Tis no hard thing t'out[795] doe the *Deuill* in:
A Boy o' thirteene yeere old made him an *Affe*   50

---

787 loud] round 1716
788 SN.] [*Exit Sledge with Pug.* G
789 O'] O W O, G
790 SN. om. G
791 [*to Everill.* G
792 I will G
793 two] to 1641
794 imploy 1641
795 t' ret. G

But t'toher[796] day.
Fit. Well, I'll beginne to practice;
And fcape the imputation of being *Cuckold*,
By mine owne act.
Mer. yo' are right.[797]
Eve. Come, you ha' put
Your felfe to a fimple coyle here, and your freinds,
By dealing with new *Agents*, in new plots.   55

Mer. No more o' that, fweet coufin.
Eve. What had you
To doe with this fame *Wittipol*, for a *Lady*?
Mer. Queftion not that: 'tis done.
Eve. You had fome ftraine'Boue E-*la*?
Mer. I had indeed.
Eve. And, now, you crack for't.
Mer. Do not vpbraid me.
Eve. Come, you muft be told on't;   60

You are fo couetous, ftill, to embrace[798]
More then you can, that you loofe all.
Mer. 'Tis right.
What would you more, then Guilty? Now, your fuccours.[799]

---

[796] t'tother 1692 t'other 1716. f.
[797] You're 1716, W right. || [*Exit Fitz*. G
[798] imbrace 1641
[799] [*Exeunt*. G

Act. V.   Scene. VI.
Shakles.   Pvg.   Iniquity.   Divel.[800]

Pug *is brought to* New-gate.
Here you are lodg'd, Sir, you muſt
ſend your garniſh,
If you'll be priuat.
Pvg. There it is, Sir, leaue me.[801]
To *New-gate*, brought? How is the name of *Deuill*
Diſcredited in me! What a loſt fiend
Shall I be, on returne? My *Cheife* will roare   5

In triumph, now, that I haue beene on earth,
A day, and done no noted thing, but brought
That body back here, was hang'd out this morning.
Well! would it once were midnight, that I knew
My vtmoſt. I thinke Time be drunke, and ſleepes;   10

He is ſo ſtill, and moues not! I doe glory
Now i'[802] my torment. Neither can I expect it,
I haue it with my fact.
Enter Iniquity *the* Vice.[803]
Ini. *Child* of hell, be thou merry:
Put a looke on, as round, boy, and red as a cherry.
Caſt care at thy poſternes; and firke i' thy fetters,   15

They are ornaments, *Baby*, haue graced thy betters:
Looke vpon me, and hearken. Our *Cheife* doth ſalute thee,
And leaſt the[804] coldyron ſhould chance to confute thee,
H'hath ſent thee, *grant-paroll*[805] by me to ſtay longer
A moneth here on earth, againſt cold *Child*, or honger.   20

Pv. How? longer here a moneth?
Ing. Yes, boy, till the *Seſſion*,
That ſo thou mayeſt[806] haue a triumphall egreſſion.
Pvg. In a cart, to be hang'd.

---

[800] SD. VJJ VII. W Act. ...] Scene IV. *A Cell in Newgate. Enter* Shakles, *with* Pvg *in chains*. G
[801] [*Exit Shackles.*
[802] i'] in W
[803] SN. (after 'fact.' 13) *the* Vice om. G
[804] the] our 1692, 1716
[805] parole G
[806] maist 1692 may'st 1716 mayst W, G

Ing. No, *Child*, in a Carre,
The charriot of Triumph, which moſt of them are.
And in the meane time, to be greazy, and bouzy,   25

And naſty, and filthy, and ragged and louzy,
With dam'n me, renounce me, and all the fine phraſes;
That bring, vnto *Tiborne*, the plentifull gazes.
Pvg. He is a *Diuell*! and may be our *Cheife*!
The great Superiour *Diuell*! for his malice: 30

Arch-diuel! I acknowledge him. He knew
What I would ſuffer, when he tie'd me vp thus
In a rogues body: and he has (I thanke him)
His tyrannous pleaſure on me, to confine me
To the vnlucky carkaſſe of a *Cutpurſe*,   35

wherein I could do nothing.
The great Deuill *enters,*[807] *and vpbraids him with all his dayes worke.*
Div. Impudent fiend,
Stop thy lewd mouth. Doeſt[808] thou not ſhame and tremble
To lay thine owne dull damn'd defects vpon
An innocent caſe, there? Why thou heauy ſlaue!
The ſpirit, that did poſſeſſe that fleſh before   40

Put more true life, in a finger, and a thumbe,
Then thou in the whole Maſſe. Yet thou rebell'ſt
And murmur'ſt? What one profer haſt thou made,
Wicked inough,[809] this day, that might be call'd
Worthy thine owne, much leſſe the name that ſent thee?   45

Firſt, thou did'ſt helpe thy ſelfe into a beating
Promptly, and with't endangered'ſt too thy tongue:
A *Diuell*, and could not keepe a body entire[810]
One day! That, for our credit. And to vindicate it,
Hinderd'ſt (for ought thou know'ſt) a deed of darkneſſe: 50

Which was an act of that egregious folly,
As no one, to'ard the *Diuel*, could ha' thought on.
This for your acting! but for suffering! Why
Thou haſt beene cheated on, with a falſe beard,
And a turn'd cloake. Faith, would your predeceſſour   55

---

[807] SN.] *Enter* Satan. G Div.] *Sat.* G
[808] Dost 1692, 1716
[809] enough 1692, f.
[810] entire W, G

The *Cutpurſe*, thinke you, ha' been ſo? Out vpon thee,
The hurt th'[811] haſt don, to let men know their ſtrength,
And that the'are[812] able to out-doe a *diuel*
Put in a body, will for euer be
A ſcarre vpon our Name! whom haſt thou dealt with,   60

Woman or man, this day, but haue out-gone thee
Some way, and moſt haue prou'd the better fiendes?
Yet, you would be imploy'd?[813] Yes, hell ſhall make you
Prouinciall o' the *Cheaters*![814] or *Bawd-ledger*,
For this ſide o' the towne! No doubt you'll render   65

A rare accompt of things. Bane o' your itch,
And ſcratching for imployment.[815] I'll ha' brimſtone
To allay it ſure, and fire to ſindge your nayles off,
But, that I would not ſuch a damn'd diſhonor
Sticke on our ſtate, as that the *diuell* were hang'd;   70

And could not ſaue a body, that he tooke
From *Tyborne*, but it muſt come thither againe:
You ſhould e'en ride. But, vp away with him—
Iniquity *takes him on his back.*
Ini. Mount, dearling of darkneſſe, my ſhoulders are broad:
He that caries the fiend, is ſure of his loade.   75

The *Diuell* was wont to carry away the euill;
But, now, the Euill out-carries the *Diuell*.[816]

---

[811] th'] thou G
[812] the'are] they are 1641, G the'are are 1692 they're 1716, W
[813] employ'd W, G
[814] Cheaters] *heaters* 1641
[815] employment W, G
[816] [*Exeunt.* [*A loud explosion, smoke, &c.* G

Act. V.   Scene. VII.
Shakles.   Keepers.

A great noise is heard in New-gate, *and the Keepers come out affrighted.*[817]

O mee!
Kee. 1. What's this?
2. A piece of Iustice HallIs broken downe.
3. Fough! what a fteeme of brimftone
Is here?[818]
4. The prifoner's dead, came in but now!
Sha. Ha? where?
4. Look here.
Kee. S'lid, I fhuld know his countenance!
It is *Gill-Cut-purfe*, was hang'd out, this morning!   5

Sha. 'Tis he!
2. The *Diuell*, fure, has a hand in this!
3. What fhall wee doe?
Sha. Carry the newes of it
Vnto the *Sherifes*.
1. And to the *Iuftices*.
4. This[819] ftrange!
3. And fauours of the *Diuell*, ftrongly!
2. I' ha' the *fulphure* of *Hell-coale* i' my nofe.   10

1. Fough.
Sha. Carry him in.
1. Away.
2. How ranke it is![820]

---

[817] SD.] *Enter* Shakles, *and the* Under-keepers, *affrighted.* G
[818] Is here?] part of line 2 W
[819] This is 1716, f.
[820] [*Exeunt with the body.* G

Act. V.   Scene. VIII.
Sir Povle.   Mere-craft.   Ever-ill.
Traines.   Pitfall.   Fitz-dottrel.

{To them}[821]
VVittipol.   Manly.   Miſtreſſe Fitz-dottrel.
Ingine.   *To them* } Gvilt-head.
Sledge. *to them* } Shackles.
The Iuſtice comes out wondring, and the reſt informing him.

This was the notableſt Conſpiracy, That ere I heard of.[822]
Mer. Sir, They had giu'n him potions,
That did enamour him on the counterfeit *Lady*—
Eve. Iuſt to the time o'[823] deliuery o' the deed—
Mer. And then the witchcraft 'gan't' appeare, for ſtreight   5

He fell into his fit.
Eve. Of rage at firſt, Sir,
Which ſince, has ſo increaſed.
Tay. Good S^r. *Poule*, ſee him,
And puniſh the impoſtors.
Pov. Therefore I come, *Madame.*
Eit. Let M^r. *Etherſide* alone, *Madame.*
Pov. Do you heare?
Call in the Conſtable, I will haue him by: 10

H'is[824] the Kings *Officer*! and ſome Cittizens,
Of credit! I'll diſcharge my conſcience clearly.
Mer. Yes, Sir, and ſend for his wife.
Eve. And the two *Sorcerers*,
By any meanes![825]
Tay. I thought one a true *Lady*,
I ſhould be ſworne. So did you, *Eyther-ſide*?   15

Eit. Yes, by that light, would I might ne'r ſtir elſe, *Tailbuſh.*
Tay. And the other a ciuill Gentleman.

---

[821] SD. Sir] To them.] Sir 1692 *to them* om. 1692, 1716, W Act. ...] Scene V. *A Room
in* Fitzdottrel's *House.* Fitzdottrel *discovered   in   bed;   Lady* Eitherside,
Tailbush, Ambler, Trains, *and* Pitfall, *standing   by   him.   Enter Sir* Paul Eitherside,
Meercraft, *and* Everill. G
[822] SN. *and*] at 1692, 1716, W The ...] om. G
[823] time o' ret. G
[824] H'is] He's 1716, f.
[825] means. [*Exit Ambler.* G

Eve. But, *Madame,*
You know what I told your *Ladyſhip.*
Tay. I now ſee it:
I was prouiding of a banquet for 'hem.
After I had done inſtructing o'[826] the fellow   20

De-uile, the Gentlemans man.
Mer. Who's[827] found a thiefe, *Madam.*
And to haue rob'd your Vsher, Maſter *Ambler,*
This morning.
Tay. How?
Mer. I'll tell you more, anon.
Fit. Gi me ſome *garlicke, garlicke, garlicke, garlicke.*
He beginnes his fit.
Mer. Harke the poore Gentleman, how he is tormented!   25

Fit. *My wife is a whore, I'll kiſſe her no more: and why?*
Ma'ſt not thou be a Cuckold, as well as I?
Ha, ha, ha, ha, ha, ha, ha, ha, &c.[828]
Pov. That is the *Diuell* ſpeakes, and laughes in him.
The Iuſtice interpret all:[829]
Mer. Do you thinke ſo, S^r.
Pov. I diſcharge my conſcience.   30

Fit. *And is not the Diuell good company? Yes, wis.*
Eve. How he changes, Sir, his voyce!
Fit. *And a Cuckold is*
Where ere hee put his head, with a a[830] *Wanion,*
If his hornes be forth, the Diuells companion!
Looke, looke, looke, elſe.
Mer. How he foames!
Eve. And ſwells!   35

Tay. O, me! what's that there, riſes in his belly!
Eit. A ſtrange thing! hold it downe:
Tra. Pit. We cannot, *Madam.*
Pov. 'Tis too apparent this!
Fit. *Wittipol, Wittipol.*[831]
Wittipol, *and* Manly *and* Mistr. Fitz-dottrel *enter.*
Wit. How now, what play ha' we here.

---

[826] o'] of W
[827] Who is G
[828] *ha,* om. W *ha, &c.* om. G
[829] SN. *interprets* 1692, 1716, W *The ...*] om. G
[830] a om. 1641, f.
[831] SN. Wittipol, *and ... enter*] *Enter* Wittipol, ... G

Man. What fine, new matters?
Wit. The *Cockſcomb*, and the *Couerlet*.
Mer. O ſtrang[832] impudēce!   40

That theſe ſhould come to face their ſinne!
Eve. And out-face*Iuſtice*, they are the parties, Sir.
Pov. Say nothing.
Mer. Did you marke, Sir, vpon their[833] comming in,
How he call'd *Wittipol.*
Eve. And neuer ſaw 'hem.
Pov. I warrant you did I, let 'hem play a while.   45

Fit. *Buz, buz, buz, buz.*
Tay. Laſſe poore Gentleman!
How he is tortur'd!
Mʳˢ. Fi. Fie, Maſter *Fitz-dottrel!*
What doe you meane to counterfait thus?
Fit. *O, ô,*
His wife[834] *goes to him.*
Shee comes with a needle, and thruſts it in,
Shee pulls out that, and ſhee puts in a pinne,   50

And now, and now, I doe not know how, nor where,
But ſhee pricks mee heere, and ſhee pricks me there: ôh, ôh:
Pov. Woman forbeare.
Wit. What, Sʳ?
Pov. A practice foule
For one ſo faire:
Wit. Hath this, then, credit with you?
Man. Do you beleeue in't?
Pov. Gentlemen, I'll diſcharge
My conſcience. 'Tis a cleare conſpiracy!   56

A darke, and diuelliſh practice! I deteſt it!
Wit. The *Iuſtice* ſure will proue the merrier man![835]
Man. This is moſt ſtrange, Sir!
Pov. Come not to confront
Authority with impudence:[836] I tell you,
I doe deteſt it.[837] Here comes the Kings *Conſtable,*
And with him a right worſhipfull *Commoner;*

---

832 strange 1641, f.
833 their] our W
834 SN. *His wife* om. G
835 prove to be the merrier? 1641
836 impudence] insolence 1641
837 it.—*Re-enter* Ambler, *with* Sledge *and* Guilthead. G

My good friend, Mafter *Guilt-head*! I am glad
I can before fuch witneffes, profeffe
My confcience, and my deteftation of it.   65

Horible! moft vnaturall! Abominable!
Eve. You doe not tumble enough.
Mer. Wallow, gnafh:
They whifper him.
Tay. O, how he is vexed!
Pov. 'Tis too manifeft.
Eve. Giue him more foap to foame with,[838] now lie ftill.
and giue him[839] foape to act with.[840]
Mer. And act a little.
Tay. What do's he now, S[r].
Pov. Shew
The taking of *Tabacco*, with which the *Diuell*
Is fo delighted.
Fit. *Hum!*
Pov. And calls for *Hum*.
You takers of ftrong[841] *Waters*, and *Tabacco*,Marke this.
Fit. *Yellow, yellow, yellow, yellow, &c.*[842]
Pov. That's *Starch*! the *Diuells* Idoll of that colour.   75

He ratifies it, with clapping of his hands.
The proofes are pregnant.
Gvi. How the *Diuel* can act!
Pov. He is the Mafter of *Players*! Master *Guilt-head*,
And *Poets*, too! you heard him talke in rime!
I had forgot to obferue it to you, ere while!   80

Tay. See, he fpits fire.
Pov. O no, he plaies at *Figgum*,
The *Diuell* is the Author of wicked *Figgum*—
Sir Poule *interprets* Figgum *to be*[843] *a Iuglers game.*[844]
Man. Why fpeake you not vnto him?
Wit. If I had
All innocence of man to be indanger'd,[845]
And he could faue, or ruine it: I'ld not breath   85

---

[838] with [*To Meer.*] G
[839] SN. *him* om. 1641
[840] SN. om. G
[841] strong om. 1641
[842] &c. om. G
[843] SN. *to be* om. 1641
[844] SN. om. G
[845] endanger'd W, G

A ſyllable in requeſt, to ſuch a foole,[846]
He makes himſelfe.
Fit. *O they whiſper, whiſper, whiſper.*[847]
Wee ſhall haue more, of Diuells a ſcore,
To come to dinner, in mee the ſinner.
Eyt. Alas, poore Gentleman!
Pov. Put 'hem aſunder.   90

Keepe 'hem one from the other.
Man. Are you phrenticke,[848] Sir,
Or what graue dotage moues you, to take part
VVith so much villany? wee are not afraid
Either of law, or triall; let vs be
Examin'd what our ends were, what the meanes?   95

To worke by, and poſſibility of thoſe meanes.
Doe not conclude againſt vs, ere you heare vs.
Pov. I will not heare you, yet I will conclude
Out of the circumſtances.
Man. VVill you ſo, Sir?
Pov. Yes, they are palpable:
Man. Not as your folly: 100

Pov. I will diſcharge my conſcience, and doe all
To the *Meridian* of Iuſtice:
Gvi. You doe well, Sir.
Fit. *Prouide mee to eat, three or foure diſhes o' good meat,*
I'll feaſt them, and their traines, a Iuſtice head and braines
Shall be the firſt.
Pov. The *Diuell* loues not Iuſtice,
There you may ſee.
Fit. *A ſpare-rib O' my wife,*   106

And a whores purt'nance! a Guilt-head *whole.*
Pov. Be not you[849] troubled, Sir, the *Diuell* ſpeakes it.
Fit. *Yes, wis, Knight, ſhite, Poule, Ioule, owle, foule, troule, boule.*
Pov. *Crambe,*[850] another of the *Diuell's* games!   110

---

[846] foole] fellow 1641
[847] He makes himselfe] I'd rather fall 1641 O they whisper, they whisper, whisper, &c.
1641
[848] phrenetic G
[849] you om. W
[850] *Crambe*] Crambo W. G

Mer. Speake. Sir, fome *Greeke*, if you can.[851] Is not the *Iuftice*
A folemne gamefter?
Eve. Peace.
Fit. **Οὶ μοὶ, κακοδαιμων,**[852]
Καὶ τρισκακοδαίμων, καὶ τετράκις, καὶ πεντάκις,[853]
Καὶ δοδεκάκις,[854] **καὶ μυριάκις.**
Pov.[855] Hee curfes.
In *Greeke*, I thinke.
Eve. Your *Spanifh*, that I taught you.   115

Fit. *Quebrémos el ojo de burlas,*
Eve. How? your reft—
Let's breake his necke in ieft, the *Diuell* faies.
Fit.[856] *Di grátia, Signòr mio fe haúete denári fataméne parte.*
Mer. What, would the *Diuell* borrow money?
Fit. *Ouy, Ouy Monfieur, ùn pàuure Diable! Diablet in!*   120

Pov. It is the *diuell*, by his feuerall langauges.
Enter the Keeper *of* New-gate.[857]
Sha. Where's S^r. *Poule Ether-fide*?
Pov. Here, what's the matter?
Sha. O! fuch an accident falne out at *Newgate*, Sir:
A great piece of the prifon is rent downe!
The *Diuell* has beene there, Sir, in the body—   125

Of the young *Cut-Purfe*, was hang'd out this morning,
But, in new clothes, Sir, euery one of vs know him.
Thefe things were found in his pocket.
Amb. Thofe[858] are mine, S^r.
Sha. I thinke he was commited on your charge, Sir.
For a new felony.
Amb. Yes.
Sha. Hee's gone, Sir, now,   130

And left vs the dead body. But withall, Sir,
Such an infernall ftincke, and fteame behinde,
You cannot fee S^t. *Pulchars Steeple*, yet.
They fmell't as farre as *Ware*, as the wind lies,   134

---

[851] can. [*Aside to Fitz.*] G
[852] κακοδάμων 1692, 1716
[853] τισ 1692, 1716
[854] δωδεκάκις W, G
[855] *Aside to Fitz.* G
[856] Fit. *Ouy,*] in line 120, 1692, f.
[857] SN.] *Enter* Shackles, *with the things found on the body of the Cut-purse.* G
[858] Those] These W

By this time, ſure.
Fit. Is this vpon your credit, friend?
Fitz-dottrel *leaues counterfaiting.*[859]
Sha. Sir, you may ſee, and ſatisfie your ſelfe.
Fit. Nay, then, 'tis time to leaue off counterfeiting.
Sir I am not bewitch'd, nor haue a *Diuell*:
No more then you. I doe defie him, I,
And did abuſe you. Theſe two Gentlemen   140

Put me vpon it. (I haue faith againſt him)[860]
They taught me all my tricks. I will tell truth,
And ſhame the *Feind*. See, here, Sir, are my bellowes,
And my falſe belly, and my *Mouſe*, and all
That ſhould ha' come forth?
Man. Sir, are not you[861] aſham'd
Now of your ſolemne, ſerious vanity?   146

Pov. I will make honorable amends to truth.
Fit. And ſo will I. But theſe are *Coozeners*,[862] ſtill;
And ha' my land, as plotters, with my wife:
Who, though ſhe be not a witch, is worſe, a whore.   150

Man. Sir, you belie her. She is chaſte, and vertuous,
And we are honeſt. I doe know no glory
A man ſhould hope, by venting his owne follyes,
But you'll ſtill be an *Aſſe*, in ſpight of prouidence.
Pleaſe you goe in, Sir, and heare truths, then iudge 'hem:
And make amends for your late raſhneſſe; when,   156

You ſhall but heare the paines and care was taken,
To ſaue this foole from ruine (his *Grace* of *Drown'd-land*)
Fit. My land is drown'd indeed—
Pov. Peace.
Man. And how much
His modeſt, and too worthy wife hath ſuffer'd   160

By miſ-conſtruction, from him, you will bluſh,
Firſt, for your owne beliefe, more for his actions!
His land is his: and neuer, by my friend,
Or by my ſelfe, meant to another vſe,
But for her ſuccours, who hath equall right.   165

---

[859] SN.] *Fitz. [starts up.]* G
[860] () ret. G
[861] not you] you not W, G
[862] Coozners 1641 *Cozeners* 1692, 1716 cozeners W, G

If any other had worfe counfells in't,[863]
(I know I fpeake to thofe can apprehend mee)[864]
Let 'hem repent 'hem, and be not detected.
It is not manly to take ioy, or pride
In humane[865] errours. (wee doe all ill things,   170

They doe 'hem worft that loue 'hem, and dwell there,
Till the plague comes) The few that haue the feeds
Of goodneffe left, will fooner make their way
To a true life, by fhame, then punifhment.[866]

THE END.[867]

---

[863] in it G
[864] () ret. G
[865] human 1692, f.
[866] [*He comes forward for the Epilogue.* G
[867] 'The End.' after line 6 1692 om. 1716 W, G

THE EPILOGUE[868]

Thus, the Proiecter, *here, is ouer-throwne.*
But I haue now a Proiect *of mine owne,*
If it may paſſe: that no man would inuite
The Poet *from vs, to ſup forth to night,*   5

If the play *pleaſe. If it diſpleaſant be,*
We doe preſume, that no man will: nor wee.[869]

---

[868] 'The Epilogue.' om. G
[869] [*Exeunt.* G

Notes

The present edition includes whatever has been considered of value in the notes of preceding editions. It has been the intention in all cases to acknowledge facts and suggestions borrowed from such sources, whether quoted verbatim, abridged, or developed. Notes signed W. are from Whalley, G. from Gifford, C. from Cunningham. For other abbreviations the Bibliography should be consulted. Explanations of words and phrases are usually found only in the Glossary. References to this play are by act, scene, and line of the Text; other plays of Jonson are cited from the Gifford-Cunningham edition of 1875. The references are to play, volume and page.

Title-Page.

THE DIUELL IS AN ASSE. 'Schlegel, seizing with great felicity upon an untranslateable German idiom, called the play *Der dumme Teufel* [Schlegel's *Werke*, ed. Böcking, 6. 340]—a title which must be allowed to be twice as good as that of the English original. The phrase 'the Devil is an ass' appears to have been proverbial. See Fletcher's *The Chances*, Act 5. Sc. 2:
Dost thou thinkThe devil such an ass as people make him?'—Ward, *Eng. Drama* 2. 372.
A still more important passage occurs in Dekker's *If this be not a good Play*, a partial source of Jonson's drama:
Scu. Sweete-breads I hold my life, that diuels an asse.—Dekker, *Wks.* 3. 328.
Jonson uses it again in *The Staple of News*, *Wks.* 5. 188:
The conjurer cozened him with a candle's end; he was an ass.
Dekker (*Non-dram. Wks.* 2. 275) tells us the jest of a citizen who was told that the 'Lawyers get the Diuell and all: What an Asse, replied the Citizen is the diuell? If I were as he I would get some of them.'
HIS MAIESTIES SERVANTS. Otherwise known as the *King's Company*, and popularly spoken of as the *King's Men*. For an account of this company see Winter, ed. *Staple of News*, p. 121; and Fleay, *Biog. Chron.* 1. 356-7; 2. 403-4.
Ficta voluptatis, etc. The quotation is from Horace, *De Art. Poet.*, line 338. Jonson's translation is:
Let what thou feign'st for pleasure's sake, be nearThe truth.
Jonson makes use of this quotation again in his note 'To the Reader' prefixed to Act 3 of *The Staple of News*.
I. B. Fleay speaks of this printer as J. Benson (*Biog. Chron.* 1. 354). Benson did not 'take up freedom' until June 30, 1631 (*Sta. Reg.* 3. 686). Later he became a publisher (1635-40; *Sta. Reg.* 5. lxxxiv). I. B. was also the printer of *Bartholomew Fair* and *Staple of News*. J. Benson published a volume of Jonson's, containing *The Masque of the Gypsies* and other poems, in 1640 (*Brit.*

Museum Cat. and Yale Library). In the same year he printed the *Art of Poetry*, 12mo, and the *Execration against Vulcan*, 4to (cf. *Pub. of Grolier Club*, N. Y. 1893, pp. 130, 132). The evidence that I. B. was Benson is strong, but not absolutely conclusive.

ROBERT ALLOT. We find by Arber's reprint of the *Stationer's Register* that Robert Allot 'took up freedom' Nov. 7, 1625. He must have begun publishing shortly after, for under the date of Jan. 25, 1625-6 we find that Mistris Hodgettes 'assigned over unto him all her estate,' consisting of the copies of certain books, for the 'some of forty-five pounds.' The first entry of a book to Allot is made May 7, 1626. In 1630 Master Blount 'assigned over unto him all his estate and right in the copies' of sixteen of Shakespeare's plays. In 1632 Allot brought out the Second Folio of Shakespeare's works. On Sept. 7, 1631 *The Staple of News* was assigned to him. The last entry of a book in his name is on Sept. 12, 1635. The first mention of 'Mistris Allott' is under the date of Dec. 30, 1635. Under date of July 1, 1637 is the record of the assignment by Mistris Allott of certain books, formerly the estate of 'Master Roberte Allotts deceased.' Among these books are '37. *Shakespeares Workes* their part. 39. *Staple of Newes* a Play. 40. *Bartholomew fayre* a Play.' I have been able to find no record of *The Devil is an Ass* in the *Stationer's Register*.

the Beare. In the Shakespeare folio of 1632 Allot's sign reads 'the Black Beare.' The first mention of the shop in the *London Street Directory* is in 1575, among the 'Houses round the Churchyard.'

Pauls Church-yard. 'Before the Fire, which destroyed the old Cathedral, St. Paul's Churchyard was chiefly inhabited by stationers, whose shops were then, and until the year 1760, distinguished by signs.'—Wh-C.

THE PERSONS OF THE PLAY.

GVILT-HEAD, A Gold-smith. The goldsmiths seem to have been a prosperous guild. (See Stow, *Survey*, ed. Thoms, p. 114.) At this time they performed the office of banking, constituting the intermediate stage between the usurer and the modern banker. 'The goldsmiths began to borrow at interest in order to lend out to traders at a higher rate. In other words they became the connecting link between those who had money to lend and those who wished to borrow for trading purposes, or it might be to improve their estates. No doubt at first the goldsmiths merely acted as guardians of their clients' hoards, but they soon began to utilize those hoards much as bankers now make use of the money deposited with them.'—*Social England* 3. 544.

AMBLER. Jonson uses this name again in *Neptune's Triumph, Wks.* 8. 32:
Grave master Ambler, news-master o' Paul's,Supplies your capon.
It reappears in *The Staple of News*.

Her Gentlemanvsher. For an exposition of the character and duties of the gentleman-usher see the notes to 4. 4. 134. 201, 215.

Newgate. 'This gate hath of long time been a gaol, or prison for felons and trespassers, as appeareth by records in the reign of King John, and of other kings.'—Stow, *Survey*, ed. Thoms, p. 14.

THE PROLOGUE.

1 The DIVELL is an Asse. 'This is said by the prologue pointing to the *title* of the play, which as was then the custom, was painted in large letters and placed in some conspicuous part of the stage.'—G.

Cf. *Poetaster, After the second sounding*: 'What's here? THE ARRAIGNMENT!' Also *Wily Beguiled*: *Prol.* How now, my honest rogue? What play shall we have here to-night?

Player. Sir, you may look upon the title.*Prol.* What, *Spectrum* once again?'

Jonson often, but not invariably, announces the title of the play in the prologue or induction. Cf. *Every Man out, Cynthia's Revels, Poetaster*, and all plays subsequent to *Bart. Fair* except *Sad Shep.*

3 Grandee's. Jonson uses this affected form of address again in *Timber*, ed. Schelling. 22. 27

4 allowing vs no place. As Gifford points out, the prologue is a protest against the habit prevalent at the time of crowding the stage with stools for the accommodation of the spectators.

Dekker in Chapter 6 of *The Guls Horne-booke* gives the gallant full instructions as to the behavior proper to the play-house. The youth is advised to wait until 'the quaking prologue hath (by rubbing) got culor into his cheekes', and then 'to creepe from behind the Arras,' and plant himself 'on the very Rushes where the Commedy is to daunce, yea, and vnder the state of Cambises himselfe.' Sir John Davies makes a similar allusion *(Epigrams*, ed. Grosart, 2. 10). Jonson makes frequent reference to the subject. Cf. *Induction* to *The Staple of News*, *Every Man out, Wks.* 2. 31; *Prologue* to *Cynthia's Revels, Wks.* 2. 210, etc.

5 a subtill thing. I. e., thin, airy, spiritual, and so not occupying space.

6 worne in a thumbe-ring. 'Nothing was more common, as we learn from Lilly, than to carry about familiar spirits, shut up in rings, watches, sword-hilts, and other articles of dress.'—G.

I have been unable to verify Gifford's statement from Lilly, but the following passage from Harsnet's *Declaration* (p. 13) confirms it: 'For compassing of this treasure, there was a consociation betweene 3 or 4 priests, *deuill-coniurers*, and 4 *discouerers*, or *seers*, reputed to carry about with them, their familiars in rings, and glasses, by whose suggestion they came to notice of those golden hoards.'

Gifford says that thumb-rings of Jonson's day were set with jewels of an extraordinary size, and that they appear to have been 'more affected by magistrates and grave citizens than necromancers.' Cf. *1 Henry IV* 2. 4: 'I could have crept into any alderman's thumb-ring.' Also *Witts Recreat., Epig.* 623:

He wears a hoop-ring on his thumb; he hasOf gravidad a dose, full in the face.

Glapthorne, *Wit in a Constable*, 1639, 4. 1: 'An alderman—I may say to you, he has no more wit than the rest of the bench, and that lies in his thumb-ring.'

8 In compasse of a cheese-trencher. The figure seems forced to us, but it should be remembered that trenchers were a very important article of table equipment in Jonson's day. They were often embellished with 'posies,' and it is possible that Jonson was thinking of the brevity of such inscriptions. Cf. Dekker, *North-Ward Hoe* 3. 1 (*Wks.* 3. 38): 'Ile have you make 12. poesies for a dozen of cheese trenchers.' Also *Honest Whore*, Part I, Sc. 13; and Middleton, *Old Law* 2. 1 (*Wks.* 2. 149); *No Wit, no Help like a Woman's* 2. 1 (*Wks.* 4. 322).

15 Like the young adders. It is said that young adders, when frightened, run into their mother's mouth for protection.

16 Would wee could stand due North. I. e., be as infallible as the compass.

17 Muscouy glasse. Cf. Marston, *Malcontent, Wks.* 1. 234: 'She were an excellent lady, but that her face peeleth like Muscovy glass.' Reed (*Old Plays* 4. 38) quotes from Giles Fletcher's *Russe Commonwealth*, 1591, p. 10: 'In the province of Corelia, and about the river Duyna towards the North-sea, there groweth a soft rock which they call Slude. This they cut into pieces, and so tear it into thin *flakes, which naturally it is apt for*, and so use it for glasse lanthorns and such like. It giveth both inwards and outwards a clearer light then glasse, and for this respect is better than either glasse or horne; for that it neither breaketh like glasse, nor yet will burne like the lanthorne.' Dekker *(Non-dram. Wks.* 2. 135) speaks of a 'Muscouie Lanthorne.' See Gloss.

22 the Diuell of Edmunton. *The Merry Devil of Edmunton* was acted by the King's Men at the Globe before Oct. 22, 1607. It has been conjecturally assigned to Shakespeare and to Drayton. Hazlitt describes it as 'perhaps the first example of sentimental comedy we have' (see *O. Pl.*, 4th ed., 10. 203 f.). Fleay, who believes Drayton to be the author, thinks that the 'Merry devil' of *The Merchant of Venice* 2. 3, alludes to this play (*Biog. Chron.* 1. 151 and 2. 213). There were six editions in the 17th century, all in quarto—1608, 1612, 1617, 1626, 1631, 1655. Middleton, *The Black Book, Wks.* 8. 36, alludes to it pleasantly in connection with *A Woman kill'd with Kindness.* Genest mentions it as being revived in 1682. Cf. also *Staple of News*, 1st Int.

26 If this Play doe not like, etc. Jonson refers to Dekker's play of 1612 (see Introduction). On the title-page of this play we find *If it be not good, The Diuel is in it*. At the head of Act. 1, however, the title reads *If this be not a good play*, etc.

ACT I.

1. 1. 1 Hoh, hoh, etc. 'Whalley is right in saying that this is the conventional way for the devil to make his appearance in the old morality-plays. Gifford objects on the ground that 'it is not the roar of terror; but the boisterous expression of sarcastic merriment at the absurd petition of Pug;' an objection, the truth of which does not necessarily invalidate Whalley's statement. Jonson of course adapts the old conventions to his own ends. See Introduction.

1. 1. 9 Entring a Sow, to make her cast her farrow? Cf. Dekker, etc., *Witch of Edmonton* (*Wks.* 4. 423): '*Countr.* I'll be sworn, *Mr. Carter*, she bewitched Gammer *Washbowls* sow, to cast her Pigs a day before she would have farried.'

1. 1. 11 Totnam. 'The first notice of Tottenham Court, as a place of public entertainment, contained in the books of the parish of St. Gile's-in-the-Fields, occurs under the year 1645 (Wh-C.). Jonson, however, as early as 1614 speaks of 'courting it to Totnam to eat cream' (*Bart. Fair*, Act 1. Sc. 1, *Wks.* 4. 362). George Wither, in the *Britain's Remembrancer*, 1628, refers to the same thing:

And Hogsdone, Islington, and Tothnam-court,For cakes and cream had then no small resort.

Tottenham Fields were until a comparatively recent date a favorite place of entertainment.

1. 1. 13 a tonning of Ale, etc. Cf. *Sad Shep.*, *Wks.* 6. 276:

The house wives tun not work, nor the milk churn.

1. 1. 15 Spight o' the housewiues cord, or her hot spit. 'There be twentie severall waies to make your butter come, which for brevitie I omit; as to bind your cherne with a rope, to thrust thereinto a red hot spit, &c.'— Scot, *Discovery*, p. 229.

1. 1. 16, 17 Or some good Ribibe ... witch. This seems to be an allusion, as Fleay suggests, to Heywood's *Wise-Woman of Hogsdon*. The witch of that play declares her dwelling to be in 'Kentstreet' (Heywood's *Wks.* 5. 294). A ribibe meant originally a musical instrument, and was synonymous with rebec. By analogy, perhaps, it was applied to a shrill-voiced old woman. This is Gifford's explanation. The word occurs again in Skelton's *Elynour Rummyng*, l. 492, and in Chaucer, *The Freres Tale*, l. 1377: 'a widwe, an old ribybe.' Skeat offers the following explanation: 'I suspect that this old joke, for such it clearly is, arose in a very different way [from that suggested by Gifford], viz. from a pun upon *rebekke*, a fiddle, and *Rebekke*, a married woman, from the mention of Rebecca in the marriage-service. Chaucer himself notices the latter in E. 1704.'

1. 1. 16 Kentish Towne. Kentish Town, Cantelows, or Cantelupe town is the most ancient district in the parish of Pancras. It was originally a small village, and as late as the eighteenth century a lonely and somewhat dangerous spot. In later years it became noted for its Assembly Rooms. In 1809 Hughson (*London* 6. 369) called it 'the most romantic hamlet in the parish of Pancras.' It is now a part of the metropolis. See Samuel Palmer's *St. Pancras*, London, 1870.

1. 1. 17 Hogsden. Stow (*Survey*, ed. Thoms, p. 158) describes Hogsden as a 'large street with houses on both sides.' It was a prebend belonging to St. Paul's. In Hogsden fields Jonson killed Gabriel Spenser in a duel in 1598. These fields were a great resort for the citizens on a holiday. The eating of cream there is frequently mentioned. See the quotation from Wither under note 1. 1. 11, and *Alchemist*, *Wks.* 4. 155 and 175:

——Ay, he would have builtThe city new; and made a ditch about itOf silver, should have run with cream from Hogsden.

Stephen in *Every Man in* dwelt here, and so was forced to associate with 'the archers of Finsbury, or the citizens that come a-ducking to Islington ponds.' Hogsden or Hoxton, as it is now called, is to-day a populous district of the metropolis.

1. 1. 18 shee will not let you play round Robbin. The expression is obscure, and the dictionaries afford little help. Round-robin is a common enough phrase, but none of the meanings recorded is applicable in this connection. Some child's game, played in a circle, seems to be referred to, or the expression may be a cant term for 'play the deuce.' Robin is a name of many associations, and its connection with Robin Hood, Robin Goodfellow, and 'Robert's Men' ('The third old rank of the Canting crew.'—Grose.) makes such an interpretation more or less probable.

M. N. G. in *N. & Q.* 9th Ser. 10. 394 says that 'when a man does a thing in a circuitous, involved manner he is sometimes said "to go all round Robin Hood's barn to do it."' 'Round Robin Hood's barn' may possibly have been the name of a game which has been shortened to 'round Robin.'

1. 1. 21 By a Middlesex Iury. 'A reproof no less severe than merited. It appears from the records of those times, that many unfortunate creatures were condemned and executed on charges of the rediculous nature here enumerated. In many instances, the judge was well convinced of the innocence of the accused, and laboured to save them; but such were the gross and barbarous prejudices of the juries, that they would seldom listen to his recommendations; and he was deterred from shewing mercy, in the last place by the brutal ferociousness of the people, *whose teeth were set on edge with't*, and who clamoured tumultuously for the murder of the accused.'—G.

1. 1. 32 Lancashire. This, as Gifford says, 'was the very hot-bed of witches.' Fifteen were brought to trial on Aug. 19, 1612, twelve of whom were convicted and burnt on the day after their trial 'at the common place of execution near to Lancaster.' The term 'Lancashire Witches' is now applied to the beautiful women for which the country is famed. The details of the Lancaster trial are contained in Potts' *Discoverie* (Lond. 1613), and a satisfactory account is given by Wright in his *Sorcery and Magic*.

1. 1. 33 or some parts of Northumberland. The first witch-trial in Northumberland, so far as I have been able to ascertain, occurred in 1628. This was the trial of the Witch of Leeplish.

1. 1. 37 a Vice. See Introduction.

1. 1. 38 To practice there-with any play-fellow. See variants. The editors by dropping the hyphen have completely changed the sense of the passage. Pug wants a vice in order that he may corrupt his play-fellows *there-with*.

1. 1. 41 ff.   **Why, any Fraud;**

   Or Couetousnesse; or Lady Vanity;

   Or old Iniquity. Fraud is a character in Robert Wilson's *The Three Ladies of London*, printed 1584, and *The Three Lords and Three Ladies of London*, c 1588, printed 1590. Covetousness appears in *Robin Conscience*, c 1530, and is applied to one of the characters in *The Staple of News, Wks.* 5. 216.

Vanity is one of the characters in *Lusty Juventus* (see note 1. 1. 50) and in *Contention between Liberality and Prodigality*, printed 1602 (*O. Pl.* 4th ed., 8. 328). She seems to have been a favorite with the later dramatists, and is frequently mentioned (*I Henry IV.* 2. 4; *Lear* 2. 2; *Jew of Malta* 2. 3, Marlowe's *Wks.* 2. 45). Jonson speaks of her again in *The Fox, Wks.* 3. 218. For Iniquity see Introduction, p. xxxviii.

The change in punctuation (see variants), as well as that two lines below, was first suggested by Upton in a note appended to his *Critical Observations on Shakespeare*. Whalley silently adopted the reading in both cases.

1. 1. 43 I'll call him hither. See variants. Coleridge, *Notes*, p. 280, says: 'That is, against all probability, and with a (for Jonson) impossible violation of character. The words plainly belong to Pug, and mark at once his simpleness and his impatience.' Cunningham says that he arrived independently at the same conclusion, and points out that it is plain from Iniquity's opening speech that *he* understood the words to be Pug's.

1. 1. 49 thy dagger. See note 1. 1. 85.

1. 1. 50 lusty Iuuentus. The morality-play of *Lusty Juventus* was written by R. Wever about 1550. It 'breathes the spirit of the dogmatic reformation of the Protector Somerset,' but 'in spite of its abundant theology it is neither ill written, nor ill constructed' (Ward, *Eng. Drama* 1. 125). It seems to have been very popular, and the expression 'a lusty Juventus' became proverbial. It is used as early as 1582 by Stanyhurst, *Aeneis* 2 (Arber). 64 and as late as Heywood's *Wise Woman of Hogsdon* (c 1638), where a gallant is apostrophised as Lusty Juventus (Act 4). (See Nares and *NED.*) Portions of the play had been revived not many years before this within the tragedy of *Thomas More* (1590, acc. to Fleay 1596) under the title of *The Mariage of Witt and Wisedome*. 'By dogs precyous woundes' is one of the oaths used by Lusty Juventus in the old play, and may be the 'Gogs-nownes' referred to here (*O. Pl.*, 4th ed., 2. 84). 'Gogs nowns' is used several times in *Like will to Like* (*O. Pl.*, 4th ed., 3. 327, 331, etc.).

1. 1. 51 In a cloake to thy heele. See note 1. 1. 85.

1. 1. 51 a hat like a pent-house. 'When they haue walkt thorow the streetes, weare their hats ore their eye-browes, like pollitick penthouses, which commonly make the shop of a Mercer, or a Linnen Draper, as dark as a roome in Bedlam.' Dekker, *West-ward Hoe, Wks.* 2. 286.

With your hat penthouse-like o'er the slope of your eyes.—*Love's Labour's Lost* 3. 1. 17.

Halliwell says (*L. L. L.*, ed. Furness, p. 85): 'An open shed or shop, forming a protection against the weather. The house in which Shakespeare was born had a penthouse along a portion of it.' In Hollyband's *Dictionarie*, 1593, it is spelled 'pentice,' which shows that the rime to 'Juventus' is probably not a distorted one.

1. 1. 52 thy doublet all belly. 'Certaine I am there was neuer any kinde of apparell euer inuented that could more disproportion the body of man then these Dublets with great bellies, ... stuffed with foure, fiue or six pound of Bombast at the least.'—Stubbes, *Anat.*, Part 1, p. 55.

1. 1. 54 how nimble he is! 'A perfect idea of his activity may be formed from the incessant skipping of the modern Harlequin.'—G.

1. 1. 56 the top of Pauls-steeple. As Gifford points out, Iniquity is boasting of an impossible feat. St. Paul's steeple had been destroyed by fire in 1561, and was not yet restored. Several attempts were made and money collected. 'James I. countenanced a sermon at *Paul's Cross* in favor of so pious an undertaking, but nothing was done till 1633 when reparations commenced with some activity, and Inigo Jones designed, at the expense of Charles I., a classic portico to a Gothic church.'—Wh-C.

Lupton, *London Carbonadoed*, 1632, writes: 'The head of St. Paul's hath twice been troubled with a burning fever, and so the city, to keep it from a third danger, lets it stand without a head.' Gifford says that 'the Puritans took a malignant pleasure in this mutilated state of the cathedral.' Jonson refers to the disaster in his *Execration upon Vulcan, U. 61, Wks.* 8. 408. See also Dekker, *Paules Steeples complaint, Non-dram. Wks.* 4. 2.

1. 1. 56 Standard in Cheepe. This was a water-stand or conduit in the midst of the street of West Cheaping, where executions were formerly held. It was in a ruinous condition in 1442, when it was repaired by a patent from Henry VI. Stow (*Survey*, ed. Thoms, p. 100) gives a list of famous executions at this place, and says that 'in the year 1399, Henry IV. caused the blanch charters made by Richard II. to be burnt there.'

1. 1. 58 a needle of Spaine. Gifford, referring to Randolph's *Amyntos* and Ford's *Sun's Darling*, points out that 'the best needles, as well as other sharp instruments, were, in that age, and indeed long before and after it, imported from Spain.' The tailor's needle was in cant language commonly termed a *Spanish pike*.

References to the Spanish needle are frequent. It is mentioned by Jonson in *Chloridia, Wks.* 8. 99; by Dekker, *Wks.* 4. 308; and by Greene, *Wks.* 11. 241. Howes (p. 1038) says: 'The making of Spanish Needles, was first taught in England by Elias Crowse, a Germane, about the eight yeare of Queene Elizabeth, and in Queen Maries time, there was a Negro made fine Spanish Needles in Cheape-side, but would neuer teach his Art to any.'

1. 1. 59 the Suburbs. The suburbs were the outlying districts without the walls of the city. Cf. Stow, *Survey*, ed. Thoms, p. 156 f. They were for the most part the resort of disorderly persons. Cf. B. & Fl., *Humorous Lieut.* 1. 1.; Massinger, *Emperor of the East* 1. 2.; Shak., *Jul. Caes.* 2. 1; and Nares, *Gloss.* Wheatley (ed. *Ev. Man in*, p. 1) quotes Chettle's *Kind Harts Dreame*, 1592: 'The suburbs of the citie are in many places no other but dark dennes for adulterers, thieves, murderers, and every mischief worker; daily experience before the magistrates confirms this for truth.' Cf. also Glapthorne, *Wit in a Constable, Wks.*, ed. 1874, 1. 219:

——make safe retreatInto the Suburbs, there you may finde cast wenches.

In *Every Man in, Wks.* 1. 25, a 'suburb humour' is spoken of.

1. 1. 60 Petticoate-lane. This is the present Middlesex Street, Whitechapel. It was formerly called Hog Lane and was beautified with 'fair hedge-rows,' but by Stow's time it had been made 'a continual building throughout of garden houses and small cottages' (*Survey*, ed. 1633, p. 120 b). Strype tells us that the house of the Spanish Ambassador, supposedly the famous Gondomar, was situated there (*Survey* 2. 28). In his day the inhabitants were French Protestant weavers, and later Jews of a disreputable sort. That its reputation was somewhat unsavory as early as Nash's time we learn from his *Prognostication* (*Wks.* 2. 149):

'If the Beadelles of Bridewell be carefull this Summer, it may be hoped that Peticote lane may be lesse pestered with ill aires than it was woont: and the houses there so cleere clensed, that honest women may dwell there without any dread of the whip and the carte.' Cf. also *Penniless Parliament, Old Book Collector's Misc.* 2. 16: 'Many men shall be so venturously given, as they shall go into Petticoat Lane, and yet come out again as honestly as they went first in.'

1. 1. 60 the Smock-allies. Petticoat Lane led from the high street, Whitechapel, to *Smock Alley* or Gravel Lane. See Hughson 2. 387.

1. 1. 61 Shoreditch. Shoreditch was formerly notorious for the disreputable character of its women. 'To die in Shoreditch' seems to have been a proverbial phrase, and is so used by Dryden in *The Kind Keeper*, 4to, 1680. Cf. Nash, *Pierce Pennilesse, Wks.* 2. 94: 'Call a Leete at *Byshopsgate*, & examine how euery second house in *Shorditch* is mayntayned; make a priuie search in *Southwarke*, and tell mee how many Shee-Inmates you fin de: nay, goe where you will in the Suburbes, and bring me two Virgins that haue vowd Chastity and Ile builde a Nunnery.' Also *ibid.*, p. 95; Gabriel Harvey, *Prose Wks.*, ed. Grosart. 2. 169; and Dekker, *Wks.* 3. 352.

1. 1. 61 Whitechappell. 'Till within memory the district north of the High Street was one of the very worst localities in London; a region of narrow and filthy streets, yards and alleys, many of them wholly occupied by thieves' dens, the receptacles of stolen property, gin-spinning dog-holes, low brothels, and putrescent lodging-houses,—a district unwholesome to approach and unsafe for a decent person to traverse even in the day-time.'—Wh-C.

1. 1. 61, 2 and so to Saint Kathernes.
To drinke with the Dutch there, and take forth their patternes.
Saint Kathernes was the name of a hospital and precinct without London. The hospital was said to have been founded by Queen Matilda, wife of King Stephen. In *The Alchemist* (*Wks.* 4. 161), Jonson speaks of its having been used 'to keep the better sort of mad-folks.' It was also employed as a reformatory for fallen women, and it is here that Winifred in *Eastward Ho* (ed. Schelling, p. 84) finds an appropriate landing-place.

From this hospital there was 'a continual street, or filthy strait passage, with alleys of small tenements, or cottages, built, inhabited by sailors' victuallers, along by the river of Thames, almost to Radcliff, a good mile from the Tower.'—Stow, ed. Thoms, p. 157.

The precinct was noted for its brew-houses and low drinking places. In *The Staple of News* Jonson speaks of 'an ale-wife in Saint Katherine's, At the Sign of the Dancing Bears' (*Wks.* 5. 226). The same tavern is referred to in the *Masque of Augurs* as well as 'the brew-houses in St. Katherine's.' The sights of the place are enumerated in the same masque.

The present passage seems to indicate that the precinct was largely inhabited by Dutch. In the *Masque of Augurs* Vangoose speaks a sort of Dutch jargon, and we know that a Flemish cemetery was located here (see Wh-C). Cf. also Sir Thomas Overbury's *Character of A drunken Dutchman resident in England*, ed. Morley, p. 72: 'Let him come over never so lean, and plant him but one month near the brew-houses of St. Catherine's and he will be puffed up to your hand like a bloat herring.' Dutch weavers had been imported into England as early as the reign of Edward III. (see Howes, p. 870 a), and in the year 1563 great numbers of Netherlanders with their wives and children fled into England owing to the civil dissension in Flanders (Howes, p. 868 a). They bore a reputation for hard drinking (cf. *Like will to Like*, O. Pl. 3. 325; Dekker, *Non-dram. Wks.* 3. 12; Nash, *Wks.* 2. 81, etc.).

The phrase 'to take forth their patternes' is somewhat obscure, and seems to have been forced by the necessity for a rhyme. Halliwell says that 'take forth' is equivalent to 'learn,' and the phrase seems therefore to mean 'take their measure,' 'size them up,' with a view to following their example. It is possible, of course, that actual patterns of the Dutch weavers or tailors are referred to.

1. 1. 63 Custome-house key. This was in Tower Street on the Thames side. Stow (ed. Thoms, pp. 51. 2) says that the custom-house was built in the sixth year of Richard II. Jonson mentions the place again in *Every Man in, Wks.* 1. 69.

1. 1. 66 the Dagger, and the Wool-sacke. These were two ordinaries or public houses of low repute, especially famous for their pies. There were two taverns called the 'Dagger,' one in Holborn and one in Cheapside. It is probably to the former of these that Jonson refers. It is mentioned again in the *Alchemist* (*Wks.* 4. 24 and 165) and in Dekker's *Satiromastix* (*Wks.* 1. 200). Hotten says that the sign of a dagger was common, and arose from its being a charge in the city arms.

The Woolsack was without Aldgate. It was originally a wool-maker's sign. Machyn mentions the tavern in 1555; and it is alluded to in Dekker, *Shoemaker's Holiday, Wks.* 1. 61. See Wh-C. and Hotten's *History of Signboards*, pp. 325 and 362.

1. 1. 69 Belins-gate. Stow (ed. Thoms, p. 78) describes Belins-gate as 'a large water-gate, port or harborough.' He mentions the tradition that the name was derived from that of Belin, King of the Britons, but discredits it. Billingsgate is on the Thames, a little below London Bridge, and is still the great fish-market of London.

1. 1. 70 shoot the Bridge. The waterway under the old London Bridge was obstructed by the narrowness of the arches, by cornmills built in some of the openings, and by the great waterworks at its southern end. 'Of the arches left open some were too narrow for the passage of boats of any kind. The widest was only 36 feet, and the resistance caused to so large a body of water on the rise and fall of the tide by this contraction of its channel produced a fall or rapid under the bridge, so that it was necessary to "ship oars" to *shoot the bridge*, as it was called,—an undertaking, to amateur watermen especially, not unattended with danger. "With the flood-tide it was impossible, and with the ebb-tide dangerous to pass through or *shoot* the arches of the bridge." In the latter case prudent passengers landed above the bridge, generally at the *Old Swan Stairs*, and walked to some wharf, generally *Billingsgate*, below it.'—Wh-C.

1. 1. 70 the Cranes i' the Vintry. These were 'three strong cranes of timber placed on the Vintry wharf by the Thames to crane up wine there (Stow, ed. Thoms, p. 00). They were situated in Three Cranes' lane, and near by was the famous tavern mentioned as one of the author's favorite resorts (*Bart. Fair* 1. 1, *Wks.* 4. 356). Jonson speaks of it again in *The Silent Woman, Wks.* 3. 376, and in the *Masque of Augurs*. Pepys visited the place on January 23, 1662, and describes the best room as 'a narrow dogg-hole' in which he and his friends were crammed so close 'that it made me loath my company and victuals, and a sorry dinner it was too.' Cf. also Dekker, (*Non-dram. Wks.* 8. 77).

1. 1. 72 the Strand. This famous street was formerly the road between the cities of Westminster and London. That many lawyers lived in this vicinity we learn from Middleton (*Father Hubburd's Tales, Wks.* 8. 77).

1. 1. 73 Westminster-hall. It was once the hall of the King's palace at Westminster, originally built by William Rufus. The present hall was formed 1397-99. Here the early parliaments were held. 'This great hall hath been the usual place of pleadings, and ministration of justice.'—Stow, ed. Thoms, p. 174.

1. 1. 75 so Veluet to Leather. Velvet seems to have been much worn by lawyers. Cf. Overbury, *Characters*, p. 72: 'He loves his friend as a counsellor at law loves the velvet breeches he was first made barrister in.'

1. 1. 85 In his long coat, shaking his wooden dagger. See Introduction.

1. 1. 93 Cokeley. Whalley says that he was the master of a puppet show, and this has been accepted by all authorities (Gifford, ed.; Nares, *Gloss.*; Alden, ed. of *Bart. Fair*). He seems, however, to have been rather an improviser like Vennor, or a mountebank with a gift of riming. He is mentioned several times by Jonson: *Bart. Fair, Wks.* 4. 422, 3: 'He has not been sent for, and sought out for nothing, at your great city-suppers, to put down Coriat and Cokely.' *Epigr.* 129; *To Mime, Wks.* 8. 229:

Or, mounted on a stool, thy face doth hitOn some new gesture, that's imputed wit?—Thou dost out-zany Cokely, Pod; nay Gue:And thine own Coryat too.

1. 1. 94 Vennor. Gifford first took Vennor to be a juggler, but corrected his statement in the *Masque of Augurs, Wks.* 7. 414. He says: 'Fenner, whom I supposed to be a juggler, was a rude kind of *improvisatore*. He was altogether ignorant; but possessed a wonderful facility in pouring out doggrel verse. He says of himself,

Yet, without boasting, let me boldly say
I'll rhyme with any man that breathes this day
Upon a subject, in *extempore*, etc.

He seems to have made a wretched livelihood by frequenting city feasts, &c., where, at the end of the entertainment, he was called in to mount a stool and amuse the company by stringing together a number of vile rhymes upon any given subject. To this the quotation alludes. Fenner is noticed by the duchess of Newcastle: "For the numbers every schoolboy can make them on his fingers, and for the *rime*, Fenner would put down Ben Jonson, and yet neither boy nor Fenner so good poets." This, too, is the person meant in the Cambridge answer to Corbet's satire:

A ballad late was made,But God knows who the penner;Some say the rhyming sculler,And others say 'twas Fenner. p. 24.

Fenner was so famed for his faculty of rhyming, that James, who, like Bartholomew Cokes, would willingly let no raree-show escape him, sent for him to court. Upon which Fenner added to his other titles that of his "Majesty's Riming Poet." This gave offense to Taylor, the Water poet, and helped to produce that miserable squabble printed among his works, and from which I have principally derived the substance of this note.'—G.

'In Richard Brome's *Covent Garden Weeded* (circ. 1638), we have: "Sure 'tis Fenner or his ghost. He was a riming souldier." (p. 42.)'—C.

The controversy referred to may be found in the Spenser Society's reprint of the 1630 folio of Taylor's *Works*, 1869, pp. 304-325. Here may be gathered a few more facts regarding the life of Fenner (or Fennor as it should be spelled), among them that he was apprenticed when a boy to a blind harper. In the quarrel, it must be confessed, Fennor does not appear markedly inferior to his derider either in powers of versification or in common decency. The quarrel between the poets took place in October, 1614, and Fennor's admittance to court seems to be referred to in the present passage.

1. 1. 95 a Sheriffes dinner. This was an occasion of considerable extravagance. Entick (*Survey* 1. 499) tells us that in 1543 a sumptuary law was passed 'to prevent luxurious eating or feasting in a time of scarcity; whereby it was ordained, that the lord-mayor should not have more than seven dishes at dinner or supper,' and 'an alderman and sheriff no more than six.'

1. 1. 96 Skip with a rime o' the Table, from New-nothing. What is meant by *New-nothing* I do not know. From the construction it would seem to indicate the place from which the fool was accustomed to take his leap, but it is possible that the word should be connected with *rime*, and may perhaps be the translation of a Greek or Latin title for some book of *facetiae* published about this time. Such wits as Fennor and Taylor doubtless produced many pamphlets, the titles of which have not been recorded. In 1622 Taylor brought out a collection of verse called 'Sir Gregory Non-sense His Newes from no place,' and it may have been this very book in manuscript that suggested Jonson's title. In the play of *King Darius*, 1106, one of the actors says: 'I had rather then my new nothing, I were gon.'

1. 1. 97 his Almaine-leape into a custard. 'In the earlier days, when the city kept a fool it was customary for him at public entertainments, to leap into a large bowl of custard set on purpose.'—W. Whalley refers also to *All's well that Ends Well* 2. 5: 'You have made a shift to run into it, boots and all, like him that leapt into the custard.'

Gifford quotes Glapthorne, *Wit in a Const.*:

The custard, with the four and twenty nooksAt my lord Mayor's feast.

He continues: 'Indeed, no common supply was required; for, besides what the Corporation (great devourers of custard) consumed on the spot, it appears that it was thought no breach of city manners to send, or take some of it home with them for the use of their ladies.' In the excellent old play quoted above, Clara twits her uncle with this practise:

Now shall you, sir, as 'tis a frequent custom,'Cause you're a worthy alderman of a ward,Feed me with custard, and perpetual white brothSent from the lord Mayor's feast.'

Cunningham says: 'Poets of a comparatively recent date continue to associate mayors and custards.' He Quotes Prior *(Alma,* Cant. 1) and a letter from Bishop Warburton to Hurd (Apr. 1766): 'I told him (the Lord Mayor) in what I thought he was defective—that I was greatly disappointed to see no custard at table. He said that they had been so ridiculed for their custard that none had ventured to make its appearance for some years.' Jonson mentions the 'quaking custards' again in *The Fox, Wks.* 3. 164., and in *The Staple of News, Wks.* 5. 196, 7.

An Almain-leap was a dancing leap. 'Allemands were danced here a few years back' (Nares). Cunningham quotes from Dyce: 'Rabelais tells us that Gargantua "wrestled, ran, jumped, not at three steps and a leap, ... nor yet at the Almane's, for, said Gymnast, these jumps are for the wars altogether unprofitable and of no use." *Rabelais,* Book 1, C. 23.'

Bishop Barlow, *Answer to a Catholike Englishman,* p. 231, Lond. 1607, says: 'Now heere the Censurer makes an Almaine leape, skipping 3 whole pages together' (quoted in *N. & Q.* 1st Ser. 10. 157).

1. 1. 97 their hoods. The French hood was still worn by citizens' wives. Thus in the *London Prodigal,* ed. 1709:

No *Frank,* I'll have thee go like a *Citizen*In a Garded Gown, and a *French* Hood.

When Simon Eyre is appointed sheriff, his wife immediately inquires for a 'Fardingale-maker' and a 'French-hood maker' (Dekker, *Wks.* 1. 39). Strutt says that French hoods were out of fashion by the middle of the 17th century *(Antiq.* 3. 93). See the frequent references to this article of apparel in *Bart. Fair.* It is interesting to notice that the hoods are worn at dinner.

1. 1. 106, 7. The readings of 'Whalley and Gifford are distinctly inferior to the original.

1. 1. 112, 3 Car-men Are got into the yellow starch. Starch was introduced in the age of Elizabeth to meet the needs of the huge Spanish ruff which had come into favor some years before (see *Soc. Eng.,* p. 386). It was frequently colored. In Middleton and Rowley's *World Tossed at Tennis* five different colored starches are personified. Stubbes says that it was 'of all collours and hues.' Yellow starch must have come into fashion not long before this play was acted, for in the *Owle's Allmanacke,* published in 1618, it is said: 'Since yellow bandes and saffroned chaperoones came vp, is not above two yeeres past.' This, however, is not to be taken literally, for the execution of Mrs. Turner took place Nov. 14, 1615. Of her we read in Howell's Letters 1. 2: 'Mistress *Turner,* the first inventress of *yellow Starch,* was executed in a Cobweb Lawn Ruff of that colour at *Tyburn;* and with her I believe that *yellow Starch,* which so much disfigured our Nation, and rendered them so ridiculous and fantastic, will receive its Funeral.' Sir S. D'Ewes *(Autobiog.* 1. 69) says that from that day it did, indeed, grow 'generally to be detested and disused.' *The Vision of Sir Thomas Overbury*, 1616 (quoted in Amos, *Great Oyer*, p. 50) speaks of

——that fantastic, ugly fall and ruff

Daub'd o'er with that base starch of yellow stuff

as already out of fashion. Its popularity must have returned, however, since Barnaby Riche in the *Irish Hubbub*,1622, p. 40, laments that 'yellow starcht bands' were more popular than ever, and he prophesies that the fashion 'shortly will be as conversant amongst taylors, tapsters, and tinkers, as now they have brought tobacco.'

D'Ewes also in describing the procession of King James from Whitehall to Westminster, Jan. 30, 1620, says that the king saw one window 'full of gentlewomen or ladies, all in yellow bandes,' whereupon he called out 'A pox take yee,' and they all withdrew in shame. In *The Parson's Wedding*, printed 1664, *O. Pl.* 11. 498, it is spoken of as out of fashion. Yellow starch is mentioned again in 5. 8. 74. 5, and a ballad of 'goose-green starch and the devil' is mentioned in *Bart. Fair, Wks.* 4. 393. Similarly, Nash speaks in *Pierce Pennilesse, Wks.* 2. 44. of a 'Ballet of Blue starch and poaking stick.' See also Dodsley's note on *Albumazar, O. Pl.* 7. 132.

1. 1. 113, 4 Chimney-sweepers To their tabacco. See the quotation from Riche in the last note and note 5. 8. 71.

1. 1. 114, 5 Hum, Meath, and Obarni. Hum is defined B. E. *Dict. Cant. Crew, Hum* or *Humming Liquor*, Double Ale, Stout, Pharoah. It is mentioned in Fletcher's *Wild Goose Chase* 2. 3 and Heywood's *Drunkard.* p. 48. Meath or mead is still made in England. It was a favorite drink in the Middle Ages, and consisted of a mixture of honey and water with the addition of a ferment. Harrison, *Description of England*, ed. Furnivall, 1. 161, thus describes it: 'There is a kind of swish swash made also in Essex, and diuerse other places, with honicombs and water, which the [homelie] countrie wiues, putting some pepper and a little other spice among, call mead, verie good in mine opinion for such as loue to be loose bodied [at large, or a little eased of the cough,] otherwise it differeth so much from the true metheglin, as chalke from cheese.'

Obarni was long a crux for the editors and dictionaries. Gifford (*Wks.* 7. 226) supplied a part of the quotation from *Pimlyco or Runne Red-Cap*, 1609, completed by James Platt, Jun. (*N. & Q.* 9th Ser. 3. 306). in which 'Mead Obarne and Mead Cherunk' are mentioned as drinks

——that whet the spitesOf Russes and cold Muscovites.

Mr. Platt first instanced the existing Russian word *obarni* or *obvarnyi* (see Gloss.), meaning 'boiling, scalding,' and C. C. B. (*N. & Q.* 9. 3. 413) supplied a quotation from the account of the voyage of Sir Jerome Bowes in 1583 (Harris's *Travels* 1. 535), in which 'Sodden Mead' appears among the items of diet supplied by the Emperor to the English Ambassador. The identification was completed with a quotation given by the *Stanford Dict.*: '1598 Hakluyt *Voy.* 1. 461 One veather of sodden mead called *Obarni.*'

1. 1. 119 your rope of sand. This occupation is mentioned again in 5. 2. 6.

1. 1. 126 Tissue gownes. Howes, p. 869. tells us that John Tuce, 'dweling neere Shorditch Church', first attained perfection in the manufacture of cloth of tissue.

1. 1. 127 Garters and roses. Howes, p. 1039, says that 'at this day (1631) men of meane rancke weare Garters, and shooe Roses, of more than fiue pound price.' Massinger, in the *City Madam, Wks.*, p. 334, speaks of 'roses worth a family.' Cf. also John Taylor's *Works*, 1630 (quoted in *Hist. Brit. Cost.*):

Weare a farm in shoe-strings edged with goldAnd spangled garters worth a copyhold.

1. 1. 128 Embroydred stockings. 'Then haue they nether-stocks to these gay hosen, not of cloth (though neuer so fine) for that is thought to base, but of *Iarnsey* worsted, silk, thred, and such like, or els at the least of the finest yarn *that* can be, and so curiouslye knit with open seam down the leg, with quirks and clocks about the ancles, and sometime (haply) interlaced with gold or siluer threds, as is wonderful to behold.'—Stubbes, *Anat.*, Part 1, p. 57. The selling of stockings was a separate trade at this time, and great attention was paid to this article of clothing. Silk stockings are frequently mentioned by the dramatists. Cf. Stephen Gosson, *Pleasant Quippes*:

These worsted stockes of bravest die, and silken garters fring'd with gold;These corked shooes to beare them hie makes them to trip it on the molde;They mince it with a pace so strange,Like untam'd heifers when they range.

1. 1. 128 cut-worke smocks, and shirts. Cf. B. & Fl., *Four Plays in One*:
——She show'd me gownes, head tires,Embroider'd waistcoats, smocks seamed with cutworks.

1. 1. 135 But you must take a body ready made. King James in his *Dæmonologie* (*Wks.*, ed. 1616, p. 120) explains that the devil, though but of air, can 'make himself palpable, either by assuming any dead bodie, and vsing the ministerie thereof, or else by deluding as well their sence of feeling as seeing.'

1. 1. 143 our tribe of Brokers. Cf. *Ev. Man in, Wks.* 1. 82:
'*Wel.* Where got'st thou this coat, I marle?*Brai.* Of a Hounsditch man, sir, one of the devil's near kinsmen, a broker.'

The pawnbrokers were cordially hated in Jonson's time. Their quarter was Houndsditch. Stow says: 'there are crept in among them [the inhabitants of Houndsditch] a base kinde of vermine, wel-deserving to bee ranked and numbred with them, whom our old Prophet and Countryman, *Gyldas*, called *Ætatis atramentum*, the black discredit of the Age, and of place where they are suffered to live.... These men, or rather monsters in the shape of men, professe to live by lending, and yet will lend nothing but upon pawnes;' etc.

Nash speaks of them in a similar strain: 'Fruits shall be greatly eaten with Catterpillers; as Brokers, Farmers and Flatterers, which feeding on the sweate of other mens browes, shall greatlye hinder the beautye of the spring.'—*Prognostication, Wks.*2. 145. 'They shall crie out against brokers, as Jeremy did against false prophets.' *Ibid.* 2. 162.

1. 1. 148 as you make your soone at nights relation. Cf.

Dekker, *Satiromastix, Wks.* 1. 187: 'Shee'l be a late sturrer soone at night sir,' and *ibid.* 223:

By this faire Bride remember soone at night.

1. 2. 1 ff. I, they doe, now, etc. 'Compare this exquisite piece of sense, satire, and sound philosophy in 1616 with Sir M. Hale's speech from the bench in a trial of a witch many years afterwards.'—Coleridge, *Notes*, p. 280.

1. 2. 1 Bretnor. An almanac maker (fl. 1607-1618). A list of his works, compiled from the catalogue of the British Museum, is given in the *DNB*. He is mentioned twice by Middleton:

This farmer will not cast his seed i' the groundBefore he look in Bretnor.— *Inner-Temple Masque, Wks.* 7. 211.

'*Chough.* I'll not be married to-day, Trimtram: hast e'er an almanac about thee? this is the nineteenth of August, look what day of the month 'tis.

Trim. 'Tis tenty-nine indeed, sir. [*Looks in almanac.Chough.* What's the word? What says Bretnor?*Trim.* The word is, sir, *There's a hole in her coat.*'— Middleton, *A Fair Quarrel, Wks.* 4. 263.

Fleay identifies him with Norbret, one of the astrologers in Beaumont and Fletcher's *Rollo, Duke of Normandy.*

1. 2. 2 Gresham. A pretended astrologer, contemporary with Forman, and said to be one of the associates of the infamous Countess of Essex and Mrs. Turner in the murder of Sir Thomas Overbury. Arthur Wilson mentions him in *The Life of James I.*, p. 70:

'Mrs. *Turner,* the Mistris of the *Work,* had lost both her supporters. *Forman,* her first prop, drop't away suddenly by death; and *Gresham* another rotten *Engin* (that succeded him) did not hold long: She must now bear up all her self.'

He is mentioned twice in Spark's *Narrative History of King James*, Somer's *Tracts* 2. 275: 'Dr. Forman being dead, Mrs. Turner wanted one to assist her; whereupon, at the countesses coming to London, one Gresham was nominated to be entertained in this businesse, and, in processe of time, was wholly interested in it; this man was had in suspition to have had a hand in the Gunpowder plot, he wrote so near it in his almanack; but, without all question, he was a very skilful man in the mathematicks, and, in his latter time, in witchcraft, as was suspected, and therefore the fitter to bee imployed in those practises, which, as they were devilish, so the devil had a hand in them.'

Ibid. 287: 'Now Gresham growing into years, having spent much time in many foule practises to accomplish those things at this time, gathers all his babies together, *viz.* pictures in lead, in wax, in plates of gold, of naked men and women with crosses, crucifixes, and other implements, wrapping them all up together in a scarfe, crossed every letter in the sacred word Trinity, crossed these things very holily delivered into the hands of one Weston to bee hid in the earth that no man might find them, and so in Thames-street having finished his evill times he died, leaving behind him a man and a maid, one hanged for a witch, and the other for a thief very shortly after.'

In the 'Heads of Charges against Robert, Earl of Somerset', drawn up by Lord Bacon, we read: 'That the countess laboured Forman and Gresham to inforce the Queen by witchcraft to favour the countess' (Howell's *State Trials* 2. 966). To this King James replied in an 'Apostyle,' *Nothing to Somerset*. This exhausts the references to Gresham that I have been able to find. See note on Savory, 1. 2. 3.

1. 2. 2. Fore-man. Simon Foreman, or Forman (1552-1611) was the most famous of the group of quacks here mentioned. He studied at Oxford, 1573-1578, and in 1579 began his career as a necromancer. He claimed the power to discover lost treasure, and was especially successful in his dealings with women. A detailed account of his life is given in the *DNB.* and a short but interesting sketch in *Social England* 4. 87. The chief sources are Wm. Lilly's *History* and a diary from 1564 to 1602, with an account of Forman's early life, published by Mr. J. O. Halliwell-Phillipps for the Camden Soc., 1843.

He is mentioned again by Jonson in *Silent Woman, Wks.* 3. 413: '*Daup.* I would say, thou hadst the best philtre in the world, and couldst do more than Madam Medea, or Doctor Foreman.' In *Sir Thomas Overbury's Vision* (Harl. Ms., vol. 7, quoted in D'Ewes' *Autobiog.*, p. 89) he is spoken of as 'that fiend in human shape.'

1. 2. 3 Francklin. Francklin was an apothecary, and procured the poison for Mrs. Turner (see Amos, *Great Oyer.* p. 97). He was one of the three persons executed with Mrs. Turner. Arthur Wilson, in his *Life of James I.* (p. 70), describes him as 'a swarthy, sallow, crooked-backt fellow, who was to be the *Fountain* whence these bitter waters came.' See also Somer's *Tracts* 2. 287. The poem already quoted furnishes a description of Francklin:

A man he was of stature meanly tall.His body's lineaments were shaped, and allHis limbs compacted well, and strongly knit.Nature's kind hand no error made in it.His beard was ruddy hue, and from his headA wanton lock itself did down dispreadUpon his back; to which while he did liveTh' ambiguous name of *Elf-lock* he did give.—Quoted in Amos. p. 50.

1. 2. 3 Fiske. 'In this year 1633, I became acquainted with Nicholas Fiske, licentiate in physick, who was borne in Suffolk, near Framingham [Framlingham] Castle, of very good parentage.... He was a person very studious, laborious, and of good apprehension.... He was exquisitely skilful in the art of directions upon nativities, and had a good genius in performing judgment thereupon.... He died about the seventy-eighth year of his age, poor.'—Lilly, *Hist.*, p. 42 f.

Fiske appears as La Fiske in *Rollo, Duke of Normandy*, and is also mentioned by Butler, *Hudibr.*, Part 2, Cant. 3. 403:

And nigh an ancient obeliskWas rais'd by him, found out by *Fisk*.

1. 2. 3 Sauory. 'And therefore, she fearing that her lord would seek some public or private revenge against her, by the advice of the before-mentioned Mrs. Turner, consulted and practised with Doctor Forman and Doctor Savory, two conjurers, about the poisoning of him.'—D'Ewes, *Autobiog.* 1. 88. 9.

He was employed after the sudden death of Dr. Forman. Wright (*Sorcery and Magic*, p. 228) says that the name is written Lavoire in some manuscripts. 'Mrs. Turner also confessed, that Dr. Savories was used in succession, after Forman, and practised many sorceries upon the Earle of Essex his person.'—

Spark, *Narrative History*, Somer's *Tracts* 2. 333.

In the *Calendar of State Papers* the name of 'Savery' appears four times. Under date of Oct. 16, 1615, we find Dr. Savery examined on a charge of 'spreading Popish Books.' 'Savery pretends to be a doctor, but is probably a conjurer.' And again under the same date he is interrogated as to his relations with Mrs. Turner and Forman. Under Oct. 24 he replies to Coke. 'Oct. ?' we find Dr. Savery questioned as to his 'predictions of troubles and alterations in Court.' This is the last mention of him.

Just what connection Gresham and Savory had with the Overbury plot is a difficult matter to determine. Both are spoken of as following Forman immediately, and of neither is any successor mentioned except the actual poisoner, Franklin. It seems probable that Gresham was the first to be employed after Forman, and that his own speedy death led to the selection of Savory. How the latter managed to escape a more serious implication in the trial it is difficult to conceive.

1. 2. 6-9 christalls, ... characters. As in other fields, Jonson is well versed in magic lore. Lumps of crystal were one of the regular means of raising a demon. Bk. 15, Ch. 16 of Scot's *Discovery of Witchcraft*, 1584, is entitled: 'To make a spirit appear in a christall', and Ch. 12 shows 'How to enclose a spirit in a christall stone.'

Lilly (*History*, p. 78) speaks of the efficacy of 'a constellated ring' in sickness, and they were doubtless considered effective in more sinister dealings. Jonson has already spoken of the devil being carried in a thumb-ring.

Charms were usually written on parchment. In Barrett's *Magus*, Bk. 2, Pt. 3. 109, we read that the pentacle should be drawn 'upon parchment made of a kid-skin, or virgin, or pure clean white paper.'

That parts of the human body belonged to the sorcerer's paraphernalia is shown by the Statute 1 Jac. I. c. xii, which contains a clause forbidding conjurors to 'take up any dead man woman or child out of his her or their grave ... or the skin bone or any other parte of any dead person, to be imployed or used in any manner of Witchcrafte Sorcerie Charme or Inchantment.'

The wing of the raven, as a bird of ill omen, may be an invention of Jonson's own. The lighting of candles within the magic circle is mentioned below (note 1. 2. 26).

Most powerful of all was the pentacle, of which Scot's *Discovery* (Ap. II, p. 533, 4) furnishes an elaborate description. This figure was used by the Pythagorean school as their seal, and is equivalent to the pentagram or five-pointed star (see *CD.*).

Dekker (*Wks.* 2. 200) connects it with the Periapt as a 'potent charm,' and Marlowe speaks of it in *Hero and Leander*, *Wks.* 3. 45:

A rich disparent pentacle she wears,Drawn full of circles and strange characters.

It will be remembered that the inscription of a pentagram on the threshold prevents the escape of Mephistopheles in Goethe's *Faust*. The editors explain its potency as due to the fact that it is resolvable into three triangles, and is thus a triple sign of the Trinity.

Cunningham says that the pentacle 'when delineated upon the body of a man was supposed to point out the five wounds of the Saviour.' W. J. Thoms (*Anecdotes*, Camden Soc., 1839, p. 97) speaks of its presence in the western window of the southern aisle of Westminster Abbey, an indication that the monks were versed in occult science.

1. 2. 21 If they be not. Gifford refers to Chrysippus, *De Divinatione, Lib. 1. § 71:* 'This is the very syllogism by which that acute philosopher triumphantly proved the reality of augury.'

1. 2. 22 Why, are there lawes against 'hem? It was found necessary in 1541 to pass an act (33 Hen. VIII. c. 8) by which—'it shall be felony to practise, or cause to be practised conjuration, witchcrafte, enchantment, or sorcery, to get money: or to consume any person in his body, members or goods; or to provoke any person to unlawful love; or for the despight of Christ, or lucre of money, to pull down any cross; or to declare where goods stolen be.' Another law was passed 1 Edward VI. c. 12 (1547). 5 Elizabeth. c. 16 (1562) gives the 'several penalties of conjuration, or invocation of wicked spirits, and witchcraft, enchantment, charm or sorcery.' Under Jas. I, anno secundo (vulgo primo), c. 12, still another law was passed, whereby the second offense was declared a felony. The former act of Elizabeth was repealed. This act of James was not repealed until 9 George II. c. 5.

Social England, p. 270, quotes from Ms. Lansdowne, 2. Art. 26, a deposition from William Wicherley, conjurer, in which he places the number of conjurers in England in 1549 above five hundred. A good idea of the character of the more disreputable type of conjurer can be got from Beaumont and Fletcher's *Fair Maid of the Inn*. See especially Act 5, Sc. 2.

1. 2. 26 circles. The magic circle is one of the things most frequently mentioned among the arts of the conjurer. Scot (*Discovery*, p. 476) has a long satirical passage on the subject, in which he enjoins the conjurer to draw a double circle with his own blood, to divide the circle into seven parts and to set at each division a 'candle lighted in a brazen candlestick.'

1. 2. 27 his hard names. A long list of the 'diverse names of the divell' is given in *The Discovery*, p. 436, and another in the Second Appendix, p. 522.

1. 2. 31, 2 I long for thee. An' I were with child by him, ... I could not more. The expression is common enough. Cf. *Eastward Hoe*: 'Ger. As I am a lady, I think I am with child already, I long for a coach so.' Dekker, *Shomakers Holiday, Wks.* 1. 17: 'I am with child till I behold this huffecap.' The humors of the longing wife are a constant subject of ridicule. See *Bart. Fair*, Act 1, and Butler's *Hudibras*, ed. 1819, 3. 78 and note.

1. 2. 39 A thousand miles. 'Neither are they so much limited as Tradition would have them; for they are not at all shut up in any separated place: but can remove millions of miles in the twinkling of an eye.'—Scot, *Discovery*, Ap. II, p. 493.

1. 2. 43 The burn't child dreads the fire. Jonson is fond of proverbial expressions. Cf. 1. 6. 125; 1. 6. 145; 5. 8. 142, 3, etc.

1. 3. 5 while things be reconcil'd. In Elizabethan English both *while* and *whiles* often meant 'up to the time when', as well as 'during the time when' (d. a similar use of 'dum' in Latin and of ἕ ος in Greek).—Abbot, §137.

For its frequent use in this sense in Shakespeare see Schmidt and note on *Macbeth* 3. 1. 51, Furness's edition. Cf. also Nash, *Prognostication, Wks.* 2. 150: 'They shall ly in their beds while noon.'

1. 3. 8, 9 those roses Were bigge inough to hide a clouen foote. Dyce (*Remarks*, p. 289) quotes Webster, *White Devil*, 1612:

—why, 'tis the devil;I know him by a great rose he wears on's shoe,To hide his cloven foot.

Cunningham adds a passage from Chapman, *Wks.* 3. 145:

Fro. Yet you cannot change the old fashion (they say)And hide your cloven feet.*Oph.* No! I can wear roses that shall spread quiteOver them.

Gifford quotes Nash, *Unfortunate Traveller, Wks.* 5. 146: 'Hee hath in eyther shoo as much taffaty for his tyings, as would serue for an ancient.' Cf. also Dekker, *Roaring Girle, Wks.* 3. 200: 'Haue not many handsome legges in silke stockins villanous splay feet for all their great roses?'

1. 3. 13 My Cater. Whalley changes to 'm'acter' on the authority of the *Sad Shep.* (vol. 4. 236):

—Go bear 'em in to MuchTh' acater.

The form 'cater', however, is common enough. Indeed, if we are to judge from the examples in Nares and *NED.*, it is much the more frequent, although the present passage is cited in both authorities under the longer form.

1. 3. 21 I'le hearken. W. and G. change to 'I'd.' The change is unnecessary if we consider the conditional clause as an after-thought on the part of Fitzdottrel. For a similar construction see 3. 6. 34-6.

1. 3. 27 Vnder your fauour, friend, for, I'll not quarrell. 'This was one of the qualifying expressions, by which, "according to the laws of the duello", the lie might be given, without subjecting the speaker to the absolute necessity of receiving a challenge.'—G.

Leigh uses a similar expression. Cf. note 2. 1. 144. It occurs several times in *Ev. Man in*:

'*Step.* Yet, by his leave, he is a rascal, under his favour, do you see.*E. Know.* Ay, by his leave, he is, and under favour: a pretty piece of civility!'—*Wks.* 1. 68.

'*Down.* 'Sdeath! you will not draw then?*Bob.* Hold, hold! under thy favour forbear!'—*Wks.* 1. 117.

'*Clem.* Now, sir, what have you to say to me?*Bob.* By your worship's favour——.'—*Wks.* 1. 140.

I have not been able to confirm Gifford's assertion.

1. 3. 30 that's a popular error. Gifford refers to *Othello* 5. 2. 286:

Oth. I look down towards his feet,—but that's a fable.—If that thou be'st a devil, I cannot kill thee.

Cf. also *The Virgin Martyr*, Dekker's *Wks.* 4. 57:

—Ile tell you what now of the Divel;He's no such horrid creature, cloven footed,Black, saucer-ey'd, his nostrils breathing fire,As these lying Christians make him.

1. 3. 34 Of Derby-shire, S^r. about the Peake. Jonson seems to have been well acquainted with the wonders of the Peak of Derbyshire. Two of his masques, *The Gipsies Metamorphosed*, acted first at Burleigh on the Hill, and later at Belvoir, Nottinghamshire, and *Love's Welcome at Welbeck*, acted in 1633 at Welbeck, Nottinghamshire, the seat of William Cavendish, Earl of Newcastle, are full of allusions to them. The Devil's Arse seems to be the cavern now known to travellers as the *Peak* or *Devil's Cavern*. It is described by Baedeker as upwards of 2,000 feet in extent. One of its features is a subterranean river known as the Styx. The origin of the cavern's name is given in a coarse song in the *Gypsies Met. (Wks.* 7. 357), beginning:

Cocklorrel would needs have the Devil his guest,And bade him into the Peak to dinner.

In *Love's Welcome* Jonson speaks again of 'Satan's sumptuous Arse', *Wks.* 8. 122.

1. 3. 34, 5.   That Hole.

Belonged to your Ancestors?Jonson frequently omits the relative pronoun. Cf. 1. 5. 21; 1. 6. 86, 87; 3. 3. 149; 5. 8. 86, 87.

1. 3. 38 Foure pound a yeere. 'This we may suppose to have been the customary wages of a domestic servant.'—C. Cunningham cites also the passage in the *Alchemist, Wks.* 4. 12; 'You were once ... the good, Honest, plain, livery-three-pound-thrum, that kept Your master's worship's house,' in which he takes the expression 'three-pound' to be the equivalent of 'badly-paid'.

1. 4. 1 I'll goe lift him. Jonson is never tired of punning on the names of his characters.

1. 4. 5 halfe a piece. 'It may be necessary to observe, once for all, that the *piece* (the double sovereign) went for two and twenty shillings.'—G. Compare 3. 3. 83, where a hundred pieces is evidently somewhat above a hundred pounds. By a proclamation, Nov. 23, 1611, the piece of gold called the Unitie, formerly current at twenty shillings was raised to the value of twenty two shillings (S. M. Leake, *Eng. Money* 2. 276). Taylor, the water-poet, tells us that Jonson gave him 'a piece of gold of two and twenty shillings to drink his health in England' (*Conversations*, quoted in Schelling's *Timber*, p. 105). In the *Busie Body* Mrs. Centlivre uses *piece* as synonymous with *guinea* (2d ed., pp. 7 and 14).

1. 4. 31 lust what it list. Jonson makes frequent use of the subjunctive. Cf. 1. 3. 9; 1. 6. 6; 5. 6. 10; etc.

1. 4. 43 Ô here's the bill, S^r. Collier says that the use of play-bills was common prior to the year 1563 (Strype, *Life of Grindall,* ed. 1821, p. 122). They are mentioned in *Histriomastix*, 1610; *A Warning for Fair Women*, 1599, etc. See Collier, *Annals* 3. 382 f.

1. 4. 50 a rotten Crane. Whalley restores the right reading, correctly explained as a pun on Ingine's name.

1. 4. 60 Good time! Apparently a translation of the Fr. *A la bonne heure,* 'very good', 'well done!' etc.

1. 4. 65 The good mans gravity. Cf. Homer, *Il.*, Γ 105:

ἄξετε δὲ Πριάμοιο βίην.

Shak., *Tempest* 5. 1: 'First, noble friend, let me embrace thine age.' *Catiline* 3. 2.: 'Trouble this good shame (good and modest lady) no farther.'

1. 4. 70 into the shirt. Cf. Dekker, *Non-dram. Wks.* 2. 244: 'Dice your selfe into your shirt.'

1. 4. 71 Keepe warme your wisdome? Cf. *Cyn. Rev., Wks.* 2. 241: '*Madam, your whole self cannot but be perfectly wise; for your hands have wit enough to keep themselves warm.*' Gifford's note on this passage is: 'This proverbial phrase is found in most (sic) of our ancient dramas. Thus in *The Wise Woman of Hogsden*: "You are the wise woman, are you? You *have wit to keep yourself warm enough*, I warrant you"'. Cf. also *Lusty Juventus*, p. 74: 'Cover your head; For indeed you have need to keep in your wit.'

1. 4. 72 You lade me. 'This is equivalent to the modern phrase, you do not spare me. You lay what imputations you please upon me.'—G.

The phrase occurs again in 1. 6. 161, where Wittipol calls Fitzdottrel an ass, and says that he cannot 'scape his lading'. 'You lade me', then, seems to mean 'You make an ass of me'. The same use of the word occurs in Dekker, *Olde Fortunatus, Wks.* 1. 125: 'I should serue this bearing asse rarely now, if I should load him'. And again in the works of Taylor, the Water Poet, p. 311: 'My Lines shall load an Asse, or whippe an Ape.' Cf. also *Bart. Fair, Wks.* 4. 421: 'Yes, faith, I have my lading, you see, or shall have anon; you may know whose beast I am by my burden.'

1. 4. 83, 4   But, not beyond,
A minute, or a second, looke for. The omission of the comma after *beyond* by all the later editors destroys the sense. Fitzdottrel does not mean that Wittipol cannot have 'beyond a minute', but that he cannot have a minute beyond the quarter of an hour allowed him.

1. 4. 96 Migniard. 'Cotgrave has in his dictionary, "*Mignard*—migniard, prettie, quaint, neat, feat, wanton, dainty, delicate." In the *Staple of News* [*Wks.* 5. 221] Jonson tries to introduce the substantive *migniardise*, but happily without success.'—G.

1. 4. 101 Prince Quintilian. The reputation of this famous rhetorician (c 35-c 97 A. D.) is based on his great work entitled *De Instiutione Oratoria Libri* XII. The first English edition seems to have been made in 1641, but many Continental editions had preceded it. The title Prince seems to be gratuitous on Jonson's part. He is mentioned again in *Timber* (ed. Schelling, 57. 29 and 81. 4).

1. 5. 2 Cf. *New Inn, Wks.* 5. 323:
'*Host.* What say you, sir? where are you, are you within?(*Strikes* Lovel *on the breast.*)'

1. 5. 8, 9. Old Africk, and the new America,
With all their fruite of Monsters. Cf. Donne, *Sat., Wks.* 2. 190 (ed. 1896):
Stranger ...Than Afric's monsters, Guiana's rarities.

Brome, *Queen's Exchange, Wks.* 3. 483: 'What monsters are bred in *Affrica*?' Glapthorne, *Hollander, Wks.*, 1874, 1. 81: 'If *Africke* did produce no other monsters,' etc. The people of London at this time had a great thirst for monsters. See Alden, *Bart. Fair*, p. 185, and Morley, *Memoirs of Bartholomew Fair*.

1. 5. 17 for hidden treasure. 'And when he is appeared, bind him with the bond of the dead above written: then saie as followeth. I charge thee N. by the father, to shew me true visions in this christall stone, if there be anie treasure hidden in such a place N. & wherein it now lieth, and how manie foot from this peece of earth, east, west, north, or south.'—Scot, *Discovery*, p. 355.

Most of the conjurers pretended to be able to recover stolen treasure. The laws against conjurers (see note 1. 2. 6) contained clauses forbidding the practice.

1. 5. 21 his men of Art. A euphemism for conjurer. Cf. B. & Fl., *Fair Maid of the Inn* 2. 2:

'*Host.* Thy master, that lodges here in my Osteria, is a rare man of art; they say he's a witch.*Clown.* A witch? Nay, he's one step of the ladder to preferment higher; he's a conjurer.'

1. 6. 10 wedlocke. Wife; a common latinism of the period.

1. 6. 14 it not concernes thee? A not infrequent word-order in Jonson. Cf. 4. 2. 22.

1. 6. 18 a Niaise. Gifford says that the side note 'could scarcely come from Jonson; for it explains nothing. A niaise (or rather an *eyas*, of which it is a corruption) is unquestionably a young hawk, but the niaise of the poet is the French term for, "a simple, witless, inexperienced gull", &c. The word is very common in our old writers.'

The last statement is characteristic of Gifford. It would have been well in this case if he had given some proof of his assertion. The derivation *an eyas > a nyas* is probably incorrect. The *Centary Dictionary* gives '*Niaise, nyas* (and corruptly *eyas*, by misdivision of *a nias*).' The best explanation I can give of the side note is this. The glossator takes the meaning 'simpleton' for granted. But Fitzdottrel has just said 'Laught at, sweet bird?' In explanation the side note is added. This, perhaps, does not help matters much and, indeed, I am inclined to believe with Gifford that the side notes are by another hand than Jonson's. See Introduction.

1. 6. 29, 30. **When I ha' seene**

All London in't, and London has seene mee. Gifford compares Pope:

Europe he saw, and Europe saw him too.

1. 6. 31 Black-fryers Play-house. This famous theatre was founded by James Burbage in 1596-7. The Burbages leased it to Henry Evans for the performances of the Children of the Chapel, and the King's Servants acted there after the departure of the children. In 1619 the Lord Mayor and the Council of London ordered its discontinuance, but the players were able to keep it open on the plea that it was a private house. In 1642 'public stage plays' were suppressed, and on Aug. 5, 1655, Blackfriars Theatre was pulled down and tenements were built in its place. See Wh-C.

Nares, referring to Shirley's *Six New Playes*, 1653, says that 'the Theatre of Black-Friars was, in Charles I.'s time at least considered, as being of a higher order and more respectability than any of those on the Bank-side.'

1. 6. 33 Rise vp between the Acts. See note 3. 5. 43.

1. 6. 33, 4   let fall my cloake,

Publish a handsome man, and a rich suite. The gallants of this age were inordinately fond of displaying their dress, or 'publishing their suits.' The play-house and 'Paul's Walk,' the nave of St. Paul's Cathedral, were favorite places for accomplishing this. The fourth chapter of Dekker's *Guls Horne-booke* is entitled 'How a Gallant should behaue himselfe in Powles walkes.' He bids the gallant make his way directly into the middle aisle, 'where, in view of all, you may publish your suit in what manner you affect most, either with the slide of your cloake from the one shoulder, and then you must (as twere in anger) suddenly snatch at the middle of the inside (if it be taffata at the least) and so by that meanes your costly lining is betrayd,' etc. A little later on (*Non-dram. Wks.* 2. 238) Dekker speaks of 'Powles, a Tennis-court, or a Playhouse' as a suitable place to 'publish your clothes.' Cf. also *Non-dram. Wks.* 4. 51.

Sir Thomas Overbury gives the following description of 'a Phantastique:' 'He withers his clothes on a stage as a salesman is forced to do his suits in Birchin Lane; and when the play is done, if you mark his rising, 'tis with a kind of walking epilogue between the two candles, to know if his suit may pass for current.' Morley, p. 73.

Stephen Gosson (*School of Abuse*, p. 29) says that 'overlashing in apparel is so common a fault, that the verye hyerlings of some of our plaiers, which stand at reversion of vi^s by the weeke, jet under gentlemens noses in sutes of silke.'

1. 6. 37, 8   For, they doe come

To see vs, Loue, as wee doe to see them. Cf. *Induction* to *The Staple of News*, *Wks.* 5. 151: 'Yes, on the stage; we are persons of quality, I assure you, and women of fashion, and come to see and to be seen.' *Silent Woman, Wks.* 3. 409: 'and come abroad where the matter is frequent, to court, ... to plays, ... thither they come to shew their new tires too, to see, and to be seen.' Massinger, *City Madam, Wks.*, p. 323:

Sir. Maur. Is there aught elseTo be demanded?*Anne.* ... a fresh habit,Of a fashion never seen before, to draw,The gallants' eyes, that sit upon the stage, upon me.

Gosson has much to say on the subject of women frequenting the theatre. There, he says (p. 25). 'everye man and his queane are first acquainted;' and he earnestly recommends all women to stay away from these 'places of suspition' (pp. 48 f.).

1. 6. 40 Yes, wusse. *Wusse* is a corruption of *wis*, OE. *gewis*, certainly. Jonson uses the forms *I wuss* (*Wks.* 1. 102), *I wusse* (*Wks.* 6. 146), and *Iwisse* (*Wks.* 2. 379. the fol. reading; Gifford changing to *I wiss*), in addition to the present form. In some cases the word is evidently looked upon as a verb.

1. 6. 58 sweet Pinnace. Cf. 2. 2. 111 f. A woman is often compared to a ship. Nares cites B. & Fl., *Woman's Pr.* 2. 6:

This pinck, this painted foist, this cockle-boat.

Cf. also *Stap. of News*, *Wks.* 5. 210:

She is not rigg'd, sir; setting forth some lady Will cost as much as furnishing a fleet.—Here she is come at last, and like a galley Gilt in the prow.

Jonson plays on the names of Pinnacia in the *New Inn*, *Wks.* 5. 384:

'*Host.* Pillage the Pinnace....*Lord B.* Blow off her upper deck. *Lord L.* Tear all her tackle.'

Pinnace, when thus applied to a woman, was almost always used with a conscious retention of the metaphor. Dekker is especially fond of the word. *Match me in London*, *Wks.* 4. 172:

—There's a Pinnace (Was mann'd out first by th' City), is come to th' Court, New rigg'd.

Also Dekker, *Wks.* 4. 162; 3. 67, 77, 78.

When the word became stereotyped into an equivalent for procuress or prostitute, the metaphor was often dropped. Thus in *Bart. Fair*, *Wks.* 4. 386: 'She hath been before me, punk, pinnace and bawd, any time these two and twenty years.' Gifford says on this passage: 'The usual gradation in infamy. A *pinnace* was a light vessel built for speed, generally employed as a tender. Hence our old dramatists constantly used the word for a person employed in love messages, a go-between in the worst sense, and only differing from a bawd in not being stationary.' A glance at the examples given above will show, however, that the term was much more elastic than this explanation would indicate.

The dictionaries give no suggestion of the origin of the metaphor. I suspect that it may be merely a borrowing from classical usage. Cf. *Menaechmi* 2. 3. 442:

Ducit lembum dierectum nauis praedatoria.

In *Miles Gloriosus* 4. 1. 986, we have precisely the same application as in the English dramatists: 'Haec celox (a swift sailing vessel) illiust, quae hinc agreditur, internuntia.'

1. 6. 62 th' are right. Whalley's interpretation is, of course, correct. See variants.

1. 6. 73 Not beyond that rush. Rushes took the place of carpets in the days of Elizabeth. Shakespeare makes frequent reference to the custom (see Schmidt). The following passage from Dr. Bulleyne has often been quoted: 'Rushes that grow upon dry groundes be good to strew in halles, chambers and galleries, to walk upon, defending apparel, as traynes of gownes and kertles from dust.' Cf. also *Cyn. Rev.* 2. 5; *Every Man out* 3. 3.

1. 6. 83 As wise as a Court Parliament. Jonson refers here, I suppose, to the famous Courts or Parliaments of Love, which were supposed to have existed during the Middle Ages (cf. Skeat, *Chaucer's Works* 7. lxxx).

Cunningham calls attention to the fact that Massinger's *Parliament of Love* was not produced until 1624. Jonson depicts a sort of mock Parliament of Love in the *New Inn*, Act 4.

1. 6. 88 And at all caracts. 'I. e., to the nicest point, to the minutest circumstance.'—G. See Gloss. and cf. *Every Man in*, *Wks.* 1. 70.

1. 6. 89, 90 as scarce hath soule, In stead of salt. Whalley refers to *Bart. Fair, Wks.* 4. 446, 7: 'Talk of him to have a soul! 'heart, if he have any more than a thing given him instead of salt, only to keep him from stinking. I'll be hang'd afore my time.' Gifford quotes the passage from B. & Fl., *Spanish Curate*:

—this soul I speake of,Or rather salt, to keep this heap of fleshFrom being a walking stench.

W. furnishes a Latin parallel: 'Sus vero quid habet praeter escam? cui quidem, ne putresceret, animam ipsam pro sale datam dicit esse Chrysippus.'—Cic. *De Natura Deor*, lib. 2.

It is to these passages that Carlyle refers in his *Past and Present*: 'A certain degree of soul, as Ben Jonson reminds us, is indispensable to keep the very body from destruction of the frightfulest sort; to 'save us,' says he, 'the expense of salt.' Bk. 2, Ch. 2.

'In our and old Jonson's dialect, man has lost the *soul* out of him; and now, after the due period,—begins to find the want of it.... Man has lost his soul, and vainly seeks antiseptic salt.' (Simpson in *N. & Q.*, 9th Ser. 4. 347, 423.)

To the same Latin source Professor Cook (*Mod. Lang. Notes*, Feb., 1905) attributes the passage in *Rabbi Ben Ezra* 43-45:

What is he but a bruteWhose flesh has soul to suit,Whose spirit works lest arms and legs want play?

and Samuel Johnson's 'famous sentence recorded by Boswell under June 19, 1784: "Talking of the comedy of *The Rehearsal*, he said: 'It has not wit enough to keep it sweet.'"'

1. 6. 97 the walks of Lincolnes Inne. One of the famous Inns of Court (note 3.1.8). It formerly pertained to the Bishops of Chichester (Stow, *Survey*, ed. 1633, p. 488a). The gardens 'were famous until the erection of the hall, by which they were curtailed and seriously injured' (Wh-C.). The Tatler (May 10, 1709, no. 13) speaks of Lincoln's Inn Walks.

1. 6. 99 I did looke for this geere. See variants. Cunningham says: 'In the original it is *geere*, and so it ought still to stand. Gear was a word with a most extended signification. Nares defines it, "matter, subject, or business in general!" When Jonson uses the word *jeer* he spells it quite differently. The *Staple of News* was first printed at the same time as the present play, and in the beginning of Act IV. Sc. 1, I find: "*Fit.* Let's *ieere* a little. *Pen.* Ieere? what's that?"'

It is so spelt regularly throughout *The Staple of News*, but in *Ev. Man in* 1. 2 (fol. 1616), we find: 'Such petulant, geering gamsters that can spare No ... subject from their jest.' The fact is that both words were sometimes spelt *geere*, as well as in a variety of other ways. The uniform spelling in *The Staple of News*, however, seems to indicate that this is the word *gear*, which fits the context, fully as well as, perhaps better than Gifford's interpretation. A common meaning is 'talk, discourse', often in a depreciatory sense. See Gloss.

1. 6. 125 Things, that are like, are soone familiar. 'Like will to like' is a familiar proverb.

1. 6. 127 the signe o' the husband. An allusion to the signs of the zodiac, some of which were supposed to have a malign and others a beneficent influence.

1. 6. 131 You grow old, while I tell you this.

Hor. [*Carm.* I. II. 8 f.]:Dum loquimur, fugerit invidaAetas, carpe diem.—G.

Whalley suggested:

Fugit Hora: hoc quod loquor, inde est.—Pers. *Sat.* 5.

1. 6. 131, 2   And such

As cannot vse the present, are not wise. Cf. *Underwoods* 36. 21:

To use the present, then, is not abuse.

1. 6. 138 Nay, then, I taste a tricke in't. Cf. 'I do taste this as a trick put on me.' *Ev. Man in, Wks.* 1. 133. See Introduction.

1. 6. 142 cautelous. For similar uses of the word cf. Massinger, *City Madam, Wks.,* p. 321, and B. & Fl., *Elder Brother, Wks.* 10. 275. Gifford gives an example from Knolles, *Hist. of the Turks,* p. 904.

1. 6. 149 MAN. Sir, what doe you meane?

153 MAN. You must play faire, S^r. 'I am not certain about the latter of these two speeches, but it is perfectly unquestionable that the former *must* have been spoken by the husband Fitzdottrel.'—C.

Cunningham may be right, but the change is unnecessary if we consider Manly's reproof as occasioned by Fitzdottrel's interruption.

1. 6. 158, 9   No wit of man

Or roses can redeeme from being an Asse. 'Here is an allusion to the metamorphosis of Lucian into an *ass*; who being brought into the theatre to shew tricks, recovered his human shape by eating some *roses* which he found there. See the conclusion of the treatise, *Lucius, sive Asinus.*'—W.

See Lehman's edition, Leipzig, 1826, 6. 215. As Gifford says, the allusion was doubtless more familiar in Jonson's day than in our own. The story is retold in Harsnet's *Declaration* (p. 102), and Lucian's work seems to have played a rather important part in the discussion of witchcraft.

1. 6. 161 To scape his lading. Cf. note 1. 4. 72.

1. 6. 180 To other ensignes. 'I. e., to horns, the Insignia of a cuckold.'—G.

1. 6. 187 For the meere names sake. 'I. e. the name of the play.'—W.

1. 6. 195 the sad contract. See variants. W. and G. are doubtless correct.

1. 6. 214 a guilt caroch. 'There was some distinction apparently between *caroch* and *coach.* I find in Lord Bacon's will, in which he disposed of so much imaginary wealth, the following bequest: "I give also to my wife my four coach geldings, and my best caroache, and her own coach mares and caroache."'—C.

Minsheu says that a carroch is a great coach. Cf. also Taylor's *Wks.,* 1630:

No coaches, or carroaches she doth crave.

Rom Alley, O. Pl., 2d ed., 5. 475:

No, nor your jumblings,In horslitters, in coaches or caroches.

Greene's Tu Quoque, O. Pl., 2d ed., 7. 28:

May'st draw him to the keeping of a coachFor country, and carroch for

London.

Cf. also Dekker, *Non-dram. Wks.* 1. 111. Finally the matter is settled by Howes (p. 867), who gives the date of the introduction of coaches as 1564, and adds: 'Lastly, euen at this time, 1605, began the ordinary use of Caroaches.' In *Cyn. Rev., Wks.* 2. 281, Gifford changes *carroch* to *coach*.

1. 6. 216 Hide-parke. Jonson speaks of coaching in Hyde Park in the *Prologue to the Staple of News, Wks.* 5. 157, and in *The World in the Moon, Wks.* 7. 343. Pepys has many references to it in his *Diary.* 'May 7, 1662. And so, after the play was done, she and The Turner and Mrs. Lucin and I to the Parke; and there found them out, and spoke to them; and observed many fine ladies, and staid till all were gone almost.'

'April 22, 1664. In their coach to Hide Parke, where great plenty of gallants, and pleasant it was, only for the dust.'

Ashton in his *Hyde Park* (p. 59) quotes from a ballad in the British Museum (c 1670-5) entitled, *News from Hide Park*, In which the following lines occur:

Of all parts of *England*, Hide-park hath the name,For Coaches and Horses, and Persons of fame.

1. 6. 216, 7 Black-Fryers, Visit the Painters. A church, precinct, and sanctuary with four gates, lying between Ludgate Hill and the Thames and extending westward from Castle Baynard (St. Andrew's Hill) to the Fleet river. It was so called from the settlement there of the Black or Dominican Friars in 1276. Sir A. Vandyck lived here 1632-1641. 'Before Vandyck, however, Blackfriars was the recognized abode of painters. Cornelius Jansen (d. 1665) lived in the Blackfriars for several years. Isaac Oliver, the miniature painter, was a still earlier resident.' Painters on glass, or glass stainers, and collectors were also settled here.—Wh-C.

1. 6. 219 a middling Gossip. 'A go-between, an *internuntia*, as the Latin writers would have called her.'—W.

1. 6. 224 the cloake is mine. The reading in the folio belonging to Dr. J. M. Berdan of Yale is: 'the cloake is mine owne.' This accounts for the variant readings.

1. 6. 230 motion. Spoken derogatively, a 'performance.' Lit., a puppet-show. The motion was a descendent of the morality, and exceedingly popular in England at this time. See Dr. Winter, *Staple of News*, p. 161; Strutt, *Sports and Pastimes*, p. 166 f.; Knight, *London* 1. 42. Jonson makes frequent mention of the motion. *Bartholomew Fair* 5. 5 is largely devoted to the description of one, and *Tale Tub* 5. 5 presents a series of them.

1. 7. 4 more cheats? See note on *Cheaters*, 5. 6. 64, and Gloss.

1. 7. 16 The state hath tane such note of 'hem. See note 1. 2. 22.

1. 7. 25 Your Almanack-Men. An excellent account of the Almanac-makers of the 17th century is given by H. R. Plomer in *N. & Q.*,6th Ser. 12. 243, from which the following is abridged:

'Almanac-making had become an extensive and profitable trade in this country at the beginning of the 17th century, and with the exception of some fifteen or twenty years at the time of the Rebellion continued to flourish until its close. There were three distinct classes of almanacs published during the seventeenth century—the common almanacs, which preceded and followed the period of the Rebellion, and the political and satirical almanacs that were the direct outcome of that event.

'The common almanacs came out year after year in unbroken uniformity. They were generally of octavo size and consisted of two parts, an almanac and a prognostication. Good and evil days were recorded, and they contained rules as to bathing, purging, etc., descriptions of the four seasons and rules to know the weather, and during the latter half of the century an astrological prediction and "scheme" of the ensuing year.

'In the preceding century the makers of almanacs were "Physitians and Preests", but they now adopted many other titles, such as "Student in Astrology", "Philomath", "Well Willer to the Mathematics." The majority of them were doubtless astrologers, but not a few were quack doctors, who only published their almanacs as advertisements.' (Almanac, a character in *The Staple of News*, is described as a 'doctor in physic.')

Among the more famous almanac-makers the names of William Lilly, John Partridge and Bretnor may be mentioned. For the last see note 2. 1. 1, and B. & Fl., *Rollo, Duke of Normandy*, where Fiske and Bretnor appear again. Cf. also *Alchemist, Wks.* 4. 41; *Every Man out, Wks.* 2. 39-40; *Mag. La., Wks.* 6. 74, 5. In Sir Thomas Overbury's *Character* of *The Almanac-Maker* (Morley, p. 56) we read: 'The verses of his book have a worse pace than ever had Rochester hackney; for his prose, 'tis dappled with ink-horn terms, and may serve for an almanac; but for his judging at the uncertainty of weather, any old shepherd shall make a dunce of him.'

ACT II.

2. 1. 1 Sir, money's a whore, etc. Coleridge, *Notes*, p. 280. emends: 'Money, sir, money's a', &c. Cunningham, on the other hand, thinks that 'the 9-syllable arrangement is quite in Jonson's manner, and that it forces an emphasis upon every word especially effective at the beginning of an act.' See variants.

Money is again designated as a whore in the *Staple of News* 4. 1: 'Saucy Jack, away: Pecunia is a whore.' In the same play Pennyboy, the usurer, is called a 'money-bawd.' Dekker (*Non-dram. Wks.* 2. 137) speaks of keeping a bawdy-house for Lady Pecunia. The figure is a common one.

2. 1. 3 Via. This exclamation is quite common among the dramatists and is explained by Nares as derived from the Italian exclamation *via!* 'away, on!' with a quibble on the literal of L. *via*, a way. The *Century Dictionary* agrees substantially with this derivation. Abundant examples of its use are given by the authorities quoted, to which may be added *Merry Devil of Edmonton* 1. 2. 5, and Marston, *Dutch Courtezan, Wks.* 2. 20:

O, yes, come, *via!*—away, boy—on!

2. 1. 5 With Aqua-vitae. Perhaps used with especial reference to line 1, where he has just called money a bawd Compare:

O, ay, as a bawd with aqua-vitae.—Marston, *The Malcontent, Wks.* 1. 294.

'Her face is full of those red pimples with drinking Aquauite, the common drinke of all bawdes.'—Dekker, *Whore of Babylon, Wks.* 2. 246.

2. 1. 17. See variants. Line 15 shows that the original reading is correct.

2. 1. 19 it shall be good in law. See note 1. 2. 22.

2. 1. 20 Wood-cock. A cant term for a simpleton or dupe.

2. 1. 21 th' Exchange. This was the first Royal Exchange, founded by Sir Thomas Gresham in 1566, opened by Queen Elizabeth in 1570-1, and destroyed in the great fire of 1666 (Wh-C.). Howes (1631) says that it was 'plenteously stored with all kinds of rich wares and fine commodities,' and Paul Hentzner (p. 40) speaks of it with enthusiasm.

It was a favorite lounging-place, especially in the evening. Wheatley quotes Hayman, *Quodlibet*, 1628, p. 6:

Though little coin thy purseless pockets line,Yet with great company thou'rt taken up;For often with Duke Humfray thou dost dine,And often with Sir Thomas Gresham sup.

'We are told in *London* and *Country Carbonadoed*, 1632, that at the exchange there were usually more coaches attendant than at church doors.' Cf. also *Bart. Fair, Wks.* 4. 357: 'I challenge all Cheapside to shew such another: Moor-fields, Pimlico-path, Or the Exchange, in a summer evening.' Also *Ev. Man in, Wks.* 1. 39.

2. 1. 30 do you doubt his eares? Ingine's speech is capable of a double interpretation. Pug has already spoken of the 'liberal ears' of his asinine master.

2. 1. 41 a string of's purse. Purses, of course, used to be hung at the girdle. A thief was called a cut-purse. See the amusing scene in *Bart. Fair, Wks.* 5. 406.

2. 1. 53, 4 at the Pan, Not, at the skirts. '*Pan* is not easily distinguished from *skirt*. Both words seem to refer to the outer parts, or extremities. Possibly Meercraft means—on a broader scale, on a more extended front.'—G.

'The pan is evidently the deepest part of the swamp, which continues to hold water when the *skirts* dry up, like the hole in the middle of the tray under a joint when roasting, which collects all the dripping. Meercraft proposed to grapple with the main difficulty at once.'—C.

I had already arrived at the same conclusion before reading Cunningham's note. The *NED.* gives: 'Pan. A hollow or depression in the ground, esp. one in which water stands.

1594 Plat, *Jewell-ho* 1. 32 Of all Channels, Pondes, Pooles, Riuers, and Ditches, and of all other pannes and bottomes whatsoeuer.'

Pan, however, is also an obsolete form of *pane*, a cloth or skirt. The use is evidently a quibble. The word *pan* suggested to Jonson the word *skirt*, which he accordingly employed not unaptly.

2. 1. 63 his black bag of papers, there, in Buckram. The buckram bag was the usual sign of the pettifogger. Cf. Marston, *Malcontent, Wks.* 1. 235:

Pass. Ay, as a pettifogger by his buckram bag.

Dekker, *If this be not a good Play, Wks.* 3. 274: 'We must all turn pettifoggers and in stead of gilt rapiers, hang buckram bags at our girdles.' Nash refers to the same thing in *Pierce Pennilesse, Wks.* 2. 17.

2. 1. 64 th' Earledome of Pancridge. Pancridge is a corruption of Pancras. The Earl of Pancridge was 'one of the "Worthies" who annually rode to Mile End, or the Artillery Ground, in the ridiculous procession called *Arthurs Shew*' (G.). Cf. *To Inigo Marquis Would-be, Wks.* 8. 115:

Content thee to be Pancridge earl the while.

Tale Tub, Wks. 6. 175:

—next our St. George,Who rescued the king's daughter, I will ride;Above Prince Arthur.*Clench.* Or our own Shoreditch duke.*Med..* Or Pancridge earl.*Pan.* Or Bevis or Sir Guy.

For *Arthur's Show* see Entick's *Survey* 1. 497; Wh-C. 1. 65; and Nares 1. 36. Cf. note 4. 7. 65·

2. 1. 71, 2 Your Borachio Of Spaine. '"*Borachio* (says Min-shieu) is a bottle commonly of a pigges skin, with the hair inward, dressed inwardly with rozen, to keep wine or liquor sweet:"—Wines preserved in these bottles contract a peculiar flavour, and are then said *to taste of the borachio*.'—G.

Florio says: 'a boracho, or a bottle made of a goates skin such as they vse in Spaine.' The word occurs somewhat frequently (see *NED.*) and apparently always with this meaning, or in the figurative sense of 'drunkard'. It is evident, however, from Engine's question, 'Of the King's glouer?' either that it is used here in a slightly different sense, or more probably that Merecraft is relying on Fitzdottrel's ignorance of the subject. Spanish leather for wearing apparel was at this time held in high esteem. See note 4. 4. 71, 2.

2. 1. 83 a Harrington. 'In 1613, a patent was granted to John Stanhope, lord Harrington, Treasurer of the Chambers, for the coinage of royal farthing tokens, of which he seems to have availed himself with sufficient liberality. Some clamour was excited on the occasion: but it speedily subsided; for the Star Chamber kept a watchful eye on the first symptoms of discontent at these pernicious indulgences. From this nobleman they took the name of Harrington in common conversation.'—G.

'Now (1613) my lord Harrington obtained a patent from the King for the making of Brasse Farthings, a thing that brought with it some contempt through lawfull.'—Sparke, *Hist. Narration*, Somer's *Tracts* 2. 294.

A reference to this coin is made in *Drunken Barnaby's Journal* in the *Oxoniana* (quoted by Gifford) and in Sir Henry Wotton's Letters (p. 558, quoted by Whalley). Cf. also *Mag. La., Wks.* 6. 89: 'I will note bate you a single Harrington,' and *ibid., Wks.* 6. 43.

2. 1. 102 muscatell. The grape was usually called *muscat.* So in Pepys' *Diary*, 1662: 'He hath also sent each of us some anchovies, olives and muscatt.' The wine was variously written *muscatel, muscadel,* and *muscadine.* Muscadine and eggs are often mentioned together (cf. Text, 2. 2. 95-96; *New Inn* 3. 1; Middleton, *Wks.* 2. 290; 3. 94; and 8. 36), and were used as an aphrodisiac (Bullen). Nares quotes Minsheu: 'Vinum muscatum, quod moschi odorem referat; for the sweetnesse and smell it resembles muske.'

2. 1. 116, 7 the receiu'd heresie, That England beares no Dukes. 'I know not when this *heresy* crept in. There was apparently some unwillingness to create dukes, as a title of honour, in the Norman race; probably because the

Conqueror and his immediate successors were dukes of Normandy, and did not choose that a subject should enjoy similar dignities with themselves. The first of the English who bore the title was Edward the black prince, (son of Edward III.) who was created duke of Cornwall, by charter, as Collins says, in 1337. The dignity being subsequently conferred on several of the blood-royal, and of the nobility, who came to untimely ends, an idea seems to have been entertained by the vulgar, that the title itself was ominous. At the accession of James I. to the crown of this country, there was, I believe, no English peer of ducal dignity.'—G.

The last duke had been created in the reign of Henry VIII., who made his illegitimate son the Duke of Richmond, and Charles Brandon, who married his sister Mary, Duke of Suffolk. After the attainder and execution of Thomas Howard, Duke of Norfolk, in 1572, there was no duke in England except the king's sons, until the creation of the Duke of Richmond in 1623. (See *New Int. Cyc.* 6. 349.)

2. 1. 144 Bermudas. 'This was a cant term for some places in the town with the same kind of privilege as the mint of old, or the purlieus of the Fleet.'—W.

'These *streights* consisted of a nest of obscure courts, alleys, and avenues, running between the bottom of St. Martin's Lane, Half-moon, and Chandos-street. In Justice Overdo's time, they were the receptacles of fraudulent debtors, thieves and prostitutes.'—G. (Note on *Bart. Fair*, *Wks.* 4. 407.)

'On Wednesday at the Bermudas Court, Sir Edwin Sandys fell foul of the Earl of Warwick. The Lord Cavendish seconded Sandys and the Earl told the Lord, "By his favour he believed he lied." Hereupon, it is said, they rode out yesterday, and, as it is thought, gone beyond sea to fight.—*Leigh to Rev. Joseph Mede*, July 18, 1623.' (Quoted Wh-C. 1. 169.) So in *Underwoods*, *Wks.* 8. 348:

turn pirates here at land,Have their Bermudas and their Streights i' the Strand.

Bart. Fair, *Wks.* 4. 407: "The Streights, or the Bermudas, where the quarrelling lesson is read."

It is evident from the present passage and the above quotations that ruffians like Everill kept regular quarters in the 'Bermudas', where they might be consulted with reference to the settlement of affairs of honor.

2. 1. 151 puts off man, and kinde. 'I. e., human nature.'—G. Cf. *Catiline*, *Wks.* 4. 212:

—so much, that kindMay seek itself there, and not find.

2. 1. 162 French-masques. 'Masks do not appear as ordinary articles of female costume in England previous to the reign of Queen Elizabeth.... French masks are alluded to by Ben Jonson in *The Devil is an Ass*. They were probably the half masks called in France 'loups,' whence the English term 'loo masks.'

Loo masks and whole as wind do blow,And Miss abroad's disposed to go.*Mundus Muliebris*, 1690.—Planché *Cycl. of Costume* 1. 365.

'Black masks were frequently worn by ladies in public in the time of Shakespeare, particularly, and perhaps universally at the theatres.'—Nares.

2. 1. 163 Cut-works. A very early sort of lace deriving its name from the mode of its manufacture, the fine cloth on which the pattern was worked being cut away, leaving the design perfect. It is supposed to have been identical with what was known as Greek work, and made by the nuns of Italy in the twelfth century. It was introduced into England during the reign of Queen Elizabeth, and continued in fashion during those of James I. and Charles I. Later it fell under the ban of the Puritans, and after that period is rarely heard of. (Abridged from Planché, *Cycl.*)

2. 1. 168 ff. nor turne the key, etc. Gifford points out that the source of this passage is Plautus, *Aulularia* [ll. 90-100]:

Caue quemquam alienum in aedis intromiseris.Quod quispiam ignem quaerat, extingui uolo,Ne causae quid sit quod te quispiam quaeritet.Nam si ignis uiuet, tu extinguere extempulo,Tum aquam aufugisse dicito, si quis petet.Cultrum, securim, pistillum, mortarium,Quae utenda uasa semper uicini rogant,Fures uenisse atque abstulisse dicito.Profecto in aedis meas me absente neminemVolo intromitti, atque etiam hoc praedico tibi,Si Bona Fortuna ueniat, ne intromiseris.

Jonson had already made use of a part of this passage:

Put out the fire, kill the chimney's heart,That it may breathe no more than a dead man.*Case is Altered* 2. 1, *Wks.* 6. 328.

Wilson imitated the same passage in his *Projectors*, Act 2, Sc. 1: 'Shut the door after me, bolt it and bar it, and see you let no one in in my absence. Put out the fire, if there be any, for fear somebody, seeing the smoke, may come to borrow some! If any one come for water, say the pipe's cut off; or to borrow a pot, knife, pestle and mortar, or the like, say they were stole last night! But harke ye! I charge ye not to open the door to give them an answer, but whisper't through the keyhole! For, I tell you again, I wilt have nobody come into my house while I'm abroad! No; no living soul! Nay, though Good Fortune herself knock at a door, don't let her in!'

2. 2. 1 I haue no singular seruice, etc. I. e., This is the sort of thing I must become accustomed to, if I am to remain on earth.

2. 2. 49, 50 Though they take Master Fitz-dottrell, I am no such foule. Gifford points out that the punning allusion of *foul* to *fowl* is a play upon the word dottrel. 'The dotterel (Fuller tells us) is avis γελοτοποιος a mirth-making bird, so ridiculously mimical, that he is easily caught, or rather catcheth himself by his over-active imitation. As the fowler stretcheth forth his arms and legs, stalking towards the bird, so the bird extendeth his legs and wings, approaching the fowler till he is surprised in the net.'—G.

This is what is alluded to in 4. 6. 42. The use of the metaphor is common. Gifford quotes Beaumont & Fletcher. *Bonduca* and *Sea Voyage*. Many examples are given in Nares and the *NED.*, to which may be added *Damon and Pithias*, *O. Pl.* 4. 68; Nash, *Wks.* 3. 171; and Butler's *Character of a Fantastic* (ed. Morley, p. 401): 'He alters his gait with the times, and has not a motion of his body that (like a dottrel) he does not borrow from somebody else.' Nares quotes *Old Couple* (*O. Pl.*, 4th ed., 12. 41):

E. Our Dotterel then is caught?*B.* He is and justAs Dotterels use to be: the lady firstAdvanc'd toward him, stretch'd forth her wing, and heMet her with all expressions.

It is uncertain whether the sense of 'bird' or 'simpleton' is the original. *Dottrel* seems to be connected with *dote* and *dotard*. The bird is a species of plover, and Cunningham says that 'Selby ridicules the notion of its being more stupid than other birds.' In *Bart. Fair* (*Wks.* 4. 445) we hear of the 'sport call'd Dorring the Dotterel.'

2. 2. 51 Nor faire one. The dramatists were fond of punning on *foul* and *fair*. Cf. *Bart. Fair* passim.

2. 2. 77 a Nupson. Jonson uses the word again in *Every Man in*, *Wks.* 1. 111: 'O that I were so happy as to light on a nupson now.' In *Lingua*, 1607, (*O. Pl.*, 4th ed., 9. 367, 458) both the forms *nup* and *nupson* are used. The etymology is uncertain. The *Century Dictionary* thinks *nup* may be a variety of *nope*. Gifford thinks it may be a corruption of Greek νηπ.

2. 2. 78 with my Master's peace. 'I. e. respectfully, reverently: a bad translation of *cum pace domini*.'—G.

2. 2. 81 a spic'd conscience. Used again in *Sejanus*, *Wks.* 3. 120, and *New Inn*, *Wks.* 5. 337.

2. 2. 90 The very forked top too. Another reference to the horned head of the cuckold. Cf. 1. 6. 179, 80.

2. 2. 93 engendering by the eyes. Cf. Song in *Merch. of V.* 3. 2. 67: 'It is engender'd in the eyes.'

2. 2. 98 make benefit. Cf. *Every Man in*, *Wks.* 1. 127.

2. 2. 104 a Cokes. Cf. Ford, *Lover's Melancholy*, *Wks.* 2. 80: 'A kind of cokes, which is, as the learned term [it], an ass, a puppy, a widgeon, a dolt, a noddy, a———.' Cokes is the name of a foolish coxcomb in *Bart. Fair*.

2. 2. 112 you neat handsome vessells. Cf. note 1. 6. 57.

2. 2. 116 your squires of honour. This seems to be equivalent to the similar expression 'squire of dames.'

2. 2. 119-125 For the variety at my times, ... I know, to do my turnes, sweet Mistresse. I. e., when for variety you turn to me, I will be able to serve your needs. Pug, of course, from the delicate nature of the subject, chooses to make use of somewhat ambiguous phrases.

2. 2. 121. Thos. Keightley, *N. & Q.* 4. 2. 603, proposes to read:
Of that proportion, or in the rule.

2. 2. 123 Picardill. Cotgrave gives: 'Piccadilles: Piccadilles; the severall divisions or peeces fastened together about the brimme of the collar of a doublet, &c.' Gifford says: 'With respect to the *Piccadil*, or, as Jonson writes it, Picardil, (as if he supposed the fashion of wearing it be derived from Picardy,) the term is simply a diminutive of picca (Span. and Ital.) a spear-head, and was given to this article of foppery, from a fancied resemblance of its stiffened plaits to the bristled points of those weapons. Blount thinks, and apparently with justice, that Piccadilly took its name from the sale of the "small stiff collars, so called", which was first set on foot in a house near the western extremity of the present street, by one Higgins, a tailor.'

As Gifford points out, 'Pug is affecting modesty, since he had not only assumed a handsome body, but a fashionable dress, "made new" for a particular occasion.' See 5. 1. 35, 36.

Jonson mentions the *Picardill* again in the *Challenge at Tilt, Wks.* 7. 217, and in the *Epistle to a Friend, Wks.* 8. 356. For other examples see Nares, *Gloss*.

2. 2. 127 f. your fine Monkey; etc. These are all common terms of endearment. The monkey is frequently mentioned as a lady's pet by the dramatists. See *Cynthia's Revels*, passim, and Mrs. Centlivre's *Busie Body*.

2. 3. 36, 7 and your coach-man bald! Because he shall be bare. See note to 4. 4. 202.

2. 3. 45 This man defies the Diuell. See 2. 1. 18.

2. 3. 46 He dos't by Ingine. I. e., wit, ingenuity, with a possible reference to the name of Merecraft's agent.

2. 3. 49 Crowland. Crowland, or Croyland is an ancient town and parish of Lincolnshire, situated in a low flat district, about eight miles north-east from Peterborough. The origin of Crowland was in a hermitage founded in the 7th century by St. Guthlac. An abbey was founded in 714 by King Ethelbald, which was twice burnt and restored.

2. 4. 6 Spenser, I thinke, the younger. Thomas (1373-1400) was the only member of the Despenser family who was an Earl of Gloucester. The person referred to here, however, is Hugh le Despenser, the younger baron, son of Hugh le Despenser, the elder. He married Eleanor, daughter of Gilbert of Clare, Earl of Gloucester, and sister and coheiress of the next Earl Gilbert. After the death of the latter, the inheritance was divided between the husbands of his three sisters, and Despenser was accordingly sometimes called Earl of Gloucester.

Despenser was at first on the side of the barons, but later joined the King's party. In 1321 a league was formed against him, and he was banished, but was recalled in the following year. In the Barons' rising of 1326 he was taken prisoner, brought to Hereford, tried and put to death.

2. 4. 8 Thomas of Woodstocke. Thomas of Woodstock, Earl of Buckingham (1355-97), the youngest son of Edward III., was made Duke of Gloucester by his nephew, Richard II., in 1385, and later acquired an extraordinary influence, dominating the affairs of England for several years. By his high-handed actions he incurred Richard's enmity. He was arrested July 10, 1397, and conveyed to Calais, where he was murdered in the following September by the king's order.

2. 4. 10 Duke Humphrey. Humphrey, called the Good Duke Humphrey (1391-1447), youngest son of Henry IV., was created Duke of Gloucester and Earl of Pembroke in 1414. During the minority of Henry VI. he acted as Protector of the kingdom. His career was similar to that of Thomas of Woodstock. In 1447 he was arrested at Bury by order of Henry VI., who had become king in 1429. Here he died in February, probably by a natural death, although there were suspicions of foul play.

2. 4. 11 Richard the Third. Richard III. (1452-1485), Duke of Gloucester and King of England, was defeated and slain in the battle of Bosworth Field, 1485.

2. 4. 12-4 MER. By ... authentique. This passage has been the occasion of considerable discussion. The subject was first approached by Malone. In a note to an essay on *The Order of Shakespeare's Plays* in his edition of Shakespeare's works (ed. 1790, 3. 322) he says: 'In *The Devil's an Ass*, acted in 1616, all his historical plays are obliquely censured.'

Again in a dissertation on *Henry VI.*: 'The malignant Ben, does indeed, in his *Devil's an Ass*, 1616, sneer at our author's historical pieces, which for twenty years preceding had been in high reputation, and probably were *then* the only historical dramas that had possession of the theatre; but from the list above given, it is clear that Shakespeare was not the *first* who dramatized our old chronicles; and that the principal events of English History were familiar to the ears of his audience, before he commenced a writer for the stage.' Malone here refers to quotations taken from Gosson and Lodge. Both these essays were reprinted in Steevens' edition, and Malone's statements were repeated in the edition by Dr. Chalmers.

In 1808 appeared Gilchrist's essay, *An Examination of the Charges ... of Ben Jonson's enmity,* etc. *towards Shakespeare.* This refutation, strengthened by Gifford's *Proofs of Ben Jonson's Malignity*, has generally been deemed conclusive. Gifford's note on the present passage is written with much asperity. He was not content, however, with an accurate restatement of Malone's arguments. He changes the italics in order to produce an erroneous impression, printing thus: 'which were probably then the *only historical dramas on the stage*: He adds: 'And this is advanced in the very face of his own arguments, to prove that there were scores, perhaps hundreds, of others on it at the time.' This is direct falsification. There is no contradiction in Malone's arguments. What he attempted to prove was that Shakespeare had had predecessors in this field, but that in 1616 his plays held undisputed possession of the stage. Gifford adds a passage from Heywood's *Apology for Actors*, 1612, which is more to the point: 'Plays have taught the unlearned the knowledge of many famous *histories*, instructed such as cannot read in the discovery of our *English Chronicles*: and what man have you now of that weake capacity that being possest of their true use, cannot discourse of any notable thing recorded even from *William the Conqueror*, until this day?'

This passage seems to point to the existence of other historical plays *contemporary* with those of Shakespeare. Besides, Jonson's words seem sufficiently harmless. Nevertheless, although I am not inclined to accept Malone's charge of 'malignity', I cannot agree with Gifford that the reference is merely a general one. I have no doubt that the 'Chronicle,' of which Merecraft speaks, is Hall's, and the passage the following: 'It semeth to many men, that the name and title of Gloucester, hath been vnfortunate and vnluckie to diuerse, whiche for their honor, haue been erected by creacion of princes, to that stile and dignitie, as Hugh Spencer, Thomas of Woodstocke, sonne to kyng Edward the third, and this duke Humfrey, which thre persones, by miserable death finished their daies, and after them kyng Richard the iii. also, duke of Gloucester, in ciuill warre was slaine and confounded: so y^t this name of Gloucester, is take for an vnhappie and vnfortunate stile, as the prouerbe speaketh of Seianes horse, whose rider was euer unhorsed, and whose possessor was euer brought to miserie.' Hall's *Chronicle*, ed. 1809, pp. 209-10. The passage in 'the Play-bookes' which Jonson satirizes is at the close of *3 Henry VI*. 2. 6:

Edw. Richard, I will create thee Duke of Gloucester,And George, of Clarence: Warwick, as ourself,Shall do and undo as him pleaseth best.*Rich.* Let me be Duke of Clarence, George of Gloucester;For Gloucester's dukedom is too ominous.

The last line, of course, corresponds to the *'Tis fatal* of Fitzdottrel. Furthermore it may be observed that Thomas of Woodstock's death at Calais is referred to in Shakespeare's *K. Rich. II.*; Duke Humphrey appears in *2 Henry IV.*; *Henry V.*; and *1* and *2 Henry VI.*; and Richard III. in *2* and *3 Henry VI.* and *K. Rich. III. 3 Henry VI.* is probably, however, not of Shakespearean authorship.

2. 4. 15 a noble house. See Introduction.

2. 4. 23 Groen-land. The interest in Greenland must have been at its height in 1616. Between 1576 and 1622 English explorers discovered various portions of its coast; the voyages of Frobisher, Davis, Hudson and Baffin all taking place during that period. Hakluyt's *Principall Navigations* appeared in 1589, Davis's *Worldes Hydrographical Description* in 1594, and descriptions of Hudson's voyages in 1612-3. The usual spelling of the name seems to have been *Groenland,* as here. I find the word spelled also *Groineland, Groenlandia, Gronland,* and *Greneland* (see Publications of the Hakluyt Society). Jonson's reference has in it a touch of sarcasm.

2. 4. 27 f. Yes, when you, etc. The source of this passage is Hor., *Sat.* 2. 2. 129 f.:

Nam propriae telluris erum natura neque illumNec me nec quemquam statuit; nos expulit ille,Ilium aut nequities, aut vafri inscitia jurisPostremo expellet certe vivacior haeres.Nunc ager Umbreni sub nomine, nuper OfelliDictus, erit nulli proprius, sed cadet in usumNunc mihi, nunc alii.

Gifford quotes a part of the passage and adds: 'What follows is admirably turned by Pope:

Shades that to Bacon might retreat afford,Become the portion of a booby lord;And Helmsley, once proud Buckingham's delight,Slides to a scrivener, or city knight.'

A much closer imitation is found in Webster, *Devil's Law Case, Wks.* 2. 37:

Those lands that were the clients art now becomeThe lawyer's: and those tenements that wereThe country gentleman's, are now grownTo be his tailor's.

2. 4. 32 not do'it first. Cf. 1. 6. 14 and note.

2. 5. 10 And garters which are lost, if shee can shew 'hem. Gifford thinks the line should read: 'can not shew'. Cunningham gives a satisfactory explanation: 'As I understand this it means that if a gallant once saw the garters he would never rest until he obtained possession of them, and they would thus be *lost* to the family. Garters thus begged from the ladies were used by the gallants as *hangers* for their swords and poniards. See *Every Man out of his Humour, Wks.* 2. 81: "O, I have been graced by them beyond all aim of affection: this is her garter my dagger hangs in;" and again p. 194. We read also in *Cynthia's Revels*, *Wks.* 2. 266, of a gallant whose devotion to a lady in such that he

Salutes her pumps,Adores her hems, her skirts, her knots, her curls,*Will spend his patrimony for a garter,*Or the least feather in her bounteous fan.'

Gifford's theory that ladies had some mode of displaying their garters is contradicted by the following:

Mary. These roses will shew rare: would 'twere in fashionThat the garters might be seen too!—Massinger, *City Madam, Wks.*, p. 317.

Cf. also *Cynthia's Revels, Wks.* 2. 296.

2. 5. 14 her owne deare reflection, in her glasse. 'They must haue their looking glasses caryed with them wheresoeuer they go, ... no doubt they are the deuils spectacles to allure vs to pride, and consequently to distruction for euer.'—Stubbes, *Anat.*, Part 1, P. 79.

2. 6. 21 and done the worst defeate vpon my selfe. *Defeat* is often used by Shakespeare in this sense. See Schmidt, and compare *Hamlet* 2. 2. 598:

—A kingUpon whose property and most dear lifeA damn'd defeat was made.

2. 6. 32 a body intire. Cf. 5. 6. 48.

2. 6. 35 You make me paint. Gifford quotes from the *Two Noble Kinsmen*: How modestly she blows and paints the sunWith her chaste blushes.

2. 6. 37 SN. 'Whoever has noticed the narrow streets or rather lanes of our ancestors, and observed how story projected beyond story, till the windows of the upper rooms almost touched on different sides, will easily conceive the feasibility of everything which takes place between Wittipol and his mistress, though they make their appearance in different houses.'—G.

I cannot believe that Jonson wished to represent the two houses as on opposite sides of the street. He speaks of them as 'contiguous', which would naturally mean side by side. Further than this, one can hardly imagine even in the 'narrow lanes of our ancestors' so close a meeting that the liberties mentioned in 2. 6. 76 SN. could be taken.

2. 6. 53 A strange woman. In *Bart. Fair, Wks.* 4. 395, Justice Overdo says: 'Rescue this youth here out of the hands of the lewd man and *the strange woman.*' Gifford explains in a note: 'The scripture phrase for an immodest woman, a prostitute. Indeed this acceptation of the word is familiar to many languages. It is found in the Greek; and we have in Terence—pro *uxore habere hanc* peregrinam: upon   which   Donatus   remarks, *hoc   nomine etiam* meretrices *nominabantur.*'

2. 6. 57-113 WIT. No, my tune-full Mistresse? etc. This very important passage is the basis of Fleay's theory of identification discussed in section D. IV. of the Introduction. The chief passages necessary for comparison are quoted below.

A CELEBRATION OF CHARIS:
In Ten Lyric Pieces.
V.
His Discourse with Cupid.

Noblest Charis, you that are
Both my fortune and my star,
And do govern more my blood,
Than the various moon the flood,
Hear, what late discourse of you,   5

Love and I have had; and true.
'Mongst my Muses finding me,
Where he chanced your name to see
Set, and to this softer strain;
Sure, said he, if I have brain,   10

This, here sung, can be no other,
By description, but my Mother!
So hath Homer praised her hair;
So Anacreon drawn the air
Of her face, and made to rise   15

Just about her sparkling eyes,
Both her brows bent like my bow.
By her looks I do her know,
Which you call my shafts. And see!
Such my Mother's blushes be,   20

As the bath your verse discloses
In her cheeks, of milk and roses;
Such as oft I wanton in:
And, above her even chin,
Have you placed the bank of kisses,   25

Where, you say, men gather blisses,
Ripen'd with a breath more sweet,
Than when flowers and west-winds meet.
Nay, her white and polish'd neck,
With the lace that doth it deck,   30

Is my mother's: hearts of slain
Lovers, made into a chain!
And between each rising breast,
Lies the valley call'd my nest,
Where I sit and proyne my wings   35

After flight; and put new stings
To my shafts: her very name
With my mother's is the same.

I confess all, I replied,
And the glass hangs by her side,   40

And the girdle 'bout her waist,
All is Venus, save unchaste.
But alas, thou seest the least
Of her good, who is the best
Of her sex: but couldst thou, Love,   45

Call to mind the forms that strove
For the apple, and those three
Make in one, the same were she.
For this beauty yet doth hide
Something more than thou hast spied.   50

Outward grace weak love beguiles:
She is Venus when she smiles:
But she's Juno when she walks,
And Minerva when she talks.

UNDERWOODS XXXVI.
AN ELEGY.

By those bright eyes, at whose immortal fires
Love lights his torches to inflame desires;
By that fair stand, your forehead, whence he bends
His double bow, and round his arrows sends;
By that tan grove, your hair, whose globy rings   5

He flying curls, and crispeth with his wings;
By those pure baths your either cheek discloses,
Where he doth steep himself in milk and roses;
And lastly, by your lips, the bank of kisses,
Where men at once may plant and gather blisses: 10

Ten me, my lov'd friend, do you love or no?
So well as I may tell in verse, 'tis so?
You blush, but do not:—friends are either none,
Though they may number bodies, or but one.
I'll therefore ask no more, but bid you love,   15

And so that either may example prove
Unto the other; and live patterns, how
Others, in time, may love as we do now.
Slip no occasion; as time stands not still,

I know no beauty, nor no youth that will.   20

To use the present, then, is not abuse,
You have a husband is the just excuse
Of all that can be done him; such a one
As would make shift to make himself alone
That which we can; who both in you, his wife,   25

His issue, and all circumstance of life,
As in his place, because he would not vary,
Is constant to be extraordinary.

THE GIPSIES METAMORPHOSED
The Lady Purbeck's Fortune, by the

Gip. Help me, wonder, here's a book,2

Where I would for ever look:
Never yet did gipsy trace
Smoother lines in hands or face:
Venus here doth Saturn move   5

That you should be Queen of Love;
And the other stars consent;
Only Cupid's not content;
For though you the theft disguise,
You have robb'd him of his eyes.   10

And to shew his envy further:
Here he chargeth you with murther:
Says, although that at your sight,
He must all his torches light;
Though your either cheek discloses   15
Mingled baths of milk and roses;
Though your lips be banks of blisses,
Where he plants, and gathers kisses;
And yourself the reason why,
Wisest men for love may die;   20

You will turn all hearts to tinder,
And shall make the world one cinder.

From
A CHALLENGE AT TILT,

At a Marriage.

Cup. What can I turn other than a Fury itself to see thy 2
impudence? If I be a shadow, what is substance? was it not I
that yesternight waited on the bride into the nuptial chamber, and,
against the bridegroom came, made her the throne of love? had I
not lighted my torches in her eyes, planted my mother's roses in 5
her cheeks; were not her eye-brows bent to the fashion of my bow,
and her looks ready to be loosed thence, like my shafts? had I not
ripened kisses on her lips, fit for a Mercury to gather, and made
her language sweeter than his upon her tongue? was not the girdle
about her, he was to untie, my mother's, wherein all the joys and 10
delights of love were woven?

1 Cup. And did not I bring on the blushing bridegroom to taste
those joys? and made him think all stay a torment? did I not
shoot myself into him like a flame, and made his desires and his
graces equal? were not his looks of power to have kept the night 15
alive in contention with day, and made the morning never wished
for? Was there a curl in his hair, that I did not sport in, or a
ring of it crisped, that might not have become Juno's fingers? His
very undressing, was it not Love's arming? did not all his kisses
charge? and every touch attempt? but his words, were they not 20
feathered from my wings, and flew in singing at her ears, like
arrows tipt with gold?

In the above passages the chief correspondences to be noted are as follows:
1. *Ch.* 5. 17; *U.* 36. 3-4; *Challenge* 6. Cf. also *Ch.* 9. 17:
Eyebrows bent, like Cupid's bow.
2. *Ch.* 5. 25-6; *U.* 36. 9-10; *DA.* 2. 6. 86-7; *Gipsies* 17-8; *Challenge* 8.
3. *Ch.* 5. 21-2; *U.* 36. 7-8; *DA.* 2. 6. 82-3; *Gipsies* 15-6; *Challenge* 5-6.
4. *Ch.* 5. 41; *Challenge* 9-10.
5. *U.* 36. 5-6; *DA.* 2. 6. 77-82; *Challenge* 17-8. Cf. also *Ch.* 9. 9-12:
Young I'd have him too, and fair, Yet a man; with crisped hair, Cast in thousand
snares and rings, For love's fingers, and his wings.
6. *U.* 36. 21; *DA.* 1. 6. 132.
7· *U.* 36. 1-2; *Gipsies* 13-4; *Challenge* 5.
8. *U.* 36. 22-3; *DA.* 2. 6. 64-5
9. *DA.* 2. 6. 84-5; *Ch.* 9. 19-20:
Even nose, and cheek withal, Smooth as is the billiard-ball.
10. *Gipsies* 19-20; *Ch.* 1. 23-4:
Till she be the reason, why, All the world for love may die.

2. 6. 72 These sister-swelling brests. 'This is an elegant and poetical
rendering of the *sororiantes mammae* of the Latins, which Festus thus
explains: *Sororiare puellarum mammae dicuntur, cum primum tumescunt.*'—
G.

2. 6. 76 SN. 'Liberties very similar to these were, in the poet's time, permitted by ladies, who would have started at being told that they had foregone all pretensions to delicacy.'—G.

The same sort of familiarity is hinted at in Stubbes, *Anatomy of Abuses* (Part 1, p. 78). Furnivall quotes *Histriomastix* (Simpson's *School of Shak.* 2. 50) and *Vindication of Top Knots*, Bagford Collection, 1. 124, in illustration of the subject. Gosson's *Pleasant Quippes* (1595) speaks of 'these naked paps, the Devils ginnes.' Cf. also *Cyn. Rev., Wks.* 2. 266, and *Case is A., Wks.* 6. 330. It seems to have been a favorite subject of attack at the hands of both Puritans and dramatists.

2. 6. 76 Downe to this valley. Jonson uses a similar figure in *Cyn. Rev., Wks.* 2. 240 and in *Charis* (see note 2. 6. 57).

2. 6. 78 these crisped groues. So Milton, *Comus*, 984: 'Along the crisped shades and bowers.' Herrick, *Hesper., Cerem. Candlemas-Eve*: 'The crisped yew.'

2. 6. 85 well torn'd. Jonson's usual spelling. See *Timber*, ed. Schelling, 64. 33; 76. 22. etc.

2. 6. 85 Billyard ball. Billiards appears to have been an out-of-door game until the sixteenth century. It was probably introduced into England from France. See J. A. Picton, *N. & Q..* 5. 5. 283. Jonson uses this figure again in *Celeb. Charis* 9. 19-20.

2. 6. 92 when I said, a glasse could speake, etc. Cf. 1. 6. 80 f.

2. 6. 100 And from her arched browes, etc. Swinburne says of this line: 'The wheeziest of barrel-organs, the most broken-winded of bagpipes, grinds or snorts out sweeter music than that.'—*Study of Ben Jonson*, p. 104.

2. 6. 104 Have you seene. Sir John Suckling (ed. 1874, p. 79) imitates this stanza:

Hast thou seen the down in the airWhen wanton blasts have tossed it?Or the ship on the sea,When ruder winds have crossed it?Hast thou marked the crocodile's weeping,Or the fox's sleeping?Or hast viewed the peacock in his pride,Or the dove by his brideWhen he courts for his lechery?O, so fickle, O, so vain, O, so false, so false is she!

2. 6. 104 a bright Lilly grow. The figures of the lily, the snow, and the swan's down have already been used in *The Fox, Wks.* 3. 195. The source of that passage is evidently Martial, *Epig.* 1. 115:

Loto candidior puella cygno,Argento, nive, lilio, ligustro.

In this place Jonson seems to have more particularly in mind *Epig.* 5. 37:

Puella senibus dulcior mibi cygnis ...Cui nec lapillos praeferas Erythraeos, ...Nivesque primas liliumque non tactum.

2. 7. 2, 3 that Wit of man will doe't. There is evidently an ellipsis of some sort before *that* (cf. Abbott, §284). Perhaps 'provided' is to be understood.

2. 7. 4 She shall no more be buz'd at. The metaphor is carried out in the words that follow, *sweet meates* 5, *hum* 6, *flye-blowne* 7. 'Fly-blown' was a rather common term of opprobrium. Cf. Dekker, *Satiromastix, Wks.* 1. 195: 'Shal distaste euery vnsalted line, in their fly-blowne Comedies.' Jonson is very fond of this metaphor, and presses it beyond all endurance in *New Inn*, Act 2. Sc. 2, *Wks.* 5. 344, 5, etc.

2. 7. 13 I am resolu'd on't, Sir. See variants. Gifford points out the quibble on the word *resolved*. See Gloss.

2. 7. 17 O! I could shoote mine eyes at him. Cf. *Fox, Wks.* 3. 305: 'That I could shoot mine eyes at him, like gun-stones!'

2. 7. 22. See variants. The *the* is probably absorbed by the preceding dental. Cf. 5. 7. 9.

2. 7. 33 fine pac'd huishers. See note 4. 4. 201.

2. 7. 38 turn'd my good affection. 'Not diverted or changed its course; but, as appears from what follows, soured it. The word is used in a similar sense by Shakespeare:

Has friendship such a faint and *milky* heart,It turns in less than two nights!*Timon*, 3. 2.'—G.

2. 8. 9, 10 That was your bed-fellow. Ingine, perhaps in anticipation of Fitzdottrel's advancement, employs a term usually applied to the nobility. Cf. *K. Henry V.* 2. 2. 8:

Nay, but the man that was his bedfellow,Whom he had cloy'd and grac'd with princely favors.

Steevens in a note on the passage points out that the familiar appellation of *bedfellow*, which appears strange to us, was common among the ancient nobility.' He quotes from *A Knack to know a Knave*, 1594; *Look about you*, 1600; *Cynthia's Revenge*, 1613; etc., where the expression is used in the sense of 'intimate companion' and applied to nobles. Jonson uses the term *chamberfellow* in *Underwoods, Wks.* 8. 353.

2. 8. 20 An Academy. With this passage compare *U.* 62, *Wks.* 8. 412:

—There is up of lateThe Academy, where the gallants meet—What! to make legs? yes, and to smell most sweet:All that they do at plays. O but first hereThey learn and study; and then practice there.

Jonson again refers to 'the Academies' (apparently schools of deportment or dancing schools) in 3. 5. 33.

2. 8. 33 Oracle-Foreman. See note 1. 2. 2.

2. 8. 59 any thing takes this dottrel. See note 2. 2. 49-50.

2. 8. 64 Dicke Robinson. Collier says: 'This player may have been an original actor in some of Shakespeare's later dramas, and he just outlived the complete and final suppression of the stage.' His death and the date at which it occurred have been matters of dispute.

His earliest appearance in any list of actors is at the end of Jonson's *Catiline*, 1611, with the King's Majesty's Servants. He was probably the youngest member of the company, and doubtless sustained a female part. Gifford believes that he took the part of Wittipol in the present play, though this is merely a conjecture. 'The only female character he is known to have filled is the lady of Giovanus in *The Second Maiden's Tragedy*, but at what date is uncertain; neither do we know at what period he began to represent male characters.' Of the plays in which he acted, Collier mentions Beaumont and Fletcher's *Bonduca, Double Marriage, Wife for a Month*, and *Wild Goose Chase* (1621); and Webster's *Duchess of Malfi*, 1622.

His name is found in the patent granted by James I. in 1619 and in that granted by Charles I. in 1625. Between 1629 and 1647 no notice of him occurs, and this is the last date at which we hear of him. 'His name follows that of Lowin in the dedication to the folio of Beaumont and Fletcher's works, published at that time.'—Collier, *Memoirs*, p. 268.

Jonson not infrequently refers to contemporary actors. Compare the *Epitaph on Salathiel Pavy, Ep.* 120; the speech of Venus in *The Masque of Christmas, Wks.* 7. 263; and the reference to Field and Burbage in *Bart. Fair* 5. 3.

2. 8. 73 send frolicks! '*Frolics* are couplets, commonly of an amatory or satirical nature, written on small slips of paper, and wrapt round a sweetmeat. A dish of them is usually placed on the table after supper, and the guests amuse themselves with sending them to one another, as circumstances seem to render them appropriate: this is occasionally productive of much mirth. I do not believe that the game is to be found in England; though the drawing on Twelfth Night may be thought to bear some kind of coarse resemblance to it. On the continent I have frequently been present at it.'—G.

The *NED.* gives only one more example, from R. H. *Arraignm. Whole Creature XIV.* § 2. 244 (1631) 'Moveable as Shittlecockes ... or as Frolicks at Feasts, sent from man to man, returning againe at last, to the first man.'

2. 8. 74, 5 burst your buttons, or not left you seame. Cf. *Bart. Fair, Wks.* 4. 359: 'he breaks his buttons, and cracks seams at every saying he sobs out.'

2. 8. 95, 103. See variants.

2. 8. 100 A Forrest moues not. 'I suppose Trains means, "It is in vain to tell him of venison and pheasant, the right to the bucks in a whole forest will not move him."'—C.

2. 8. 100 that forty pound. See 3. 3. 148.

2. 8. 102 your bond Of Sixe; and Statute of eight hundred! I. e., of six, and eight hundred pounds. 'Statutes merchant, statutes staple, and recognizances in the nature of a statute staple were acknowledgements of debt made in writing before officers appointed for that purpose, and enrolled of record. They bound the lands of the debtor; and execution was awarded upon them upon default in payment without the ordinary process of an action. These securities were originally introduced for the encouragement of trade, by providing a sure and speedy remedy for the recovery of debts between merchants, and afterwards became common assurances, but have now become obsolete.'—S. M. Leake, *Law of Contracts*, p. 95.

Two of Pecunia's attendants in *The Staple of News* are *Statute* and *Band* (i. e. Bond, see *U.* 34). The two words are often mentioned together. In Dekker's *Bankrouts Banquet* (*Non-dram. Wks.* 3. 371) statutes are served up to the bankrupts.

Trains is evidently trying to impress Fitzdottrel with the importance of Merecraft's transactions.

ACT III.

3. 1. 8 Innes of Court. 'The four Inns of Court, Gray's Inn, Lincoln's Inn, the Inner, and the Middle Temple, have alone the right of admitting persons to practise as barristers, and that rank can only be attained by keeping the requisite number of terms as a student at one of those Inns.'—Wh-C.

Jonson dedicates *Every Man out of his Humor* 'To the Noblest Nurseries of Humanity and Liberty in the Kingdom, the Inns of Court.'

3. 1. 10 a good man. Gifford quotes *Merch. of Ven.* 1. 3. 15: 'My meaning in saying he is a good man, is, to have you understand me, that he is sufficient.' Marston, *Dutch Courtesan, Wks.* 2. 57. uses the word in the same sense.

3. 1. 20 our two Pounds, the Compters. The London Compters or Counters were two sheriff's prisons for debtors, etc., mentioned as early as the 15th century. In Jonson's day they were the Poultry Counter and the Wood Street Counter. They were long a standing joke with the dramatists, who seem to speak from a personal acquaintance with them. Dekker (*Roaring Girle, Wks.* 3. 189) speaks of 'Wood Street College,' and Middleton (*Phoenix, Wks.* 1. 192) calls them 'two most famous universities' and in another place 'the two city hazards, Poultry and Wood Street.' Jonson in *Every Man in* (*Wks.* 1. 42) speaks of them again as 'your city pounds, the counters', and in *Every man out* refers to the 'Master's side' (*Wks.* 2. 181) and the 'two-penny ward,' the designations for the cheaper quarters of the prison.

3. 1. 35 out of rerum natura. *In rerum natura* is a phrase used by Lucretius 1. 25. It means, according to the *Stanford Dictionary*, 'in the nature of things, in the physical universe.' In some cases it is practically equivalent to 'in existence.' Cf. *Sil. Wom., Wks.* 3. 382: 'Is the bull, bear, and horse, in *rerum natura* still?'

3. 2. 12 a long vacation. The long vacation in the Inns of Court, which Jonson had in mind, lasts from Aug. 13 to Oct. 23. In *Staple of News, Wks.* 5. 170, he makes a similar thrust at the shop-keepers:

Alas I they have had a pitiful hard time on't, A long vacation from their cozening.

3. 2. 22 I bought Plutarch's liues. T. North's famous translation first appeared in 1579. New editions followed in 1595, 1603, 1610-12, and 1631.

3. 2. 33 Buy him a Captaines place. The City Train Bands were a constant subject of ridicule for the dramatists. They are especially well caricatured by Fletcher in *The Knight of the Burning Pestle*, Act 5. In addition to the City Train Bands, the Fraternity of Artillery, now called The Honorable Artillery Company, formed a separate organization. The place of practice was the Artillery Garden in Bunhill Fields (see note 3. 2. 41). In spite of ridicule the Train Bands proved a source of strength during the Civil War (see Clarendon, *Hist. of the Rebellion*, ed. 1826, 4. 236 and Wh-C., *Artillery Ground*).

Jonson was fond of poking fun at the Train Bands. Cf. *U. 62, Wks.* 8. 409; *Ev. Man in, Wks.* 1. 88; and *Alchemist, Wks.* 4. 13. Face, it will be remembered, had been 'translated suburb-captain' through Subtle's influence.

The immediate occasion of Jonson's satire was doubtless the revival of military enthusiasm in 1614, of which Entick (*Survey* 2. 115) gives the following account:

'The military genius of the *Londoners* met with an opportunity, about this time, to convince the world that they still retained the spirit of their forefathers, should they be called out in the cause of their king and country. His majesty having commanded a general muster of the militia throughout the kingdom, the city of *London* not only mustered 6000 citizens completely armed, who performed their several evolutions with surprizing dexterity; but a martial spirit appeared amongst the rising generation. The children endeavoured to imitate their parents; chose officers, formed themselves into companies, marched often into the fields with colours flying and beat of drums, and there, by frequent practice, grew up expert in the military exercises.'

3. 2. 35 Cheapside. Originally Cheap, or West Cheap, a street between the Poultry and St. Paul's, a portion of the line from Charing Cross to the Royal Exchange, and from Holborn to the Bank of England.

'At the west end of this Poultrie and also of Buckles bury, beginneth the large street of West Cheaping, a market-place so called, which street stretcheth west till ye come to the little conduit by Paule's Gate.'—Stow, ed. Thoms, p. 99.

The glory of Cheapside was Goldsmith's Row (see note 3. 5. 2). It was also famous in early times for its 'Ridings,' and during Jonson's period for its 'Cross,' its 'Conduit,' and its 'Standard' (see note 1. 1. 56 and Wh—C.).

3. 2. 35 Scarfes. 'Much worn by knights and military officers in the sixteenth and seventeenth centuries.'—Planché.

3. 2. 35 Cornehill. Cornhill, between the Poultry and Leadenhall Street, an important portion of the greatest thoroughfare in the world, was, says Stow, 'so called of a corn market time out of mind there holden.' In later years it was provided with a pillory and stocks, a prison, called the Tun, for street offenders, a conduit of 'sweet water', and a standard. See Wh-C.

3. 2. 38 the posture booke. A book descriptive of military evolutions, etc. H. Peacham's *Compleat Gentleman*, 1627 (p. 300, quoted by Wheatley, *Ev. Mall in*), gives a long list of 'Postures of the Musquet' and G. Markham's *Souldier's Accidence* gives another. Cf. *Tale Tub, Wks.* 6. 218:

—All the posturesOf the train'd bands of the country.

3. 2. 41 Finsbury. In 1498, 'certain grounds, consisting of gardens, orchards, &c. on the north side of *Chiswell-street*, and called *Bunhill* or *Bunhill-fields*, within the manor of *Finsbury*, were by the mayor and commonalty of *London*, converted into a large field, containing 11 acres, and 11 perches, now known by the name of the *Artillery-ground*, for their train-bands, archers, and other military citizens, to exercise in.'— Entick, *Survey* 1. 441.

In 1610 the place had become neglected, whereupon commissioners were appointed to reduce it 'into such order and state for the archers as they were in the beginning of the reign of King Henry VIII.' (*Ibid.* 2. 109). See also Stow, *Survey*, ed. Thoms, p. 159.

Dekker (*Shomaker's Holiday, Wks.* 1. 29) speaks of being 'turnd to a Turk, and set in Finsburie for boyes to shoot at', and Nash (*Pierce Pennilesse, Wks.* 2.

128) and Jonson (*Bart. Fair, Wks.* 4. 507) make precisely similar references. Master Stephen in *Every Man in* (*Wks.* 1. 10) objects to keeping company with the 'archers of Finsbury.' Cf. also the elaborate satire in *U.* 62, (*Wks.* 8. 409).

3. 2. 45   to traine the youth

Of London, in the military truth. Cf. *Underwoods* 62:

Thou seed-plot of the war! that hast not spar'dPowder or paper to bring up the youthOf London, in the military truth.

Gifford believes these lines to be taken from a contemporary posture-book, but there is no evidence of quotation in the case of *Underwoods*.

3. 3. 22, 3   This comes of wearing

Scarlet, gold lace, and cut-works! etc. Webster has a passage very similar to this in the *Devil's Law Case, Wks.* 2. 37 f.:

'*Ari.* This comes of your numerous wardrobe.*Rom.* Ay, and wearing cut-work, a pound a purl.*Ari.* Your dainty embroidered stockings, with overblown roses, to hide your gouty ankles.*Rom.* And wearing more taffata for a garter, than would serve the galley dung-boat for streamers....*Rom.* And resorting to your whore in hired velvet with a spangled copper fringe at her netherlands.*Ari.* Whereas if you had stayed at Padua, and fed upon cow-trotters, and fresh beef to supper.' etc., etc.

For 'cut-works' see note 1. 1. 128.

3. 3. 24 With your blowne roses. Compare 1. 1. 127, and B. & Fl., *Cupid's Revenge*:

No man to warm your shirt, and blow your roses.

and Jonson, *Ep.* 97, *Wks.* 8. 201:

His rosy ties and garters so o'erblown.

3. 3. 25 Godwit. The godwit was formerly in great repute as a table delicacy. Thomas Muffett in *Health's Improvement*, p. 99, says: 'A fat godwit is so fine and light meat, that noblemen (yea, and merchants too, by your leave) stick not to buy them at four nobles a dozen.'

Cf. also Sir T. Browne, *Norf. Birds, Wks.*, 1835, 4. 319: God-wyts ... accounted the daintiest dish in England; and, I think, for the bigness of the biggest price.' Jonson mentions the godwit in this connection twice in the *Sil. Wom.* (*Wks.* 3. 350 and 388), and in Horace, *Praises of a Country Life* (*Wks.* 9. 121) translates 'attagen Ionicus' by 'Ionian godwit.'

3. 3. 26 The Globes, and Mermaides! Theatres and taverns. Mr. Halliwell-Phillipps has proved that the Globe Theatre on the Bankside, Southwark, the summer theatre of Shakespeare and his fellows, was built in 1599. It was erected from materials brought by Richard Burbage and Peter Street from the theatre in Shoreditch. On June 29, 1613, it was destroyed by fire, but was rebuilt without delay in a superior style, and this time with a roof of tile, King James contributing to the cost. Chamberlaine, writing to Alice Carleton (June 30, 1614), calls the Globe Playhouse 'the fairest in England.' It was pulled down Apr. 15, 1644.

Only the Lord Chamberlain's Company (the King's Men) seems to have acted here. It was the scene of several of Shakespeare's plays and two of Jonson's, *Every Man out* and *Every Man in* (Halliwell-Phillips, *Illustrations*, p.

43). The term 'summer theatre' is applicable only to the rebuilt theatre (*ibid.*, p. 44). In *Ev. Man out* (quarto, *Wks.* 2. 196) Johnson refers to 'this fair-fitted *Globe*', and in the *Execration upon Vulcan* (*Wks.* 8. 404) to the burning of the 'Globe, the glory of the Bank.' In *Poetaster* (*Wks.* 2. 430) he uses the word again as a generic term: 'your Globes, and your Triumphs.'

There seem to have been two Mermaid Taverns, one of which stood in Bread Street with passage entrances from Cheapside and Friday Street, and the other in Cornhill. They are often referred to by the dramatists. Cf. the famous lines written by *Francis Beaumont to Ben Jonson*, B. & Fl., *Wks.*, ed. 1883, 2. 708; *City Match*, *O. Pl.* 9. 334, etc. Jonson often mentions the Mermaid. Cf. *Inviting a Friend, Wks.* 8. 205:

Is a pure cup of rich Canary Wine,Which is the Mermaid's now, but shall be mine.

On the famous Voyage, Wks. 8. 234:

At Bread-Street's Mermaid having dined, and merry,Proposed to go to Holborn in a wherry.

Bart. Fair, Wks. 4. 356-7: 'your Three Cranes, Mitre, and Mermaid-men!'

3. 3. 28 In veluet! Velvet was introduced into England in the fifteenth century, and soon became popular as an article of luxury (see Hill's *Hist. of Eng. Dress* 1. 145 f.).

3. 3. 30 I' the Low-countries. 'Then went he to the Low Countries; but returning soone he betook himself to his wonted studies. In his service in the Low Countries, he had, in the face of both the campes, killed ane enemie and taken *opima spolia* from him.'—*Conversations with William Drummond, Wks.* 9. 388.

In the Epigram *To True Soldiers* Jonson says:

—I loveYour great profession, which I once did prove.*Wks.* 8. 211.

3. 3. 32 a wench of a stoter! See variants. The word is not perfectly legible in the folios, which I have consulted, but is undoubtedly as printed. Cunningham believes 'stoter' to be a cheap coin current in the camps. This supplies a satisfactory sense, corresponding to the '*Sutlers* wife, ... of two blanks' in the following line.

3. 3. 33 of two blanks! 'Jonson had Horace in his thoughts, and has, not without some ingenuity, parodied several loose passages of one of his satires.'—G. Gifford is apparently referring to the close of Bk. 2. Sat. 3.

3. 3. 51 vn-to-be-melted. Cf. *Every Man in, Wks.* 1. 36: 'and in un-in-one-breath-utterable skill, sir.' *New Inn, Wks.* 5. 404: you shewed a neglect Un-to-be-pardon'd.'

3. 3. 62 Master of the Dependances! See Introduction. pp. <u>lvi</u>, <u>lvii</u>.

3. 3. 69 the roaring manner. Gifford defines it as the 'language of bullies affecting a quarrel' (*Wks.* 4. 483). The 'Roaring Boy' continued under various designations to infest the streets of London from the reign of Elizabeth until the beginning of the eighteenth century. Spark (Somer's *Tracts* 2. 266) says that they were persons prodigall and of great expence, who having runne themselves into debt, were constrained to run into factions to defend themselves from danger of the law.' He adds that divers of the nobility afforded them maintenance, in return for which 'they entered into many desperate enterprises.'

Arthur Wilson (*Life of King James I.*, p. 28), writing of the disorderly state of the city in 1604, says: 'Divers *Sects* of *vitious Persons* going under the Title of *Roaring Boyes, Bravadoes, Roysters*, &c. commit many insolences; the Streets swarm night and day with bloody quarrels, private *Duels* fomented,' etc.

Kastril, the 'angry boy' in the *Alchemist*, and Val Cutting and Knockem in *Bartholomew Fair* are roarers, and we hear of them under the title of 'terrible boys' in the *Silent Woman* (*Wks.* 3. 349). Cf. also Sir Thomas Overbury's *Character of a Roaring Boy* (ed. Morley, p. 72): 'He sleeps with a tobacco-pipe in his mouth; and his first prayer in the morning is he may remember whom he fell out with over night.'

3. 3. 71 the vapours. This ridiculous practise is satirized in *Bart. Fair*, *Wks.* 4. 3 (see also stage directions).

3. 3. 77 a distast. The quarrel with Wittipol.

3. 3. 79 the hand-gout. Jonson explains the expression in *Magnetic Lady*, *Wks.* 6. 61.

You cannot but with trouble put your handInto your pocket to discharge a reckoning,And this we sons of physic do call *chiragra*,A kind of cramp, or hand-gout.

Cf. also Overbury's *Characters*, ed. Morley, p. 63: 'his liberality can never be said to be gouty-handed.'

3. 3. 81 Mint. Until its removal to the Royal Mint on Tower Hill in 1810, the work of coinage was carried on in the Tower of London. Up to 1640, when banking arose, merchants were in the habit of depositing their bullion and cash in the Tower Mint, under guardianship of the Crown (see Wh-C. under *Royal Mint*, and *History of Banking in all the Leading Nations*, London, 1896, 2. 1).

3. 3. 86-8 let ... hazard. Merecraft seems to mean: 'You are in no hurry. Pray therefore allow me to defer your business until I have brought opportune aid to this gentleman's distresses at a time when his fortunes are in a hazardous condition.' The pregnant use of the verb *timing* and the unusual use of the word *terms* for a period of time render the meaning peculiarly difficult.

3. 3. 106 a Businesse. This was recognized as the technical expression. Sir Thomas Overbury ridicules it in his *Characters*, ed. Morley, p. 72: 'If any private quarrel happen among our great courtiers, he (the Roaring Boy) proclaims the business—that's the word, the business—as if the united force of the Roman Catholics were making up for Germany.' Jonson ridicules the use of the word in similar fashion in the Masque of *Mercury Vindicated from the Alchemists*.

3. 3. 133 hauings. Jonson uses the expression again in *Ev. Man in*, *Wks.* 1. 29, and *Gipsies Met.*, *Wks.* 7. 364. It is also used in *Muse's Looking Glasse*, *O. Pl.* 9. 175.

3. 3. 147 such sharks! Shift in *Ev. Man in* is described as a 'threadbare shark.' Cf. also Earle, *Microcosmography*, ed. Morley, p. 173.

3. 3. 148 an old debt of forty. See 2. 8. 100.

3. 3. 149 the Bermudas. See note 2. 1. 144. Nares thinks that the real Bermudas are referred to here.

3. 3. 155 You shall ha' twenty pound on't. As Commission on the two hundred. 'Ten in the hundred' was the customary rate at this period (see *Staple of News, Wks.* 5. 189).

3. 3. 165 St. Georges-tide? From a very early period the 23d of April was dedicated to St. George. From the time of Henry V. The festival had been observed with great splendor at Windsor and other towns, and bonfires were built (see Shak, *1 Henry VI.* 1. 1). The festival continued to be celebrated until 1567, when Elizabeth ordered its discontinuance. James I., however, kept the 23d of April to some extent, and the revival of the feast in all its glories was only prevented by the Civil War. So late as 1614 it was the custom for fashionable gentlemen to wear blue coats on St. George's Day, probably in imitation of the blue mantle worn by the Knights of the Garter, an order created at the feast of St. George in 1344 (see Chambers' *Book of Days* 1. 540).

The passages relating to this custom are *Ram Alley, O. Pl.*, 2d ed., 5. 486:

By Dis, I will be knight,Wear a blue coat on great St. George's day,And with my fellows drive you all from Paul'sFor this attempt.

Runne and a great Cast, Epigr. 33:

With's coram nomine keeping greater swayThan a court blew-coat on St. George's day.

From these passages Nares concludes 'that some festive ceremony was carried on at St. Paul's on St. George's day annually; that the court attended; that the *blue-coats*, or attendants, of the courtiers, were employed and authorised to keep order, and drive out refractory persons; and that on this occasion it was proper for a knight to officiate as *blue coat* to some personage of higher rank'.

In the *Conversations with Drummond*, Jonson's *Wks.* 9. 393, we read: 'Northampton was his mortal enimie for beating, on a St. George's day, one of his attenders.' Pepys speaks of there being bonfires in honor of St. George's Day as late as Apr. 23, 1666.

3. 3. 166 chaines? PLV. Of gold, and pearle. The gold chain was formerly a mark of rank and dignity, and a century before this it had been forbidden for any one under the degree of a gentleman of two hundred marks a year to wear one (*Statutes of the Realm*, 7 Henry VIII. c. 6). They were worn by the Lord Mayors (Dekker, *Shomaker's Holiday, Wks.* 1. 42), rich merchants and aldermen (Glapthorne, *Wit for a Constable, Wks.*, ed. 1874, 1. 201-3), and later became the distinctive mark of the upper servant in a great family, especially the steward (see Nares and *Ev. Man out, Wks.* 2. 31). Massinger (*City Madam, Wks.*, p. 334) speaks of wearing a chain of gold 'on solemn days.' With the present passage cf. *Underwoods* 62, *Wks.* 8. 410:

If they stay here but till St. George's day.All ensigns of a war are not yet dead,Nor marks of wealth so from a nation fled,But they may see gold chains and pearl worn then,Lent by the London dames to the Lords' men.

3. 3. 170 take in Pimlico. 'Near Hoxton, a great summer resort in the early part of the 17th century and famed for its cakes, custards, and Derby ale. The references to the Hoxton Pimlico are numerous in our old dramatists.'—Wh— C. It is mentioned among other places in *Greene's Tu Quoque, The City Match,* fol. 1639, *News from Hogsdon*, 1598, and Dekker, *Roaring Girle, Wks.* 3. 219, where it is spoken of as 'that nappy land of spice-cakes.' In 1609 a tract was published, called *Pimlyco or Runne Red-Cap, 'tis a Mad World at Hogsdon.*

Jonson refers to it repeatedly. Cf. *Alch., Wks.* 4. 155:

—Gallants, men and women.And of all sorts, tag-rag, been seen to flock here,In threaves, these ten weeks, as to a second Hogsden,In days of Pimlico and Eye-bright.

Cf. also *Alch., Wks.* 4. 151; *Bart. Fair, Wks.* 4. 357; and this play 4. 4. 164. In *Underwoods* 62 the same expression is used as in this passage:

What a strong fort old Pimlico had been!How it held out! how, last, 'twas taken in!—

Take in in the sense of 'capture' is used again in *Every Man in, Wks.* 1. 64, and frequently in Shakespeare (see Schmidt). The reference here, as Cunningham suggests, is to the Finsbury sham fights. Hogsden was in the neighborhood of Finsbury, and the battles were doubtless carried into its territory.

3. 3. 173 Some Bristo-stone or Cornish counterfeit. Cf. Heywood, *Wks.* 5. 317: 'This jewell, a plaine *Bristowe* stone, a counterfeit.' See Gloss.

3. 3. 184, 5 **I know your Equiuocks:**
You'are growne the better Fathers of 'hem o' late.

'Satirically reflecting on the Jesuits, the great patrons of *equivocation.*'— W.

'Or rather on the Puritans, I think; who were sufficiently obnoxious to this charge. The Jesuits would be out of place here.'—G.

Why the Puritans are any more appropriate Gifford does not vouchsafe to tell us. So far as I have been able to discover the Puritans were never called 'Fathers,' their regular appellation being 'the brethren' (cf. *Alch.* and *Bart. Fair*). The Puritans were accused of a distortion of Scriptural texts to suit their own purposes, instances of which occur in the dramas mentioned above. On the whole, however, equivocation is more characteristic of the Jesuits. They were completely out of favor at this time. Under the generalship of Claudio Acquaviva, 1581-1615, they first began to have a preponderatingly evil reputation. In 1581 they were banished from England, and in 1601 the decree of banishment was repeated, this time for their suspected share in the Gunpowder Plot.

3. 3. 206, 7 Come, gi' me Ten pieces more. The transaction with Guilthead is perhaps somewhat confusing. Fitzdottrel has offered to give his bond for two hundred pieces, if necessary. Merecraft's 'old debt of forty' (3. 3. 149), the fifty pieces for the ring, and the hundred for Everill's new office (3. 3. 60 and 83) 'all but make two hundred.' Fitzdottrel furnishes a hundred of this in cash, with the understanding that he receive it again of the gold-smith when he signs the bond (3. 3. 194). He returns, however, without the gold, though he seals the bond (3. 5. 1-3). Of the hundred pieces received in cash, twenty go to Guilthead as commission (3. 3. 155). This leaves forty each for Merecraft and Everill.

3. 3. 213 how th' Asse made his diuisions. See *Fab.* cix, *Fabulae*

Aesopicae, Leipzig, 1810, *Leo, Asinus et Vulpes*. Harsnet (*Declaration*, p. 110) refers to this fable, and Dekker made a similar application in *Match me in London*, 1631, *Wks.* 4. 145:

King. Father Ile tell you a Tale, vpon a timeThe Lyon Foxe and silly Asse did jarre.Grew friends and what they got, agreed to share:A prey was tane, the bold Asse did diuide itInto three equall parts, the Lyon spy'd it.And scorning two such sharers, moody grew,And pawing the Asse, shooke him as I shake you ...And in rage tore him peece meale, the Asse thus dead,The prey was by the Foxe distributedInto three parts agen; of which the LyonHad two for his share, and the Foxe but one:The Lyon (smiling) of the Foxe would knowWhere he had this wit, he the dead Asse did show.*Valasc.* An excellent Tale.*King.* Thou art that Asse.

3. 3. 214 Much good do you. So in *Sil. Wom.*, *Wks.* 3. 398: 'Much good do him.'

3. 3. 217 And coozen i' your bullions. Massinger's *Fatal Dowry*, *Wks.*, p. 272, contains the following passage: 'The other is his dressing-block, upon whom my lord lays all his clothes and fashions ere he vouchsafes them his own person: you shall see him ... at noon in the Bullion,' etc. In a note on this passage (*Wks.* 3. 390, ed. 1813) Gifford advanced the theory that the *bullion* was 'a piece of finery, which derived its denomination from the large globular gilt buttons, still in use on the continent.' In his note on the present passage, he adds that it was probably 'adopted by gamblers and others, as a mark of wealth, to entrap the unwary.'

Nares was the next man to take up the word. He connected it with '*bullion*; Copper-plates set on the Breast-leathers and Bridles of Horses for ornament' (Phillips 1706). 'I suspect that it also meant, in colloquial use, copper lace, tassels, and ornaments in imitation of gold. Hence contemptuously attributed to those who affected a finery above their station.'

Dyce (B. & Fl., *Wks.* 7. 291) was the first to disconnect the word from *bullion* meaning uncoined gold or silver. He says: '*Bullions*, I apprehend, mean some sort of hose or breeches, which were *bolled* or *bulled*, i. e. swelled, puffed out (cf. *Sad. Shep.*, Act 1. Sc. 2, *bulled* nosegays').'

The *NED.* gives 'prob. a. F. *bouillon* in senses derived from that of "bubble."'

Besides the passages already given, the word occurs in B. & Fl., *The Chances*, *Wks.* 7. 291:

Why should not bilbo raise him, or a pair of bullions?

Beggar's Bush, *Wks.* 9. 81:

In his French doublet, with his blister'd(1st fol. *baster'd*) bullions.

Brome, *Sparagus Garden*, *Wks.* 3. 152:

—shaking yourOld Bullion Tronkes over my Trucklebed.

Gesta Gray in Nichols' *Prog. Q. Eliz.* 3. 341 A, 1594: 'A bullion-hose is best to go a woeing in; for tis full of promising promontories.'

3. 3. 231 too-too-vnsupportable! This reduplicated form is common in Shakespeare. See *Merch. of Ven.* 2. 6. 42; *Hamlet* 1. 2. 129; and Schmidt, *Dict.* Jonson uses it in *Sejanus*, *Wks.* 3. 54, and elsewhere. It is merely a strengthened form of *too*. (See Halliwell in *Sh. Soc. Papers*, 1884, 1. 39, and *Hamlet*, ed. Furness, 11th ed., 1. 41.) Jonson regularly uses the hyphen.

3. 4. 13 Cioppinos. Jonson spells the word as if it were Italian, though he says in the same sentence that the custom of wearing chopines is Spanish. The *NED.*, referring to Skeat, *Trans. Phil. Soc.*, 1885-7, p. 79, derives it from Sp. *chapa*, a plate of metal, etc. 'The Eng. writers c 1600 persistently treated the word as Italian, even spelling it *cioppino*, pl. *cioppini*, and expressly associated it with Venice, so that, although not recorded in Italian Dicts. it was app. temporarily fashionable there.' The statement of the *NED.* that 'there is little or no evidence of their use in England (except on the stage)' seems to be contradicted by the quotation from Stephen Gosson's *Pleasant Quippes* (note 1. 1. 128). References to the chopine are common in the literature of the period (see Nares and *NED.*). I have found no instances of the Italianated form earlier than Jonson, and it may be original with him. He uses the plural *cioppini* in *Cynthia's Revels*, *Wks.* 2. 241. See note 4. 4. 69.

3. 4. 32 your purchase. Cf. *Alch.*, *Wks.* 4. 150, and *Fox, Wks.* 3. 168: 'the cunning purchase of my wealth.' Cunningham (*Wks.* 3. 498) says: 'Purchase, as readers of Shakespeare know, was a cant term among thieves for the plunder they acquired, also the act of acquiring it. It is frequently used by Jonson.'

3. 4. 35 Pro'uedor. Gifford's change to provedoré is without authority. The word is *provedor*, Port., or *proveedor*, Sp., and is found in Hakluyt, *Voyages*, 3. 701; G. Sandys, *Trav.*, p. 6 (1632); and elsewhere, with various orthography, but apparently never with the accent.

3. 4. 43 Gentleman huisher. For the gentleman-usher see note 4. 4. 134. The forms *usher* and *huisher* seem to be used without distinction. The editors' treatment of the form is inconsistent. See variants, and compare 2. 7. 33.

3. 4. 45-8 wee poore Gentlemen ... piece. Cf. Webster, *Devil's Law Case, Wks.* 2. 38: 'You have certain rich city chuffs, that when they have no acres of their own, they will go and plough up fools, and turn them into excellent meadow.' Also *The Fox* 2. 1:

—if ItalyHave any glebe more fruitful than these fellows,I am deceived.

As source of the latter Dr. L. H. Holt (*Mod. Lang. Notes*, June, 1905) gives Plautus, *Epidicus* 2. 3. 306-7:

nullum esse opinor ego agrum in agro Atticoaeque feracem quam hic est noster Periphanes.

3. 5. 2 the row. Stow (*Survey*, ed. 1633, p. 391) says that Goldsmith's Row, 'betwixt *Breadstreete* end and the Crosse in *Cheap*,' is 'the most beautifull Frame of faire houses and shops, that be within the Wals of *London*, or elsewhere in England.' It contained 'ten faire dwelling houses, and fourteene shops' beautified with elaborate ornamentation. Howes (ed. 1631, p. 1045) says that at his time (1630) Goldsmith's Row 'was much abated of her wonted store of Goldsmiths, which was the beauty of that famous streete.' A similar complaint is made in the *Calendar of State Papers*, 1619-23, p. 457, where Goldsmith's Row is characterized as the 'glory and beauty of Cheapside.' Paul Hentzner (p. 45) speaks of it as surpassing all the other London streets. He mentions the presence there of a 'gilt tower, with a fountain that plays.'

3. 5. 29, 30   answering
With the French-time, in flexure of your body.
This may mean bowing in the deliberate and measured fashion of the French, or perhaps it refers to French musical measure. See Gloss.

3. 5. 33 the very Academies. See note 2. 8. 20.

3. 5. 35 play-time. Collier says that the usual hour of dining in the city was twelve o'clock, though the passage in *Case is Altered*, *Wks.* 6. 331, seems to indicate an earlier hour:

Eat when your stomach serves, saith the physician,Not at eleven and six.

The performance of plays began at three o'clock. Cf. *Histriomastix*, 1610:

Come to the Town-house, and see a play:At three a'clock it shall begin.

See Collier, *Annals* 3. 377. Sir Humphrey Mildmay, in his Ms. Diary (quoted *Annals* 2. 70), speaks several times of going to the play-house after dinner.

3. 5. 39 his Damme. *NED.* gives a use of the phrase 'the devil and his dam' as early as Piers Plowman, 1393. The 'devil's dam' was later applied opprobriously to a woman. It is used thus in Shakespeare, *Com. Err.* 4. 3. 51. The expression is common throughout the literature of the period.

3. 5. 43 But to be seene to rise, and goe away. Cf. Dekker, *Guls Horne-booke*, *Non-dram. Wks.* 2. 253: 'Now sir, if the writer be a fellow that hath either epigrammd you, or hath had a flirt at your mistris, ... you shall disgrace him worse then by tossing him in a blancket ... if, in the middle of his play, ... you rise with a screwd and discontented face from your stoole to be gone: no matter whether the Scenes be good or no; the better they are the worse do you distast them.'

3. 5. 45, 6   **But say, that he be one,**
Wi' not be aw'd! but laugh at you. In the Prologue to Massinger's *Guardian* we find:

—nor dares he profess that whenThe critics laugh, he'll laugh at them agen.(Strange self-love in a writer!)

Gifford says of this passage: 'This Prologue contains many sarcastick allusions to Old Ben, who produced, about this time, his *Tale of a Tub*, and his *Magnetic Lady*, pieces which failed of success, and which, with his usual arrogance, (*strange self-love in a writer!*) he attributed to a want of taste in the audience.'—Massinger's (*Wks.*, ed. 1805, 4. 121.)

The *Guardian* appeared in 1633, two years after the printing of *The Devil is an Ass*. It seems certain that the reference is to the present passage.

3. 5. 47 pay for his dinner himselfe. The custom of inviting the poet to dinner or supper seems to have been a common one. Dekker refers to it in the *Guls Horne-booke*, *Non-dram. Wks.* 2. 249. Cf. also the Epilogue to the present play.

3. 5. 47 Perhaps, He would doe that twice, rather then thanke you. 'This ill-timed compliment to himself, Jonson might have spared, with some advantage to his judgment, at least, if not his modesty.'—G.

3. 5. 53. See variants. Gifford's change destroys the meaning and is palpably ridiculous.

3. 5. 77 your double cloakes. 'I. e., a cloake adapted for disguises, which might be worn on either side. It was of different colours, and fashions. This turned cloke with a false beard (of which the cut and colour varied) and a black or yellow peruke, furnished a ready and effectual mode of concealment, which is now lost to the stage. '—G.

3. 6. 2 canst thou get ne'r a bird? Throughout this page Merecraft and Pug ring the changes on Pitfall's name.

3. 6. 15, 16 TRA.   You must send, Sir.

The Gentleman the ring. Traines, of course, is merely carrying out Merecraft's plot to 'achieve the ring' (3. 5. 67). Later (4. 4. 60) Merecraft is obliged to give it up to Wittipol.

3. 6. 34-6 What'll you do, Sir? ...

Run from my flesh, if I could. For a similar construction cf. 1. 3. 21 and note.

3. 6. 38, 9 Woe to the seuerall cudgells,

Must suffer on this backe! Adapted from Plautus, *Captivi* 3. 4. 650:
Vae illis uirgis miseris, quae hodie in tergo morientur meo.
(Gifford mentions the fact that this is adapted from the classics. I am indebted for the precise reference to Dr. Lucius H. Holt.)

3. 6. 40 the vse of it is so present. For other Latinisms cf. *resume*, 1. 6. 149; *salts*, 2. 6. 75; *confute*, 5. 6. 18, etc.

3. 6. 61 I'll ... See variants. The original reading is undoubtedly wrong.

ACT IV

4. 1. 1 referring to Commissioners. In the lists of patents we frequently read of commissions specially appointed for examination of the patent under consideration. The King's seal was of course necessary to render the grant valid.

4. 1. 5 S^r. Iohn Monie-man. See Introduction.

4. 1. 37 I will haue all piec'd. Cf. *Mag. La.*, *Wks.* 6. 50:
Item. I heard they were out. *Nee.* But they are pieced, and put together again.

4. 1. 38 ill solder'd! Cf. *The Forest*, 12, *Epistle to Elizabeth*, etc.; 'Solders cracked friendship.'

4. 2. 11 Haue with 'hem. 'An idea borrowed from the gaming table, being the opposite of "have at them."'—C.

4. 2. 11 the great Carroch. See note 1. 6. 214.

4. 2. 12 with my Ambler, bare. See note 4. 4. 202.

4. 2. 22 I not loue this. See note 1. 6. 14.

4. 2. 26 Tooth-picks. This was an object of satire to the dramatists of the period. Nares says that they 'appear to have been first brought into use in Italy; whence the travellers who had visited that country, particularly wished to exhibit that symbol of gentility.' It is referred to as the mark of a traveller by Shakespeare, *King John*, 1. 1 (cited by Gifford):
—Now your traveller, He, and his tooth-pick, at my worship's mess.
Overbury (*Character* of *An Affected Traveller*, ed. Morley, p. 35) speaks of

the *pick-tooth* as 'a main part of his behavior.'

It was also a sign of foppery. Overbury (p. 31) describes the courtier as wearing 'a pick-tooth in his hat,' and Massinger, *Grand Duke of Florence*, Act 3 (quoted by Nares), mentions 'my case of tooth-picks, and my silver fork' among the articles 'requisite to the making up of a signior.' John Earle makes a similar reference in his *Character* of *An Idle Gallant* (ed. Morley, p. 179), and Furnivall (Stubbes' *Anatomy*, p. 77) quotes from *Laugh and lie downe*: or *The worldes Folly*, London, 1605, 4to: 'The next was a nimble-witted and glib-tongu'd fellow, who, having in his youth spent his wits in the Arte of love, was now become the jest of wit.... The picktooth in the mouth, the flower in the eare, the brush upon the beard; ... and what not that was unneedefull,' etc.

It is a frequent subject of satire in Jonson. Cf. *Ev. Man out, Wks.* 2. 124; *Cyn. Rev., Wks.* 2. 218, 248; *Fox, Wks.* 3. 266. See also Dekker, *Wks.* 3. 280.

4. 2. 63 What vile Fucus is this. The abuse of face-painting is a favorite subject of satire with the moralists and dramatists of the period. Stubbes (*Anatomy of Abuses*, Part 1, pp. 64-8) devotes a long section to the subject. Dr. Furnivall in the notes to this passage, pp. 271-3, should also be consulted. Brome satirizes it in the *City Wit, Wks.* 2. 300. Lady Politick Would-be in the *Fox* is of course addicted to the habit, and a good deal is said on the subject in *Epicoene*. Dekker (*West-ward Hoe, Wks.* 2. 285) has a passage quite similar in spirit to Jonson's satire.

4. 2. 71 the very Infanta of the Giants! Cf. Massinger and Field, *Fatal Dowry* 4. 1: 'O that I were the infanta queen of Europe!' Pecunia in the *Staple of News* is called the 'Infanta of the mines.' Spanish terms were fashionable at this time. Cf. the use of *Grandees*, 1. 3. It is possible that the reference here is to the Infanta Maria. See Introduction.

4. 3. 5, 6 It is the manner of Spaine, to imbrace onely, Neuer to kisse. Cf. Minsheu's *Pleasant and Delightfull Dialogues,* pp. 51-2: '*W.* I hold that the greatest cause of dissolutenesse in some women in England is this custome of kissing publikely.... *G.* In Spaine doe not men vse to kisse women? *I.* Yes the husbands kisse their wiues, but as if it were behinde seuen walls, where the very light cannot see them.'

4. 3. 33 f. Decayes the fore-teeth, that should guard the tongue; etc. Cf. *Timber*, ed. Schelling, 13. 24: 'It was excellently said of that philosopher, that there was a wall or parapet of teeth set in our mouth, to restrain the petulancy of our words; that the rashness of talking should not only be retarded by the guard and watch of our heart, but be fenced in and defended by certain strengths placed in the mouth itself, and within the lips.'

Professor Schelling quotes Plutarch, *Moralia, de Garrulitate* 3, translated by Goodwin: 'And yet there is no member of human bodies that nature has so strongly enclosed within a double fortification as the tongue, entrenched within a barricade of sharp teeth, to the end that, if it refuses to obey and keep silent when reason "presses the glittering reins" within, we should fix our teeth in it till the blood comes rather than suffer inordinate and unseasonable din' (4. 223).

4. 3. 39 Mad-dames. See variants. The editors have taken out of the jest whatever salt it possessed, and have supplied meaningless substitutes. Gifford followed the same course in his edition of Ford (see Ford's *Wks.* 2. 81), where, however, he changes to Mad-dam. Such gratuitous corruptions are inexplicable. Cf. *Tale Tub, Wks.* 6. 172:

Here is a strange thing call'd a lady, a mad-dame.

4. 3. 45 Their seruants. A common term for a lover. Cf. *Sil. Wom., Wks.* 3. 364.

4. 3. 51. See variants. There are several mistakes in the assignment of speeches throughout this act. Not all of Gifford's changes, however, are to be accepted without question. Evidently, if the question *where?* is to be assigned to Wittipol, the first speech must be an aside, as it is inconceivable that Merecraft should introduce Fitzdottrel first under his own name, and then as the 'Duke of Drown'd-land.'

My conception of the situation is this: Pug is playing the part of gentleman usher. He enters and announces to Merecraft that Fitzdottrel and his wife are coming. Merecraft whispers: 'Master Fitzdottrel and his wife! where?' and then, as they enter, turns to Wittipol and introduces them; 'Madame,' etc.

4. 4. 30 Your Allum Scagliola, etc. Many of the words in this paragraph are obscure, and a few seem irrecoverable. Doubtless Jonson picked them up from various medical treatises and advertisements of his day. I find no trace of *Abezzo*, which may of course be a misprint for Arezzo. The meanings assigned to *Pol-dipedra* and *Porcelletto Merino* are unsatisfactory. Florio gives '*Zucca*: a gourd; a casting bottle,' but I have been unable to discover *Mugia*. The loss of these words is, to be sure, of no moment. Two things illustrative of Jonson's method are sufficiently clear. (1) The articles mentioned are not, as they seem at first, merely names coined for the occasion. (2) They are a polyglot jumble, intended to make proficiency in the science of cosmetics as ridiculous as possible. It is worth while to notice, however, that this list of drugs is carefully differentiated from the list at 4. 4. 142 f., which contains the names of sweetmeats and perfumes.

4. 4. 32, 3 Soda di leuante, Or your Ferne ashes. Soda-ash is still the common trade name of sodium carbonate. In former times soda was chiefly obtained from natural deposits and from the incineration of various plants growing by the sea-shore. These sources have become of little importance since the invention of artificial soda by Leblanc toward the end of the eighteenth century (see *Soda* in *CD.*). Florio's definition of soda is: 'a kind of Ferne-ashes whereof they make glasses.' Cf. also W. Warde, Tr. *Alessio's Secr.*, Pt. 1 fol. 78[m] 1°: 'Take an vnce of Soda (which is asshes made of grasse, whereof glassemakers do vse to make their Cristall).' In Chaucer's *Squire's Tale* (11. 254 f.) the manufacture of glass out of 'fern-asshen' is mentioned as a wonder comparable to that of Canacee's ring.

4. 4. 33 Beniamin di gotta. The *Dict. d'Histoire Naturelle*, Paris, 1843, 2. 509, gives: 'Benjoin. Sa teinture, étendue d'eau, sert à la toilette sous le nom de *Lait virginal*.' See 4. 4. 52.

4. 4. 38 With a piece of scarlet. Lady Politick Would-be's remedies in the *Fox* are to be 'applied with a right scarlet cloth.' Scarlet was supposed to be of great efficacy in disease. See Whalley's note on the *Fox, Wks.* 3. 234.

4. 4. 38, 9 makes a Lady of sixty Looke at sixteen. Cunningham thinks this is a reference to the *In decimo sexto* of line 50.

4. 4. 39, 40 the water Of the white Hen, of the Lady Estifanias! The Lady Estifania seems to have been a dealer in perfumes and cosmetics. In *Staple of News, Wks.* 5. 166, we read: 'Right Spanish perfume, the lady Estifania's.' Estefania is the name of a Spanish lady in B. & Fl.'s *Rule a Wife*.

4. 4. 47 galley-pot. Mistresse Gallipot is the name of a tobacconist in Dekker's and Middleton's *Roaring Girle.*

4. 4. 50 In decimo sexto. This is a bookbinder's or printer's term, 'applied to books, etc., a leaf of which is one-sixteenth of a full sheet or signature.' It is equivalent to '16mo.' and hence metaphorically used to indicate 'a small compass, miniature' (see *Stanford*, p. 312). In *Cyn. Rev., Wks.* 2. 218, Jonson says: 'my braggart in decimo sexto!' Its use is well exemplified in John Taylor's *Works*, sig. L₁ v⁰/¹: 'when a mans stomache is in Folio, and knows not where to haue a dinner in Decimo sexto.' The phrase is fairly common in the dramatic literature. See Massinger, *Unnat. Combat* 3. 2; Middleton, *Father Hubburd's Tales, Wks.* 8 64, etc. In the present passage, however, the meaning evidently required is 'perfect: 'spotless,' and no doubt refers to the comparative perfection of a sexto decimo, or perhaps to the perfection naturally to be expected of any work in miniature.

4. 4. 52 Virgins milke for the face. Cf. John French, *Art Distill.*. Bk. 5. p. 135 (1651): 'This salt being set in a cold cellar on a marble stone, and dissolved into an oil, is as good as any *Lac virginis* to clear, and smooth the face.' *Lac Virginis* is spoken of twice in the *Alchemist*, Act 2, but probably in neither case is the cosmetic referred to. See Hathaway's edition, p. 293. Nash speaks of the cosmetic in *Pierce Pennilesse, Wks.* 2. 44: 'She should haue noynted your face ouer night with *Lac virginis*.'

4. 4. 55 Cataputia. Catapuce is one of the laxatives that Dame Pertelote recommended to Chauntecleer in Chaucer's *Nonne Preestes Tale*, l. 145.

4. 4. 63 Doe not you dwindle. The use of *dwindle* in this sense is very rare. *NED.* thinks it is 'probably a misuse owing to two senses of *shrink*.' It gives only a single example, *Alch., Wks.* 4. 163: 'Did you not hear the coil about the door? *Sub.* Yes, and I dwindled with it.' Besides the two instances in Jonson I have noticed only one other, in Ford, *Fancies chaste and noble, Wks.* 2. 291: '*Spa.* Hum, how's that? is he there, with a wanion! then do I begin to dwindle.'

4. 4. 69 Cioppino's. The source of this passage, with the anecdote which follows, seems to be taken from Coryat's *Crudities* (ed. 1776, 2. 36, 7): 'There is one thing vsed of the Venetian women, and some others dwelling in the cities and towns subject to the Signiory of Venice, that is not to be obserued (I thinke) amongst any other women in Christendome: which is so common in Venice, that no woman whatsoeuer goeth without it, either in her house or abroad; a thing made of wood, and couered with leather of sundry colors, some with white, some redde, some yellow. It is called a Chapiney, which they weare vnder their shoes. Many of them are curiously painted; some also I haue seene fairely gilt: so vncomely a thing (in my opinion) that it is pitty this foolish custom is not cleane banished and exterminated out of the citie. There are many of these Chapineys of a great heigth, euen half a yard high, which maketh many of their women that are very short, seeme much taller then the tallest women we haue in England. Also I haue heard that this is obserued amongst them, that by how much the nobler a woman is, by so much the higher are her Chapineys. All their Gentlewomen, and most of their wiues and widowes that are of any wealth, are assisted and supported eyther by men or women when they walke abroad, to the end they may not fall. They are borne vp most commonly by the left arme, otherwise they might quickly take a fall. For I saw a woman fall a very dangerous fall as she was going down the staires of one of the little stony bridges with her high Chapineys alone by her selfe: but I did nothing pitty her, because shee wore such friuolous and (as I may truely term them) ridiculous instruments, which were the occasion of her fall. For both I myselfe, and many other strangers (as I haue obserued in Venice) haue often laughed at them for their vaine Chapineys.'

4. 4. 71, 2 Spanish pumps Of perfum'd leather. Pumps are first mentioned in the sixteenth century (Planché). A reference to them occurs in *Midsummer Night's Dream*, 1593-4, 4. 2. They were worn especially by footmen.

Spanish leather was highly esteemed at this time. Stubbes (*Anat. of Abuses*, Part 1, p. 77) says: 'They haue korked shooes, pinsnets, pantoffles, and slippers, ... some of spanish leather, and some of English lether.' Marston (*Dutch Courtezan, Wks.* 2. 7) speaks of a 'Spanish leather jerkin,' and Middleton (*Father Hubburd's Tales, Wks.* 8. 70) of 'a curious pair of boots of King Philip's leather,' and a little farther on (*Wks.* 8. 108) of Spanish leather shoes. Fastidious Brisk's boots are made of the same material (*Ev. Man out, Wks.* 2. 147). Cf. also Dekker, *Wks.* 2. 305.

Perfumes were much in fashion, and Stubbes' *Anatomy* has a great deal to say on the subject. We hear of perfumed jerkins in Marston's *Malcontent* (*Wks.* 1. 314) and in *Cynthia's Revels* (*Wks.* 2. 325). Spanish perfume for gloves is spoken of in the latter play (p. 328) and in the *Alchemist* (*Wks.* 4. 131) 'your Spanish titillation in a glove' is declared to be the best perfume.

4. 4. 77, 8 The Guardo-duennas, such a little old man,

As this. Minsheu gives the definition: 'Escudero, m. An Esquire, a Seruingman that waits on a Ladie or Gentlewoman, in Spaine neuer but old men and gray beards.'

4. 4. 81 flat spred, as an Vmbrella. The umbrella of the seventeenth century seems to have been used exclusively to protect the face from the sun. Blount, *Glossographia*, 1670, gives: '*Umbrello* (Ital. Ombrella), a fashion of round and broad Fans, wherewith the Indians (and from them our great ones) preserve themselves from the heat of the sun or fire; and hence any little shadow, Fan, or other thing wherewith women guard their faces from the sun.'

It was apparently not in use in England when Coryat published his *Crudities*, which contains the following description (1. 135): 'Also many of them doe carry other fine things of a far greater price, that will cost at the least a duckat, which they commonly call in the Italian tongue *vmbrellaes*, that is, things that minister shadow unto them for shelter against the scorching heate of the sunne. These are made of leather something answerable to the forme of a little cannopy, & hooped in the inside with diuers little wooden hoopes that extend the *vmbrella* in a pretty large compasse.'

'As a defense from rain or snow it was not used in western Europe till early in the eighteenth century.'—*CD*.

4. 4. 82 Her hoope. A form of the farthingale (fr. Sp. *Verdugal*) was worn in France, Spain, and Italy, and in England as early as 1545. It gradually increased in size, and Elizabeth's farthingale was enormous. The aptness of the comparison can be appreciated by reading Coryat's description of the umbrella above.

4. 4. 87 An Escudero. See note 4. 4. 77, 8.

4. 4. 97 If no body should loue mee, but my poore husband. Cf. *Poetaster*, *Wks.* 2. 444: 'Methinks a body's husband does not so well at court; a body's friend, or so—but, husband! 'tis like your clog to your marmoset,' etc.

4. 4. 134 your Gentleman-vsher. 'Gentleman-Usher. Originally a state-officer, attendant upon queens, and other persons of high rank, as, in Henry VIII, Griffith is gentleman-usher to Queen Catherine; afterwards a private affectation of state, assumed by persons of distinction, or those who pretended to be so, and particularly ladies. He was then only a sort of upper servant, out of livery, whose office was to hand his lady to her coach, and to walk before her bare-headed, though in later times she leaned upon his arm.'—Nares.

Cf. Dekker, *West-ward Hoe*, *Wks.* 2. 324: 'Weare furnisht for attendants as Ladies are, We have our fooles, and our Vshers.'

The sources for a study of the gentleman-usher are the present play, *The Tale of a Tub*, and Chapman's *Gentleman Usher*. In the *Staple of News* the Lady Pecunia is provided with a gentleman-usher. The principal duties of this office seem to have consisted in being sent on errands, handing the lady to her coach, and preceding her on any occasion where ceremony was demanded. In Chapman's play Lasso says that the disposition of his house for the reception of guests was placed in the hands of this servant (cf. Chapman, *Wks.* 1. 263 f.). Innumerable allusions occur in which the requirement of going bare-headed is mentioned (see note on 4. 4. 202). Another necessary quality was a fine pace, which is alluded to in the present character's name (see also note 4. 4. 201). An excellent description of the gentleman-usher will be found in Nares' *Glossary,* quoting from Lenton's *Leasures*, a book published in 1631, and now very rare.

4. 4. 142 the Dutchesse of Braganza. Braganza is the ruling house of Portugal. Dom John, Duke of Braganza, became king of Portugal in 1640.

4. 4. 143 Almoiauna. The *Stanford Dictionary* gives: 'Almojabana, Sp. fr. Arab. *Al-mojabbana*: cheese-and-flour cake. Xeres was famed for this dainty, which is named from Arabic *jobn* = "cheese."'

4. 4. 147 Marquesse Muja. Apparently a Spanish marquise, occupying a position in society similar to that of Madame Récamier.

4. 4. 156 A Lady of spirit. With this line and lines 165 f. cf. *U. 32, Wks.* 8. 356:

To be abroad chanting some bawdy song,And laugh, and measure thighs, then squeak, spring, itch,Do all the tricks of a salt lady bitch!—For these with her young company she'll enter,Where Pitts, or Wright, or Modet would not venture;(Fol. reads 'venter')And come by these degrees the style t'inheritOf woman of fashion, and a lady of spirit.

4. 4. 164 Pimlico. See note 3. 3. 170.

4. 4. 164 daunce the Saraband. The origin of the saraband is in doubt, being variously attributed to Spain and to the Moors. It is found in Europe at the beginning of the sixteenth century, and its immoral character is constantly referred to. Grove (*Dict. of Music* 3. 226) quotes from chapter 12, 'Del baile y cantar llamado Zarabanda,' of the *Tratado contra los Juegos Publicos* ('Treatise against Public Amusements') of Mariana (1536-1623): 'Entre las otras invenciones ha salido estos años un baile y cantar tan lacivo en las palabras, tan feo en las meneos, que basta para pegar fuego aun á las personas muy honestas' ('amongst other inventions there has appeared during late years a dance and song, so lascivious in its words, so ugly in its movements, that it is enough to inflame even very modest people'). 'This reputation was not confined to Spain, for Marini in his poem "L'Adone" (1623) says:

Chiama questo suo gioco empio e profanoSaravanda, e Ciaccona, il nuova Ispano.

Padre Mariana, who believed in its Spanish origin, says that its invention was one of the disgraces of the nation, and other authors attribute its invention directly to the devil. The dance was attacked by Cervantes and Guevara, and defended by Lope de Vega, but it seems to have been so bad that at the end of the reign of Philip II. it was for a time suppressed. It was soon, however, revived in a purer form and was introduced at the French court in 1588' (Grove 3. 226-7).

In England the saraband was soon transformed into an ordinary country-dance. Two examples are to be found in the first edition of Playford's *Dancing Master*, and Sir John Hawkins (*Hist. of the Science and Practice of Music*, 1776) speaks of it several times. 'Within the memory of persons now living,' he says, a Saraband danced by a Moor was constantly a part of the entertainment at a puppet-show' (4. 388). In another place (2. 135), in speaking of the use of castanets at a puppet-show, he says: 'That particular dance called the Saraband is supposed to require as a thing of necessity, the music, if it may be called so, of this artless instrument.'

In the *Staple of News, Wks.* 5. 256, Jonson speaks of 'a light air! the bawdy Saraband!'

4. 4. 165 Heare, and talke bawdy; laugh as loud, as a larum. Jonson satirizes these vices again in *U. 67* (see note 4. 4. 156) and *Epigrams* 48 and *115*. Dekker (*Guls Horne-booke, Non-dram. Wks.* 2. 238) advises the young gallant to 'discourse as lowd as you can, no matter to what purpose, ... and laugh in fashion, ... you shall be much obserued.'

4. 4. 172 Shee must not lose a looke on stuffes, or cloth. It being the fashion to 'swim in choice of silks and tissues,' plain woolen cloth was despised.

4. 4. 187 Blesse vs from him! Preserve us. A precaution against any evil that might result from pronouncing the devil's name. Cf. *Knight of the Burning Pestle* 2. 1: Sure the devil (God bless us!) is in this springald!' and Wilson, *The Cheats*, Prologue:

No little pug nor devil,—bless us all!

4. 4. 191, 2 What things they are? That nature should be at leasure
Euer to make 'hem! Cf. *Ev. Man in*, *Wks.* 1. 119: 'O manners that this age should bring forth such creatures! that nature should be at leisure to make them!'

4. 4. 197 Hee makes a wicked leg. Gifford thinks that *wicked* here means 'awkward or clownish.' It seems rather to mean 'roguish,' a common colloquial use.

4. 4. 201 A setled discreet pase. Cf. 3. 5. 22; 2. 7. 33; and Dekker, *Guls Horne-booke, Non-dram. Wks.* 2. 238: 'Walke vp and downe by the rest as scornfully and as carelesly as a Gentleman-Usher.'

4. 4. 202 a barren head, Sir. Cf. 2. 3. 36, 7 and 4. 2. 12. Here again we have a punning allusion to the uncovered head of the gentleman-usher. 'It was a piece of state, that the servants of the nobility, particularly the gentleman-usher, should attend bare-headed.' Nares, *Gloss.* For numerous passages illustrating the practice both in regard to the gentleman-usher and to the coachman, see the quotations in Nares, and Ford, *Lover's Melancholy, Wks.* 1. 19; Chapman, *Gentleman-Usher, Wks.* 1. 263; and the following passage, *ibid.* 1. 273:

Vin. I thanke you sir. Nay pray be couerd; O I crie you mercie, You must be bare. *Bas.* Euer to you my Lord. *Vin.* Nay, not to me sir, But to the faire right of your worshipfull place.

A passage from Lenton (see note 4. 4. 134) may also be quoted: 'He is forced to stand bare, which would urge him to impatience, but for the hope of being covered, or rather the delight hee takes in shewing his new-crisp't hayre, which his barber hath caused to stand like a print hedge, in equal proportion.'

The dramatists ridiculed it by insisting that the coachman should be not only bare-headed, but bald. Cf. 2. 3. 36 and Massinger, *City Madam, Wks.* p. 331: 'Thou shalt have thy proper and bald-headed coachman.' Jonson often refers to this custom. Cf. *Staple of News, Wks.* 5. 232:

Such as are bald and barren beyond hope, Are to be separated and set by For ushers to old countesses: and coachmen To mount their boxes reverently, etc.

New Inn, Wks. 5. 374:

Jor. Where's thy hat?...*Bar.* The wind blew't off at Highgate, and my lady Would not endure me light to take it up; But made me drive bareheaded in the rain. *Jor.* That she might be mistaken for a countess?

Cf. also *Mag. La., Wks.* 6. 36, and *Tale Tub, Wks.* 6. 217 and 222.

4. 4. 204 his Valley is beneath the waste. 'Waist' and 'waste' were both spelled *waste* or *wast.* Here, of course, is a pun on the two meanings.

4. 4. 206 Dulnesse vpon you! Could not you hit this? Cf. *Bart.*

Fair, *Wks.* 4. 358: 'Now dullness upon me, that I had not that before him.'

4. 4. 209 the French sticke. Walking-sticks of various sorts are mentioned during the sixteenth and seventeenth centuries. 'In Chas. II.'s time the French walking-stick, with a ribbon and tassels to hold it when passed over the wrist, was fashionable, and continued so to the reign of George II.' (Planché).

4. 4. 215, 6 report the working, Of any Ladies physicke. In Lenton's *Leasures* (see note 4.4.134) we find: 'His greatest vexation is going upon sleevelesse arrands, to know whether some lady slept well last night, or how her physick work'd i' th' morning, things that savour not well with him; the reason that ofttimes he goes but to the next taverne, and then very discreetly brings her home a tale of a tubbe.'

Cf. also B. & Fl., *Fair Maid of the Inn* 2. 2: '*Host.* And have you been in England?... But they say ladies there take physic for fashion.'

Dekker, *Guls Horne-booke, Non-dram. Wks.* 2. 255, speaks of 'a country gentleman that brings his wife vp to learne the fashion, see the Tombs at Westminster, the Lyons in the Tower, or to take physicke.' In the 1812 reprint the editor observes that in Jonson's time 'fanciful or artful wives would often persuade their husbands to take them up to town for the advantage of *physick*, when the principal object was dissipation.'

4. 4. 219 Corne-cutter. This vulgar suggestion renders hopeless Pug's pretensions to gentility. Corncutters carried on a regular trade (see *Bart. Fair* 2. 1.), and were held in the greatest contempt, as we learn from Nash (*Four Letters Confuted, Wks.* 2. 211).

4. 4. 232 The Moone. I. e., see that the moon and zodiacal sign are propitious.

4. 4. 235 Get their natiuities cast! Astrology was a favorite subject of satire. Cf. Massinger, *City Madam* 2. 2; B. & Fl., *Rollo Duke of Normandy* 4. 2, etc.

4. 5. 31, 2 his valour has At the tall board bin question'd. *Tall board* is, I think, the same as *table-board*, a gaming-table. In Dyce's edition of Webster's *Devil's Law Case* (*Wks.* 2. 38) we read: 'shaking your elbow at the table-board.' Dyce says in a note that the old folio reads *Taule-board. Tables* is derived from Lat. *Tabularum lusus* › Fr. *Tables.* The derivation, *table › tavl › taul › tall*, presents no etymological difficulties. A note from Professor Joseph Wright of Oxford confirms me in my theory.

The passage seems to mean that Merecraft was accused of cheating, and, his valor not rising to the occasion, his reputation for honesty was left somewhat in doubt.

4. 6. 38-41 intitle Your vertue, to the power, vpon a life

... Euen to forfeit. Wittipol is 'wooing in language of the pleas and bench.' Cf. 4. 7. 62.

4. 6. 42 We haue another leg-strain'd, for this Dottrel. See variants, and note 2. 2. 49, 50.

4. 6. 49 A Phrentick. See note 5. 8. 91-2.

4. 7. 37-40. See variants. Gifford silently follows Whalley's changes, which are utterly unwarrantable. Cunningham points out the wrong division in

37, 8. The scansion is thus indicated by Wilke (*Metrische Untersuchungen*, p. 3):

Of a/ most wor/thy gen/tleman./ Would oneOf worth/ had spoke/ it: whence/ it comes,/ it isRather/ a shame/ to me,/ ᵗhen/ a praise.

The missing syllable in the third verse is compensated for by the pause after the comma. This is quite in accordance with Jonson's custom (see Wilke, p. 1 f.).

4. 7. 45 Publication. See 3. 3. 137.

4. 7. 54 I sou't him. See variants. Gifford says that he can make nothing of *sou't* but *sought* and *sous'd*, and that he prefers the latter. Dyce (*Remarks*) confidently asserts that the word is the same as *shue*, 'to frighten away poultry,' and Cunningham accepts this without question. There seems, however, to be no confirmation for the theory that the preterit was ever spelt *sou't*. Wright's *Dialect Dictionary* gives: '*Sough.* 19. to strike; to beat severely,' but the pronunciation here seems usually to be *souff*. Professor Wright assures me that *sous'd* is the correct reading, and that the others are 'mere stupid guesses.'

4. 7. 62 in possibility. A legal phrase used of contingent interests. See note 4. 6. 38, 9.

4. 7. 65 Duke O' Shore-ditch. 'A mock title of honour, conferred on the most successful of the London archers, of which this account is given:

When Henry VIII became king, he gave a prize at Windsor to those who should excel at this exercise, (archery) when Barlo, one of his guards, an inhabitant of Shoreditch, acquired such honor as an archer, that the king created him *duke of Shoreditch*, on the spot. This title, together with that of marquis of Islington, earl of Pancridge, etc., was taken from these villages, in the neighborhood of Finsbury fields, and continued so late as 1683. Ellis's *History of Shoreditch*, p. 170.

The latest account is this: In 1682 there was a most magnificent entertainment given by the Finsbury archers, when they bestowed the title of *duke of Shoreditch*, etc., upon the most deserving. The king was present. *Ibid.* 173.'—Nares, *Gloss.*

Entick (*Survey* 2. 65) gives an interesting account of a match which took place in 1583. The Duke of Shoreditch was accompanied on this occasion by the 'marquises of *Barlow*, *Clerkenwell*, *Islington*, *Hoxton*, and *Shaklewell*, the earl of *Pancras*, etc. These, to the number of 3000, assembled at the place appointed, sumptuously apparelled, and 942 of them had gold chains about their necks. They marched from merchant-taylors-hall, preceded by whifflers and bellmen, that made up the number 4000, besides pages and footmen; performing several exercises and evolutions in *Moorfields*, and at last shot at the target for glory in *Smithfield*.'

4. 7. 69 Ha'. See variants. The original seems to me the more characteristic reading.

4. 7. 84 after-game. Jonson uses the expression again in the *New Inn, Wks.* 5. 402:

And play no after-games of love hereafter.

ACT V.

5. 1. 28 Tyborne. This celebrated gallows stood, it is believed, on the site of Connaught Place. It derived the name from a brook in the neighborhood (see Minsheu, Stow, etc.).

5. 1. 29 My L. Majors Banqueting-house. This was in Stratford Place, Oxford Street. It was 'erected for the Mayor and Corporation to dine in after their periodical visits to the Bayswater and Paddington Conduits, and the Conduit-head adjacent to the Banqueting-House, which supplied the city with water. It was taken down in 1737, and the cisterns arched over at the same time.'—Wh-C.

Stow (ed. 1633, pp. 475-6) speaks of 'many faire Summer houses' in the London suburbs, built 'not so much for use and profit, as for shew and pleasure.'

The spelling *Major* seems to be a Latin form. Mr. Charles Jackson (*N. & Q.* 4. 7. 176) mentions it as frequently used by the mayors of Doncaster in former days. Cf. also Glapthorne (*Wks.* 1. 231) and *Ev. Man in* (Folio 1616, 5. 5. 41).

5. 1. 41 my tooth-picks. See note 4. 2. 26.

5. 1. 47 Saint Giles's. 'Now, without the postern of Cripplesgate, first is the parish church of Saint Giles, a very fair and large church, lately repaired, after that the same was burnt in the year 1545.'—Stow, *Survey*, ed. Thoms, p. 112.

5. 1. 48 A kind of Irish penance! 'There is the same allusion to the *rug gowns* of the wild Irish, in the *Night Walker* of Fletcher:

We have divided the sexton's household stuffAmong us; one has the *rug*, and he's turn'd *Irish*.'—G.

Cf. also Holinshed, *Chron.* (quoted *CD.*):'As they distill the best aqua-vitæ, so they spin the choicest *rug* in Ireland.' Fynes Moryson (*Itinerary*, fol. 1617, p. 160) says that the Irish merchants were forbidden to export their wool, in order that the peasants might 'be nourished by working it into cloth, namely, Rugs ... & mantles generally worn by men and women, and exported in great quantity.'

Jonson mentions rug as an article of apparel several times. In *Alch.*, *Wks.* 4. 14, it is spoken of as the dress of a poor man and *ibid.* 4. 83 as that of an astrologer. In *Ev. Man out* (*Wks.* 2. 110) a similar reference is made, and here Gifford explains that rug was 'the usual dress of mathematicians, astrologers, &c., when engaged in their sublime speculations.' Marston also speaks of rug gowns as the symbol of a strict life (*What You Will*, *Wks.* 2. 395):

Lamp-oil, watch-candles, rug-gowns, and small juice,Thin commons, four o'clock rising,—I renounce you all.

5. 2. 1 ff. put me To yoaking foxes, etc. Several at least of the following employments are derived from proverbial expressions familiar at the time. Jonson speaks of 'milking he-goats' in *Timber,* ed. Schelling, p. 34, which the editor explains as 'a proverbial expression for a fruitless task.' The occupation of lines 5-6 is adapted from a popular proverb given by Cotgrave: 'J'aymeroy autant tirer vn pet d'un Asne mort, que. I would as soone vndertake to get a fart of a dead man, as &c.' Under *Asne* he explains the same proverb as meaning 'to worke impossibilities.' This explains the passage in *Staple of News* 3. 1., *Wks.* 5. 226. The proverb is quoted again in *Eastward Ho*, Marston, *Wks.* 3. 90, and in Wm. Lilly's Observations,' *Hist.*, pp. 269-70. 'Making ropes of sand' was Iniquity's occupation in 1. 1. 119. This familiar proverb first appears in Aristides 2. 309: ἐκ ψάμμου σχοινίον πλέκειν. In the *New Inn, Wks.* 5. 394, Lovel says: 'I will go catch the wind first in a sieve.' Whalley says that the occupation of 'keeping fleas within a circle' is taken from Socrates' employment in the *Clouds* of Aristophanes (ll. 144-5). Gifford, however, ridicules the notion. Jonson refers to the passage in the *Clouds* in *Timber* (ed. Schelling, 82. 33), where he thinks it would have made the Greeks merry to see Socrates 'measure how many foot a flea could skip geometrically.' But here again we seem to have a proverbial expression. It occurs in the morality-play of *Nature*, 642. II (quoted by Cushman, p. 116):

I had leiver keep as many flese,Or wyld hares in an opyn lese,As undertake that.

5. 2. 32. Scan:

And three/ pence. ⌐Give me/ an an/swer. Sir.

Thos. Keightley, *N. & Q.* 4. 2. 603, suggests:

And your threepence, etc.

5. 2. 35 Your best songs Thom. O' Bet'lem. 'A song entitled "Mad Tom" is to be found in Percy's *Reliques*; Ballad Soc. Roxb. Ball., 2. p. 259; and Chappell's *Old Pop. Mus.* The exact date of the poem is not known.'—H. R. D. Anders, *Shakespeare's Books*, p. 24-5.

Bethlehem Royal Hospital was originally founded 'to have been a priory of canons,' but was converted to a hospital for lunatics in 1547. In Jonson's time it was one of the regular sights of London, and is so referred to in Dekker's *Northward Hoe, Wks.* 3. 56 f.; *Sil. Wom., Wks.* 3. 421; *Alch., Wks.* 4. 132.

5. 3. 6 little Darrels tricks. John Darrel (fl. 1562-1602) was born, it is believed, at Mansfield, Nottinghamshire, about 1562. He graduated at Cambridge, studied law, and then became a preacher at Mansfield. He began to figure as an exorcist in 1586, when he pretended to cast out an evil spirit from Catherine Wright of Ridgway Lane, Derbyshire. In 1596 he exorcised Thomas Darling, a boy of fourteen, of Burton-on-Trent, for bewitching whom Alice Goodrich was tried and convicted at Derby. A history of the case was written by Jesse Bee of Burton (Harsnet, *Discovery*, p. 2). The boy Darling went to Merton College, and in 1603 was sentenced by the Star-chamber to be whipped, and to lose his ears for libelling the vice-chancellor of Oxford. In March, 1596-7, Darrel was sent for to Clayworth Hall, Shakerly, in Leigh parish, Lancashire, where he exorcised seven persons of the household of Mr. Nicholas Starkie, who accused one Edmund Hartley of bewitching them, and succeeded in getting the latter condemned and executed in 1597. In November, 1597, Darrel was invited to Nottingham to dispossess William Somers, an apprentice, and shortly after his arrival was appointed preacher of St. Mary's in that town, and his fame drew crowded congregations to listen to his tales of devils and possession. Darrel's operations having been reported to the Archbishop of York, a commission of inquiry was issued (March 1597-8), and he was prohibited from preaching. Subsequently the case was investigated by Bancroft, bishop of London, and S. Harsnet, his chaplain, when Somers, Catherine Wright, and Mary Cooper confessed that they had been instructed in their simulations by Darrel. He was brought before the commissioners and examined at Lambeth on 26 May 1599, was pronounced an impostor, degraded from the ministry and committed to the Gatehouse. He remained in prison for at least a year, but it is not known what became of him. (Abridged from *DNB*.)

Jonson refers to Darrel again in *U*. 67, *Wks.* 8. 422:

This age will lend no faith to Darrel's deed.

5. 3. 27 That could, pitty her selfe. See variants.

5. 3. 28 in Potentiâ. Jonson uses the phrase again in the *Alchemist*, *Wks.* 4. 64: 'The egg's ... a chicken *in potentia*.' It is a late Latin phrase. See Gloss.

5. 4. 17 my proiect o' the forkes. Forks were just being introduced into England at this time, and were a common subject of satire. The first mention of a fork recorded in the *NED.* is: '1463 *Bury Wills* (Camden) 40, I beqwethe to Davn John Kertelynge my silvir forke for grene gyngour.'

Cf. Dekker, *Guls Horne-booke, Non-dram. Wks.* 2. 211: 'Oh golden world, the suspicious Venecian carued not his meate with a siluer pitch-forke.' B. & Fl., *Queen of Corinth* 4. 1 (quoted by Gifford):

It doth express th' enamoured courtier, As full as your fork-carving traveler.

Fox, Wks. 3. 261:

—Then must you learn the useAnd handling of your silver fork at meals, The metal of your glass; (these are main mattersWith your Italian;)

Coryat has much to say on the subject (*Crudities* 1. 106): 'I obserued a custome in all those Italian Cities and Townes through the which I passed, that is not vsed in any other country that I saw in my trauels, neither doe I thinke that any other nation of Christendome doth vse it, but only Italy. The Italian and also most strangers that are commorant in Italy, doe alwaies in their meales vse a little forke when they cut their meate. For while with their knife which they hold in one hand they cut the meate out of the dish, they fasten their forke which they hold in their other hand vpon the same dish, so that whatsoeuer he be that sitting in the company of any others at meale, should vnadvisedly touch the dish of meate with his fingers from which all at the table doe cut, he will giue occasion of offence vnto the company, as hauing transgressed the lawes of good manners.... This forme of feeding I vnderstand is generally vsed in all places of Italy, their forkes being for the most part made of yron or steele, and some of siluer, but those are vsed only by Gentlemen.' Coryat carried this custom home with him to England, for which a friend dubbed him *furcifer*. This passage is doubtless the source of Jonson's lines. Compare the last sentence of the quotation with lines 30, 31 of this scene.

5. 4. 23, 4 on my priuate, By cause. See variants. There is no necessity for change. Cf. 1616 Sir R. Dudley in *Fortesc. Papers* 17: 'Nor am I so vaine ... bycause I am not worth so much.' The same form occurs in *Sad*

Shepherd (Fol. 1631-40, p. 143):

But, beare yee Douce, bycause, yee may meet mee.

Gabriel Harvey uses both the forms *by cause* and *bycause*. *Prose Wks.* 1. 101; 102; et frequenter.

5. 4. 34 at mine owne ap-perill. The word is of rare occurrence. Gifford quotes *Timon of Athens* 1. 2: 'Let me stay at thine apperil, Timon;' and refers to *Mag. La., Wks.* 6. 109: 'Faith, I will bail him at mine own apperil.' It occurs again in *Tale Tub, Wks.* 6. 148: 'As you will answer it at your apperil.'

5. 5. 10, 11 I will leaue you To your God fathers in Law. 'This seems to have been a standing joke for a jury. It is used by Shakespeare and by writers prior to him. Thus Bulleyn, speaking of a knavish ostler, says, "I did see him ones aske blessyng to xii godfathers at ones." *Dialogue*, 1564.'—G.

The passage from Shakespeare is *Merch. of Ven.* 4. 1. 398:

In christening, shalt thou have two godfathers:Had I been judge, thou should'st have had ten more,To bring thee to the gallows, not the font.

Cf. also *Muse's Looking Glass, O. Pl.* 9. 214: 'Boets! I had rather zee him remitted to the jail, and have his twelve godvathers, good men and true contemn him to the gallows.'

5. 5. 50, 51 A Boy O' thirteene yeere old made him an Asse

But t'toher day. Whalley believed this to be an allusion to the 'boy of Bilson,' but, as Gifford points out, this case did not occur until 1620, four years after the production of the present play. Gifford believes Thomas Harrison, the 'boy of Norwich,' to be alluded to. A short account of his case is given in Hutchinson's *Impostures Detected*, pp. 262 f. The affair took place in 1603 or 1604, and it was thought necessary to 'require the Parents of the said Child, that they suffer not any to repair to their House to visit him, save such as are in Authority and other Persons of special Regard, and known Discretion.' Hutchinson says that Harrison was twelve years old. It is quite possible, though not probable, that Jonson is referring again to the Boy of Burton, who was only two years older. See note 5. 3. 6.

5. 5. 58, 59 You had some straine 'Boue E-la? Cf. 1593 Nash, *Christ's Tears, Wks.* 4. 188: 'You must straine your wits an Ela aboue theyrs.' Cf. also Nash, *Wks.* 5. 98 and 253; Lyly, *Euphues*, Aij; and Gloss.

5. 6. 1 your garnish. 'This word *garnish* has been made familiar to all time by the writings of John Howard. "A cruel custom," says he, "obtains in most of our gaols, which is that of the prisoners demanding of a newcomer *garnish*, footing, or (as it is called in some London gaols) chummage. *Pay* or *strip* are the fatal words. I say fatal, for they are so to some, who, having no money, are obliged to give up part of their scanty apparel; and if they have no bedding or straw to sleep on, contract diseases which I have known to prove mortal."'—C.

Cf. Dekker, *If this be not a good Play, Wks.* 3. 324:

Tis a strong charme gainst all the noisome smelsOf Counters, Iaylors, garnishes, and such hels.

and Greene, *Upstart Courtier*, Dija: 'Let a poore man be arrested ... he shal be almost at an angels charge, what with garnish, crossing and wiping out of the book ... extortions ... not allowed by any statute.'

The money here seems to have been intended for the jailer, rather than for Pug's fellow-prisoners. The custom was abolished by 4 George IV. c. 43, § 12.

5. 6. 10 I thinke Time be drunke, and sleepes. Cf. 1. 4. 31. For the metaphor cf. *New Inn*, *Wks.* 5. 393:

If I but knew what drink the time now loved.

and *Staple of News*, *Wks.* 5. 162:

—Now sleep, and rest;Would thou couldst make the time to do so too.

5. 6. 18 confute. 'A pure Latinism. *Confutare* is properly to pour cold water in a pot, to prevent it from boiling over; and hence metaphorically, the signification of *confuting*, reproving, or controuling.'—W.

For the present use cf. T. Adams in Spurgeon, *Treas. Dav.*, 1614, Ps. lxxx. 20: 'Goliath ... shall be confuted with a pebble.' R. Coke, *Justice Vind.* (1660) 15: 'to be confuted with clubs and hissing.'

5. 6. 21 the Session. The general or quarter sessions were held regularly four times a year on certain days prescribed by the statutes. The length of time for holding the sessions was fixed at three days, if necessity required it, but the rule was not strictly adhered to. See Beard, *The Office of the Justice of the Peace in England*, pp. 158 f.

5. 6. 23 In a cart, to be hang'd. 'Theft and robbery in their coarsest form were for many centuries capital crimes.... The question when theft was first made a capital crime is obscure, but it is certain that at every period some thefts were punished with death, and that by Edward I.'s time, at least, the distinction between grand and petty larceny, which lasted till 1827, was fully established.'—Stephen, *Hist. Crim. Law* 3. 128 f.

5. 6. 24 The charriot of Triumph, which most of them are. The procession from Newgate by Holbom and Tyburn road was in truth often a 'triumphall egression,' and a popular criminal like Jack Sheppard or Jonathan Wild frequently had a large attendance. Cf. Shirley, *Wedding* 4. 3, *Wks.*, ed. Gifford, 1. 425: 'Now I'm in the cart, riding up Holborn in a two-wheeled chariot, with a guard of Halberdiers. *There goes a proper fellow*, says one; good people pray for me: now I am at the three wooden stilts,' etc.

5. 6. 48 a body intire. Jonson uses the word in its strict etymological sense.

5. 6. 54 cheated on. Dyce (*Remarks*) points out that this phrase is used in Mrs. Centlivre's *Wonder*, Act 2. Sc. 1. Jonson uses it again in *Mercury vindicated*: 'and cheat upon your under-officers;' and Marston in *What You Will*, *Wks.* 2. 387.

5. 6. 64 Prouinciall o' the Cheaters! *Provincial* is a term borrowed from the church. See Gloss. Of the *cheaters* Dekker gives an interesting account in the *Bel-man of London, Non-dram. Wks.* 3. 116 f.: 'Of all which *Lawes*, the *Highest* in place, and the *Highest* in perdition is the *Cheating* Law or the Art of winning money by false dyce: Those that practise this studie call themselues *Cheators*, / the dyce *Cheaters*, and the money which they purchase [see note 3. 4. 31, 2.] *Cheates* [see 1.7.4 and Gloss.]: borrowing the tearme from our common Lawyers, with whome all such casuals as fall to the Lord at the holding of his *Leetes*, as *Waifes*, *Strayes*, & such like, are sayd to be *Escheated to the Lords vse* and are called *Cheates*.'

5. 6. 64 Bawd-ledger. Jonson speaks of a similar official in *Every Man out*, *Wks.* 2. 132: 'He's a leiger at Horn's ordinary (cant name for a bawdy-house) yonder.' See Gloss.

5. 6. 68 to sindge your nayles off. In the fool's song in *Twelfth Night* we have the exclamation to the devil: 'paire thy nayles dad' (Furness's ed., p. 273). The editor quotes Malone: 'The Devil was supposed from choice to keep his nails unpared, and therefore to pare them was an affront. So, in Camden's *Remaines*, 1615: "I will follow mine owne minde, and mine old trade; who shall let me? the divel's nailes are unparde."'

Compare also *Henry V.* 4. 4. 76: 'Bardolph and Nym had ten times more valor than this roaring devil i' the old play, that every one may pare his nails with a wooden dagger.'

5. 6. 76 The Diuell was wont to carry away the euill. Eckhardt, p. 100, points out that Jonson's etymology of the word *Vice*, which has been a matter of dispute, was the generally accepted one, that is, from *vice* = evil.

5. 7. 1 Iustice Hall. 'The name of the Sessions-house in the Old Bailey.'— G. Strype, B. 3. p. 281 says that it was 'a fair and stately building, very commodious for that affair.' 'It standeth backwards, so that it hath no front towards the street, only the gateway leading into the yard before the House, which is spacious. It cost above £6000 the building. And in this place the Lord Mayor, Recorder, the Aldermen and Justices of the Peace for the County of Middlesex do sit, and keep his Majesty's Sessions of Oyer and Terminer.' It was destroyed in the Gordon Riots of 1780.—Wh-C.

5. 7. 9 This strange! See variants. The change seriously injures the metre, and the original reading should be preserved. Such absorptions (*this* for *this is* or *this's*) are not uncommon. Cf. *Macbeth* 3. 4. 17, ed. Furness, p. 165: 'yet he's good' for 'yet he is as good.'

5. 8. 2 They had giu'n him potions. Jonson perhaps had in mind the trial of Anne Turner and her accomplices in the Overbury Case of the previous year. See Introduction. For a discussion of love-philtres see Burton, *Anat. of Mel.* (ed. Bullen), 3. 145 f.

5. 8. 33 with a Wanion. This word is found only in the phrases 'with a wanion,' 'in a wanion,' and 'wanions on you.' It is a kind of petty imprecation, and occurs rather frequently in the dramatists, but its precise signification and etymology are still in doubt. Boswell, *Malone*, 21. 61, proposed a derivation from *winnowing*,'a beating;' Nares from *wanung*, Saxon, 'detriment;' Dyce (Ford's *Wks.* 2. 291) from wan (vaande, Dutch, 'a rod or wand'), 'of which *wannie* and *wannion* are familiar diminutives.' The *CD.* makes it a later form of ME. *waniand*, 'a waning,' spec. of the moon, regarded as implying ill luck.

5. 8. 34 If his hornes be forth, the Diuells companion! The jest is too obvious not to be a common one. Thus in *Eastward Ho* Slitgut, who is impersonating the cuckold at Horn-fair, says: 'Slight! I think the devil be abroad. in likeness of a storm, to rob me of my horns!',—Marston's *Wks.* 3. 72. Cf. also *Staple of News, Wks.* 5. 186: 'And why would you so fain see the devil? would I say. Because he has horns, wife, and may be a cuckold as well as a devil.'

5. 8. 35 How he foames! For the stock indications of witchcraft see Introduction.

5. 8. 40 The Cockscomb, and the Couerlet. Wittipol is evidently selecting an appropriate name for Fitzdottrel's buffoonery after the manner of the puppet-shows. It is quite possible that some actual *motion* of the day was styled 'the Coxcomb and the Coverlet.'

5. 8. 50 shee puts in a pinne. Pricking with pins and needles was one of the devil's regular ways of tormenting bewitched persons. They were often supposed to vomit these articles. So when Voltore feigns possession, Volpone cries out: 'See! He vomits crooked pins' (*The Fox*, *Wks.* 3. 312).

5. 8. 61 the Kings Constable. 'From the earliest times to our own days, there were two bodies of police in England, namely, the parish and high constables, and the watchmen in cities and boroughs. Nothing could exceed their inefficiency in the 17th century. Of the constables, Dalton (in the reign of James I.) observes that they "are often absent from their houses, being for the most part husbandmen." The charge of Dogberry shows probably with no great caricature what sort of watchmen Shakespeare was familiar with. As late as 1796, Colquhoun observes that the watchmen "were aged and often superannuated men." '—Sir J. Stephen, *Hist. Crim. Law* 1. 194 f.

5. 8. 71 The taking of Tabacco, with which the Diuell

Is so delighted. This was an old joke of the time. In Middleton's *Black Book*, *Wks.* 8. 42 f. the devil makes his will, a part of which reads as follows: 'But turning my legacy to you-ward, Barnaby Burning-glass, arch-tobacco-taker of England, in ordinaries, upon stages both common and private, and lastly, in the lodging of your drab and mistress; I am not a little proud, I can tell you, Barnaby, that you dance after my pipe so long, and for all counter-blasts and tobacco-Nashes (which some call railers), you are not blown away, nor your fiery thirst quenched with the small penny-ale of their contradictions, but still suck that dug of damnation with a long nipple, still burning that rare Phoenix of Phlegethon, tobacco, that from her ashes, burned and knocked out, may arise another pipeful.'

Middleton here refers to Nash's *Pierce Pennilesse* and King James I.'s *Counterblast to Tobacco*. The former in his supplication to the devil says: 'It is suspected you have been a great *tobacco*-taker in your youth.' King James describes it as 'a custom loathsome to the eye, hateful to the nose, harmful to the brain, dangerous to the lungs, and in the black stinking fume thereof, nearest resembling the horrid stygian smoke of the pit that is bottomless.'

The dramatists seem never to grow tired of this joking allusion to the devil and his pipe of tobacco. Cf. Dekker, *If this be not a good Play*, *Wks.* 3. 293: 'I think the Diuell is sucking Tabaccho, heeres such a Mist.' *Ibid.* 327: 'Are there gentleman diuels too? this is one of those, who studies the black Art, thats to say, drinkes Tobacco.' Massinger, *Guardian*, *Wks.*, p. 344:

—You shall fry firstFor a rotten piece of touchwood, and give fireTo the great fiend's nostrils, when he smokes tobacco!

Dekker (*Non-dram. Wks.* 2. 89) speaks of 'that great *Tobacconist* the

Prince of Smoake & darknes, *Don Pluto.*'

The art of *taking* or *drinking* tobacco was much cultivated and had its regular professors. The *whiff,* the *ring,* etc., are often spoken of. For the general subject see Dekker, *Guls Horne-booke*; Barnaby Riche, *Honestie of this Age,* 1613; Harrison, *Chronology,* 1573; *Every Man in,* etc. An excellent description of a tobacconist's shop is given in *Alchemist, Wks.* 4. 37. For a historical account of its introduction see Wheatley. *Ev. Man in,* p. xlvii.

Jonson's form *tabacco* is the same as the Italian and Portuguese. See Alden, *Bart. Fair,* p. 169.

5. 8. 74, 5 yellow, etc.

That's Starch! the Diuell's Idoll of that colour. For the general subject of yellow starch see note 1. 1. 112, 3. Compare also Stubbes, *Anat. of Abuses,* p. 52: 'The deuil, as he in the fulness of his malice, first inuented these great ruffes, so hath hee now found out also two great stayes to beare vp and maintaine this his kingdome of great ruffes.... The one arch or piller whereby his kingdome of great ruffes is vnderpropped, is a certaine kinde of liquide matter which they call *starch,* wherein the devil hath willed them to wash and diue his ruffes wel.'

'Starch hound' and 'Tobacco spawling (spitting)' are the names of two devils in Dekker's *If this be not a good Play, Wks.* 3. 270. Jonson speaks of 'that idol starch' again in the *Alchemist, Wks.* 4. 92.

5. 8. 78 He is the Master of Players. An evident allusion to the Puritan attacks on the stage. This was the period of the renewed literary contest. George Wither had lately published his *Abuses stript and whipt,* 1613. For the whole subject see Thompson, E. N. S., *The Controversy between the Puritans and the Stage,* New York, 1903.

5. 8. 81 Figgum. 'In some of our old dictionaries, *fid* is explained to caulk with oakum: figgum, or fig'em, may therefore be a vulgar derivative from this term, and signify the lighted flax or tow with which jugglers stuff their mouths when they prepare to amuse the rustics by breathing out smoke and flames:

—a nut-shellWith tow, and touch-wood in it, to spite fire (5. 3. 4. 5).'   —
G.

5. 8. 86, 7 to such a foole, He makes himselfe. For the omission of the relative adverb cf. 1. 3. 34, 35.

5. 8. 89 To come to dinner, in mee the sinner. The conception of this couplet and the lines which Fitzdottrel speaks below was later elaborated in Cocklorrel's song in the *Gipsies Metamorphosed.* Pluto in Dekker's *If this be not a good Play, Wks.* 3. 268, says that every devil should have 'a brace of whores to his breakfast.' Such ideas seem to be descended from the mediæval allegories of men like Raoul de Houdanc, Ruteboeuf, etc.

5. 8. 91, 2 Are you phrenticke, Sir, Or what graue dotage moues you. 'Dotage, fatuity, or folly, is a common name to all the following species, as some will have it.... *Phrenitis,* which the Greeks derive from the word φρήν, is a disease of the mind, with a continual madness or dotage, which hath an acute fever annexed, or else an inflammation of the brain, or the membranes or kells of it, with an acute fever, which causeth madness and dotage.'—

Burton, *Anat. of Mel.*, ed. Shilleto, 1. 159-60.

5. 8. 112 f. Οἰ μοὶ κακοδαίμων, etc. See variants. 'This Greek is from the Plutus of Aristophanes, Act 4, Sc. 3.'—W.

Accordingly to Blaydes's edition, 1886, 11. 850-2. He reads Οἴμοι κακοδαίμων, etc. (Ah! me miserable, and thrice miserable, and four times, and five times, and twelve times, and ten thousand times.)

5. 8. 116 Quebrémos, etc. Let's break his eye in jest.

5. 8. 118 Di grátia, etc. If you please, sir, if you have money, give me some of it.

5. 8. 119 f. Ouy, Ouy Monsieur, etc. Yes, yes, sir, a poor devil! a poor little devil!

5. 8. 121 by his seuerall languages. Cf. Marston, *Malcontent, Wks.* 1. 212: '*Mal.* Phew! the devil: let him possess thee; he'll teach thee to speak all languages most readily and strangely.'

5. 8. 132 Such an infernall stincke, etc. Dr. Henry More says that the devil's 'leaving an ill smell behind him seems to imply the reality of the business', and that it is due to 'those adscititious particles he held together in his visible vehicle being loosened at his vanishing' (see Lowell, *Lit. Essays* 2. 347).

5. 8. 133 St. Pulchars Steeple. St. Sepulchre in the Bailey (occasionally written St. 'Pulcher's) is a church at the western end of Newgate Street and in the ward of Farringdon Without. A church existed here in the twelfth century. The church which Jonson knew was built in the middle of the fifteenth century. The body of the church was destroyed in the Great Fire of 1666.

It was the custom formerly for the clerk or bellman of St. Sepulchre's to go under Newgate on the night preceding the execution of a criminal, and, ringing his bell, to repeat certain verses, calling the prisoner to repentance. Another curious custom observed at this church was that of presenting a nosegay to every criminal on his way to Tyburn (see Wh-C.). The executed criminals were buried in the churchyard (d. Middleton, *Black Book, Wks.* 8. 25).

Cunningham says that 'the word *steeple* was not used in the restricted sense to which we now confine it. The *tower* of St. Sepulchre's in Jonson's time, must have been very much like what we now see it as most carefully and tastefully restored.'

5. 8. 134 as farre as Ware. This is a distance of about 22 miles. Ware is an ancient market-town of Herts, situated in a valley on the north side of the river Lea. The 'great bed of Ware' is mentioned in *Twelfth Night* 3. 2. 51, and the town is characterized as 'durty Ware' in Dekker's *North-ward Hoe, Wks.* 3. 53.

5. 8. 142, 3 I will tell truth, etc. Jonson uses this proverb again in *Tale Tub, Wks.* 6. 150: 'tell troth and shame the devil.'

GLOSSARY

This glossary is designed to include obsolete, archaic, dialectal, and rare words; current words used in obsolete, archaic, or exceptional senses; and, so far as practicable, obsolete and archaic phrases. Current words in current uses have occasionally been included to avoid confusion, as well as technical words unfamiliar to the ordinary reader. Favorite words have been treated, for the sake of illustration, with especial fullness.

For most words treated in its volumes published up to March, 1905, Murray's *New English Dictionary* is the chief authority. For words not reached by that work the *Century Dictionary* has been preferred. The *Stanford Dictionary* has been found especially useful for anglicized words. It has often been necessary to resort to contemporary foreign dictionaries in the case of words of Romance origin.

It has been thought best to refer to all or nearly all important passages. Etymologies are given only in cases of especial interest.

A dagger [†] before a word or definition indicates that the word or the particular meaning is obsolete; parallel lines [||] before a word, that it has never become naturalized in English; an interrogation point [?], that the case is doubtful.

A, *prep.* [Worn down from OE. preposition *an, on.*] With *be*: engaged in. *Arch.* or *dial.* 5. 1. 4.

†**A'**, *prep.* Worn down from *of.* 5. 2. 38.

Aboue, *adv.* Surpassing in degree; exceedingly. 3. 6. 33.

Abuse, *v.* †To impose upon, deceive. 5. 8. 140; 4. 2. 41; 4. 7. 80.

Academy, *n.*? A school of deportment. 2. 8. 20; 3. 5. 33.

Access, *n.* †Approach; advance. 2. 6. 68.

Accompt, *n.* [Form of *account.*] A report. 2. 7. 28.

Accomptant, †*a.* [Form of *accountant.*] Liable to give an account; accountable. 5. 2. 11.

Account, *n.* †Reckoning, consideration. Phr. *make account*: To reckon, consider. 4. 1. 10.

Acknowledge, *v.* To recognize a service as (from a person). 4. 3. 19.

Admire, *v.* †*intr.* To feel or express surprise; to wonder. 1. 1. 77.

Aduise, *v.* To warn, dissuade †(from a course). 5. 4. 43.

Aërie, *a.* [Form of *airy.*] Lively, vivacious. 4. 4. 157. aëry. 3. 5. 13.

Affection, *n.* †Mental tendency; disposition. 4. 4. 126.

Afore, *prep.* In the presence of. *Arch.* or *dial.* 4. 4. 167; 5. 5. 7.

Aforehand, *adv. Arch.* In advance. 1. 3. 41.

After-game, *n.* '*Prop.*, a second game played in order to reverse or improve the issues of the first; hence, "The scheme which may be laid or the expedients which are practised after the original game has miscarried; methods taken after the first turn of affairs" (Johnson).' *NED.* 4. 7. 84.

||**Alcorça**, *n.* Sp. 'A conserue.' Minsheu.

Alcorea, *n.* pr. for *Alcorça*, *q. v.* 4. 4. 144.

||**Allum Scagliola**, *n.* It.? Rock alum. 4. 4. 30.

†**Almaine-leape**, *n.* A dancing-leap. 1. 1. 97.

Almanack-Man, *n.* †A fortune-teller, foreteller. 1. 7. 25.

||**Almoiauana**, *n.* Sp. 'A kinde of cheese-cake.' Minsheu. 4. 4. 143.

Almond milke, *n.* 'Chambers *Cycl. Supp.*, *Almond-milk* is a preparation made of sweet blanched almonds and water, of some use in medicine, as an emollient.' *NED.* 1. 6. 222.

||**Aluagada**, *n. pr.* same as *Alvayálde*, *q. v.* 4. 4. 27.

||**Aluayalde** or **Albayalde**, *n.* Sp. 'A white colour to paint womens faces called ceruse.' Minsheu.

Ancient, *a.*? Belonging to an old family. 1. 2. 17.

And, *conj.* †If. 3. 5. 39. and'. 1. 3. 23. an'. 1. 2. 31.

Angel, *n.* 'An old English gold coin, called more fully at first the Angel-noble, being originally a new issue of the Noble, having as its device the archangel Michael standing upon, and piercing the dragon.' *NED.* Pr. about 10 s. 2. 1. 138.

Anone, *adv.* Now again. P. 10.

†**Ap-perill**, *n.* Risk. 5. 4. 34.

||**Aqua nanfa**, *n.* Sp. [Corruption of *acqua nanfa.*] 'Sweet water smelling of muske and Orenge-leaves.' Florio. 4. 4. 146.

||**Aqua-vitæ**, *n.* Any form of ardent spirits. 2. 1. 5.

Arbitrary, *a. Law.* Discretionary; not fixed. 3. 3. 75.

||**Arcana**, *n.* [*Pl.* of L. *a. arcanum*, used *subst.*] Secrets, mysteries. 4. 4. 151.

||**Argentata**, *n.* It. 'A painting for women's faces.' Florio. 4. 4. 28.

Argument, *n.* Subject-matter of discussion or discourse; theme, subject. *Obs.* or *arch.* 1. 6. 10.

Arras, *n.* [Arras, name of a town in Artois, famed for its manufacture of the fabric.] A hanging screen of a rich tapestry fabric formerly placed around the walls of household apartments. 1. 2. 46.

Art, *n.* 1. A contrivance. 1. 7. 24. †2. Magic art. 1. 5. 21.

Artist, *n.* †A professor of magic arts; an astrologer. 1. 2. 22.

As, *conj.* †With finite verb: That. 1. 4. 30; 1. 6. 61; 3. 2. 23.

As, *adv.* Phr. *as that*: Even as (in parallel clause, introducing a known circumstance with which a hypothesis is contrasted). 5. 1. 20.

Assure, *v.* †To secure. 3. 5. 68.

At, *prep.* Upon. 1. 6. 114.

Atchieue, *v.* [Form of *achieve.*] †To gain, win (a material acquisition). 3. 5. 67.

Attemp, *n.* [Form of *attempt.*] Endeavor to win over. 2. 2. 30.

Attempt, *v.* To try to win over, or seduce. *Arch.* 4. 5. 7.

Audit, *n.* A statement of account. *Fig., arch.* 3. 3. 229.

Aye, *adv.* At all times, on all occasions. (Now only *Sc.* and north *dial.*) 1. 6. 220.

Ayre, *n.* [Form of *air.*] Manner; sort. 2. 7. 21.

    Baffle, *v.* †To treat with contempt. 4. 7. 73 SN.

Bag, *n.* The sac (of the bee) containing honey. 2. 6. 112.

Bailie, *n.* [Form of *bailiff*.] An officer of justice under a sheriff; a warrant officer. 3. 3. 38.

Bane, *n.* 1. Poison. 2. 7. 18.

†2. As *exclam.* 'Plague.' 5. 6. 66.

Banke, *n.* †An artificial earthwork, an embankment. 2. 1. 56.

Bare, *a.* Bare-headed. *Arch.* 2. 3. 37.

Bate, *v.* †1. To deprive (*of*). 4. 1. 56.

†2. To make a reduction (*of*); to deduct. 2. 1. 83; 2. 1. 104.

Baudy, 2. 8. 73. See *Bawdy*.

Bawd-ledger, *n.* Resident minister to the bawds (a mock title coined by Jonson). 5. 6. 64.

Bawdry, *n. Arch.* Lewd talk; obscenity. 4. 1. 176.

Bawdy, *a.* 1. Lewd. 2. 1. 167. 2. *absol. quasi-sb.* Lewd language, obscenity. 4. 4. 165. baudy. 2. 8. 73.

Be, *v. pl.* Are. *Obs.* or *dial.* 2. 8. 63.

Bed-fellow, *n.* †Intimate companion. 2. 8. 9.

Behaue, *v. †trans.* To manage. 2. 8. 71.

Benefit, *n.* Advantage. †Phr. *make benefit of*: To take advantage of. ?*Obs.* 2. 2. 98.

Beniamin, *n.* Gum benzoin, an aromatic resin obtained from the *Styrax benzoin*, a tree of Sumatra, Java, and the neighboring islands, used in medicine, perfumery, and chemistry.

‖**Beniamin di gotta**, *n.* ?Gum benzoin in drops. See *Beniamin*. 4. 4. 33.

Bespeake, *v. trans.* w. *refl.* To engage. 1. 6. 214.

Bestow, *v.* To deposit. *Arch.* 3. 2. 9.

Black-water, *n.* 3. 3. 179. See-*water*.

Blanck manger, *n.* [Form of *blancmange*.] †'A dish composed usually of fowl, but also of other meat, minced with cream, rice, almonds, sugar, eggs, etc.' *NED.* 1. 6. 240.

Blank, *n.* 'A small French coin, originally of silver, but afterwards of copper; also a silver coin of Henry V. current in the parts of France then held by the English. According to Littré, the French *blanc* was worth 5 deniers. The application of the name in the 17th Cen. is uncertain.' *NED.* 3. 3. 33.

Blesse, *v.* †To protect, save (from). 4. 4. 187.

Blocke, *n.* A mould. *Spec. Brokers blocke*: A mould for clothes in a pawnbroker's shop. 2. 7. 15.

Blocke-head, *n.* †A wooden block for hats or wigs; hence, a blockish or stupid head. 3. 5. 65.

Board, *n.* Phr. *tall board*: ?A gaming table. 4. 5. 32. See note.

Booke, *n.* †A charter or deed; a written grant of privileges. 3. 3. 67; 3. 3. 79.

‖**Borachio**, *n. Obs.* 'A large leather bottle or bag used in Spain for wine or other liquors.' *NED.* 2. 1. 71.

Bound, *ppl. a.* Under obligations of gratitude. 4. 1. 11.

Bouzy, *a.* [Form of *bousy*.] Sotted. 5. 6. 25.

Brach, *n. Arch.* A bitch-hound. 4. 4. 229.

Braue, *a.* 1. Finely-dressed. *Arch.* 1. 4. 16; 2. 5. 11.

2. A general epithet of admiration or praise. *Arch.* 1. 2. 52; 2. 6. 75; 3. 4. 12; 4. 6. 29.

†*interj.* 3. Capital! 1. 1. 67.

Brauery, *n.* †A fine thing; a matter to boast or be proud of. 3. 6. 47.

Breake, *v.* †To speak confidentially (*with* a person *of* a thing). 3. 4. 62.

Bring, *v.* Phr. *bring up*: ?Augment, increase. 1. 4. 96.

Bristo-stone, *n.* 'A kind of transparent rock-crystal found in the Clifton limestone near Bristol, resembling the diamond in brilliancy.' *NED.* 3. 3. 173.

Broker, *n.* 1. A pawnbroker. 1. 1. 143; 1. 4. 19.

2. With added function of agent or intermediary. 1. 4. 4.

Brooke, *v.* †To endure; not to discredit; to be sufficiently appropriate for. 2. 8. 63.

Buckram, *a.* A kind of coarse linen or cloth stiffened with gum or paste. 2. 1. 63.

Bullion, *n.* †More fully, *bullion-hose*: Trunk-hose, puffed out at the upper part, in several folds. 3. 3. 217.

Bush, *n.* A branch of ivy used as vintner's sign; hence, the sign-board of a tavern. 3. 3. 170.

Businesse, *n.* †1. Affectedly used for an 'affair of honor,' a duel. 3. 3. 106.

†2. A misunderstanding, quarrel. 4. 1. 18.

Busse, *v.* *Arch.* and *dial.* To kiss. 3. 6. 1.

Buzz, *v.* Phr. *buzz at*: 1. To hum about, as an insect.

†2. To whisper to; incite by suggestions. Used quibblingly in both senses. 2. 7. 4.

†**By cause**, phr. used as *conj.* Because. 5. 4. 24.

Cabbin, *n.* †A small room, a boudoir. 1. 6. 238.

Cabinet, *n.* A small chamber or room; a boudoir. *Arch.* or *obs.* 4. 4. 152.

Campheere, *n.* [Form of *camphor*.] 4. 4. 22.

Can, *v.* †*tr.* To have at one's command; to be able to supply, devise or suggest (a pregnant use). 3. 6. 39.

Caract, *n.* [Form of *carat*. Confused with *caract*=Character.] †Value, estimate. Phr. *at all caracts*: 'To the minutest circumstance.' Gifford. 1. 6. 88.

†**Caravance**, *n.* 'Name of sundry kinds of peas and small beans.' *Stanford.*

†**Carrauicins**, *n.* perh.=*caravance*, *q. v.* 4. 4. 45.

Care, *v.* To take care. Now only *dial.* 1. 1. 29.

Carefull, *a.* Anxious, solicitous. *Arch.* 1. 6. 10.

†**Caroch**, *n.* A coach or chariot of a stately or luxurious kind. 1. 6. 214. Carroch. 4. 2. 11.

Carry, *v.* 1. *tr.* To conduct, manage. *Arch.* 3. 5. 53.

?†2. *intr.* To be arranged. 3. 3. 126.

Case, *n.* 1. The body (as enclosing the soul, etc.). 5. 6. 39.

2. Condition, supposition. Phr. *in case to*: In a condition or position to; prepared, ready. *Arch.* 4. 7. 85. *Put case*: Suppose. ?*Arch.* 4. 4. 228.

Cast, *v.* †1. To estimate. 2. 1. 81.

†2. To devise. 2. 8. 42.

Castle-soape, *n.* *Obs.* form of *Castile soap.* 5. 3. 3.

||**Cataputia**, *n.* [In Med. L. and It.] 'The hearbe spurge.' Florio. 4. 4. 55.

†**Cater**, *n.* 'A buyer of provisions or "cates"; in large households the officer who made the necessary purchases of provisions.' *NED.* 1. 3. 13.

Catholike, *a.* †Universally efficient. 1. 4. 35.

†**Cause**, *conj. Obs.* exc. *dial.* [An elliptic use of the noun for *because*.] Because. 2. 8. 28; 4. 6. 34. Phr. *by cause.* See *By cause.*

†**Cautelous**, *a.* Crafty. 1. 6. 142.

Caution, *n.* 1. Security; guarantee. 3. 4. 30; 58.
    2. A word of warning. 4. 5. 28.

Ceruse, *n.* [White lead.] A paint or cosmetic for the skin; used vaguely. 4. 4. 53.

Challengee, *n. Rare* (perh. coined by Jonson). One who is challenged. 3. 3. 141.

Character, *n.* A cabalistic or magical sign. 1. 2. 9.

Charge, *n.* Expenses; outlay. *Arch.* 2. 1. 49; 1. 6. 172.

Chartell, *n.* [Form of *cartel.*] A written challenge. 3. 3. 140.

Chaw, *v.* A common by-form of *chew* in the 16-17th c. 4. 2. 53.

Cheat, *n.* †Any product of conquest or robbery; booty, spoil. 1. 7. 4.

Cheat, *v.* Phr. *cheat on*: To cheat. 5. 6. 54.

Cheater, *n.* †A dishonest gamester; a sharper. 5. 6. 64.

Check, *n.* †Reproof, censure. 3. 6. 44.

Cheese-trencher, *n.* A wooden plate for holding or cutting cheese. P. 8.

Christall, *n.* [Form of *crystal.*] A piece of rock-crystal or similar mineral used in magic art. 1. 2. 6.

†**Cioppino**, *n.* [Italianated form of *chopine.*] A kind of shoe raised above the ground by means of a cork sole or the like; worn about 1600 in Spain and Italy, esp. at Venice, where they were monstrously exaggerated. 3. 4. 13 (see note); 4. 4. 69.

Cipher, *n.* A means of conveying secret intelligence: used vaguely. 2. 1. 167·

Circle, *n.* 1. An embrace. 1. 4. 94.
    2. Sphere (of influence, etc.). 1. 6. 96.
    3. A circular figure (of magic). 1. 2. 26.

Cloake-charge, *n.* The expense of a cloak (coined by Jonson). 2. 2. 42.

Cockscomb, *n.* †A simpleton. 5. 8. 40.

Cock-stone, *n.* †A name of the kidney-bean. 1. 1. 53.

Cog, *v.* To cheat, esp. at dice or cards. 1. 1. 48.

†**Cokes**, *n.* A simpleton, one easily 'taken in.' 2. 2. 104.

Collect, *v.* To infer, deduce. *Rare.* 1. 6. 234.

Come, *v.* Phr. *come off*: (in imperative as a call of encouragement to action) Come! come along! 3. 5. 27.

Comming, *ppl. a.* Inclined to make or meet advances. 4. 4. 180.

Commoner, *n.* †A member of the general body of a town-council. 2. 1. 42.

Complement, *n.* †1. Anything which goes to make up or fully equip. 3. 4. 33.
    †2. Polite or ceremonious greetings. 3. 5. 15.

Complexion, *n.* †1. The combination of the four 'humors' of the body in a certain proportion; 'temperament.' 2. 2. 122.

†2. Bodily habit or constitution. 5. 1. 18.

?3. Appearance of the skin. 1. 4. 63 (or perh. as 2).

†4. A coloring preparation, cosmetic. 4. 4. 12.

5. Appearance, aspect (*fig.*). 2. 6. 50.

Comport, *v.* Phr. *comport with*: †To act in accordance with. 2. 8. 17.

‖**Compos mentis**, *a. phr.* [L. f. *com-potis*.] Of sound mind. 5. 3. 12.

Compter, *n.* Old spelling of *Counter*. The name of certain city prisons for debtors; esp. the two London Compters. 3. 1. 20 (see note).

Conceit, *n.* †1. Idea, device. 2. 8. 23. conceipt.

†2. Personal opinion. 4. 4. 200.

3. Phr. *Out of conceipt*: Out of patience, dissatisfied. 2. 8. 18.

Concerne, *v.* †*intr.* To be of importance. 3. 3. 113.

Concurrence, *n.* A juncture: a condition: used vaguely. 2. 6. 54.

Conduit-head, *n.* †A structure from which water is distributed or made to issue: a reservoir. 5. 1. 27.

Confine, *v.* Imprison. Const. †*to*. 5. 6. 34.

Confute, *v.* To put to silence (by physical means). 5. 6. 18.

Content, *a.* †Willing. 1. 1. 133.

Conuenient, *a.* †1. Due, proper. 1. 4. 79.   †2. Suitable. 4. 4. 230.

Conuey, *v.* To carry from one place to another (†used of small objects and with connotation of secrecy). 2. 1. 164.

Coozen, *v.* [Form of *cozen*.] To cheat. 3. 1. 22. cossen. 5. 2. 29.

Coozener, *n.* [Form of *cozener*.] Impostor. 5. 8. 148.

‖**Coquetta**, *n.* Sp. A small loaf. 4. 4. 143.

Corn-ground, *n. Arch.* A piece of land used for growing corn; corn-land. 3. 1. 17.

Cornish, *a.* Phr. *C. counterfeit*: referring to the 'Cornish stone' or 'diamond.' a variety of quartz found in Cornwall. 3. 3. 173.

Cossen, *v.* 5. 2. 29. See *Coozen*.

Councell, *n. Obs.* form of *council*. 3. 1. 34; 5. 2. 20.

Court, *v.* Phr. *court it*: To play or act the courtier. 3. 4. 56.

Court-ship, *n.* †An act of courtesy (used in *pl.*) 1. 6. 201.

Coyle, *n.* [Form of *coil*.] ?An embarrassing situation; a 'mess.' 5. 5. 54.

Crack, *v. intr.* To break the musical quality of the voice (used *fig.*) 5. 5. 59.

Cracke, *n.* †A lively lad; a 'rogue' (playfully), a wag. 2. 8. 58.

†**Crambe**, *n.* [Form of *crambo*.] 'A game in which one player gives a word or line of verse to which each of the others has to find a rime.' *NED*. 5. 8. 110.

Creak, *v.* To exhibit the characteristics of; to betray (a *fig.* use of the *lit.* meaning). 2. 2. 87.

Credit, *n.* †1. Authority. 1. 4. 29.

†2. Repute. 5. 6. 49.

Crisped, *ppl. a.* Closely curled; as applied to trees of uncertain significance. 2. 6. 78 (see note).

Cunning, *a.* †Learned; versed in. 2. 4. 12.

Custard, *n.* †'Formerly, a kind of open pie containing pieces of meat or fruit covered with a preparation of broth or milk, thickened with eggs, sweetened, and seasoned with spices, etc.' *NED.* 1. 1. 97.

Cutpurse, *n.* One who steals by cutting purses; hence, a thief. 1. 1. 140.

Cut-work, *n.* †1. 'A kind of openwork embroidery or lace worn in the latter part of the 16th and in the 17th c.' *NED.* 2. 1. 163; 3. 3. 23.

   †2. *attrib.* 1. 1. 128. cut-worke.

   Danger, *n.* †Mischief, harm. 2. 6. 30.

†**Daw**, *v. Rare.* To frighten, torment. 4. 4. 208.

Dearling, *n. Obs.* form of *darling.* 5. 6. 74.

Decimo sexto. ?*Obs.* 'A term denoting the size of a book, or of the page of a book, in which each leaf is one-sixteenth of a full sheet; properly Sexto-decimo (usually abbreviated 16mo.).' *NED.* Also applied *fig.* to a diminutive person or thing: hence, ?An exquisite or perfect condition. 4. 4. 50.

Deed of Feoffment, *phr.* 4. 6. 44. See *Feoffment.*

Defeate, *n.* †Undoing, ruin. Phr. *do defeate upon*: To do injury to; to bring about the ruin of. 2. 6. 21.

Defend, *v.* †To prohibit, forbid. *Obs.* exc. *dial.* 1. 4. 97.

Degree, *n.* 1. A high degree or quality. 2. 1. 89.   2. Any degree. 4. 3. 26.

Delicate, *a.* †1. Charming

   †2. Voluptuous. 2. 2. 103; 2. 2. 126.

Both meanings seem to be present.

Delude, *v.* †To frustrate the aim or purpose of. 1. 6. 54.

†**Deneer**, *n.* [Form of *Denier*, *obs.* or *arch.*] A French coin, the twelfth of a sou; originally of silver, but from the 16th c. of copper. Hence (esp. in negative phrases) used as the type of a very small sum. 3. 3. 188.

Deny, *v.* ?Prove false to. 1. 4. 91.

Depart, *v.* †Phr. *depart with*: To part with; give up. 1. 4. 58; 1. 4. 83.

Dependance, *n.* †A quarrel or affair 'depending,' or awaiting settlement. 3. 3. 130.

Devil, *n.* Jonson uses the following forms: Deuill. 5. 5. 49, etc.; Diuel. 5. 5. 20; Diuell. Titlepage, etc.

Diligence, *n.* †*pl.* Labors, exertions. 2. 2. 106.

Discourse, *n.* †Conversational power. 4. 4. 225.

Discourse, *v.* To discuss. *Arch.* 4. 2. 40.

Dishonesty, *n.* †Unchastity. 4. 4. 158.

†**Displeasant**, *a.* Displeasing; disagreeable. Epilogue 6.

Distast, *n.* †Quarrel. 3. 3. 77.

Diuident, *n.* [Erron. spelling of *dividend.*] †The share (of anything divided among a number of persons) that falls to each to receive. 2. 1. 123; 3. 3. 201.

Dotage, *n.* Infatuation. 5. 8. 92 (see note).

Dottrel, *n.* 1. A species of plover (Eudromias morinellus).

   2. A silly person; one easily 'taken in.' 2. 8. 59. See note 2. 2. 49-50.

Doublet, *n.* A close-fitting body-garment, with or without sleeves, worn by men from the 14th to the 18th centuries. *Obs.* exc. *Hist.* 1. 1. 52. Phr. *hose and doublet*: as the typical male attire. 1. 6. 151.

Doubt, *n.* †Apprehension; fear. 5. 1. 8.

Doubt, *v.* †To suspect; have suspicions about. 2. 6. 47.

Dough-bak'd, *ppl. a.* Now *dial.* Imperfectly baked, so as to remain doughy. 4. 4. 20.

Doxey, *n.* 'Originally the term in Vagabonds' Cant for the unmarried mistress of a beggar or rogue: hence. *slang*, a mistress, prostitute.' *NED.* 2. 8. 38.

Draw, *v.* †1. To pass through a strainer; to bring to proper consistence. 1. 6. 222.

2. To frame, draw up (a document). 3. 3. 67.

†3. *intr.* To withdraw. 2. 1. 127.

4. Phr. *draw to*: To come upon; to catch up with. 2. 6. 24.

Dwindle, *v.* †'To shrink (with fear.) *Obs., rare.* (Prob. a misuse owing to two senses of shrink.)' *NED.* 4. 4. 63.

Effectuall, *a.* ?Earnest. 2. 2. 107.

†**E-la**, *n. Mus. Obs.* exc. *Hist.* [f. E+La; denoting the particular note E which occurred only in the seventh Hexachord, in which it was sung to the syllable *la.*] 'The highest note in the Gamut, or the highest note of the 7th Hexachord of Guido, answering to the upper E in the treble.' *NED. Fig.* of something very ambitious. 5. 5. 59.

Employ, *v.* †Phr. *employ out*: To send out (a person) with a commission. 5. 5. 46.

Engag'd, *ppl. a.* 1. Morally bound. 4. 6. 9.

†2. Involved, hampered. 1. 2. 41.

†3. Made security for a payment; rendered liable for a debt. 3. 3. 90.

Enlarge, *v.* †Phr. *enlarge upon, refl. absol.*: To expand (oneself) in words, give free vent to one's thoughts. 2. 1. 128.

Ensigne, *n.* †Token; signal displayed. ?*Obs.* 1. 6. 210.

Enter, *v.* Phrases. †1. *Enter a bond*: To enter into a bond; to sign a bond. 1. 7. 17.

†2. *Enter trust with*: To repose confidence in. 3. 4. 36.

Entertaine, *v.* †1. To give reception to; receive (a person). 1. 2. 44.

†2. To take into one's service; hire. 3. 5. 19.

Enter-view, *n. Obs.* form of *interview*. 2. 6. 23.

Enuious, *a.* †Hateful. 1. 6. 196.

Enuy, *n.* †Ill-will, enmity. 2. 6. 20.

Enuy, *v. trans.* †To begrudge (a thing). 1. 6. 13.

Equiuock, *n.* [*Obs.* form (or misspelling) of *equivoke.*] The use of words in a double meaning with intent to deceive:=Equivocation. *Rare.* 3. 3. 184.

Erect, *v.* †To set up, establish, found (an office). *Obs.* or *arch.* exc. in *Law.* 3. 3. 67.

||**Escudero**, *n.* Sp. An attendant; a lady's page. 4. 4. 87.

Euill, *n.* The Vice, *q. v.* 5. 6. 76.

Exchequer, *n.* The office of the Exchequer; used hyperbol. for the source of wealth. 3. 3. 81.

Extraordinary, †*adv.* Extraordinarily. 1. 1. 116.

Extreme, †*adv.* Extremely. 1. 7. 27.

Extremity, *n.* ?An extreme instance. 1. 5. 15.

Face, *n.* Attitude (towards); reception (of). P. 21.

Fact, *n.* †1. The making, manufacture. 3. 4. 49.

2. Phr. *with one's fact*: as an actual experience. 5. 6. 13.

Faine, *v. Obs.* form of *feign*. 5. 5. 28.

Fauour, *n.* †1. Leave, permission. Phr. *under* (your) *fauour*: with all submission, subject to correction. *Obs.* or *arch.* 1. 3. 27.

2. ?Comeliness; ?face. 4. 6. 49.

Feate, *n.* A business transaction. 3. 3. 227.

Fellow, *n.* Phr. *good fellow*: Of a woman. A term of familiar address. 5. 1. 5.

Feoffee, *n.* The person to whom a freehold estate in land is conveyed by a feoffment. 3. 5. 60.

Feoffment, *n.* 'The action of investing a person with a fief or fee. In technical language applied esp. to the particular mode of conveyance (originally the only one used, but now almost obsolete) in which a person is invested in a freehold estate in lands by livery of seisin (at common law generally, but not necessarily, evidenced by a deed, which, however, is not required by statute).' *NED.* 4. 5. 15; 4. 7. 7.

Phr. *Deed of Feoffment*: 'The instrument or deed by which corporeal hereditaments are conveyed.' *NED.* 4. 6. 44.

Fetch, *v.* 1. To earn; get (money). 2. 1. 72.

†2. To perform, take (a leap). 1. 1. 55.

†3. Phr. *Fetch again*: To revive, restore to consciousness. 2. 1. 4.

†**Figgum**, *n.* ?Juggler's tricks (not found elsewhere). 5. 8. 82.

Finenesse, *n.* †'Overstrained and factitious scrupulousness.' Gifford. 3. 3. 104.

Firke, *v.* †To frisk about; ?to hitch oneself (Cunningham). 5. 6. 15.

Fixed, *ppl. a.* Made rigid or immobile (by emotion). 1. 5. 2.

Fizzling, *vbl. sb.* †Breaking wind without noise. 5. 3. 2.

Flower, *n.* †*Anc. Chem.* (*pl.*): 'The pulverulent form of any substance, esp. as the result of condensation after sublimation.' *NED.* 4. 4. 19.

Fly, *v.* Of a hawk: To pursue by flying: used *fig.* 4. 7. 53.

Flye-blowne, *a.* Tainted. With a quibble on the literal meaning. 2. 7. 7.

Fool, *v.* Phr. *fool off*: To delude, baffle. 2. 6. 25.

Forbeare, *v. trans.* †To keep away from or from interfering with; to leave alone. 1. 3. 22.

Forked, *a.* 'Horned,' cuckolded. 2. 2. 90.

Foyle, *n.* [Form of *foil*.] A thin leaf of some metal placed under a precious stone to increase its brilliancy. 3. 3. 180.

French-masque, *n.* pr. the 'Loo,' or 'Loup,' a half-mask of velvet, worn by females to protect the complexion. 2. 1. 162.

French-time, *n.* ?Formal and rhythmic measure (as characteristic of the French, in contrast to Italian, music). 3. 5. 30.

Frolick, *n.* †?Humorous verses circulated at a feast. 2. 8. 73.

‖**Fucus**, *n.* †Paint or cosmetic for beautifying the skin; a wash or coloring for the face. 3. 4. 50; 4. 2. 63.

Fustian, *n.* †A kind of coarse cloth made of cotton and flax. 3. 3. 30.

'Gainst, *prep.* [Form of *against*.] In anticipation of. *Arch.* 1. 1. 19.

'Gainst, *conj.* In anticipation that; in case that. *Arch.* or *dial.* 1. 1. 73; 3. 2. 39.

Gallant, *n.* 1. A man of fashion and pleasure; a fine gentleman. *Arch.* 1. 7. 27; 4. 4. 167.

    †2. Of a woman: A fashionably attired beauty. 3. 4. 8.

Gallant, *a.* Loosely, as a general epithet of admiration or praise: Splendid. Cf. *Brave.* Now *rare.* 2. 1. 58.

Gallery, *n.* 1. A long narrow platform or balcony on the outside of a building. 2. 2. 54.

    2. A room for pictures. 2. 5. 13.

Galley-pot, *n.* [Form of *gallipot.*] 'A small earthen glazed pot, esp. one used by apothecaries for ointments and medicines.' *NED.* 4. 4. 47.

Garnish, *n. slang.* 'Money extorted from a new prisoner, either as drink money for the other prisoners, or as a jailer's fee. *Obs.* exc. *Hist.*' *NED.* 5. 6. 1 (see note).

Geere, *n.* [Form of *gear.*] ?Discourse, talk; esp. in depreciatory sense, 'stuff.' Or possibly *obs.* form of *jeer.* 1. 6. 99 (see note).

Gentleman, *n.* 'A man of gentle birth, or having the same heraldic status as those of gentle birth; properly, one who is entitled to bear arms, though not ranking among the nobility. Now chiefly *Hist.*' *NED.* 3. 1. 1.

Gentleman huisher, *n.* 3. 4. 43. Same as *Gentleman-vsher, q. v.*

Gentleman-vsher, *n.* A gentleman acting as usher to a person of superior rank. 4. 4. 134. Gentleman huisher. 3. 4. 43. See note 4. 4. 134.

Gentlewoman, *n.* 1. A woman of gentle birth. 3. 3. 164.   2. A female attendant upon a lady of rank. Now chiefly *Hist.* 5. 1. 26.

Gleeke, *n.* 'A game at cards, played by three persons: forty-four cards were used, twelve being dealt to each player, while the remaining eight formed a common "stock."' *NED.* Phr. *three peny Gleeke.* 5. 2. 31.

Glidder, *v. Obs.* exc. *dial.* To glaze over. 4. 4. 47.

Globe, *n.* The name of a play-house; hence, used as a generic term for a play-house. 3. 3. 26.

Go, *v.* Phrases. 1. *Goe on*: as an expression of encouragement, Come along! advance! 3. 5. 27.

    2. *Goe with*: Agree with. 4. 4. 133.

God b'w'you [God be with you], *Phr.* Good-bye. 1. 6. 223.

Godwit, *n.* A marsh-bird of the genus Limosa. Formerly in great repute, when fattened, for the table. 3. 3. 25.

†**Gogs-nownes**, *n.* A corrupt form of 'God's wounds' employed in oaths. 1. 1. 50.

Gold-smith, *n.* A worker in gold, who (down to the 18th c.) acted as banker. 2. 8. 84.

Googe, *v.* [Form of *gouge.*] To cut out. 2. 1. 94.

Gossip, *n.* A familiar acquaintance, chum (applied to women). Somewhat *arch.* 1. 6. 219; 2. 8. 69.

Grandee, *n.* A Spanish or Portuguese nobleman of the highest rank; hence, †A term of polite address. P. 3.

†**Grant-paroll** [Fr. *grande parole*], *n.* Full permission (?not found elsewhere). 5. 6. 19.

||**Grasso di serpe**, *n.* It. ?'Snake's †fat.' *Stanford.* 4. 4. 34.

Gratulate, *v.* Now *arch.* and *poet.* †1. To rejoice. Phr. *gratulate with*: rejoice with, felicitate. 4. 1. 14.

2. *tr.* To rejoice at. 5. 1. 51.

Groat, *n.* A denomination of coin which was recognized from the 13th c. in various countries of Europe. The English groat was coined 1351(2)-1662, and was originally equal to four pence. †The type of a very small sum (cf. *Deneer*). 5. 4. 6.

Groome, *n.* 1. A serving man. *Obs.* or *arch.* 2. 2. 65.

†2. With added connotation of contempt. 2. 2. 87.

||**Guarda-duenna**, *n.* Sp. A lady's attendant. 4. 4. 83.

||**Guardo-duenna**, *n.* 4. 4. 77. See *Guarda-duenna.*

Gueld, *v.* [Form of *Geld.*] †*transf.* and *fig.* To mutilate: impair. 1. 1. 65.

Guilt, *ppl. a.* [Form of *gilt.*] Gilded. 1. 6. 214.

Hand-gout, *n.* Gout in the hand; used *fig.* of an unwillingness to grant favors without a recompense; hard-fistedness. 3. 3. 79.

Hand-kercher, *n.* Form of *handkerchief. Obs.* exc. *dial.* and vulgar. Common in literary use in 16-17th c. 4. 4. 89.

Handsomenesse, *n.* †Decency. 4. 3. 26.

Hang, *v.* Phr. *hang out*: †To put to death by hanging. 5. 6. 8.

Hap', *v.* Shortened form of *happen*. Phr. *may hap' see*: May chance to see (in process of transition to an adverb). 3. 2. 8.

†**Hard-wax**, *n.* ?Sealing-wax. 5. 1. 39.

Harness, *v.* †To dress, apparel. 2. 5. 6.

†**Harrington**, *n. Obs.* exc. *Hist.* 'A brass farthing token, coined by John, Lord Harrington, under a patent granted him by James I. in 1613.' *NED.* 2. 1. 83.

Ha's, *v.* Has. (Prob. a recollection of earlier forms, *hafs, haves.* Mallory.) 5. 3. 9; 4. 6. 43.

Heare, *v.* Phr. *heare ill of* (it): To be censured for. ?*Obs.* or ?*colloq.* 2. 7. 28.

Heauy, *a.* †Dull, stupid. 5. 6. 39.

Hedge, *v.* †Phr. *hedge in*: To secure (a debt) by including it in a larger one for which better security is obtained; to include a smaller debt in a larger. 2. 8. 104; 3. 2. 6.

Height, *n.* 1. A superior quality; a high degree. 2. 1. 70.

2. The highest point; the most important particular. 4. 4. 212.

3. Excellence; perfection of accomplishment. 2. 8. 59.

4. Phr. *at height*: In the highest degree; to one's utmost satisfaction. 5. 3. 22.

Here by, *adv.* †Close by; in this neighborhood. 3. 4. 41.

His, *poss. pron. 3d sing.* †*neut.* Its. 2. 1. 103.

Hold, *v.* Phr. *hold in with*: To keep (one) on good terms with. ?*Obs.* 3. 3. 221.

Honest, *a.* Chaste, virtuous. *Arch.* 4. 4. 161.

Honour, *n.* †An obeisance; a bow or curtsy. 3. 5. 27.

Hood, *n.* 'French hood, a form of hood worn by women in the 16th and 17th centuries, having the front band depressed over the forehead, and raised in folds or loops over the temples.' *NED.* 1. 1. 99.

Hooke, *v.* 1. *intr.* To get all one can; to display a grasping nature. 3. 3. 156.

  2. Phr. *hooke in*: To secure by hook or by crook. 3. 3. 150.

Hope, *v.* Phr. *hope †o'*: To have hope of; hope for. 1. 5. 1.

Horne, *n.* In *pl.*, the supposed insignia of a cuckold. 5. 8. 34.

Hose, *n.* †Breeches. Phr. *hose and doublet*. 1. 6. 151.

†Huisher, *n. Obs.* form of *usher*. 2. 7. 33. See *Gentleman-vsher*.

Hum, *n.* †A kind of liquor; strong or double ale. 1. 1. 114; 5. 8. 72.

Humour, *v.* To take a fancy to. *?Obs.* 1. 7. 13.

  I, *Obs.* form of *ay*. 1. 2. 1: *passim*.

I, *prep.* In. 2. 4. 41.

‖Incubus, *n.* 'A feigned evil spirit or demon (originating in personified representations of the nightmare) supposed to descend upon persons in their sleep, and especially to seek carnal intercourse with women. In the middle ages, their existence was recognized by the ecclesiasical and civil law.' *NED*. 2. 3. 26.

‖In decimo sexto, *phr.* 4. 4. 50. See *Decimo sexto*.

‖Infanta, *n.* 1. A daughter of the King and queen of Spain or Portugal; *spec.* the eldest daughter who is not heir to the throne.

  2. †*transf.* Applied analogously or fancifully to other young ladies. 4. 2. 71.

Ingag'd, *ppl. a. Obs.* form of Engag'd. 4. 4. 168. See *Engag'd* 1.

Ingenious, *a.* †Able; talented; clever. 2. 8. 75.

Ingine, *n.* †1. Skill in contriving, ingenuity. 2. 3. 46.

  †2. Plot; snare, wile. 2. 2. 87. With play on 3.

  3. Mechanical contrivance, machine; †trap.

Ingrate, *a.* Ungrateful. *Arch.* 1. 6. 174.

Iniquity, *n.* The name of a comic character or buffoon in the old moralities; a name of the Vice, *q. v.* 1. 1. 43; 1. 1. 118.

Inquire, *v.* †To seek information concerning, investigate. 3. 1. 11.

Innes of Court, *sb. phr.* The four sets of buildings belonging to the four legal societies which have the exclusive right of admitting persons to practise at the bar, and hold a course of instruction and examination for that purpose. 3. 1. 8. (see note).

Intend, *v.* †To pay heed to; apprehend. 4. 4. 127.

Intire, *a. Obs.* form of *entire*. [Fr. *entier* ‹ L. *integer*, untouched.] Untouched, uninjured. 2. 6. 32; 5. 6. 48.

Intitle, *v.* [Form of *entitle*.] To give (a person) a rightful claim (to a thing). 4. 6. 38.

Intreat, *v.* [Form of *entreat*.] †To prevail on by supplication; to persuade. 3. 6. 44.

Iacke, *n.* 1. The name of various mechanical contrivances. 1. 4. 50.

  †2. A term of familiarity; pet. 2. 2. 128.

Iewes-trumpe, *n.* Now *rare*. Jews' harp (an earlier name, and formerly equally common in England). 1. 1. 92.

Joynt-stoole, *v.* A stool made of parts joined or fitted together; a stool made by a   joiner   as   distinguished   from   one   of   more   clumsy

workmanship. *Obs.* exc. *Hist.* 1. 1. 92.
Iump, *v.* †1. *intr.* Act hurriedly or rashly. 4. 1. 5.
      †2. *trans.* To effect or do as with a jump; to dispatch. 4. 1. 6.
Iust, *a.* †1. Complete in character. 1. 5. 10.
      2. Proper, correct. 2. 2. 122.
Iuuentus, *n.* 1. 1. 50. See *Lusty.*
†**Kell**, *n.* The web or cocoon of a spinning caterpillar. *Obs.* exc. *dial.* 2. 6. 79.
Kinde, *n.* (One's) nature. Now *rare.* Phr. *man and kinde*: ?Human nature. 2. 1. 151.
Know, *v.* 1. To know how. ?*Obs.* 1. 2. 44.
      ?2. *pass. be known*: Disclose. 2. 1. 145.
Knowledge, *n.* †1. Cognizance, notice. Phr. *Take knowledge* (with clause): To become aware. 4. 4. 61.
      2. A matter of knowledge; a known fact (a licentious use). 1. 6. 82.
Lade, *v.* To load with obloquy or ridicule (as an ass with a burden; the consciousness of the metaphor being always present in the mind of the speaker). 1. 4. 72.
Lading, *vbl. sb.* A burden of obloquy or ridicule. 1. 6. 161. See *Lade.*
Lady-President, *n.* 4. 4. 9. See *President.*
Larum, *n.* †An apparatus attached to a clock or watch, to produce a ringing sound at any fixed hour. 4. 4. 165.
Lasse, *int.* Aphetic form of *Alas.* 5. 8. 46.
Lay, *v.* †To expound, set forth. 2. 8. 72.
Leaguer, *n.* A military camp. 3. 3. 33.
Leaue, *v.* To cease. Now only *arch.* 2. 2. 79; 4. 4. 125.
Leg, *n.* An obeisance made by drawing back one leg and bending the other; a bow, scrape. Esp. in phr. *to make a leg.* Now *arch.* or jocular. 4. 4. 97. legge. 2. 8. 22.
||**Lentisco**, *n.* Sp. and It. Prick-wood or Foule-rice, some call it Lentiske or Mastike-tree.' Florio. (Pistacia lentiscus.) 4. 4. 35.
Letter of Atturney, *sb. phr.* A formal document empowering another person to perform certain acts on one's behalf (now more usually 'power of attorney'). 4. 5. 15.
Lewd, *a.* †Ignorant (implying a reproach). 5. 6. 37.
Liberall, *a.* Ample, large. Somewhat *rare.* 1. 6. 179.
Lift, *v.* To raise (as by a crane). Used *fig.* (a metaphor borrowed from Ingine's name). 1. 4. 1.
Like, *v.* †To be pleasing, be liked or approved. P. 26.
Limb, *n.* 1. A leg (a part of the body).
      ?2. A leg (curtsy. See *Leg*). A quibble on the two >meanings. 1. 6. 218.
Limon, *n. Obs.* form of *lemon.* 4. 4. 25.
Liuery and seisen, *sb. phr.* erron. for *Livery of seisin* (AF. *livery de seisin*): 'The delivery of property into the corporal possession of a person; in the case of a house, by giving him the ring, latch or key of the door; in case of land, by delivering him a twig, a piece of turf, or the like.' *NED.* 4. 5. 16.
Loose, *v. Obs.* form of *lose.* 4. 7. 79.

Lords-man, *n.* A lord's man; an attendant on a lord. ?*Obs.* 3. 3. 166.
Lose, *v.* †To be deprived of the opportunity (to do something). 3. 4. 26.
Lusty, *a.* Merry; healthy, vigorous. Phr. *lusty Iuuentus*: the title of a morality play produced c 1550; often used allusively in the 16-17th c. 1. 1. 50.
Light, *int.* A shortened form of the asseveration *by this light*, or *by God's light*. 2. 6. 15.
Mad-dame, *n.* A whimsical spelling of *Madame*. †A courtesan, prostitute. 4. 3. 39.
Make, *v.* Phr. *make away*: To make away with; to kill. 2. 4. 9.
Manage, *v. intr.* ?To administer the affairs of a household. 4. 4. 193.
Manager, *n.* ?One capable of administering the affairs of a household. 4. 4. 138.
‖Mantecada (for *Mantecado*), *n.* Sp. 'A cake made of honey, meal, and oil; a wafer.' Pineda, 1740. 4. 4. 143.
Mary, *int.* [< ME. *Mary*, the name of the Virgin, invoked in oaths.] Form of *Marry*. Indeed! 1. 4. 28.
Masque, *n.* A masquerade. 2. 2. 110.
Masticke, *n.* 'A resinous substance obtained from the common mastic-tree, *Pistacia Lentiseus*, a small tree about twelve feet high, native in the countries about the Mediterranean. In the East mastic is chewed by the women.' *CD.* 4. 2. 54.
Match, *n.* †An agreement; a bargain. 1. 4. 67.
Mathematicall, *a.* ?Mathematically accurate; skillful to the point of precision. 1. 4. 4.
Meath, *n.* [Form of *Mead.*] A strong liquor. 1. 1. 115 (see note).
Med'cine, *v.* To treat or affect by a chemical process. 2. 1. 70.
Mercat, *n.* [Form of *market.*] 1. 1. 10.
Mere, *a.* †Absolute, unqualified. 2. 3. 12. meere. 1. 4. 54.
Mermaide, *n.* The name of a tavern; hence, used as a generic term for a tavern. 3. 3. 26.
Mettall, *n.* 1. Metal.
    2. Mettle. A quibble on the two meanings. 2. 8. 105.
Middling, *a.* †One performing the function of a go-between. Phr. *middling Gossip*: A go-between. 1. 6. 219.
Mill, *n.* A lapidary wheel. 3. 3. 176.
†Migniard, *a.* Delicate, dainty, pretty. 1. 4. 96.
Missiue, *a.* Sent or proceeding, as from some authoritative or official source. 3. 3. 35.
Moiety, *n.* A half share. 2. 1. 46. moyety. 2. 1. 48.
Monkey, *n.* A term of endearment; pet. ?*Obs.* 2. 2. 127.
†Moon-ling, *n.* A simpleton, fool. 1. 6. 158.
Motion, *n.* †A puppet-show. 1. 6. 230.
Much about, *prep. phr.* Not far from; very near. ?*Obs.* 4. 4. 153.
Mungril, *a. Obs.* form of *mongrel*. 3. 1. 39.
Mure, *v.* Phr. *mure up*: To inclose in walls; immure. 2. 2. 91.
Muscatell, *a.* [Form of *muscadel.*] Of the muscadel rape. 2. 1. 102.

Muscatell, *n.* A sweet wine. 2. 1. 102; 2. 2. 95. See above.

Muscouy glasse, *n.* Muscovite; common or potash mica; the light colored mica of granite and similar rocks. P. 17.

||**Mustaccioli**, *n.* It. [For *Mostaciuolli.*] 'A kind of sugar or ginger bread.' Florio. 4. 4. 144.

Muta, *n.* [?L. *mutare*, to change.] ?A dye (?coined by Jonson). 4. 4. 56.

†**Neale**, *n.* To temper by heat; anneal. 2. 1. 88.

Neare, *adv.* In *fig.* sense, Nigh. Phr. *go neare* (to). 5. 1. 7.

Need, *v. intr.* Be necessary. ?*Arch.* 2. 8. 106.

Neither, *adv.* Also not; no again. ?*Obs.* 4. 7. 68.

†**Niaise**, *n.* 1. A young hawk; an eyas.

2. A simpleton. pr. with quibble. 1. 6. 18.

Note, *n.* Mark, token, sign. ?*Arch.* 3. 3. 101.

Noted, *a.* Notable; worthy of attention. ?*Obs.* 5. 6. 7.

†**Nupson**, *n.* A fool; a simpleton. 2. 2. 77.

O', *prep.* Shortened form of *of.* 1. Of. 1. 1. 108. etc. Phr. *hope o'* 1. 5. 1. See *Hope.*

†2. With. 1. 3. 21.

O', *prep.* Shortened form of *on.* 1. On; upon. 4. 2. 61.

†2. Into. 1. 4. 88.

||**Obarni**, *n. Obs.* [Russ. *obvarnyi*, scalded, prepared by scalding.] 'In full, *mead obarni*, i. e. "scalded mead," a drink used in Russia, and known in England c 1600.' *NED.* 1. 1. 115.

Obserue, *v.* †To be attentive to; look out for. 1. 2. 45.

Obtaine, *v.* To obtain a request; with obj. cl. expressing what is granted. Now *rare* or *obs.* 3. 3. 86.

Occasion, *n.* †A particular, esp. a personal need, want or requirement. Chiefly in *pl.*=needs, requirements. 3. 3. 57; 3. 3. 85.

Of, *prep.* †From (after the *vb. Fetch*). 2. 1. 73. **Off**, *adv.* [Used with ellipsis of *go*, etc., so as itself to function as a verb.] Phr. *to off on* (one's bargain): To depart from the terms of; to break. 1. 5. 25.

Offer, *v.* †1. To make the proposal; suggest. 2. 8. 46.

†2. *intr.* Phr. *offer at*: To make an attempt at; to attempt. 3. 6. 30.

||**Oglio reale**, *n.* It. ?Royal oil. 4. 4. 52.

On, *prep.* In senses now expressed by *of.* 'In *on't* and the like, common in literary use to c 1750; now *dial.* or vulgar.' *NED.* 2. 8. 55; 2. 8. 61; 3. 3. 7; 3. 3. 144. etc.

On, *pron. Obs.* form of *One.* 5. 2. 40.

Order, *n.* Disposition of measures for the accomplishment of a purpose. Phr. *take order*: To take measures, make arrangements. *Obs.* or *arch.* 1. 6. 209.

||**Ore-tenus**, *adv.* [Med. L.] *Law.* By word of mouth. 3. 3. 140.

Paint, *v. intr.* †To change color; to blush. 2. 6. 35.

Pan, *n.* 1. [Form of *pane.*] †A cloth; a skirt.

2. A hollow, or depression in the ground, esp. one in which water stands. With quibble on 1. 2. 1. 53.

Paragon, *n.* A perfect diamond; now applied to those weighing more than a hundred carats. ('In quot. 1616 *fig.* of a person.' *NED.* This statement is entirely incorrect.) 3. 3. 177.

Parcel-, *qualifying sb.* Partially, in part. *Obs.* since 17th c. until revived by Scott. 2. 3. 15.

Part, *n.* Share of action; allotted duty. In *pl.* ?*Obs.* 4. 4. 116.

||**Pastillo**, *n.* It. 'Little pasties, chewets.' Florio. 4. 4. 142.

Pattent, *n.* Letters patent; an open letter under the seal of the state or nation, granting some right or privilege; spec. such letters granting the exclusive right to use an invention. 2. 1. 41; 4. 2. 38.

Peace, *n.* Leave; permission. Phr. *with his peace*: With his good leave; respectfully. (A translation of L. *cum eius pace* or *eius pace*; ?not found elsewhere.) 2. 2. 78.

||**Pecunia**, *n.* L. Money. 2. 1. 3.

||**Peladore**, *n.* Sp. A depilatory; preparation to remove hair. 4. 4. 145.

Pentacle, *n.* A mathematical figure used in magical ceremonies, and considered a defense against demons. 1. 2. 8 (see note).

†**Perse'line**, *n. Obs.* form of ?*parsley*, or of ?*purslane.* 4. 4. 24.

Perspectiue, *n.* †A reflecting glass or combination of glasses producing some kind of optical delusion when viewed in one way, but presenting objects in their true forms when viewed in another; used *fig.* 2. 6. 63.

Phantasy, *n.* Whimsical or deluded notion. ?*Obs.* 2. 3. 60.

Phantsie, *n.* [Form of *fancy*.] Imagination. 1. 4. 88.

†**Phrentick**, *n.* A frantic or frenzied person; one whose mind is disordered. 4. 6. 49.

Phrenticke, *a.* [Form of *frantic*.] Insane. Now rare. 5. 8. 91.

Physicke, *n.* †Natural philosophy; physics. 2. 2. 122.

†**Picardill**, *n.* [Form of *Piccadill*.] A large stiff collar in fashion about the beginning of the reign of James I. 2. 2. 123 (see note).

Piece, *n.* †1. A gold piece, pr. 22 shillings (Gifford). 1. 4. 5; 3. 3. 83.

    2. Phr. *at all pieces*: At all points; in perfect form. 2. 7. 37.

Piece, *v.* To reunite, to rejoin (a broken friendship). ?*Arch.* 4. 1. 37.

Pinnace, *n.* 1. A small sailing vessel.

    †2. Applied *fig.* to a woman, usually to a prostitute (sometimes, but not often, with complete loss of the metaphor). 1. 6. 58.

||**Pipita** [?For *pepita*], *n.* Sp. or It. 'A seed of a fruit, a pip, a kernel.' *Stanford.* 4. 4. 45.

||**Piueti**, *n.* Sp. 'A kinde of perfume.' Minsheu. 4. 4. 150.

Plaine, *a.* Unqualified, downright. ?*Arch.* 4. 4. 158.

Plume, *v.* To strip off the plumage of; to pluck. ?*Arch.* 4. 4. 43.

||**Pol-dipedra** [?*Polvo di pietra*], n. It. ?Rock-alum. 4. 4. 30.

Politique, *a.* [Form of *politic*.] Crafty, artful. 2. 2. 76.

||**Porcelletto marino**, *n.* It.?'The fine Cockle or Muscle shels which painters put their colours in.' Florio. 4. 4. 34.

Possesse, *v.* †To acquaint. Phr. *possesse with*: To inform of. 5. 5. 44.

Posterne, *n.* ?A back door or gate. Phr. *at one's posternes*: Behind one. 5. 6. 15.

†**Posture booke**, *n.* ?A book treating of military tactics, describing the

'postures' of the musket, etc. 3. 2. 38 (see note).

‖**Potentia**, *n.* L. 'Power;' potentiality. 5. 3. 28.

Power, *n. Law.* Legal authority conferred. 4. 6. 39.

Pownce. [Form of *pounce.*] A claw or talon of a bird of prey. 4. 7. 55.

Pox, *n.* Irreg. spelling of *pocks, pl.* of *pock.* †Phr. *pox vpon*: A mild imprecation. 3. 3. 38. *pox o'.* 4. 2. 61.

Practice, *n.* 1. A plot. ?*Arch.* 5. 8. 57.

    2. Treachery. ?*Arch.* 4. 7. 80.

Practice, *v.* †1. To tamper with; corrupt. 1. 1. 38.

    2. *intr.* To plot; conspire. 5. 3. 10; 5. 51.

Pragmaticke, *a.* Pragmatical. 1. 6. 56.

Pregnant, *a.* †Convincing; clear. 5. 8. 77.

Present, *a.* Immediate (fr. L. *praesens*). 3. 6. 40.

Present, *n.* †1. The money or other property one has on hand. 1. 5. 20.

    2. The existing emergency; the temporary condition. 2. 6. 70.

President, *n.* †A ruling spirit. 3. 5. 38.

Presume, *v.* To rely (upon). 2. 2. 30.

Pretend, *v.* 1. To lay claim (to). 2. 4. 16; 3. 3. 102.

    †2. To aspire to. 1. 6. 36.

Price, *n.* Estimated or reputed worth; valuation. 2. 8. 105.

Priuate, *n.* †Priuate account. 5. 4. 23.

Processe, *n. Law.* Summons; mandate. 3. 3. 72; 3. 3. 139.

Prodigious, *a.* †Portentous; disastrous. 2. 7. 19.

Profer, *n.* †An essay, attempt. 5. 6. 43.

Proiect, *v.* 1. *tr.* To devise. 1. 8. 10.

    †2. *intr.* To form projects or schemes. 3. 3. 42.

Proiector, *n.* One who forms schemes or projects for enriching men. 1. 7. 9. See the passage.

Pronenesse, *n.* Inclination, *spec.* to sexual intercourse. 4. 4. 233.

Proper, *a.* Well-formed. Now only prov. Eng. 1. 6. 218.

Proportion, *n.* 1. Allotment; share. 2. 3. 36.

    2. Calculation; estimate. 2. 1. 90; 3. 3. 127.

Prostitute, *a.* Debased; worthless. 3. 2. 19.

‖**Pro'uedor**, *n.* [Sp. *proveedor*=Pg. *provedor*.] A purveyor. 3. 4. 35.

Prouinciall, *n.* "In some religious orders, a monastic superior who has the general superintendence of his fraternity in a given district called a province." *CD.* 5. 6. 64.

‖**Prouocado**, *n.* [< Sp. *provocar*, to challenge.] Challengee; one challenged. 3. 3. 143.

‖**Prouocador**, *n.* [< Sp. *provocador, provoker*.] Challenger. 3. 3. 142.

Pr'y thee. [A weakened form of *I pray thee.*] Jonson uses the following forms: Pray thee. 1. 2. 30. Pr'y thee. 2. 1. 78. 'Pr'y the. 1. 3. 22.

Publication, *n.* Notification; announcement: *spec.* the notification of a 'depending' quarrel by a preliminary settlement of one's estate. 3. 3. 137.

Pug, *n.* †1. An elf; a spirit; a harmless devil. The Persons of the Play.

    2. A term of familiarity or endearment. ?*Obs.* 2. 2. 128.

Pui'nee, *a.* [For *puisne*, *arch.* form of *puny*, retained in legal use.]
    1. *Law.* Inferior in rank.
    2. Small and weak; insignificant; pr. with a quibble on 1. 1. 1. 5.
†**Punto**, *n.* ?*Obs.* Eng. fr. Sp. or It. *punto.* A delicate point of form, ceremony, or etiquette; the 'pink' of style. 4. 4. 69.
Purchase, *n.* †Plunder; ill-gotten gain. 3. 4. 32.
Purt'nance, *n.* The inwards or intestines. ?*Arch.* 5. 8. 107.
Put, *v.* 1. *intr.* To move; to venture. 1. 1. 24.
Phrases. 1. *Put downe*: To put to rout, vanquish (in a contest). 1. 1. 93.
    2. *Put off*: To dismiss (care, hope, etc.). 2. 2. 48; 3. 4. 25. To turn aside, turn back; divert (one from a course of action). 1. 4. 68.
    3. *Put out*: To invest; place at interest. 3. 4. 23.
    4. *Put vpon*: To instigate; incite. 5. 8. 141.To foist upon; palm off on. 3. 3. 174.
    Quality, *n.* 1. Character, nature. Now *rare.* 3. 4. 37.
    2. High birth or rank. Now *arch.* 1. 1. 111.
Quarrell, *v.* To find fault with (a person); to reprove angrily. *Obs.* exc. Sc. (Freq. in 17th c.). 4. 7. 12.
Quit, *v.* †To free, rid (of). 3. 6. 61.
Read, *v.* †To discourse. 4. 4. 248.
Repaire, *v.* To right; to win reparation or amends for (a person). ?*Obs.* 2. 2. 59.
‖**Rerum natura**, *phr.* L. The nature of things; the physical universe. 3. 1. 35.
Resolu'd, *ppl. a.* 1. Determined. 2. 7. 13. With quibble on 2.
    2. Convinced.
Retchlesse, *a.* [Form of *reckless.*] †Careless; negligent. 3. 6. 34.
Reuersion, *n.* A right or hope of future possession or enjoyment; hence, phr. in *reuersion*: In prospect; in expectation. 5. 4. 44.
Rhetorique, *n.* Rhetorician. ?*Obs.* 1. 4. 102.
†**Ribibe**, *n.* A shrill-voiced old woman. 1. 1. 16.
Right, *a.* True; real; genuine. *Obs.* or *arch.* 2. 2. 103.
Roaring, *a.* †Roistering, quarreling. Phr. *roaring manner*: The fashion of picking a quarrel in a boisterous, disorderly manner. 3. 3. 69.
Rose, *n.* A knot of ribbon in the form of a rose used as ornamental tie of a shoe. 1. 3. 8.
†**Rose-marine**, *n.* [The older and more correct form of *rosemary* < OF. *rosmarin* L. *rosmarinus*, lit. 'sea-dew.'] Rosemary. 4. 4. 19.
‖**Rouistico** [Same as *ligustro*], *n.* It. 'Priuet or prime-print ... also a kind of white flower.' Florio. 'Pianta salvatico.' Bassano. 4. 4. 55.
Royster, *n.* A rioter; a 'roaring boy'. *Obs.* or *arch.* 1. 1. 68.
Rug, *n.* †A kind of coarse, nappy frieze, used especially for the garments of the poorer classes; a blanket or garment of this material. 5. 1. 47.
†**Salt**, *n.* [L. *Saltus.*] A leap. 2. 6. 75.
Sample, *v.* †To place side by side for comparison; compare. 5. 1. 3.
Saraband, *n.* A slow and stately dance of Spanish or oriental origin, primarily for a single dancer, but later used as a contra-dance. It was originally accompanied by singing and at one time severely censured for its immoral

character 4. 4. 164 (see note).

Sauour, *v. tr.* To exhibit the characteristics of. *?Arch.* 4. 1. 49.

†'Say, *v.* [By apheresis from *essay*.] Phr. *'say on*: To try on. 1. 4. 37 SN.

†Scape, *v.* [Aphetic form of escape, common in England from 13-17th c.]
    1. To escape. 1. 6. 161.
    2. To miss. *?Obs.* 1. 4. 33.
    3. To avoid. 5. 5. 52.

Sciptick, *n.* [A humorous misspelling of *sceptic*.] ?One who doubts as to the truth of reality; applied humorously to one made doubtful of the reality of his own perceptions. 5. 2. 40.

Scratching, *vbl. sb.* Eager striving; used contemptuously. *?Colloq.* 5. 6. 67.

'Sdeath, *int.* [An abbr. of *God's death*.] An exclamation, generally of impatience. 1. 2. 25.

Seaming, *a. Phr. seaming lace*: 'A narrow openwork braiding, gimp, or insertion, with parallel sides, used for uniting two breadths of linen, instead of sewing them directly the one to the other; used for garments in the 17th c.' *CD.* 2. 5. 9.

Seisen, 4. 5. 16. See *Liuerie and seisen*.

†Sent, *v.* An old, and historically more correct, spelling of *scent*. 2. 6. 26.

Seruant, *n.* †A professed lover. 4. 3. 45.

Session, *n. Law.* A sitting of justices in court. 5. 6. 21.

Shame, *v.* To feel ashamed. *?Obs.* or *arch.* 5. 6. 37.

Shape, *n.* Guise; dress; disguise. *?Arch.* 5. 3. 18.

†Shop-shift, *n.* A shift or trick of a shop-keeper. 3. 5. 4.

Shrug, *v. refl.* Phr. *shrug up*: To hitch (oneself) up (into one's clothes). 1. 4. 80 SN.

Signe, *n.* One of the twelve divisions of the zodiac. 4. 4. 233. Used *fig.* 1. 6. 127.

Signet, *n.* A seal. Formerly one of the seals for the authentication of royal grants in England, and affixed to documents before passing the privy seal. 5. 4. 22.

Sirah, *n.* A word of address, generally equivalent to 'fellow' or 'sir.' *Obs.* or *arch.* 1. 4. 45; 3. 5. 25. sirrah (addressed to a woman). 4. 2. 66.

†'Slid, *int.* An exclamation, app. an abbreviation of *God's lid*. 1. 3. 33.

†'Slight, *int.* A contraction of *by this light* or *God's light*. 1. 2. 15. S'light. 2. 7. 16; 2. 8. 81.

Smock, *n.* 1. A woman's shirt. 1. 1. 128.
    ?2. A woman. 4. 4. 190.

||Soda di leuante, *n.* It. ?Soda from the East. 4. 4. 32 (see note).

Soone, *a.* Early. Phr. *soone at night*: Early in the evening. 1. 1. 148.

†Sope of Cyprus, *n.* ?Soap made from the 'cyprus' or henna shrub. 4. 4. 45.

Sou't, *v. pret.* Pr. for *sous'd*, pret. of *souse*, to swoop upon (like a hawk). 4. 7. 54 (see note).

†Spanish-cole, *n.* A perfume; fumigator. 4. 4. 150.

Spic'd, *ppl. a.* †Scrupulous; squeamish. 2. 2. 81.

Spring-head, *n.* A fountain head; a source. 3. 3. 124.

†Spruntly, *adv.* Neatly; gaily; finely. 4. 2. 61.

Spurne, *v.* To jostle, thrust. P. 11.

Squire, *n.* 1. A servant. 2. 2. 131.

    2. A gallant; a beau. 2. 2. 116.

    3. A gentleman who attends upon a lady; an escort. *?Arch.* 5. 3. 19.

Stalking, *n.* In *sporting*, the method of approaching game stealthily or under cover. 2. 2. 51.

Stand, *v.* Phrases. 1. *Stand for 't*: To enter into competition; to make a claim for recognition. 1. 6. 36.

    2. *Stand on*: To insist upon. 3. 3. 83.

    3. *Stand vpon*: To concern; to be a question of. 3. 3. 60.

Standard, *n.* †A water-standard or conduit; *spec.* the Standard in Cheap. 1. 1. 56.

State, *n.* †Estate. 4. 5. 30; 5. 3. 13.

Stay, *v. tr.* 1. To delay; detain. 2. 2. 20.

    2. To maintain. *?Arch.* 3. 1. 7.

    3. To retain. *?Arch.* 2. 4. 26.

Still, *adv.* 1. Ever; habitually. 1. 5. 23.   2. Continually. 3. 3. 27.

Stoter, *n.* ?A small coin. Cunningham. (Considered by W. and G. a misprint for *Storer*.) 3. 3. 32.

Straine, *n.* A musical note. Used *fig.* 5. 5. 58.

Strange, *a.* Immodest; unchaste. 2. 6. 53 (see note).

Strength, *n.* In *pl.*: abilities; resources. 1. 1. 24; 1. 4. 35.

Strong-water, *n.* 1. 1. 114. See *Water*.

Subtill, *a.* 1. Tenuous; dainty; airy. P. 5.

    2. Cunningly devised; ingenious. 1. 1. 116.

Subtilty, *n.* 1. Fineness; fine quality; delicacy. 2. 1. 86.

    2. An artifice; a stratagem. 2. 2. 4.

    3. Cunning; craftiness. 1. 1. 144; 2. 2. 12.

Subtle, *a.* Intricate. 2. 1. 114; 2. 2. 12.

Sufficiency, *n.* Efficiency. *?Arch.* 3. 5. 56.

    Tabacco, *n. Obs.* form of *tobacco*. (Cf. Sp. *Tabaco*; Port. and It. *Tabacco*). 1. 1. 114; 5. 8. 73.

Table-booke, *n.* †A memorandum-book. 5. 1. 39.

Taile, *n.* Phr. *in taile of*: At the conclusion of. 1. 1. 95.

Take, *v.* 1. To catch (in a trap).

    2. To captivate. With quibble on 1. 3. 6. 13.

    3. To catch; surprise. 2. 1. 147; 4. 1. 27.

    4. To take effect. 1. 4. 36. Phrases.

    5. *take forth*: ?To learn. *Dial.* 1. 1. 62.

    †6. *take in*: To capture. 3. 3. 170.

    7. *take vp*: To borrow. 3. 6. 15.

Taking, *n.* †Consumption; smoking (the regular phrase). 5. 8. 71.

Talke, *n.* Phr. *be in talke*: To be discussing or proposing. 3. 5. 52.

Tall, *a.* 4. 5. 32. See *Board*, and note.

Tasque [< OF. *tasque*], *n. Obs.* form of *task*. Business. 5. 1. 14.

Taste, *v.* 1. To perceive; recognize. 1. 6. 138.

2. To partake of; enjoy (tast). 4. 4. 93.

†**Tentiginous**, *a.* Excited to lust. 2. 3. 25.

Terme, *n.* 1. A period of time; time. 3. 3. 88.

2. An appointed or set time. *Obs.* in general sense. 1. 1. 6.

Then, *conj. Obs.* form of than. P. 10; etc.

Thorow, *prep. Obs.* form of *through*. 1. 1. 145.

Thorowout, *prep. Obs.* form of *throughout*. 2. 1. 50.

Thought, *n.* ?Device. 2. 2. 30.

Thumbe-ring, *n.* A ring designed to be worn upon the thumb; often a seal-ring. P. 6.

Ticket, *n.* †A card; a brief note. 2. 8. 90.

Time, *n.* Phr. *good time!*: Very good; very well. 1. 4. 60.

Time, *v.* ?To regulate at the proper time; to bring timely aid to. 3. 3. 97.

Tissue, *n.* 'A woven or textile fabric; specifically, in former times, a fine stuff, richly colored or ornamented, and often shot with gold or silver threads, a variety of cloth of gold.' *CD.* Used *attrib.* 1. 1. 126.

To night, *adv.* †During the preceding night; last night. 4. 1. 18.

†**Too-too-**, *adv.* Quite too; altogether too: noting great excess or intensity, and formerly so much affected as to be regarded as one word, and so often written with a hyphen. 3. 3. 231.

Top, *n.* 1. Summit; used *fig.* 2. 2. 89.

2. The highest example or type. *?Arch.* or *obs.* 4. 4. 244.

Torn'd, *ppl. a.* Fashioned, shaped (by the wheel, etc.). *Transf.* and *fig.* 2. 6. 85.

Tother, *indef. pron.* [A form arising from a misdivision of *that other*, ME. also *thet other*, as *the tother*.] Other; usually preceded by *the*. 1. 3. 37.

Toy, *n.* 1. A trifle. 2. 8. 2; 2. 8. 50.

2. A trifling fellow. 4. 7. 24; 4. 7. 57.

?3. Thing; trouble; used vaguely. 3. 3. 222.

Tract, *n.* 1. A level space; *spec.* of the stage. P. 8.

†2. Attractive influence, attraction. 2. 2. 10.

Trauell, *v.* To labor; toil. 3. 4. 52.

Trauell, *n.* †Toil; anxious striving. 1. 6. 119.

Treachery, *n.* An act of treachery. *?Obs.* 3. 6. 49.

Troth, *int.* In troth; in truth. 4. 1. 21.

Trow, *v.* To think, suppose. As a phrase added to questions, and expressions of indignant or contemptuous surprise; nearly equivalent to 'I wonder.' 5. 2. 36.

Turn, *v.* To sour; *fig.* to estrange. 2. 7. 38.

Turne, *n.* 1. Humor; mood; whim. 2. 2. 37.

2. Act of service. 2. 2. 125.

3. Present need; requirement. 3. 3. 192.

Vmbrella, *n.* †A portable shade, probably a sort of fan, used to protect the face from the sun. 4. 4. 81.

Vndertaker, *n.* One who engages in any project or business. *?Arch.* 2. 1. 36.

Vnder-write, *v.* To subscribe; to put (one) down (for a subscription). 3. 3. 145.

†**Vnquiet**, *v.* To disquiet. 4. 1. 20.

Vntoward, *a.* Perverse, refractory. *?Arch.* 2. 8. 16.

Vp, *adv.* Set up: established. 3. 5. 54.

Vpon, *prep.* 1. Directed towards or against; with reference to. 1. 1. 13; 1. 6. 112.

2. Immediately after. 3. 3. 123.

3. After and in consequence of. 1. 1. 39.

Vrge, *v.* To charge. Phr. *vrge with*: To charge with; accuse of. *?Arch.* 4. 1. 44.

Vse, *v.* To practise habitually. 1. 3. 42.

Vtmost, *n.* The extreme limit (of one's fate or disaster). 5. 6. 10.

Valor, *n.* Courage; used in *pl.* 4. 1. 32.

Vapours, *n. pl.* †A hectoring or bullying style of language or conduct, adopted by ranters and swaggerers with the purpose of bringing about a real or mock quarrel. 3. 3. 71 (see note).

Veer, *v. Naut.* To let out; pay out; let run. 5. 5. 46.

Venery, *n.* Gratification of the sexual desire. 3. 6. 7.

†**Vent**, *v.* To sell. 3. 4. 61.

Vent, *v.* 1. To publish; promulgate. 2. 3. 24.

2. To give expression to. 2. 3. 5; 2. 1. 166; 5. 8. 153.

Venter, *n. Obs.* form of *venture*. 1. 6. 175.

†**Venting**, *vbl. sb.* Selling; sale. 3. 4. 49.

Vernish, *n.* Older and *obs.* form of *varnish*. ?A wash to add freshness and lustre to the face; a cosmetic. 4. 4. 36.

||**Vetus Iniquitas**, *n.* L. 'Old Iniquity,' a name of the 'Vice' in the morality plays. 1. 1. 47.

||**Via**, *int.* It. Away! off! 2. 1. 3 (see note).

Vice, *n.* 1. Fault.

†2. The favorite character in the English morality-plays, in the earlier period representing the principle of evil, but later degenerating into a mere buffoon. 1. 1. 44; 1. 1. 84; etc. With quibble on 1. P. 9. See also Introduction.

Vierger, *n. Obs.* form of *verger*. 4. 4. 209.

Vindicate, *v.* †To avenge; retaliate for. 5. 6. 49.

Virgins milke, *n.* A wash for the face; a cosmetic. 4. 4. 52.

†**Wanion**, *n.* 'A plague;' 'a vengeance.' Phr. *with a wanion*: A plague on him; bad luck on him. 5. 8. 33.

Wanton, *a.* Playful; sportive. 2. 6. 75.

Ward-robe man, *n.* A valet. 1. 3. 13.

Ware, *v.* Beware of; take heed to. *Arch.* 5. 5. 5.

Wast, *n. Obs.* form of *waist*. 1. 4. 95. waste (with quibble on *waste*, a barren place). 4. 4. 204.

Water, *n.* 1. Essence; extract. 4. 4. 39.

2. *-water*: The property of a precious stone in which its beauty chiefly consists, involving its transparency, refracting power and color. 3. 3. 179: 181.

3. *strong-water*: A distilled liquor. 1. 1. 14.

Wedlocke, *n.* †A wife. 1. 6. 10; 2. 3. 18.

Well-caparison'd, *ppl. a.* Well furnished with trappings; also *fig.*, well decked out. Involving a quibble. 2. 5. 7.

Wench, *n.*

1. A mistress; strumpet. *Obsolescent.* 5. 2. 21.

†2. A term of familiar address; friend. 4. 1. 60.

While, *conj.* Till; until. Now prov. Eng. and U. S. 1. 3. 5.

Wicked, *a.* ?Roguish. 4. 4. 197.

Widgin, *n.* [Form of *widgeon.*] A variety of wild duck. 5. 2. 39.

Wis, *adv.* [< ME. wis.] 5. 8. 31. See *Wusse.*

Wish, *v.* To desire (one to do something); to pray, request. ?*Arch.* 2. 2. 52.

Wit, *n.* 1. Intellect. 1. 4. 29; 1. 4. 64.

2. Intelligence. 3. 2. 13.

3. Ingenuity; ingenious device. 2. 2. 86.

Withall, *adv.* Besides; in addition; at the same time. 2. 2. 27; 3. 5. 16. with-all. 2. 2. 73.

Wiue-hood, *n. Obs.* form of *wifehood.* 1. 6. 50.

Worshipfull, *a.* Worthy of honor or respect. 4. 7. 75. Used in sarcasm. 2. 2. 89; 3. 3. 8.

Wrought, *ppl. a.* Embroidered. ?*Arch.* 1. 2. 47.

†**Wusse**, *adv.* [Corruption of *wis* < ME. *wis,* by apheresis from *iwis*; sure, certain.] Certainly; truly; indeed. 1. 6. 40.

Yellow-water, *n.* 3. 3. 181. See-*water.*

Zuccarina, *n.* It. 'A kind of bright Roche-allum.' Florio.

Zuccarino, *n.* 4. 4. 31. ?For *Zuccarina, q. v.*

Zucche Mugia, *n.* It. ?A perfume. 4. 4. 35.

BIBLIOGRAPHY

Abbott, E. A. A Shakespearian Grammar. Lond. 1891.

Alden, Carroll Storrs. Edition of Bartholomew Fair. N. Y. 1904.

Amos, Andrew. The Great Oyer of Poisoning. The Trial of the Earl of Somerset for the Poisoning of Sir Thomas Overbury. Lond. 1846.

Arber, Edward (ed.). A Transcript of the Registers of the Company of Stationers of London; 1554-1640. 5 vols. Birmingham, 1894.

Bates, Katherine Lee, and Godfrey, Lydia Boker. English Drama. A Working Basis. Wellesley College, 1896.

Baudissin, Wolf (Graf Von). Ben Jonson und seine Schule. Leipzig, 1836.

Beaumont and Fletcher. Dramatic Works. Ed. A. Dyce. 11 vols. Lond. 1843.

Boccaccio, Giovanni. Opere volgari. 17 vols. Firenze, 1827-34.

Brandl, Alois. Quellen des weltlichen Dramas in England vor Shakespeare. Quellen u. Forschungen 80. Strassburg, 1889. [Contains thirteen plays, among which are Heywood's *Love* and *The Weather*, *Respublica*, *King Darius*, and *Horestes*.]

Brome, Richard. Dramatic Works. 3 vols. Lond. 1873.

Burton, Robert. The Anatomy of Melancholy. Ed. A. R. Shilleto. Lond. and N. Y. 1893.

Butler, Samuel. Hudibras, with Dr. Grey's Annotations. Lond. 1819.

———— Characters. See Morley.

Carpenter, Frederic Ives. Metaphor and Simile in the Minor Elizabethan Drama. Chicago, 1895. Jonson, pp. 125-156.

CD. Century Dictionary.

Chambers, E. K. The Mediæval Stage. 2 vols. Oxford, 1903.

Chambers, R. (ed.). Book of Days: A Miscellany of Popular Antiquities. 2 vols. Edinburgh, 1864.

Coleridge, Samuel Taylor. Shakespeare, Ben Jonson, Beaumont and Fletcher. Notes and Lectures. Liverpool, 1874.

Collier, John Payne. Memoirs of the Principal Actors in the Plays of Shakespeare. Lond. 1846.

———— The History of English Dramatic Poetry to the Time of Shakespeare; and Annals of the Stage to the Restoration. 3 vols. Lond. 1831.

Coryat, Thomas. Crudities; repr. from the ed. of 1611. 2 vols. Lond. 1776.

Cotgrave, Randle. A Dictionarie of the French and English Tongues. Lond. 1632.

Craik, George Lillie. The History of British Commerce. 3 vols. Lond. 1844.

Cunningham, W. The Growth of English Industry and Commerce in Modern Times. Part I. The Mercantile System. Cambridge Univ. Press, 1903.

Cushman, Lysander William. The Devil and the Vice in the English Dramatic Literature before Shakespeare. Studien zur Englischen Philologie.

Halle, 1900.

DA. The Devil is an Ass.

Darrel, John. A Detection of that sinnful, shamful, lying and ridiculous Discours, of Samuel Harshnet, entituled: A Discoverie of the frauudulent Practises of Iohn Darrell. Imprinted 1600.

———— A true Narration of that strange and grevous Vexation by the Devil of seven Persons in Lancashire and William Somers of Nottingham. —— 1600. In Somer's Tracts, vol. 3. Lond. 1810.

Dekker, Thomas. Dramatic Works. 4 vols. Lond. 1873.

———— Non-dramatic Works. 5 vols. Ed. A. B. Grosart. Lond. 1885.

D'Ewes, Sir Simonds. A compleat Journal ... both of the House of Lords and House of Commons. Lond. 1693.

———— The Autobiography and Correspondence. Ed. J. O. Halliwell. Lond. 1845.

DNB. Dictionary of National Biography.

Dodsley, Robert. A Select Collection of Old Plays. With Notes. Ed. T. Coxeter. Lond. 1744.

———— Same. 2d ed. Ed. J. Reed. Lond. 1780.

———— Same. 4th ed. Ed. W. Carew Hazlitt. Lond. 1874.

Doran, John. History of Court Fools. Lond. 1858.

Douce, Francis. Illustrations of Shakespeare and of Ancient Manners. 2 vols. Lond. 1807.

Downes, John. Roscius Anglicanus, or an Historical Review of the Stage from 1660 to 1706. Repr. by Joseph Knight. Lond. 1886.

Dyce, Alexander. Remarks on Collier's and Knight's Editions of Shakespeare. Lond. 1844.

Eckhardt, Eduard. Die Lustige Person im älteren englischen Drama (bis 1642). Palaestra 17. Berlin, 1902.

Entick, John. A New and Accurate History and Survey of London, Westminster, Southwark, and Places adjacent. 4 vols. Lond. 1766.

Fleay, Frederic Gard. Biographical Chronicle of the English Drama 1559-1642. 2 vols. Lond. 1891.

———— A Chronicle History of the London Stage, 1559-1642. Lond. 1890.

Florio, John. Queen Anna's new World of Words, or Dictionarie of the Italian and English Tongues. Lond. 1611.

Ford, John. Works. Ed. A. Dyce. 3 vols. Lond. 1869.

Furness, Horace Howard. A New Variorum Edition of Shakespeare. Phila. 1871-1904.

Genest, John. Some Account of the English Stage from the Restoration in 1660 to 1830. 10 vols. Bath, 1832.

Grose, Francis. Lexicon Balatronicum. 2d ed. Lond. 1811.

Halliwell, James Orchard. A Dictionary of Archaic and Provincial Words. 2 vols. Lond. 1847.

Halliwell-Phillipps, James Orchard. Illustrations of the Life of Shakespeare. Lond. 1874.

Harrison, Rev. William. Description of England in Shakespeare's Youth. Ed. F. J. Furnivall. Lond. 1877-81.

Harsnet, Samuel. A Declaration of egregious Popish Impostures ... Newly printed by Ia. Roberts. dwelling in Barbican. 1605. (Repr. from the original edition of 1603.)

Hathaway, Charles M. Edition of The Alchemist. N. Y. 1903.

Hawkins, Sir John. A General History of the Science and Practice of Music. Lond. 1776.

Hazlitt, William Carew. Second Series of Bibliographical Collections and Notes on Early English Literature, 1474-1700. Lond. 1882.

————— Tales and Legends of National Origin or Widely Current in England from Early Times. Lond. 1892.

Hentzner, Paul. A Journey into England. In the year 1598. Printed at Strawberry Hill 1757.

Herford, Charles Harold. Studies in the Literary Relations of England and Germany in the Sixteenth Century. Cambridge, 1886.

Heywood, Thomas. Dramatic Works. 6 vols. Lond. 1874.

Hindley, Charles. The Old Book Collector's Miscellany. 3 vols. Lond. 1871-3.

Hollstein, Ernst. Verhältnis von Ben Jonson's 'The Devil is an Ass' und John Wilson's 'Belphegor, or the Marriage of the Devil' zu Machiavelli's Novelle vom Belfagor. Halle, 1901.

Hotten, John Camden, and Larwood, Jacob. The History of Signboards. Lond. 1867.

Howell, James. Epistolae Ho-elianae. The Familiar Letters of J. Howell. Ed. J. Jacobs. Lond. 1892.

Howes, Edmvnd. Annales, or, A General Chronicle of England. Begun by John Stow: continued and augmented ... unto the end of this present yeere, 1631. Lond. 1631.

Hughson, David. London; being an Accurate History and Description of the British Metropolis and its Neighborhood. 6 vols. Lond. 1805-09.

Hulme, E. W. History of the Patent System. In Law Quarterly Review, vols. 12 and 16.

Hutchinson, Francis. Historical Essay concerning Witchcraft. 2d ed. Lond. 1720.

James I., King of England, and VI. of Scotland. Workes. Lond. 1616.

Jonson, Benjamin. References are to the Gifford-Cunningham Edition 1875. For other editions, see Introduction A .

Knight, Charles. Popular History of England. 8 vols. Lond. 1867-8.

Koeppel, Emil. Quellen Studien zu den Dramen Ben Jonson's, John Marston's und Beaumont's und Fletcher's. Erlangen u. Leipzig, 1895. Münchener Beiträge, vol. 11.

————— Studien zur Geschichte der italienischen Novelle in der englischen Litteratur des 16. Jahrhunderts. (Quellen und Forschungen 70.) Strassburg, 1892.

Langbaine, Gerard. An Account of the English Dramatick Poets. Oxford,

1691.

Lilly, William. History of his Life and Times, in 'The Liues of those Eminent Antiquaries Elias Ashmole, Esquire, and Mr. Wm. Lilly, written by themselves.' Lond. 1774.

Lupton, Donald. London and the Countrey Carbonadoed and Quartred into severall Characters. Lond. 1632. In Harleian Miscellany, vol. 9. Lond. 1812.

Machiavelli, Niccolò. Opere. Milano, 1805. [Vol. 9, pp. 39-55, contains 'Novella Piacevolissima' (Belfagor).]

Mallory, Herbert S. Edition of Poetaster. N. Y. 1905.

Malone, Edmond. Edition of Shakespeare's Works. 10 vols. Lond. 1790.

Marlowe, Christopher. Works. Ed. A. H. Bullen. Boston, 1885.

Marston, John. Works. Ed. A. H. Bullen. Boston, 1887.

Massinger, Philip. Dramatic Works of Massinger and Ford. Ed. Hartley Coleridge. Lond. 1839.

Middleton, Thomas. Works. Ed. A. H. Bullen. Boston, 1885.

Minsheu, John. A Dictionary of Spanish and English. [Contains also 'A Spanish Grammar' and 'Pleasant and Delightfull Dialogues in Spanish and English.'] Lond. 1623.

Morley, Henry (ed.). Character Writings of the Seventeenth Century. Lond. 1891.

Moryson, Fynes. An Itinerary, Written in the Latine Tongue, and then translated by him into English. Lond. 1617.

N. & Q. Notes and Queries.

Nares, Robert. Glossary. New Edition by Halliwell and Wright. Lond. 1859.

Nashe, Thomas. Complete Works. Ed. A. B. Grosart. 4 vols. Lond. and Aylesbury, 1883-4.

NED. The New English Dictionary.

Nicholson, Brinsley. Ben Jonson's Folios and the Bibliographers. Notes and Queries, 4th Ser. 5. 573.

O. Pl. See Dodsley.

Overbury, Sir Thomas. See Morley.

Pepys, Samuel. Diary and Correspondence. Lond. 1875-9.

Planché, James Robinson. A Cyclopædia of Costume or Dictionary of Dress. Lond. 1876-9.

Potts, Thomas. Discovery of Witches in the County of Lancaster. 1613. Repr. by J. Crossley. Manchester, 1845.

Rapp, Moriz. Studien über das englische Theater. Tübingen, 1862.

Ray, John. Collection of English Proverbs. Cambridge, 1678.

Reed. See Dodsley.

Reinsch, Dr. Hugo. Ben Jonson's Poetik und seine Beziehungen zu Horaz. Münchener Beiträge 16. Erlangen u. Leipzig, 1899.

Roskoff, Gustav. Geschichte des Teufels. 2 vols. Leipzig, 1869.

Schelling, Felix E. Edition of Jonson's Timber. Boston, 1892.

Schmidt, Alexander. Shakespeare-Lexicon. Berlin, 1874-5.

Scot, Reginald. The Discoverie of Witchcraft. 1584. Repr. by Brinsley

Nicholson. Lond. 1886.

Sharp, Thomas. On the Pageants or Dramatic Mysteries anciently performed at Coventry. Coventry, 1825.

Soc. Eng. See Traill.

Soldan, Wilhelm Gottlieb. Geschichte der Hexenprozesse. Stuttgart, 1880.

Spalding, Thomas Alfred. Elizabethan Demonology. Lond. 1880.

Sparke, Michael. Truth brought to Light and discouered by Time, or A Discourse and Historicall Narration of the first xiiii Yeares of King Iames Reigne. Lond. 1651. Repr. Somer's Tracts, vol. 2. 1809.

Stephen, Sir James Fitzjames. A History of Criminal Law of England. Lond. 1883.

Stow, John. The Survey of London. Written In 1598. Enlarged by A. M., H. D. and others. Lond. 1633.

———— New ed. by W. J. Thoms. Lond. 1842.

Strutt, Joseph. *Antiq.* A compleat View of the Manners, etc.... of the Inhabitants of England. 3 vols. Lond. 1775-76.

———— The Sports and Pastimes of the People of England. Lond. 1801.

Stubbes, Philip. Anatomy of Abuses in England in Shakespeare's Youth, A. D. 1583. Ed. F. J. Furnivall. Lond. 1877-82.

Swinburne, Algernon Charles. A Study of Ben Jonson. N. Y. 1889.

Taylor, John. Works, comprised in the folio ed. of 1630. Spenser Soc. Pub. Manchester, 1868-9.

Taylor, John. Works not included in the fol. vol. of 1630. Spencer Soc. Pub. 5 vols. Lond. 1870-8.

Thoms, William J. Early English Prose Romances, with bibliographical and historical introductions. 3 vols. 2d ed. Lond. 1858. [Vol. I contains the legend of Friar Rush, repr. from the 1620 ed.]

Traill, Henry Duff (ed.). Social England. 6 vols. N. Y. and Lond. 1896.

Upton, John. Critical Observations on Shakespeare. 2d ed. Lond. 1748.

Ward, Adolphus William. A History of English Dramatic Literature to the Death of Queen Anne. 3 vols. Lond. and N. Y. 1899.

Webster, John. Works. Ed. A. Dyce. 4 vols. Lond. 1830.

Wh-C. Wheatley, Henry B., and Cunningham, Peter. London Past and Present. Lond. and N. Y. 1891.

Wheatley, H. B. Edition of Every Man in his Humor. Lond. 1877.

Wilke, Friedrich Wilhelm. Metrische Untersuchungen zu Ben Jonson. Halle, 1884.

Wilson, Arthur. The History of Great Britain, being the Life and Reign of King Iames the First. Lond. 1653.

Wilson, John. Dramatic Works. Lond. 1874.

Winter, De. Edition of The Staple of News. N. Y. 1905.

Woodbridge, Elisabeth. Studies in Jonson's Comedy. Boston and N. Y. 1898.

Wright, Thomas. Dictionary of Obsolete and Provincial English. Lond. 1857.

———— History of Caricature and Grotesque in Literature and Art. Lond.

1864.

——————— Narrations of Sorcery and Magic. N. Y. 1852.